CASS TIMBERLANE

A NOVEL OF HUSBANDS AND WIVES

BY

SINCLAIR LEWIS

British Library Cataloguing-in-Publication Data
A catalogue record for this book is available from the
British Library

CONTENTS

SINCLAIR LEWIS

Sinclair Lewis was born in Sauk Centre, Minnesota, USA in 1885. A lonely and socially awkward child, Lewis tried unsuccessfully to run away from home, before entering Yale University in 1903. It was here that, in the *Yale Courant* and the *Yale Literary Magazine,* Lewis had his first works – mostly romantic poetry and short sketches – published. After graduating, he drifted for a while, while continuing to write, and sold shallow, popular stories to magazines. In 1912, he published a potboiler called *Hike and the Aeroplane,* before producing three serious novels: *Our Mr. Wrenn: The Romantic Adventures of a Gentle Man* (1914), *The Trail of the Hawk: A Comedy of the Seriousness of Life* (1915), and *The Job* (1917).

In 1920, while living in Washington D.C., Lewis had his first major success with the novel *Main Street.* Selling around two million copies within a few years, it catapulted Lewis into fame and riches, and he followed it with the critically acclaimed *Babbitt* (1922), and *Arrowsmith* (1925) – for which he received, but refused, the Pulitzer Prize. Lewis went on to publish more than ten more novels, as well as a vast amount o short fiction. His 1929 novel *Dodsworth* was adapted into a highly successful film, and in 1930 Lewis became the first American author to ever win the Nobel Prize in Literature. His

1947 novel, *Kingsblood Royal,* is seen as an early and powerful contribution to the then burgeoning Civil Rights Movement. Lewis died in Rome, aged 65, from advanced alcoholism.

TO

P. M. R.

The scene of this story, the small city of Grand Republic in Central Minnesota, is entirely imaginary, as are all the characters.

But I know that the characters will be "identified," each of them with several different real persons in each of the Minnesota cities in which I have happily lingered: in Minneapolis, St. Paul, Winona, St. Cloud, Mankato, Fergus Falls and particularly, since it is only a little larger than "Grand Republic" and since I live there, in the radiant, sea-fronting, hillside city of Duluth.

All such guesses will be wrong, but they will be so convincing that even the writer will be astonished to learn how exactly he has drawn some judge or doctor or banker or housewife of whom he has never heard, or regretful to discover how poisonously he is supposed to have described people of whom he is particularly fond.

SINCLAIR LEWIS

CASS TIMBERLANE

1

UNTIL JINNY MARSHLAND was called to the stand, the Judge was deplorably sleepy.

The case of Miss Tilda Hatter *vs.* the City of Grand Republic had been yawning its way through testimony about a not very interesting sidewalk. Plaintiff's attorney desired to show that the city had been remarkably negligent in leaving upon that sidewalk a certain lump of ice which, on February 7, 1941, at or about the hour of 9:37 P.M., had caused the plaintiff to slip, to slide, and to be prone upon the public way, in a state of ignominy and sore pain. There had been an extravagant amount of data as to whether the lump of ice had been lurking sixteen, eighteen, or more than eighteen feet from the Clipper Hardware Store. And all that May afternoon the windows had been closed, to keep out street noises, and the court room had smelled, as it looked, like a schoolroom.

Timberlane, J., was in an agony of drowsiness. He was

faithful enough, and he did not miss a word, but he heard it all as in sleep one hears malignant snoring.

He was a young judge: the Honorable Cass Timberlane, of the Twenty-Second Judicial District, State of Minnesota. He was forty-one, and in his first year on the bench, after a term in Congress. He was a serious judge, a man of learning, a believer in the majesty of the law, and he looked like a tall Red Indian. But he was wishing that he were out bass-fishing, or at home, reading *Walden* or asleep on a cool leather couch.

Preferably asleep.

All the spectators in the room, all five of them, were yawning and chewing gum. The learned counsel for the plaintiff, Mr. Hervey Plint, the dullest lawyer in Grand Republic, a middle-aged man with a miscellaneous sort of face, was questioning Miss Hatter. He was a word-dragger, an uh'er, a looker to the ceiling for new thoughts.

"Uh—Miss Hatter, now will you tell us what was the—uh—the purpose of your going out, that evening—I mean, I mean how did you happen to be out on an evening which—I think all the previous testimony agrees that it was, well, I mean, uh, you might call it an inclement evening, but not such as would have prevented the, uh, the adequate cleaning of the thorough-fares——"

"Jekshn leading quest," said the city attorney.

"Jekshn stained," said the Court.

"I will rephrase my question," confided Mr. Plint. He was

a willing rephraser, but the phrases always became duller and duller and duller.

Sitting above then? on the bench like Chief Iron Cloud, a lean figure of power, the young father of his people, Judge Timberlane started to repeat the list of presidents, a charm which usually would keep him awake. He got through it fairly well, stumbling only on Martin Van Buren and Millard Fillmore, as was reasonable, but he remained as sleepy as ever.

Without missing any of Miss Hatter's more spectacular statements, His Honor plunged into the Counties of Minnesota, all eighty-seven of them, with their several county-seats:

Aitkin—Aitkin

Anoka—Anoka

Becker—Detroit Lakes

Beltrami—Bemidji

He had reached "Olmsted—Rochester" when he perceived that Miss Hatter had gone back to her natural mummy-case, and the clerk was swearing in a witness who pricked His Honor into wakefulness.

——How did I ever miss seeing her, in a city as small as this? Certainly not four girls in town that are as pretty, he reflected.

The new witness was a half-tamed hawk of a girl, twenty-

7

three or -four, not tall, smiling, lively of eye. The light edged gently the clarity of her cheeks, but there was something daring in her delicate Roman nose, her fierce black hair. Her gray suit indicated prosperity, which in Grand Republic was respectability.

——Be an exciting kid to know, thought Timberlane, J., that purist and precisionist and esteemed hunter of ducks, that chess-player and Latinist, who was a man unmarried—at least, unmarried since his recent and regrettable divorce.

The young woman alighted on the oak witness-chair like a swallow on a tombstone.

Counselor Plint said gloomily, "Will you please just give us your, uh, your name and profession and address, please?"

"Jinny Marshland—Virginia Marshland. I'm draftsman and designer for the Fliegend Fancy Box and Pasteboard Toy Manufacturing Company, and a kind of messenger—man of all work."

"Residence, please."

"I live up in Pioneer Falls, mostly. I was born there, and I taught school there for a while. But you mean here in Grand Republic? I live with Miss Hatter, at 179 1/2 West Flandrau Street."

Profoundly, as one who doubts the eternal course of the planets, Mr. Plint worried, "You *board* with Miss Hatter?"

"Yes, sir."

Jinny and Judge Cass Timberlane looked at each other.

He had been approving her voice. He loved his native city of Grand Republic, and esteemed the housewifery and true loyal hearts of its 43,000 daughters, but it disturbed him that so many of them had voices like the sound of a file being drawn across the edge of a sheet of brass. But Miss Marshland's voice was light and flexible and round.

——I *would* fall for a girl merely because she has fine ankles and a clear voice, I who have maintained that the most wretched error in all romances is this invariable belief that because a girl has a good nose and a smooth skin, therefore she will be agreeable to live with and—well, make love to. The insanity that causes even superior men (meaning judges) to run passionately after magpies with sterile hearts. This, after the revelations of female deception I've seen in divorce proceedings. I am corrupted by sentimentality.

Mr. Plint was fretting his bone. "Now, uh, Miss—Miss Marshland. Oh, yes, precisely. Now as I was saying, Miss Marshland, several people have testified that there was a party—anyway, there were several guests at the Hatter residence that evening, and there was more or less eating and drinking, and what we want to know is, was there any sign—uh—I mean any sign of intoxicating beverages being consumed, I mean, particularly by Miss Hatter herself?"

"No, she drank a coke. I might take a cocktail sometimes, but I'm sure Miss Hatter never touches a drop."

Charles Sayward, the city attorney, was roused from slumber

to protest, "I move the testimony be stricken, as hearsay and irrelevant."

Judge Timberlane said gravely, "I must grant that motion, Mr. Sayward, but don't you think you're being a little technical?"

"It is my humble understanding of court procedure, Your Honor, that it is entirely technical."

(On the Heather Club golf course they called each other "Charles" and "Cass.")

"On the other hand, Mr. City Attorney, you know that here in the Middlewest we pride ourselves on being less formal than the stately tribunals of Great Britain and our traditional East. I may be so bold as to say that even in court, we're almost human, and that on a day like this—you may not have noticed it, Mr. City Attorney, but it is somewhat somnolent—then we frequently permit any testimony that will give this jury—" He smiled at the honest but bored citizens, "an actual picture of the issue. However," and now he smiled at Jinny, "I think you'd better confine yourself to answering the questions, without comment, Miss Marshland. Motion granted. Continue, Mr. Plint."

As Jinny went on, without noticeably obeying the Court's command, Cass felt that the court-room air was fresher, that there might actually be some life and purpose to court proceedings. She was perhaps twenty-four to his forty-one, but he insisted that Jinny and he were young together, and in antagonism to the doddering Mr. Plint, the cobwebbed and molding Charles Sayward (who was thirty-five, by the records) and the Assyrian antiquity of the jury.

He wanted to lean over the sharp oak edge of his lofty desk and demand of Jinny, "See here. You know the jury will give the Hatter woman approximately half of whatever she's suing for, no matter what nonsense we grind out. Let's go off and forget all this. I want to talk to you, and make it clear that I can be light-minded and companionable."

But it came to him that this would not be the way to impress Jinny. She thought that he was a judge and a venerable figure; she probably thought that he was more columnar than her young suitors with their dancing and babble. He straightened, he placed his right forefinger senatorially against his cheek, he cleared his throat, and for her, glancing down to see if he was successfully fooling her, he pretended that he was a judge on a bench.

She was explaining, to Mr. Plint's prompting, that she boarded at Miss Hatter's, along with Tracy Oleson (secretary to that industrial titan, Mr. Wargate), Lyra Coggs the librarian, Eino Roskinen, and three other young people. They were artistic and pretty refined. No indeed, they never got drunk, and if Tilda Hatter slipped on any ole lump of ice, that lump of ice was meant to be slipped on. Yes, she liked working for the Fliegend Company. She wasn't, she beamed, much of a draftsman, but Mr. and Mrs. Fliegend were so kind. She liked it better than schoolteaching; you had to be so solemn in school.

She was not loquacious so much as gay and natural. It was all fantastically irregular, but City Attorney Sayward had given up trying to check her, and he looked up at Judge Timberlane with humorous helplessness. The jury yearned over her as though they were her collective parent, and Counselor Plint had a notion, though he didn't know how in the world it had come about, that she was a useful witness.

Only George Hame, the court reporter, was unmoved, as he made his swift symbols in a pulpy-looking notebook. To George, all accents and all moods, the shrieks of the widows of murdered bootleggers, the droning of certified accountants explaining crooked ledgers, the grumble of Finnish or Polish homesteaders, were the same. What was said never seemed the important thing to George, but whether he got it all down. The Judge, his captain, could be unprofessionally enlivened by an unnecessary girl witness, after only five months on the bench, but George did not believe in women. He had a wife unremittingly productive of babies, for whose assembly-belt production he felt only accidentally responsible, and after sixteen years of court reporting, all witnesses, pretty or otherwise, were to him merely lumps of potato in a legal hash that was nourishing but tedious.

Jinny Marshland finished her testimony, smiled at Cass, smiled at Tilda Hatter, and slipped out of the court room like a trout flicking down a stream. The case reverted to mumbling, and the Judge reverted to the list of Minnesota counties and to a sleepiness which made his shoulders ache, his eyes feel dusty and swollen. With his right hand, the large hand of a woodsman or a hunter, he gravely stroked the lapel of his dark-gray jacket, smoothed his painfully refined dark-blue tie, as he repeated:

Otter Tail County—Fergus Falls
Pennington—Thief River Falls
Pine—Pine City
Pipestone—Pipestone

Till half an hour ago he had been proud of the court room; of his high oak desk, jutting into the room like a prow, with a silken American flag, topped with a small gold eagle, erected beside the Judge's leather chair. He had been proud of the carved seal of Minnesota on the oak paneling behind the bench; of the restful dark-gray plaster walls; of the resplendently shiny oak benches, though they were hard upon the restless anatomy of the aching public. He had felt secure and busy, for this was his workshop, his studio, his laboratory, in which he was an artist-scientist, contributing to human progress and honor.

Now it was a stuffy coop, absurdly small for a court room, barely able to hold eighty people when crowded. Such portions of the Eternal Law as were represented by the Statutes of the

State of Minnesota seemed dreary today, and he wanted to be out in the May breeze, walking with Jinny Marshland.

Cass was considered a conscientious judge, but he adjourned today at five minutes before the usual four o'clock. He could eat no more bran.

Before he could hasten out into the open air, however, he still had half an hour of chamber work. He was rather proud of Chambers No. 3, Radisson County Court House. On his election, when he had taken the room over, it already looked scholarly and solid, with a cliff of law-books, a long oak table, a council of black leather chairs, and he had added the framed photographs of Justices Holmes, Cardozo, and Brandeis . . . and of the historic bag of ducks that Dr. Roy Drover and he had shot in 1939. On his portly desk was a handsome bronze inkwell which he never used, and a stupendous bronze automatic cigar-lighter—a gift—which he had always disliked.

He had to sign an injunction, to talk with a Swede who desired to be naturalized. Young Vincent Osprey, who overlaid with a high Yale Law School gloss a dullness almost equal to that of Mr. Hervey Plint, brought in a woman client, on the theory that she wanted wholesome advice about her coming divorce suit. She did not want advice; she wanted to get rid of her present spouse so that she could marry another with a more powerful kiss. But in most judicial districts of Minnesota, domestic-relations procedure is as fatherly and informal as a physician's consultation, and Cass held forth to her.

"Mrs. Nelson, a woman or a man has only four or five real friendships in his whole life. To lose one of them is to lose a chance to give and to trust. Am I being too discursive?"

"I t'ink so."

"Well look, Mrs. Carlson——"

"Mrs. Nelson."

"——Nelson. Look. In a divorce, the children are terrified. Have you any children?"

"Not by Nelson."

Judge Timberlane glanced at Mr. Osprey and shook his head. The lawyer yelped, "All right, Mrs. Nelson, you skip along now. That's all His Honor has to say."

When they were alone, Cass turned to Osprey, and it was to be seen that Osprey was his admirer.

"No use, Vince. Let it go through. I figure she's hot to gallop to another marriage-bed. Otherwise I'd give her a red-hot lecture on the humiliations of divorce. I will facilitate any divorce, in case of cruelty—or extreme boredom, which is worse—but, Vince, divorce is hell. Don't you ever divorce Cerise, no matter how extravagant you say she is."

"You bet your life I wouldn't, Chief. I'm crazy about that girl."

"You're lucky. If it weren't for my work, my life would be as empty as a traitor's after a war. Ever since Blanche divorced me—why, Vince, I have nobody to show my little tin triumphs

15

to. I envy Cerise and you. And I don't seem to find any girl that will take Blanche's place."

As he spoke, Cass was reflecting that, after all, Jinny Marshland was just another migratory young woman.

"But what about Christabel Grau, Chief? I thought you and she were half engaged," bubbled Vincent Osprey.

"Oh, Chris is a very kind girl. I guess that's the trouble. I apparently want somebody who's so intelligent that she'll think I'm stupid, so independent that she'll never need me, so gay and daring that she'll think I'm slow. That's my pattern, Vince; that's my fate."

2

THE CITY of Grand Republic, Radisson County, Minnesota, eighty miles north of Minneapolis, seventy-odd miles from Duluth, has 85,000 population.

It is large enough to have a Renoir, a school-system scandal, several millionaires, and a slum. It lies in the confluent valleys where the Big Eagle River empties into the Sorshay River, which flows west to the Mississippi.

Grand Republic grew rich two generations ago through the uncouth robbery of forests, iron mines, and soil for wheat. With these almost exhausted, it rests in leafy quiet, wondering whether to become a ghost town or a living city. The Chamber of Commerce says that it has already become a city, but, in secret places where the two bankers on the school board cannot hear them, the better schoolteachers deny this.

At least there is in Grand Republic a remarkable number of private motor cars. It was a principal cause of his reputation for eccentricity that Cass Timberlane, on amiable spring days, walked the entire mile and a quarter from the court house to his home.

He climbed up Joseph Renshaw Brown Way to Ottawa Heights, on which were the Renoir and the millionaires and most of the houses provided with Architecture.

He looked down on the Radisson County Court House, in which was his own court room, and he did not shudder. He was fondly accustomed to its romanticism and blurry inconvenience.

It had been built in 1885 from the designs of an architect who was drunk upon Howard Pyle's illustrations to fairy tales. It was of a rich red raspberry brick trimmed with limestone, and it displayed a round tower, an octagonal tower, a minaret, a massive entrance with a portcullis, two lofty flying balconies of iron, colored-glass windows with tablets or stone petals in the niches above them, a green and yellow mosaic roof with scarlet edging, and the breathless ornamental stairway from the street up to the main entrance without which no American public building would be altogether legal.

Cass knew that it was as archaic as armor and even less comfortable, yet he loved it as a symbol of the ancient and imperial law. It was his Westminster, his Sorbonne; it was the one place in which he was not merely a male in vulgar trousers, but a spiritual force such as might, with a great deal of luck and several hundreds of years, help to make of Grand Republic another Edinburgh.

He had, too, an ancestral proprietary right in this legal palace, for his father had started off his furniture business (wholesale as well as retail, and therefore noble) by providing most of the chairs and desks for the court house.

When he had reached Varennes Boulevard, circling along

18

the cliffs on top of Ottawa Heights, Cass could see the whole city, the whole valley, with the level oat and barley fields on the uplands beyond. The Big Eagle River came in from the south, bearing the hot murmurous air from the great cornfields, from the country of the vanquished Sioux; the Sorshay River, which had been called the Sorcier by the *coureurs de bois*, two hundred years ago, wound from a northern darkness of swamp and lakes and impenetrable jackpine thickets, the country of the tawny Chippewas.

At the junction of the rivers was the modern city, steel and cement and gasoline and electricity, as contemporary as Chicago if but one-fortieth the size and devoid of the rich raucousness of the Loop. The limestone magnificence of the Wargate Memorial Auditorium and the titanic Blue Ox National Bank Building (no less than twelve stories), the carved and educated granite of the Alexander Hamilton High School, the Pantheon of the Duluth & Twin Cities Railroad Station, the furnaces and prodigious brick sheds of the Wargate Wood Products Corporation plant and a setting of smaller factories, were all proofs of the Chamber of Commerce's assertion that in a short time, perhaps twenty years or twenty centuries, Grand Republic would have a million inhabitants.

But beyond the tracks, along the once navigable Sorshay River, the wooden warehouses and shaky tenements were so like the frontier village of seventy-five years ago that you imagined the wooden sidewalks of the 1860's and the streets a churning of mud, with Chippewa squaws and Nova Scotia lumbermen in crimson jackets and weekly murder with axe handles. Very untidy.

Indeed Mrs. Kenny Wargate, Manhattan-born and cynical daughter-in-law of the Ruling Family, asserted that Grand Republic had leaped from clumsy youth to senility without ever having a dignified manhood. She jeered, "Your Grand Republic slogan is: tar-paper shanty to vacant parking lot in three generations."

But Judge Timberlane and his friends, loving the place as home, believed that just now, after woes and failures and haste and waste and experiment, Grand Republic was beginning to build up a kind of city new to the world, a city for all the people, a city for decency and neighborliness, not for ecclesiastical display and monarchial power and the chatter of tamed journalists and professors drinking coffee and eating newspapers in cafés. And if so many of the pioneers had been exploiters and slashers of the forest, the Wargates had been and now were builders of industries that meant homes and food for hundreds of immigrant families from the fiords, from New England hills.

Cass often pondered thus as he walked along Varennes Boulevard. As he rounded a curve of the bluff-top, he could look northward, and there, at the city's edge, was the true Northland, in the stretches of pine and birch and poplar that framed the grim eye of Dead Squaw Lake. And he loved it as he could never love the lax and steamy and foolishly laughing isles he had once seen in the Caribbean.

Through all of his meditation ran his startled remembrance of Jinny Marshland on the witness stand. He was still indignant that in a city so small as Grand Republic he had never seen her.

But he knew that, for all his talk at public dinners about Midwestern Democracy, the division between the proprietors and the serfs was as violent in Grand Republic as in London. The truckdriver might call Boone Havock, the contractor, "Boone," when they met in the Eitelfritz Brauhaus (as with remarkable frequency they did meet), but he would never enter Boone's house or his church, and as for Boone's asylum, the Federal Club, neither the truckdriver nor any Scandinavian or Finn with less than $10,000 income nor any recognizable Jew whatever would be allowed even to gawk through the leaded-glass windows (imported).

Even Lucius Fliegend, Jinny's Jewish employer, that fine and sensitive old man, could not belong to the Federal Club, but had to play his noontime chess in the Athletic Club. And as a professing member of Democracy, Cass was ashamed that not since he had been elected judge had he once been in the Athletic Club.

He would remedy that right away. Tomorrow.

He was abnormally conscious of the universal and multiple

revolution just then, in the early 1940's, from sulfa drugs and surrealism and semantics to Hitler, but he was irritated by all the Voices, by the radio prophets and the newspaper-column philosophers. He had had two competent years in Washington as a Member of Congress. Sick of the arguments, he had refused to be re-elected, yet now that he was back in his native town, sometimes he missed the massacres in the Coliseum, and felt a little bored and futile.

And ever since his divorce from the costly and clattering Blanche, he had been lonely. Could a Jinny Marshland cure his loneliness, his confusions in the skyrocketing world?

Then he rebuked himself.

Why should a charming girl, probably a dancer to phonographs, have any desire to cure the lonelinesses of forty-year-old single gentlemen? There was tenderness and loyalty in Jinny, he felt, but what would she want with a judge whom she would find out not to be a judge at all but another gaunt and early-middle-aged man who played the flute? Thus he raged and longed as he neared his house. It is understood that the newer psychiatrists, like the older poets, believe that patients do fall in love at first sight.

Cass's house was sometimes known as "Bergheim" and sometimes as "the old Eisenherz place." It had been built as a summer residence—in those days it had seemed to be quite out in the country—by Simon Eisenherz, greatest of the

Radisson County pioneers, in 1888, and purchased by Cass's father, Owen Timberlane, in 1929. Owen had died there, less than a year later, leaving it jointly to his wife, Marah, and to Cass, along with a local fortune of forty or fifty thousand dollars.

The house was somber and somehow tragic, and when Cass's mother died there, also, and he took Blanche, his wife, to it, she had hated it as much as he himself loved it. As a boy he had considered it the wonderful castle, the haunt of power and beauty, which no ordinary mortal like a Timberlane could ever hope to own complete. He still felt so.

George Hame, his court reporter, said that Bergheim was a wooden model of the court house, and it did have a circular tower and an octagonal conservatory, now called the "sun room." It was painted a dark green, merely because it had always been painted dark green. Over the porches there were whole gardens of jig-saw blossoms, and two of the windows were circular, and one triangular, with ruby glass. Cass admitted everything derisive that was said about this monstrosity, and went on loving it, and explaining that if you opened all of the windows all of the time, it wasn't airless inside—not very—not on a breezy day.

As he came up the black-and-white marble walk to the bulbous carriage-porch, a black kitten, an entire stranger, was sitting on a step. It said "meow," not whiningly but in a friendly mood, as between equals, and it looked at Cass in a

23

way that dared him to invite it in for a drink.

He was a lover of cats, and he had had none since the ancient and misanthropic Stephen had died, six months before. He had a lively desire to own this little black clown, all black, midnight black, except for its sooty yellow eyes. It would play on the faded carpets when he came home from the court room to the still loneliness that, in the old house, was getting on his nerves.

"Well, how are you, my friend?" he said.

The kitten said she was all right. And about some cream now——?

"Kitten, I can't steal you from some child who's out looking for you. It wouldn't be right to invite you in."

The kitten did not answer anything so naive and prudish. It merely said, with its liquid and trusting glance, that Cass was its god, beyond all gods. It frisked, and dabbled at a fly with its tiny black paw, and looked up at him to ask, "How's that?"

"You are a natural suborner of perjury and extremely sweet," admitted Cass, as he scooped it up and took it through the huge oak door, down the dim hallway to the spacious kitchen and to Mrs. Higbee, his cook-general.

Mrs. Higbee was sixty years old, and what is known as "colored," which meant that she was not quite so dark of visage as Webb Wargate after his annual Florida tanning. She was graceful and sensible and full of love and loyalty. She was in no way a comic servant; she was like any other wholesome Middle-Class American, with an accent like that of any other emigree from Ohio. It must be said that Mrs. Higbee was not singularly intelligent; only slightly more intelligent than Mrs. Boone Havock or Mrs. Webb Wargate; not more than twice as intelligent as Mrs. Vincent Osprey. She was an Episcopalian, and continued to be one, for historic reasons, though she was not greatly welcomed in the more fashionable temples of that faith. Judge Timberlane depended on her good sense rather more than he did on that of George Hame or his friend Christabel Grau.

Mrs. Higbee took the black kitten, tickled it under the chin, and remarked. "Our cat?"

"I'm afraid so. I've stolen it."

"Well, I understand a black cat is either very good luck or very bad luck, I forget which, so we can take a chance on it. What's its name?"

"What is it? A her?"

"Let's see. Um, I think so."

"How about 'Cleo'? You know—from Cleopatra. The Egyptians worshiped cats, and Cleopatra was supposed to be thin and dark and uncanny, like our kitten."

But he was not thinking of Queen Cleopatra. He was thinking of Jinny Marshland, and the thought was uneasy with him.

"All right, Judge. You, Cleo, I'm going to get those fleas off you right away tomorrow, and no use your kicking."

Cass marveled, "Has she got fleas?"

"Has—she—got—fleas! Judge, don't you ever take a real good look at females?"

"Not often. Oh, Mrs. Higbee, you know I'm dining out tonight—at Dr. Drover's."

"Yes. You'll get guinea hen. And that caramel ice cream. And Miss Grau. You won't be home early."

"Anything else I ought to know about the party?"

"Not a thing. . . . Will you look at that Cleo! She knows where the refrigerator is, already!"

In Cass's set, which was largely above the $7000 line, it was as obligatory to dress for party dinners as in London, and anyway, he rather liked his solid tallness in black and white. He dawdled in his bedroom, not too moonily thinking of Jinny yet conscious of her. A bright girl like that would do things with this room which, he admitted, habit and indifference and too much inheritance of furniture had turned into a funeral vault. It was a long room with meager windows and a fireplace bricked-up years ago.

The wide bed was of ponderous black walnut, carved with cherubs that looked like grapes and grapes that looked like cherubs, and on it was a spread of yellowed linen. The dresser was of black walnut also, with a mortuary marble slab; the wardrobe was like three mummy-cases on end, though not so gay; and littered over everything were books on law and economics and Minnesota history.

"It is a gloomy room. No wonder Blanche insisted on sleeping in the pink room."

He heard a friendly, entirely conversational "Meow?" and saw that the gallant Cleo had come upstairs to explore. All cats have to know about every corner of any house they choose to honor, but sometimes they are timid about caves under furniture. There have, indeed, been complaining and tiresome cats. But Cleo talked to him approvingly about her new home.

For so young and feminine a feline, she was a complete Henry M. Stanley. She looked at the old bedspread and patted its fringe. She circulated around under the old Chinese teakwood chair, in which no one had ever sat and which no one even partly sane would ever have bought. She glanced into the wardrobe, and cuffed a shoelace which tried to trip her.

She said, "All right—fine" to Cass, and went on to the other rooms.

In that stilly house he continued to hear her jaunty cat-slang till she had gone into the gray room, the last and largest of the six master's-bedrooms. Then he jumped, at a long and terrified moan. He hurried across the hall. Cleo was crouched, staring at the bed upon which had died his mother, that silent and bitter woman christened Marah Nord.

The tiny animal shivered and whimpered till he compassionately snatched it up and cuddled it at his neck. It shivered once more and, as he took it back to his own den, it began timidly to purr, in a language older than the Egyptian.

"Too many ghosts in this house, Cleo. You must drive them out—you and *she*. I have lived too long among shadows."

3

BOUND FOR DR. DROVER'S and the presumable delights of dinner, he walked down Varennes Boulevard, past the houses of the very great: the red-roofed Touraine château of Webb Wargate, the white-pillared brick Georgian mansion (with a terrace, and box-trees in wine jars) of the fabulous contractor, Boone Havock, and the dark granite donjon and the bright white Colonial cottage (oversize) in which dwelt and mutually hated each other the rival bankers Norton Trock and John William Prutt.

On his judge's salary, without the inheritance from his father, Cass could never have lived in this quarter. It was the Best Section; it was Mayfair, where only Episcopalians, Presbyterians, Congregationalists, and the more Gothic Methodists—all Republicans and all golf-players—lived on a golden isle amid the leaden surges of democracy.

He turned left on Schoolcraft Way, into a neighborhood not so seraphic yet still soundly apostolic and Republican, and came to the square yellow-brick residence of his friend, Dr. Roy Drover. Roy said, and quite often, that his place might not be so fancy as some he knew, but it was the only completely air-conditioned house in town, and it had, in the Etruscan catacombs of its basement, the most powerful oil furnace and the best game-room, or rumpus room—with a red-and-silver bar, a billiard table, a dance-floor, and a rifle-range—in all of Grand Republic, which is to say in all of the Western Hemisphere.

With the possible exception of Bradd Criley the lawyer, Dr. Drover was Cass's closest friend.

Roy was two years older than Cass, who was two years older than Bradd, and it is true that in boyhood, four years make a generation, yet from babyhood to college days, Cass and Roy and Bradd had formed an inseparable and insolently exclusive gang, to the terror of all small animals within hiking distance of Grand Republic. They did such pleasurable killing together; killing frogs, killing innocent and terrified snakes, killing gophers, and later, when they reached the maturity of shotguns, killing ducks and snipe and rabbits. Like Indians they had roamed this old Chippewa Indian land, familiars of swamp and crick (not creek), cousins to the mink and mushrat (not muskrat), heroes of swimming hole and ice-skating and of bobsledding down the long, dangerous Ottawa Heights. And once, finding a midden filled with stone slivers, they had been very near to their closest kin, the unknown Indians of ten thousand years ago, who came here for stone weapons when the last glacier was retreating.

Growing older, they had shown variations of civilization and maturity. Bradd Criley had become a fancy fellow, wavy-haired and slick about his neckties, a dancing man and a seducer of girls, adding industry to his natural talents for the destruction of women. Cass Timberlane had gone bookish and somewhat moral. Only Roy Drover, graduating from medical school and becoming a neat surgeon, a shrewd diagnostician, a skillful investor of money and, before forty, a rich man, had remained entirely unchanged, a savage and a small boy.

He preferred surgery, but in a city as small as Grand Republic, he could not specialize entirely, and he kept up his practice as a physician.

At forty-three, Dr. Drover looked fifty. He was a large man, tall as Cass Timberlane and much thicker, with a frontier mustache, a long black 1870-cavalryman mustache, a tremendous evangelical voice, and a wide but wrinkled face.

In a way, he was not a doctor at all. He cared nothing for people except as he could impress them with his large house, his log fishing-lodge, named "Roy's Rest," in the Arrowhead Lake Region, and his piratical airplane trips to Florida, where he noisily played roulette and, taking no particular pains to conceal it from his wife, made love to manicure girls posing as movie actresses and completely fooling the contemptuously shrewd Dr. Drover.

When Roy was drunk—that did not happen often, and never on a night before he was to operate—he got into fights with doormen and taxi-drivers, and always won them, and always got forgiven by the attendant policeman, who recognized him as one of their own hearty sort, as a medical policeman.

He played poker, very often and rather late, and he usually won. He read nothing except the *Journal of the American Medical Association*, the newspapers, and his ledger. Because he liked to have humble customers call him "Doc," he believed that he was a great democrat, but he hated all Jews, Poles, Finns, and people from the Balkans, and he always referred to Negroes as "darkies" or "smokes."

He said loudly, "Speaking as a doctor, I must tell you that it is a scientifically proven fact that all darkies, without exception, are mentally just children, and when you hear of a smart one, he's just quoting from some renegade white man. Down South, at Orlando, I got to talking to some black caddies, and they said, 'Yessir, Mr. White Man, you're dead right. We don't want to go No'th. Up there, they put you to work!' All the darkies are lazy and dumb, but that's all right with me. They'll never have a better friend than I am, and they all know it, because they can see I understand 'em!"

Roy's most disgusted surprise had been in meeting a New York internist who told him that in that Sidon there was an orchestra made up of doctors, who put their spare time in on Mozart instead of duck-hunting.

From land investments, which he made in co-operation with Norton Trock, Roy had enough capital to make sure that his two sons would not have to be driven and martyred doctors, like him, but could become gentlemanly brokers.

Roy and his pallid wife, Lillian, were considered, in Grand Republic, prime examples of the Happy Couple.

She hated him, and dreaded his hearty but brief embraces, and prayed that he would not turn the two boys, William Mayo Drover and John Erdmann Drover, into his sort of people, Sound, Sensible, Successful Citizens with No Nonsense about Them.

Cass Timberlane knew, in moments of mystic enlightenment, that whether or not Roy Drover was his best friend, there was no question but that Roy was his most active enemy.

He had for years mocked Cass's constant reading, his legal scruples, his failure to make slick investments, and his shocking habit of listening to Farmer-Laborites. After Cass had become a judge, Roy grumbled, "I certainly wish I could make my money as easy as that guy does—sitting up there on his behind and letting the other fellows do the work." Tonight, Cass sighed that Roy would certainly ridicule Jinny Marshland, if he ever met that young woman.

But Roy had been his intimate since before he could remember. There had never been any special reason for breaking with him and, like son with father, like ex-pupil with ex-teacher, Cass had an uneasy awe of his senior and a longing—entirely futile—to make an impression on him. Cass's pride in being elected to Congress and the bench was less than in being a better duck-shot than Roy.

There were present, for dinner and two tables of bridge, the Drovers, Cass, Christabel Grau, the Boone Havocks, and the Don Pennlosses.

Chris Grau was the orphaned daughter of a wagon-manufacturer. She was much younger than the others, and she was invited as an extra-woman partner for Cass. She was a plump and rather sweet spinster of thirty-two who, until the recent taking off, had suffered from too much affectionate mother. She not only believed that in the natural course of events Cass would fall in love with her and marry her, but also that there is any natural course of events. Rose Pennloss, wife of the rather dull and quite pleasant Donald, the grain-dealer, was Cass's sister, but Cass and she liked each other and let each other alone.

It was Boone Havock and his immense and parrot-squawking wife Queenie who were the great people, the belted earl and terraced countess, of the occasion; they were somewhat more energetic and vastly more wealthy than Dr. Drover, and it was said that Boone was one of the sixteen most important men in Minnesota.

He had started as a lumberjack and saloon-bouncer and miner and prizefighter—indeed, he had never left off, and his success in railroad-contracting, bridge-building, and factory-construction was due less to his knowledge of how to handle steel than to his knowledge of how to battle with steel-workers. But he owned much of the stock in the genteel

Blue Ox National Bank, and he was received with flutters in the gray-velvet and stilly office of the bank-president, Norton Trock.

Queenie Havock had the brassiest voice and the most predictable anti-labor prejudices in Grand Republic; her hair looked like brass, and her nose looked somewhat like brass, and she was such a brass-hearted, cantankerous, vain, grasping, outrageous old brazen harridan that people describing her simply had to add, "But Queenie does have such a sense of humor and such a kind heart."

It was true. She had the odd and interesting sense of humor of a grizzly bear.

For a town which was shocked by the orgies of New York and Hollywood, there was a good deal of drinking in Grand Republic. All of them, except Chris Grau and Roy Drover, had three cocktails before dinner. Roy had four.

Throughout dinner, and during vacations from the toil of bridge, the standard conversation of their class and era was carried on. If Cass and his sister, Rose, did not chime in, they were too accustomed to the liturgy to be annoyed by it.

This was the credo, and four years later, the war would make small difference in its articles:

Maids and laundresses are now entirely unavailable; nobody at all has any servants whatsoever; and those who do have, pay too much and get nothing but impertinence.

Strikes must be stopped by law, but the Government must never in any way interfere with industry.

All labor leaders are crooks. The rank and file are all virtuous, but misled by these leaders.

The rank and file are also crooks.

Children are now undisciplined and never go to bed till all-hours, but when we were children, we went to bed early and cheerfully.

All public schools are atrocious, but it is not true that the teachers are underpaid, and, certainly, taxes must be kept down.

Taxes, indeed, are already so oppressive that not one of the persons here present knows where his next meal or even his next motor car will come from, and these taxes are a penalty upon the industrious and enterprising, imposed by a branch of the Black Hand called "Bureaucracy."

America will not get into this war between Hitler and Great Britain, which will be over by June, 1942.

But we are certainly against Fascism—because why?—because Fascism just means Government Control, and we're against Government Control in Germany *or* in the United States! When our Government quits interfering and gives Industry the green light to go ahead, then we'll show the world what the American System of Free Enterprise can do to provide universal prosperity.

Boone Havock can still, at sixty, lick any seven Squareheads in his construction gangs; he carries on his enterprises not for profit—for years and years that has been entirely consumed by these taxes—but solely out of a desire to give work to the common people. He once provided a fine running shower-bath for a gang in Kittson County, but none of the men ever used it, and though he himself started with a shovel, times have changed since then, and all selfless love for the job has departed.

Dr. Drover also carries on solely out of patriotism.

The wife of President Franklin D. Roosevelt, a woman who has so betrayed her own class that she believes that miners and Negroes and women are American citizens, ought to be compelled by law to stay home.

We rarely go to the movies, but we did just happen to see a pretty cute film about gang-murder.

The Reverend Dr. Quentin Yarrow, pastor of St. Anselm's P.E., is a fine man, very broad-minded and well-read, and just as ready to take a drink or shoot a game of golf as any regular guy.

Jay Laverick, of the flour mills, is a fine man, a regular guy, always ready to shoot a game of golf or take a drink, but he has been hitting up the hard stuff pretty heavy since his little wife passed away, and he ought to remarry.

Cass should certainly remarry, and we suspect that it is Chris Grau, also present, whom Cass has chosen and already kissed—at least.

You can't change human nature.

We don't fall for any of these 'isms.

While we appreciate wealth—it shows that a man has ability—maybe Berthold Eisenherz, with his brewery and half the properties on the Blue Ox Range that are still producing iron ore, and this damn showy picture of his by some Frenchman named Renoir, is *too* wealthy. He never shoots golf or shoots ducks, which looks pretty queer for a man rich as that. What the devil does he do with himself?

Some of these smart-aleck critics claim that Middlewestern businessmen haven't changed much since that book—what's its name?—by this Communist writer, Upton Sinclair— "Babbitt," is it?—not changed much since that bellyache appeared, some twenty years ago. Well, we'd like to tell those fellows that in these twenty-odd years, the American businessman has changed completely. He has traveled to Costa Rica and Cuba and Guatemala, as well as Paris, and in the *Reader's Digest* he has learned all about psychology and modern education. He's been to a symphony concert, and by listening to the commentators on the radio, he has now become intimate with every branch of Foreign Affairs.

"As an ex-Congressman, don't you think that's true?" demanded Don Pennloss.

"Why, I guess it is," said Cass.

He had tried to bring into the conversation the name of

Jinny Marshland, but he had found no links between her and taxes or Costa Rica. Now he blurted, "Say, I had a pleasant experience in court today."

Roy Drover scoffed, "You mean you're still working there? The State still paying you good money for just yelling 'Overruled!' every time a lawyer belches?"

"They seem to be. Well, we had a pretty dull sidewalk case, but one witness was an unusually charming girl——"

"We know. You took her into your chambers and conferred with her!" bellowed Boone Havock.

"He did not. He's no fat wolf like you, you lumberjack!" screamed Queenie.

"Good gracious, I didn't know it was so late. Quarter past eleven. Can I give you a lift, Cass?" said Chris Grau.

4

"I'LL DROP YOU at your house, and if you ask me very prettily, I'll come in for a night-cap," said Chris, outside the Drovers'.

"No, I'll tell you: I'll drive you home in your car, and then walk back to my house."

"Walk? Back? At this time of night? Why, it's almost two miles!"

"People have walked two miles."

"Not unless they were playing golf."

"All right, I'll borrow a cane from Roy and a condensed-milk can and knock it all the way back."

"Cassy, you are the most contrary man living!"

He hated being called "Cassy," like a slave in Harriet Beecher Stowe, and he did not want Chris at his house. For the hour or two before he went to bed, late as usual, he wanted to be alone. He had to look after the welfare of his new friend, Cleo. He wanted to think, at least to think of what it was that he wanted to think about. And, like most men who sometimes complain of being lonely, he just liked to be alone.

Chris did not go on teasing him. He had to admit that, fusser and arranger and thwarted mother though she was, Chris liked to do whatever her men wanted.

At thirty-two, Christabel Grau was a round and soft and taffy-colored virgin with strands of gray. If Jinny Marshland was like Cleo, a thin and restless and exciting young cat, Chris was the serene tabby cuddled and humming on the hearth.

As they drove to her home, she speculated, with an unusual irritation, "Didn't you think they were dull tonight?"

"I thought they talked about as usual."

"No, you didn't. For some reason, you were sizing them up tonight, and that started me noticing that——Oh, they're all darlings, and so smart—my, I bet there isn't a doctor at the Mayos' that's as clever as Roy—but they always make the same jokes, and they're so afraid of seeming sentimental. Roy wouldn't ever admit how he loves his collection of Florida shells, and of course Boone is as moony as a girl about his Beethoven records, and Queenie says he'll sit by himself for hours listening to 'em, even the hard quartets, and he's read all the lives of the composers, but he pretends he just has the records to show off. We're all so scared of getting out of the groove here, don't you think?"

"Yes—yes," said Cass, who hadn't heard a word.

"But I do love Grand Republic so."

"Yes."

Chris lived on the top floor of her ancestral mansion on Beltrami Avenue South, in the old part of town, in the valley. And on that street Cass had been born. Forty years ago it had been the citadel of the select residential district, where dwelt all that was rich and seemly. Cass's present home, Bergheim, was aged, but the other houses on Ottawa Heights had been built since 1900. These new mansions did well in the matter of Mount Vernon pillars and lumpy French-farmhouse towers, but they were plain as warehouses compared with the Beltrami Avenue relics, which had an average of twenty-two wooden gargoyles apiece, and one of which exhibited not only a three-story tower but had a Tudor chimney running through it.

Many of these shrines had been torn down to save taxes, and others turned into a home for nuns, a home for pious Lutheran old ladies, a business college, a Y.W.C.A. In seventy years, the Belgravia of Grand Republic had been built and become an historic ruin, and men whose own frail tissues had already lasted more than eighty years, looking upon a granite castle now become a school for the anxious daughters of improbable gentry, whispered in awe, "Why, that house is old as the hills—almost seventy-five years old!"

But Chris Grau, after her mother's death, had thriftily remodeled their three-story-and-basement residence into seven apartments, keeping the top floor for herself and renting the rest. "Chris is an A 1 business-woman," said Roy Drover, and Roy would know.

Cass was "just coming in for a second, for one drink," but he felt relaxed, he felt at home, and wanted to linger in that room, feminine yet firm, lilac-scented, with soft yellow walls and chairs in blue linen, with many flowers and a Dutch-tile fireplace and all the newest new books about psychology and Yugoslavian prime ministers, many of which Chris had started to read.

She mixed a highball for him, without talking about it. She had excellent Bourbon—she was a good and intelligent woman. She sat on the arm of his chair, a chair that was just deep enough for him; she smoothed his hair, without ruffling it, she kissed his temple, without being moist, and she slipped away and sat casually in her own chair before he had time to think about whether he had any interest in caresses tonight.

"Yes, we were all awfully obvious, tonight," she meditated. "Why didn't you bawl us out?"

"I'm not an uplifter, Chris. People are what they are. You learn that in law-practice. I haven't the impertinence to tell old friends how I think they ought to talk."

"You pretend to be nothing but scholarship and exactness, but you're really all affection for the people you know."

"You'll be saying I'm a sentimentalist next, Chris."

"Well, aren't you? You even love cats."

"Hate 'em!"

——Why did I lie like that?

"Cassy, I——Oh, I'm sorry, *Cass*!"

——She even sees when I'm offended, without my having to rub her nose in it. I could be very solid and comfortable if I married her. She'd give warmth to that chilly old house. We

43

belong together; we're both Old Middlewest, informal but not rackety. Let's see: Chris must be nine years younger than I am, and——

She was talking on: "Speaking of uplift, I'll never give up hoping that some day you'll be a United States Senator or on the Supreme Court Bench. There isn't a man in the United States who has more to give the public."

"No, no, Chris, that's sheer illusion. I'm simply a backwoods lawyer. You know, any legal gent looks considerably larger and brighter, up there on the bench."

"I won't have you——"

"Besides, I feel lost in Washington. One brown rabbit doesn't mean much in that menagerie of cassowaries."

"What *is* a cassowary?"

"Eh? Damned if I know. I think it's a bird."

"I'll look it up, right now."

"Not now. I really want to talk to you."

"Well, it's about time!"

They smiled, secretly and warmly. She seemed to him as intimate and trusty as his own self when she went on:

"Maybe it was because Blanche was so ambitious that you disliked Washington. An impossible wife for you!"

"I didn't dislike the place—people walking under the trees in the evening, like a village. It's just that I have some kind of an unformulated idea that I want to be identified with Grand Republic—help in setting up a few stones in what may be a new Athens. It's this northern country—you know, stark and clean—and the brilliant lakes and the tremendous prairies to the westward—it may be a new kind of land for a new kind of people, and it's scarcely even started yet."

"Oh, I know!"

——She loves this place, too. She has roots, where Blanche has nothing but aerial feelers. Hm. She's thirty-two. She could still have half a dozen children. I'd like children around me, and not just Mrs. Higbee and Cleo and a radio and a chessboard.

Chris came, not too impulsively, to kneel before him and clasp both his hands, as she said trustingly:

"Of course you know best. The only reason why I'd like to see you in the Senate is that Grand Republic would be so proud of you!" Her eyes were all his, her voice was gentle, and her lips were not far from his. "Though maybe that's silly, Cass, because I guess the town couldn't be any prouder of you than it is already—no prouder than I am, right now!"

There was a scent of apple-blossoms about her. He leaned forward. Without moving, she seemed to be giving herself to him. Her hand was at her soft bosom and her lips lifted.

Then, from far off, he heard the wailing of a frightened kitten, gallant but hard-pressed.

Without willing it, he was on his feet, blurting good night, hastening home to the small black absurdity of Cleo.

5

HIS PANIC was gone before he had stepped like a soldier eight blocks in that nipping northern air and begun to mount the Heights. The streets were friendly with the fresh-leaved elms and maples for which Grand Republic was notable; the cherries were in blossom, and the white lilacs and mountain ash.

There were dark groves along the way, and alleys that rose sharply and vanished around curves, there were gates in brick walls and hedges; a quality by night which was odd and exciting to Cass Timberlane, a life to be guessed at, not too plain. This was no prairie town, flat and rectangular, with every virtue and crusted sin exposed.

As he climbed, he could see the belated lights of farmhouses on the uplands across the valley, the lights of buses down on Chippewa Avenue, and in simplicity he loved his city now instead of fretting that its typical evening conversation was dull—as dull as that of Congressmen in the cloakroom or newspaper correspondents over the poker table. But he fretted over himself and his perilous single state, with nervousness about the fact that Chris Grau was likely at any time to pick him up and marry him.

——No, I'll never marry again. I'd never be a good

husband. I'm too solemn—maybe too stuffy. I'm too devoted to the law.

——Am I?

——I must get married. I can't carry on alone. Life is too meaningless when you have no one for whom you want to buy gifts, or steal them.

——If I did marry, I think that this time I could make a go of it. I understand women a *little* better now. I shouldn't have minded Blanche's love of tinsel, but just laughed at her. And Chris thinks of other people. With her, I'd be happier and happier as the years went by——

——Lord, that sounds so aged! It was her youth that I liked so much in that girl on the witness-stand yesterday—or today, was it? What was her name again—Virginia something? . . . Curious. I can't see her any more!

In law-school, at the University of Minnesota, Cass had listened to a lecture by that great advocate, Hugo Lebanon of Minneapolis, had gone up glowingly to talk with him, and had been invited to dinner at the Lebanon marble palace on Lake of the Isles. There was a tall, pale, beautiful daughter named Blanche.

So Cass married the daughter.

She was emphatic about being a pure Anglo-Saxon who went right back, even if Warwickshire remained curiously unstirred about her going right back, to a gray stone house in Warwick.

She was the more vigorously pure about it because there were whispers of Jewish blood. She found it hard to put up with the mongrel blood of the furniture-dealing Timberlanes, and she was revolted when Cass estimated that through his father, he was three-eighths British stock, one-sixteenth French Canadian, and one-sixteenth Sioux Indian—whence, he fondly believed, came his tall, high-cheeked spareness—and through his mother he was two-eighths Swedish, one-eighth German, one-eighth Norwegian.

Blanche did not, after the magnitude and salons of Minneapolis, much like Grand Republic. When she came there as a bride, in 1928, the Renoir had not yet arrived, so there was no one to talk to.

She encouraged Cass to run for Congress; she served rye, with her own suave hands, to aldermen and county commissioners. Cass and she attained Washington, and she loved it like a drunkard, and loved the chance of meeting—at least of being in the same populous rooms with—French diplomats and Massachusetts senators and assorted Roosevelts. When Cass felt swamped, as a lone representative among more than four hundred, when he longed for the duck pass and his law-office and the roaring of Roy Drover, when he refused to run for reelection, Blanche rebelled. She was not going back to listen to Queenie Havock shrieking about her love-life, she shouted, and Cass could not blame her, though he did sigh that there were also other sounds audible in Grand Republic.

There was a mild, genial Englishman, Fox Boneyard, an importer of textiles, who lived in New York but was often about Washington; he had the unfortunate illusions about beautiful American women that Englishmen sometimes do have, and he also had more money than the Honorable Cass Timberlane.

Blanche married him.

During the divorce, Cass did have sense enough to refuse to pay alimony to a woman who was marrying a richer man, and who had never consented to having children. But he still loved Blanche enough to hate her, and to hate convulsively the sight of a coat she had left behind, and the wrinkles in it that had come from her strong shoulders. He underwent the familiar leap from partisanship and love to enmity and a sick feeling that he had been betrayed.

He grimly finished his last days in Congress, and then quite dramatically went to pieces. He was a feeling man, and with a whisky breath and unshaved, he was an interesting figure in water-front cafés in Trinidad and Cartagena, and to his white cruel love he paid the tribute of being sick in toilets and talking to other saintly idiots about having lost his soul.

But even love for Blanche could not keep Cass Timberlane at this romantic business for more than two months, and after another six, most of them sedately spent in and about the Temple in London, he returned to the affection of Grand Republic, and practised law for three more years before he was elected to the bench.

Election was not easy. The routine politicians disliked him because he had left Congress, because he could not be guided and because he made fun of all clauses in political speeches beginning with "than whom." The churches, particularly the Lutherans, who were powerful in Radisson County, disapproved of him because he had been divorced. The Republicans were doubtful about him because he had been amiable with Farmer-Labor leaders, and the Farmer-Laborites distrusted him because he lived in a large house. In fact, there was really no reason for his being elected except that he was known to be honest, courageous, and learned, and that he had once lent a grateful and active Norwegian farmer five dollars.

But he was a judge now, and the district had the fixed habit of him, and if he would only marry a sound churchwoman, like Christabel Grau, and give a little more attention to the Chamber of Commerce and to his bridge game, he might go on forever, a sound and contented Leading Citizen.

6

HE WAS THINKING of Chris Grau as he entered the long hallway of Bergheim, lit only by a bogus-ancient pierced-brass lamp. Then Cleo, the midnight-colored kitten, was galloping up to him, warming his ankles, purring frantically, and with that ecstatic rhythm there came back to him Jinny Marshland's name and the vision of her face that he had lost: the surprising smallness of her face, the absurd hawk nose, the jaunty hair hanging to her shoulders, the bright curiosity in her eyes, her plunging youthful walk.

He lifted Cleo and thought how light Jinny would be to lift. Cleo sat in his lap while he worked out a chess-problem for nightcap; she moaned only a little when he played the flute for a moment; and when he put her back into the box filled with clipped paper that Mrs. Higbee had provided behind the kitchen stove, Cleo made a business of curling round and sleeping, as a cat who belonged there and liked it.

"A very sound kitten," Cass pronounced, and went comfortably up to bed, pleasant in the thought that tomorrow the kitten would be here, that some time this week he could most certainly see Jinny.

He awoke rigid under the familiar torture which some dozen times a year the mysterious Enemy inflicted upon him: the torture of being bored by the too-frequent presence of his own self, bored to cold emptiness by the inescapable and unchanging sight and sound of Cass Timberlane, a man whom he usually respected, sometimes found slightly funny, but of whose complaints and futile plans, round and round in the mind, of whose demands for incessant attention, of whose mirrored gawky face, of whose heavy voice, a murky cloud forever in the air about him, he was sick to a state of fury. Could he never get away from that man? Was he condemned forever to awaken to the sight of that thick brown plowman's-hand on the blanket, to the intrusiveness of that man's inevitable whining daydream: "I will find my companion; I'll go on a journey somewhere and I'll find her; I'll tell her about Grand Republic and she'll want to come here, and we'll have a real family, with trust and serenity, and I'll be a judge that—people will say, 'His court is the model of fairness and mercy,' and she will be glad of it; *she*——"

Oh, so that intrusive man was going to fall in love now, was he, with his "Look at me! How exciting I am!" If he could only forget the name and essence of Cass Timberlane and be blissfully submerged, not in some rainbow-striped Oversoul but in the tenderness of one other person.

Then he was sick of being sick of too-much-self, and with the bright thought of Jinny he drove out his tired brooding upon his brooding.

She actually did exist. He had seen her. In her was tolerant friendship, and in her fresh cheeks and young bosom there was promise of salvation by passion. With her he could escape into the refuge of the Quiet Mind, away equally from the lonely Cass and from a world of booming politics and oratory.

Was Jinny too young for him? Nonsense! He was only forty-one, and stronger than any of these jazz-mad youngsters. And she would make him still younger, along with her.

He went to sleep in dreams of a Jinny to whom, actually, he had never said anything whatever except, "I think you'd better confine yourself to answering the questions, without comment, Miss Marshland."

There was nothing of the repining hermit in the Cass who leaped up in the morning, greeted Cleo, who considered his toes very funny, had a shower-bath and a scrupulous shave (telling himself, as always, that the electric razor was a very fine Modern Invention), greeted Mrs. Higbee, wolfed griddle cakes and sausages, and tramped out upon the fresh May morning and the courts of law.

George Hame, his court-reporter, greeted him filially, though George was only three years younger, and filled his inkwell and his water carafe and opened his mail.

The mail was of the usual: sixteen widows who had been cheated, of whom seven sounded as though they ought to have been; and sixteen organizations which desired the Judge to send in a little contribution.

The other two judges of the district came in cordially:

Judge Stephen Douglas Blackstaff, the Old Roman, and Judge Conrad Flaaten, who was Lutheran but gay. Judge Blackstaff wanted a cigarette and Judge Flaaten wanted advice, and between them and the mail and George Hame's admiration, Cass felt like his own man again, resolute and happy in his workshop.

When he marched out into the court room and the bailiff pounded his table and the nine persons present, besides the jury and the officers of court, all made motions somewhat like rising in his honor, then all the dread of too-much-self had gone out of Cass, along with much of his excitement about a stray young woman named Marshland, and he was again the tribal chieftain on his leather throne.

The case of Miss Tilda Hatter *vs.* the City of Grand Republic was concluded, and her many friends will be pleased to know that the jury was out for only sixteen minutes and awarded her $200 out of the $500 for which she had sued. Judge Timberlane reflected that Miss Hatter was almost certain to put on a spread for Jinny and her other boarders, with Bourbon, Coca-Cola, liverwurst, stuffed olives, and chocolate layer cake.

He went for lunch not to the proper Federal Club, where bankers and lawyers and grain-dealers sat around being high-class, but to the Athletic Club, which admitted Jews and Unitarians. He hoped to see Lucius Fliegend, the pasteboard-toy manufacturer, Jinny's boss.

On his way he went along Chippewa Avenue and saw the humble magnificence of the town's business center: the up-rearing limestone and aluminum of the Blue Ox National Bank, the bookshop that with a building of imitation half-timber tried to suggest the romance and antiquity of England, the one complete department store, Tarr's Emporium, with four vast floors crammed with treasures from Burma and Minneapolis, and the Bozard Beaux Arts Women's Specialty Shops, which everyone said was just as smart as New York or Halle Brothers of Cleveland.

Among the bustling citizens who looked like everybody else on every principal avenue from Bangor to Sacramento, there were trout-fishermen in high boots and Finnish section-hands and Swedish corn-planters from the prairie.

Grand Republic was metropolitan-looking in its black-glass and green-marble shop fronts, its uniformed traffic policemen with Sam Browne belts and pistol holsters, its florists' windows and La Marquise French Candy Shop, but it was small enough so that he was greeted—usually as "Judge," often as "Cass," occasionally as "Jedge"—five times on every block, while the policemen touched their caps in salute. Grand Republic was small enough so that a Mrs. George Hame had at least met a Mrs. Webb Wargate, and ventured to say, in church lobby, "Well, how is your boy Jamie doing in school, Mrs. Wargate?" It was small enough so that the Judge could know how the whole city worked, but it was also small enough so that Harley

Bozard, coming out of his shop, already knew that Cass had taken Chris Grau home last evening, and leered, "What's this I hear you're going to drive into the matrimonial slew again, Cass?"

It was all friendly; it restored his soul. He was too used to them to note the hideousness of a black old stone hotel with massive portals and torn lace curtains, and the car-parking lots that were like sores on the wholesome limbs of the streets, or to reflect that the only design for planning the city had always been the dollar-sign. What of that, when he could be greeted "H' are you, old boy!" by Frank Brightwing, the real-estate man, who was melodiously drunk on every Saturday evening and on every Sunday morning, at the Baptist Church, was as unaffectedly pious and hopeful as the cherubs he so much resembled.

The moment Cass was inside the railroad-station noisiness of the Athletic Club, he hunted up Lucius Fliegend, a gentle person with a thin beard, who might have been a professor of Greek.

He confessed, "Lucius, I'm ashamed that I haven't been around here lately, looking for a game of chess."

"You young fellows, you politicians, don't appreciate chess. In the good old days here, the lumbermen and the gamblers in iron-leases used to go out and steal a million dollars and come home and drink a quart of red-eye and sit down to six hours of chess. Now, they steal only a thousand, and then play bridge and drink gin, a lady's drink. Will you choose your pawn?"

After the game (which Lucius won), Cass spoke abruptly, for this was an honest and understanding man. "Yesterday in court I saw a young lady who says she works for you. Miss Marshland. I'd like to really meet her."

"Jinny is a lovely girl. Erica and I are fond of her. She is ambitious, but not in the sharp, bitter way of so many of these young career women. She's quite a good draftsman. She has a nice fantastic taste—she does some very funny pasteboard dolls for me. And she's beautiful, but she's also a frail, over-engined girl who will either burn herself out or fall in love with some appealing scamp who'll break her heart, unless some solid man traps her first."

"But would she *like* a solid man?"

"I doubt it. And, though he'd find it interesting, I don't know how much he'd enjoy nursing a young black panther."

"She's probably already engaged."

"I don't think so; merely has a lot of young men friends. But with all her fire, she's domestic. Her father is a druggist up here in Pioneer Falls, a pleasant fellow. He taught Jinny her Latin at the age of ten. Of course she forgot it at the age of twelve. She's a good girl and——"

"When will you invite us to dinner together?"

"Some time soon."

"No! Much sooner than that!"

57

"Very well. Next Saturday evening, provided Jinny isn't out canoeing with some handsome young man."

"Excellent!"

He was thinking of that "handsome young man" and astonished to find in himself a jealousy not coy but bitter and real. He hated jealousy and all its rotten fruits, as he had seen them in court, hated that sour suspiciousness which ferments in love, yet over a girl to whom he had once said just fourteen words, he was mildly homicidal toward an imaginary young man.

"I seem to be falling in love," he thought profoundly.

7

CASS WAS DISAPPOINTED when Mrs. Fliegend telephoned to him not to dress for dinner. He would have liked to show Jinny how stately he could be. But she reported that Jinny was "so thrilled to meet you; she thinks you were wonderful on the bench—so wise—and of course Lucius and I do, too, Judge."

He stroked Cleo, and sounded like her.

After pondering on precedents, he decided that it was far enough on in the spring for him to wear his white-flannel suit, with the tie from Marshall Field's. While he put these on, gravely, as though he were studying a brief, he wondered how much he was going to like Jinny. So far, he merely loved her.

Would she be one of these Professional Youths? Would she reek with gum and with the slang suitable to it: "Oh boy!" and "No soap" and "That's what you think"?

"Oh, quit it!" he said, aloud—and Cleo promised that she would.

He was so elegant tonight that he drove to the Fliegends', instead of walking.

The Fliegends' bulky old brown house was on South Beltrami, a block from Chris Grau's.

He felt guilty of disloyalty to Chris in loving young Jinny, but he felt even wickeder as he reflected that though he had been born only three blocks from the Fliegends', he had not been in their house since boyhood, and could not remember its rooms. Probably Chris and Bradd Criley and Boone Havock had never been inside it. In "Hie Friendly City," as we call it, we don't shoot Jews and Catholics and Socialists and saints. We just don't go calling on them.

Then Mrs. Fliegend was beaming on him at the door, while he imagined her saying, "You phony politician! You've never condescended to come to our house till you wanted us to play procurers for you. You, the great Anglo-Saxon judge and gentleman—you Sioux bastard! Get out!"

Mrs. Fliegend must have wondered why Judge Timberlane seemed so pleased by her mild greeting.

Looking past his hosts into the square living-room which made up half the first floor, he saw no Jinny, but only a great blankness where she should have been.

——Maybe she isn't coming? Ditched me for that young man in the canoe?

Mrs. Fliegend was soothing him, "Oh, she'll be here, Judge!"

——Is my youthful romance as obvious as all that?

Remembering it only from childhood, he had expected the interior of the Fliegend house to be Oriental and over-rich. But it was the elder German and Yankee pioneers who had satin-brocaded walls and Tudor fireplaces. Here, the walls were of white paneled wood, dotted with old maps of Minnesota and portraits of its early heroes: Ramsey, Sibley, Steele, Pike, Taliaferro.

"I didn't know you were such a collector of Minnesota items," said Cass.

——That sounded fatuous and condescending. I didn't mean to be.

Lucius explained, "I was born in Minnesota, in Long Prairie, and my father before me, near Marine Mills, where my grandfather settled. He fought through the Civil War, in the Third Minnesota. We are of the old generation."

Cass was meditating upon his rare gifts of ignorance when Jinny Marshland flew into the room.

She was no wild little hawk now, but a young lady. Her hair was put up, sleek and tamed, and she wore a dress of soft black with, at her pleated black girdle, one silver rose. She was quick-moving and friendly, and her greeting was almost excessive: "I'm terrified to meet you, Judge, after seeing you in court. I thought you were going to send me to Stillwater for contempt. You won't now, will you?"

Yet no spark came to him from her, and she was just another pretty girl, another reed bending to the universal south wind.

The other guests, a couple who came in with shy bumptiousness, made him feel as guilty at his neglect of them as had the Fliegends. They were Dr. Silbersee, refugee Jewish eye-ear-throat specialist from Vienna, 'cellist in the amateur double-quartet that was Grand Republic's only musical wonder, and his wife Helma, who was equally serious about the piano, Apfelkuchen, and the doctrines of the post-Freudian psychoanalysts.

Cass had been fretting all week, after his session with Chris Grau, that the local conversation was dull. He had wished, for the benefit of his unconscious protégée Jinny, to exhibit what he conceived to be a real European conversazione, complete with Rhine wine and seltzer. He got it, too, this evening, and he didn't care much for it. He realized again, as he had in Washington and in waterfront dives in Trinidad, that most conversation is dull. Aside from shop-talk, which includes the whispering of lovers, anything printed, a time-table or the rich prose of a tomato-catsup label, is more stimulating than any talk, even the screaming of six economists and an intellectual actress.

At dinner, the Fliegends and the Silbersees said that this fellow Hitler was no good, that it had been warm today, that it might be warmer tomorrow, that Toscanini was a good conductor, that rents in Grand Republic were very high just now, and that there was a Little Armenian Restaurant in Milwaukee.

It was, in perfection, New York, minus the taxi horns, and still Cass was not satisfied, and, so far as he could see, neither was Jinny.

At first, as the conversation took fire, she hadn't so much as a chip to throw into it. She sat mute, with her hands folded small and flat and meek, and she had no observations on the subject of Debussy, regarding which Lucius had represented her as highly eloquent. Cass decided that she was stupid, and that there wasn't much to be said for himself either.

But he noticed how quickly her dark eyes turned from speaker to speaker; how she weighed, and did not think very much of, her ponderous elders. Slowly he was hypnotized by her again; he felt her independence and her impatience to do things. Restless under this middle-aged droning, he wanted to be on her side. And he was a little afraid of her.

But he made a good deal of progress in his romance. To his original fourteen words of address to her, he had now added sixty-seven others, including, "No, no, you weren't late. I think I was ahead of time. I guess my watch is fast." No flowery squire could have said it more colorfully.

The Fliegends were lenient hosts, and after dinner (roast goose and potato pancakes, such heavenly stuff as Grand Republic rarely knew), they wedged the Silbersees in beside the grand piano, and sent Cass and Jinny "out to see the garden."

Like most houses in Grand Republic, where the first settlers huddled together instead of taking ten acres for each garden, the Fliegend abode was too close to its neighbors. But they had planted cedar hedges, and made a pool surrounded with wicker benches that were, surprisingly, meant to be sat upon.

Cass and Jinny did sit upon them, and he did not in the least feel that he was sitting upon a pink cloud. He was anxious to find out, while still posing as a big superior man, whether Jinny considered him a stuffy old party.

"Nice dinner," he said.

"Wasn't it?"

"This, uh, this Roy Harris they were talking about—do you know his music?"

"Just a little."

"Uh——"

"I've just heard some of it played."

"Yes, uh——I guess—I guess Dr. Silbersee is a very fine musician."

"Yes, isn't he."

"Yes."

"You've heard him play, Judge?"

"Yes, uh—oh yes, I've heard him play. A very fine 'cellist."

"Of course I don't know music well enough to tell, but I think he must be and——"

Then it broke:

"Jinny! Were you bored tonight?"

"How?"

"Our pompous talk."

"Why, I thought it was lovely talk. I was so interested about the conductors: Mitropoulos and Bruno Walter."

"Oh. You like musicians?"

"Love 'em. If I really knew any. But one thing did bother me."

"What?"

"I thought *you* were bored. I was watching you, Judge."

"And I was watching you."

"Two kids among the grown-ups!"

They both laughed very much, and he was grateful for being included in her conspiracy of youth.

The silent Jinny talked enough now. "I thought they were all so nice, and oh boy! are they ever learned! I guess the people in Vienna must be like them. But I wanted to hear *you* talk."

"Why?" It was too flagrant even to be called "fishing."

"I wanted to know how do criminals get that way, and can you help them, and——I'll bet they're awed by you."

"Not much."

"I would be. I was sort of disappointed by the court room, though. I thought there'd be a whole mob, holding their breaths, and sixteen reporters writing like mad, but they were—oh, as if they were waiting for a bus. But then when I looked at you—honestly, you scared me, Judge!"

"Now, now!"

"You *did*!"

"How could I? Judge Blackstaff might, but I'm just a hometown lawyer."

"You are not a home-town lawyer! Oh, I mean you are, of course, but I mean—you aren't *any* home-town lawyer!" She sounded proud of him, and eager. "On the bench, you looked as if you knew everything, and maybe you might be kind of sorry for me, for having murdered my Aunt Aggie and stolen the sewing-machine oil-can, but you'd put me away for ten years, for the good of society. Wouldn't you?"

"No, I'm afraid I'd resign from the bench first, Jinny."

"M!" She sounded gratified, and with some energy he kept himself from seizing her hand. It was fated that he should now take the next step, with "You came by bus, didn't you? May I drive you home?"

He, it seemed, might.

He said good night to the Fliegends and Silbersees with a feeling of having enlarged his knowledge of Grand Republic. When Jinny was beside him in his car, the major purposes of his life seemed to have been accomplished, even if he could express the ultimate glory only by a hesitating, "It was a very pleasant evening, didn't you think?"

8

THE BOARDING-HOUSE of Miss Tilda Hatter was the hobohemia of Grand Republic. It occupied the two upper floors of a senile brick building near Paul Bunyan Avenue, in a land of railroad sidings and six-man factories. On the ground floor of the building was the Lilac Lady Lunchroom: T. Hatter, Prop., at whose counter and four tousled tables eternal and poetic Youth could drink coffee and eat blueberry pie à la mode, with ice cream disgustingly but sweetly melting down into the blue-smeared debris, and talk about the high probability of their going to Minneapolis and singing on the radio, or going to Chicago and studying interior decorating.

Above the restaurant were a dozen bedrooms, with one bath, and a living-room agreeably littered with skis, skates, unstrung tennis rackets, stenographers' note-books, manuals on air-conditioning and gas-engine construction, burnt-out portable radio sets, empty powder compacts, empty gin bottles, and the *Poetic Works* of John Donne, with the covers missing. These upper rooms were reached by a covered wooden outside staircase.

The building had once been a dry-goods store and once the offices of a co-operative farmers' insurance company, and once a butcher-shop with a fancy-house above it, in which two young ladies had murdered the melancholy butcher. But now it was all orderly as a Y.W.C.A., and rather like it in the excessive amount of cigarette-smoking.

As Cass and Jinny drove up to it, she insisted, "You must come up a minute and say hello to Miss Hatter. She's convinced the jury gave her all that money only because you told them to, and she's one person that really worships you."

"Meaning that somebody else doesn't?"

His wheedling tone, the distractedness with which he turned his face toward her and so ran the car up on the curb as he was parking, were not to be distinguished from the large idiocies of any other injudicious young lover. She answered only, "You'd be surprised! Come, it's one flight up."

He had a daring hope that this girl, so desirable, with her bright face and young breast, did see him as the great man scattering nobility from the high throne of the bench. He knew that he wasn't anything of the kind, but merely a business umpire in a dusty hall. Yet if she could have such faith in him, she might lift him to whatever greatness she imagined in him. With solemnity and love he followed her up the flat-sounding steps and into the boarding-house salon.

Miss Hatter was mixing a heady beverage of gin, Coca-Cola, crème de rose, and tea, standing at a sloppy pine table, while four young people sat near her on the floor—not because there were no chairs but because they were at the age and intellectual claimancy when one does sit on the floor.

Miss Hatter screamed, "Oh, Judge!" As though he were a bishop or a movie star. "Jinny said she'd try to get you to drop in, but I never dreamed she *would!*"

——So this young woman had planned to have me drive her home. Am I gratified or do I feel let down? Anyway, she looks so charming, in fact, well, so aristocratic in her little black dress and that one silver rose, among these hit-or-a-miss yearners here.

Miss Hatter was going on: "Folks, this is Judge Timberlane. My, this is an honor. I'll say it is!"

Jinny introduced her four companions of the arts as they sulkily rose and dusted their knees. They were not too young—twenty-four to thirty—but the placid disregard of them by Grand Republic still kept them youthful and belligerent. They were Lyra Coggs, assistant city librarian, Wilma Gunton, head of the cosmetics department at Tarr's Emporium, Tracy Oleson, secretary to powerful Webb Wargate and a young man who seemed to Cass interesting enough to be looked at with suspicion, Eino Roskinen, aged twenty-four, butter-maker at the Northward Co-operative Dairy but, as Jinny explained, a born theater director.

Eino was a darkly serious young Finn; he looked at Jinny with what Cass nervously saw to be the greatest fondness and at Cass with the greatest dislike, so that Cass felt like an old windbag, though he had as yet said nothing more than, "Well! Good evening."

——So the struggle for her has started already. And I'm not going to give her up even to you, my Byronic young friend.

He was certain that Eino was an evil whelp, who meant no good to Jinny. He sat on a chair, near Miss Hatter, the only other person of his age and uncomfortable dignity, while all five of the young people were on the floor, chattering—especially the Jinny who had been so silent at the Fliegends':

"You know, Judge, we think we have an intellectual center here. Oh, we're tremendous. Wilma is going to New York to start a cosmetics company there—green lip-sticks—as soon as she can save enough money to ride there in a box-car. But our star is Eino. He has Theories. He says that the new America isn't made up of British stock and Irish and Scotch, but of the Italians and Poles and Icelanders and Finns and Hungarians and Slovaks. People like you and me are the Red Indians of the country. We'll either pass out entirely or get put on reservations, where we can do our Yankee tribal dances and wear our native evening clothes undisturbed. Isn't that the idea, Eino?"

"Not entirely, Jinx. We may allow full citizenship to some of the Yankee tribesmen, if they learn the principles of cooperation and give up their medicine-men—pastors they call 'em, I believe. But judges, now—I don't know about them. They're too corrupted by the native voodoo. I don't know whether they can learn to speak the American language."

"Don't you dare to say anything against Judge Timberlane!"

screamed Miss Hatter, and wondered why they all laughed at her, though Cass's contributory laughter was on the pale side.

He was deciding, with a thrill of reality, that he hated Eino.

——That fatuous young pup! Daring to call her "Jinx." Or even "Jinny," for that matter. "Miss Virginia" is good enough for you, my friend. You and your Hunkies! Just try bucking us Yankees! By—the—way, my friend, do you happen to know that I'm scarcely Yankee at all, that I'm part Scandinavian and part Sioux? Of course you don't! And it makes me sick, when I wonder whether this Eino has ever dared to put his arms around Jinny or kiss her lips. Sick!

All the while he knew that he did not mean any of it, that Eino was probably an excellent fellow.

——Funny. I never was jealous like this about Blanche. Wonder where she is now. I'll bet she's keeping that poor English husband of hers busy digging out viscounts for her!

Miss Hatter, addressing him constantly as "Your Honor," was explaining the wonderful things she was going to do with her litigious $200, including false teeth for an aged cousin resident in Beloochistan, Minnesota. Tracy Oleson talked about canoe trips in the Crane Lake country. Jinny alleged that Dr. Silbersee had once absently tried to remove tonsils from his 'cello. But Eino was scornful and still.

Cass was a friendly villager, and accustomed to friendliness from others. Even the forger whom he condemned to the state penitentiary seemed to feel that it was all very reasonable, and Cass was dismayed now to feel hostility in the Eino to whom he was entirely hostile! Suddenly Cass wanted to run off to the security of slippers and Cleo and a chess-problem. In a wondrously nervous state, between humble haughtiness and haughty humbleness before a dramaturgic butter-maker, he tacked successfully for an hour, and he was rewarded, when he said that it was time to go, by Jinny's coming down the outside staircase with him.

The step at the foot of the stairs was no romantic site; it was a scuffed and scabby plank which creaked. In the small yard outside, an old hen of a maple tree perched amid patchy short grass, and the rusty old iron fence smelled of rusty old iron. Across the street, a man in a lighted upper window stood scratching himself.

But she was in the half-darkness with him; he saw her throat above the soft black dress, he caught the scent of her hair, surely a different scent from any other in the world. She was herself different from anyone else, a complete individual, courageous and joyful and yet so fragile that she must be protected. He held her hand, and quaked with the feeling of it. There was no doubt now, he decided, that he was utterly in love with her, that her small dim presence was a vast blazing temple. She was not something that he had imagined in his loneliness. She was life.

He stumbled, "Look, Jinny. Have you ever been to the Unstable for dinner?"

"Just once."

"Like it?"

"It's fun."

"Will you dine with me there, next Tuesday or Wednesday?"

"I'd be glad to—say Tuesday."

The fact that she had chosen the earlier day was enough to send him home singing "Mandalay," with much feeling and no tune.

After one in the morning, he sat in his leather chair and Cleo sat on the hearth. He was posing for himself a legal question: Was he trying to seduce Jinny?

That would be extremely agreeable, if it could be accomplished, and not much more criminal than setting fire to a children's hospital. Reputable men did do it. It was obvious, he thought, that she was a little too young and too spirited to marry him, and even if she would accept him, would it not be a wickedness to introduce her in that dullest of all sets in Grand Republic, to which, by habit, he belonged? He had seen girls, lively and defiant, marry householders on Ottawa Heights, and within ten years become faintly wrinkled at the neck, and given to stating as rigidly as their own horrid grandmothers that all servants are thankless brutes.

And how well did Jinny understand him? Would she be able to endure it if he took off the grave judicial manner which he wore for protection, and betrayed himself as a Midwestern Don Quixote, one-sixteenth Sioux and one-sixteenth poet: a bridge-player who thought that bridge was dull, a Careful Investor who sympathized with hoboes, a calm and settled householder who envied Thoreau his cabin and Villon his wild girls?

"I ought to marry some woman who likes what I'm trying to do. Though I suppose I ought to find out first just what I am trying to do!"

He ended his brooding with a cry that made Cleo leap protesting into the air:

"I do love that girl so!"

9

THE UNSTABLE had been a stable and it had been a speakeasy and now it was the local Pré-Catelan, nine miles out of town, on the bank of the Big Eagle River, facing the rugged bluffs. The interior was in bright green, with chairs of polished steel and crimson composition tables decorated with aluminum blossoms, in semi-circular booths, and it had an orchestra of piano, saxophone, violin, and drum. By day, piano was a dry-goods clerk, saxophone was a Wargate warehouse-hand, violin was a lady hair-dresser, and drum was asleep. Its food Was the standard Steak & Chicken, but its whisky was excellent. Its most pious contribution to living was that in this land where autumn too often trips on the heels of spring and, except on picnics, people dine inside, it did have outdoor tables, not of composition but of honest, old-fashioned, beer-stained pine.

At such a table, in a grape-arbor, Cass and Jinny had dined slowly, looking at each other oftener than at the crisp chicken, the fresh radishes. They had talked of their childhoods, and they seemed united by fate when they found that he had, as a boy, hunted prairie chickens in the vast round of wheat stubble just beyond her native village of Pioneer Falls.

He urged, "You know what I'd like most to do, besides learning a little law and maybe having a farm way up in the hills above the Sorshay Valley? I'd like to paddle a canoe, or at least my half of the canoe, from New York City to Hudson's Bay, by way of the Hudson and the Great Lakes and the old fur-trappers' trail at Grand Portage, up here on Lake Superior. It would take maybe six months, camping out all that time. Wouldn't that be exciting?"

"Ye-es."

"Do you think you'd like to go along?"

"I don't know——I'm afraid I've never planned anything like that."

"You can come in imagination, can't you?"

"Oh—maybe. Provided we could go to New Orleans—in imagination!—to rest up afterward, and live in the French Quarter in a flat with an iron balcony, and eat gumbo. Could we do that?"

"Why not!"

They saw that they need not all their lives stick to courts and factories and city streets, but actually do such pleasant, extravagant things . . . if they shaped life together.

He cried, "Approval from the higher court! Look!"

The moon had come out from a black-hearted, brazen-edged cloud, to illuminate the wide barley-fields on the uplands across the river, with one small yellow light in a farmhouse, and the fantastically carved and poplar-robed bluffs of the Big Eagle. Wild roses gave their dusty scent, and inside the rackety roadhouse, the jukebox softly played Jerome Kern. It was everything that was most Christmas-calendar and banal: June, moon, roses, song, a man and a girl; banal as birth and death and war, banal and eternal; the Perfect Moment which a man knows but a score of times in his whole life. All respectable-citizen thoughts about whether they should be married, and should they keep the maple bedstead in the gray room, were burned out of him, and he loved the maid as simply and fiercely as any warrior. He ceased to be just Cass Timberlane; he was a flame-winged seraph guarding the gentle angel. They floated together in beauty. They were not doing anything so common as to hold hands; ifcwas their spirits that reached and clung, made glorious by the moment that would die.

When the moon was gone under a marbled cloud and the music ceased and there was only silence and lingering awe, she whispered, so low that he was not quite sure that she had said it, "That frightened me! It was too beautiful. 'On such a night——' Oh, Cass!"

She was chatty and audible enough afterward, and she carefully called him "Judge," but he knew that they were intimates.

As they drove home she prattled, "Judge, I have an important message. Tilda Hatter wants to give a party for you at the boarding-house—all of us do, of course."

"Except Eino, who objects?"

She giggled. "But don't you think his objection is flattering? I've only heard him object before to Henry James and

Germany and stamp-collecting. . . . You will come? You'll love Lyra Coggs."

"I'm sure I will. She's a great girl. . . . What are you snickering at?"

"You do try so hard not to be the judge, tolerating us noisy brats!"

"I swear that's not so. Surely you're onto me by now. More than anything else, I'm still the earnest schoolboy that wants to learn everything. And there's so much you can teach me. I certainly don't regard myself as aged, at only forty-one, but still *you*—you were born the year of the Russian revolution, you've always known airplanes and the radio. I want to understand them as you do."

"And the things *I* want to learn! Biology and hockey and Swedish!"

"How about anthropology and crop-rotation?"

"Okay. And fencing and flower-arrangement and gin-rummy and Buddhism."

"Do most of the kids at Miss Hatter's want to learn anything? They sound smug to me."

"They are not! If you knew how we talk when we're alone! Oh, maybe too much slang and cursing and talk about sex."

He winced. He did not care for the picture of Eino Roskinen "talking about sex" with a helpless Jinny . . . if she was helpless.

"But that's because we're sick of the pompous way that

all you older people go on, over and over, about politics and
affairs in Europe and how you think we drink too much."

"Well, don't you?"

"Maybe. But *we* know how to handle *our* liquor."

"I doubt it."

"So do I!" She laughed, and he was in love with her again,
after a measureless five seconds during which he had detested
her for the egotism of youth. She piped on, "But I do think
we're a terribly honest lot."

"You don't think I'm the kind of politician that hates
honesty?"

She said her "Oh, you're different," and the good man found
the wisdom to stop talking and to feel the magic of having her
there cozily beside him: her smooth arms, her hands folded in
her lap, her thin corn-yellow dress and the small waist belted
with glittering jet whose coolness his hand wanted to follow.
She was there with him, this girl who was different from any
female since Eve, and he was thus sanctified. . . . And did it
really matter when she unfolded the fairy hands and smoked
her seventh cigarette that evening?

Didn't the vestal Chris smoke too much?

The intrusion of Chris worried him. She had no hold on
him but—well—if Chris saw him driving with this girl, there
would be trouble.

——Why should there be trouble? I'm independent of her
and of everybody else—well, maybe not of Jinny.

He said aloud, "What about your drafting at Fliegends'? I suppose you want to go study in Paris, and become a famous artist."

"No, I have no real ideas. I'm just a fair workman, at best. I'll never have what they call a 'career.' "

He was so little Feminist as to be pleased.

As they drove up to Miss Hatter's he wound up all the tinsel of his thoughts in one bright ball and tossed it to her: "I certainly have enjoyed this evening!"

She answered with equal poesy, "So have I!"

He tentatively kissed her hand. She could not have noticed it, for she said only, "You'll come to our party, week from Thursday, then?"

"Yes, sweet. Good night."

10

THE SURPRISING OBJECTS that you see when you leave your own Grand Republic and go traveling—pink snakes and polar bears—are nothing beside what you find when you stay at home and have a new girl and meet her friends, whose resentment of you is only less than your amazement that there are such people and that she likes them.

At Tilda Hatter's party, Cass was first uncomfortable because he was the only Elder Statesman present and the young people showed their independence by unduly ignoring him. Then the gods presiding over that form of torture called social gatherings switched to the opposite ordeal, and he found himself the rival of another celebrity, of whom, just to be difficult, the bright young people did make much.

Besides the boarders, Jinny, Eino, Tracy Oleson, and the efficient Miss Gunton and Miss Coggs, there were present a couple of schoolteachers, the leftist county agricultural agent, and a young Norwegian-American grain expert who had once run for the Legislature. They sat tremendously upon the floor and talked, and all of them, including Jinny, to Cass's delicate distress, had Bourbon highballs.

Their talk was tempestuous. They said that America should join Great Britain in its war against Germany, but that many of the Rich Guys on Ottawa Heights were Isolationists. They said that it was okay—that was how they put it—for a man and a woman to live together without clerical license. Cass was shocked when he heard the pure young novice, Jinny, chirping, "Old people today are just as afraid of Sex as their grandfathers were."

They all looked at Cass, but forbiddingly did not ask him what he thought. Eino Roskinen, squatted beside Jinny, drew her toward him, and she leaned with her back against his shoulder, and Cass violently did not notice.

He did not understand their family words and jokes. One of them had only to say "Hail the Hippopotamus!" for the whole tribe to guffaw. He was not too old for them—he was perhaps eight years older than Wilma or Tracy—but he felt too bookish, too responsible, too closely shaved, too alone.

He had become used to his *de facto* banishment when Lucius and Erica Fliegend and Sweeney Fishberg came in.

Sweeney Fishberg was perhaps the most remarkable man in the cosmos of Grand Republic and surrounding terrain.

He was an attorney, of liberal tastes, equally likely to take a labor-union case for nothing or to take the most fraudulent of damage suits for a contingent fee which, to the fury of his Yankee wife, he was likely to give to a fund for strikers—any strikers on any strike. He was a saint and a shyster; part Jewish and part Irish and part German; he had once acted in a summer stock company, and once taught Greek in a West

Virginia college; he was a Roman Catholic, and a mystic who bothered his priest with metaphysical questions; he was in open sympathy with the Communist Party.

For twenty years, ever since he had come to Grand Republic from his natal Massachusetts at the age of thirty, he had been fighting all that was rich and proud and puffy in the town; and he had never won a single fight nor lost his joy in any of them, and he was red-headed and looked like a Cockney comedian. He was nine years older than Cass, and no lawyer in the district ever brought such doubtful suits into court, yet no lawyer was more decorous, more co-operative with the judge, and Cass believed that Sweeney had thrown to him all the votes he could influence in Cass's elections as congressman, judge, and member of the Aurora Borealis Bock Beer and Literary Association.

It was Sweeney Fishberg who was Cass's rival as celebrity of the evening and who led the hazing.

Pretending not to know that Cass had even heard of them, Sweeney and the Fliegends and Tracy Oleson and the county agent agreed that Dr. Roy Drover was a butcher, that Bradd Criley was a Fascist, and that the Reverend Dr. Lloyd Garrison Gadd, Cass's distant cousin and his pastor, was a "phony liberal" who loved the wage-workers but underpaid his cook. It was clear to Cass that he was being drawn, but whenever he wanted to be angry, he remembered that this was the malice with which Roy and Bradd talked of Sweeney

Fishberg and would have talked of Mr. Fliegend had they ever considered him important enough to mention. With prayer and resolution, Cass got through his hazing, and all of them began to look at him in a fond and neighborly way—all but Eino. Not Eino, ever.

On the ground of helping mix the highballs, Cass followed Jinny to the kitchen, a coop shocking with dirty dishes. He spoke savagely. "Did you plan to have all those Robespierres gang up on me?"

"Not really. And they've often ganged up on me, for what they think is my innocence."

"Are you in love with that Roskinen? Now, please, I don't mean to sound rude, but I must know. Are you engaged to him or anything?"

"Not anything."

"Are you engaged to anybody?" His arm circled her shoulder.

"Not just now. Don't, Cass. You're choking me."

"I almost could choke you when you let that Roskinen— Oh, I suppose he's a decent-enough boy, but I'm furious when you let him maul you, put his hand on your breast."

She flared, as if she hated him, "You have a vile mind!" But when he jerked back like a slapped five-year-old, she softened. "Honestly, darling, it doesn't mean a thing, with a colt like Eino, but if you want me to act like a lady, I'll try, and how I dread it!"

He kissed her, long and seriously, surprised by the soft fleshiness of her lips. She squeezed away from him with an embarrassed "Well!" and fled from him, carrying back into the living-room the still-unwashed glasses she had brought with her. As Cass leaned against the untidy sink, overwhelmed, feeling guilty but assuring himself that she had responded to his kiss, Eino Roskinen came in, glaring.

"Now this is going to be melodrama," Cass thought protestingly.

Eino was in his uniform as a young radical: dark jacket, soft shirt, small black bow tie; and he was militant.

"I want to ask you something, sir."

"Need you call me 'sir'?"

"Maybe. Look. I'm very fond of Virginia. I'm kind of her brother. I notice you hanging around her, and you don't belong down here in the slums."

"Slums?"

"I guess they're that to you. You belong on the Heights. I want to know what the idea is. I guess, aside from your being a judge, that you could break me in two—you're a sporting gent, I suppose. But if I found out that you were just having a little fun trying to make her, I'd take a chance on killing you."

"Eino, that's funny."

"How?"

"Because that's the way I've been thinking about you! I'm

in love with Jinny. I want to marry her, if I can. You're in love with her, too?"

"And how! Except when she gets frivolous when I talk about the principles of co-operative distribution." Eino sighed. "But I can't marry anybody, for years."

"So——"

"Oh, you probably win. You would!"

"Eino!" The boy was astonished by Cass's fervor. "There's nobody else to whom I can say this. I worship that girl, and I hope you'll be my friend as you are hers."

"Okay," said Eino, tragically.

Cass said good-bye to her at one-thirty, in the presence of the entire underground. Before going to bed, he spent half an hour in stroking Cleo and wanting to telephone to Jinny. But he held off till next evening and then demanded, Would she take a walk with him tomorrow evening?

Yes. Without reservations.

He hoped the Bunch hadn't been too hard on him after he had crawled away——

"Judge, you never crawled!"

"*Cass!*"

"Cass."

"Tomorrow at eight? And a movie afterwards?"

"*And* a movie. And a caramel sundae."

With that telephone conversation, touching on the deeper issues of life and passion, he felt satisfied. He was irritated but too canny to say anything about it when Mrs. Higbee (with the aid of Cleo) brought him an evening toddy and looked ribald and knowing.

"I can't run this big house all by myself," inwardly complained Cass, who never yet had run it.

11

BERGHEIM, CASS'S HOUSE, the old Eisenherz country place, looked out over the bluffs. It had neither a city nor a suburban aspect, but suggested a comfortable village. At the back, where the grass was more like an ancient pasture than a prim lawn, there was a green-painted wooden well, and the white-painted stable, with its pert cupola, suggested a print of the 1880's and long gentlemen with whiskers and driving-gloves, lace ladies with parasols, and spotted coach-dogs with their tails aloft in that fresher breeze. But what to Cass had always been, still was, a last touch of European elegance in Bergheim was that it had walnut-colored Venetian blinds.

Across the street from Cass was the abode of Scott and Juliet Zago, who had for years been notorious as being happily married. They called their house, which displayed fake half-timbering, and wavy shingles imitating thatch, sometimes "The Playhouse" and sometimes "The Dolls House," Juliet, you see, being the doll. She was thirty-five to Scott's fifty, but she let people think that the gap was ten years greater. She was the chronic child-wife; she talked baby-talk and wriggled and beamed and poked her forefinger at things; and she often pretended to be the big sister of her two small daughters.

Scott dealt in insurance, and he made jokes and made

puns. Juliet read all the books about China and Tibet and gave you her condensed version of them—not much condensed, at that—with her own system of pronunciation of Chinese proper names.

Yet Cass, who disliked puns and was readily sickened by baby-talk, did not detest the Zagos, and theirs was the only house in the neighborhood to which Cleo ever wandered. For they were the kindest of neighbors, as affectionate as parakeets.

On one side of Cass's place lived the Perfect Prutts.

John William Prutt, the father, was a banker; the most first-rate second-rate banker in the entire state. He was president of the Second National Bank. It could just as well have been called the First National Bank, since the institution once so named had perished, but Mr. Prutt's bank would have to be a second, never a first nor yet a last. He was fifty years old and always had been. He was perfect; in everything that was second-class he was perfect. He was a vestryman, but not the leading vestryman, of St. Anselm's Church; he had been a vice-president but never the president of the Federal Club. He was tall and solemnly handsome, and he never split an infinitive or a bottle.

His wife, Henrietta Prutt, his son, Jack Prutt, his daughter, Margaret Prutt, his dog, Dick Prutt, and even his Buick car, the Buick of the Prutts, were as full of perfection and Pruttery as John William Prutt himself.

The Prutts lived in a supposedly little white Colonial cottage that had somehow grown into a huge white Colonial army-barracks, yet still breathed the purity of Jonathan Edwards, and just beyond it, in a hulk of grim dark native stone, lived another banker, Norton Trock, who collected china and sounded like a lady.

On the other side of Cass's house was the blindingly white, somewhat Spanish and somewhat packing-box, stucco residence of Gregory Marl, owner of the presumably liberal and Independent Republican newspapers, the *Banner* and the *Evening Frontier*, with the *Sunday Frontier-Banner*, the only English-language newspapers in Grand Republic. He was ar large, quiet, secretly industrious man of thirty-five; he had inherited the paper but had raised their circulations; he was a rose-grower and a Bermuda yachtsman. The star of his household, and a bright and menacing November star, was his wife Diantha, who was on every committee in town, and who knew something and talked a great deal about painting and the drama and a mystery called Foreign Affairs. But her major art was as hostess, and as the Marls had no children, Diantha could spend weeks in planning a party. She was the rival of Madge Dedrick as the general utility duchess and Mrs. Astor of the city.

Madge Dedrick, relict of Sylvanus Dedrick, the lumber baron, lived a little beyond the Prutts, in a handsome, high-pillared Georgian house that had exactly the same lines (condensed) as Boone Havock's and did not in the least look like it. Madge's half-dozen small flower-gardens looked like gardens of flowers, while Mr. Havock's looked like paper posies, the larger size, bought last night and pinned on crooked in the darkness.

At seventy, Mrs. Dedrick was small and soft-voiced, powdery of cheek, with tiny plump hands and great powers, held shrewdly under control, of derision and obscenity. Now living with her was her tall, doe-eyed, aloof, divorced daughter, Eve Dedrick Champeris, who had been reared in Grand Republic, Farmington, New York, Cannes, and Santa Barbara, and who had divorced the charming Mr. Raymond Champeris on the good, old-fashioned grounds of drinking like a sot and passing out at costly parties. It seemed like such a waste of champagne, Eve explained.

Diantha Marl tempted society with high intellectual conversation plus string quartets and dynamite cocktails; Madge and Eve Dedrick with cool Rhine wines in a low-lit, satin-paneled room filled with silver and crystal and cushions and exquisite legs and lively spitefulness, so that the Wargates, who had ten times as much money, politely accepted the invitations of both Diantha and the Dedricks.

On all these rulers of Grand Republic Cass meditated, while he fretted the question of whether Jinny would really like being lifted from her boarding-house to the stuffy elegance of Ottawa Heights. He wanted to persuade himself that she would like Boone Havock and Eve Champeris better than Eino Roskinen and Sweeney Fishberg. It was hard to play Prince to the Cinderella when he suspected that all the windows in Castle Charming were glued shut. He conducted extensive imaginary conversations with her, trying to give both sides, which is likely to be confusing.

"Scott and Juliet—jolly people—wonderful at an outdoor barbecue," he heard himself informing Jinny, who snapped back, "Silly pair of clowns!"

"Gregory and Diantha Marl—leaders in public thought."

"Scared conservatives throwing calico babies to the union wolves!"

"Bradd Criley and Jay Laverick and Frank Brightwing—very amusing fellows."

"That's something *like* it. Just let me meet them, and you keep the others."

——Now what kind of a mind have I got, to give a non-existent antagonist the best of an argument? As I'm making the whole thing up anyway, why don't I have Jinny vanquished and humble and adoring?

If he ever married Jinny, he would have to lure in new dinner-guests without offending the old ones, and then, probably, Jinny would not like the novelties. He thought of a party at which he introduced the Rev. Dr. Evan Brewster, Negro pastor of an unpainted Baptist church in the North End, and Ph.D. of Columbia, to Dr. Drover and Eve Champeris, and how bored Dr. Brewster would be by their patter and how much danger there would be that Jinny would too openly agree.

Then, "Oh dry up!" said Cass to his imagination.

When the spring term of court was over, he was free for all summer, except for special sessions and a few days in the outlying towns of the district. They wound up with a solemn meeting of Judges Blackstaff, Flaaten, and Timberlane *in re* the portentous question: should the judges of this district, when on the bench, wear silk robes, as in Minneapolis?

The three dignitaries sat about the long oak table in Judge Blackstaff's chambers, smoking unaccustomed cigars, the gift of their host, and grew red-faced with the ardor of their debate.

"It's a matter of dignity," maintained Judge Blackstaff, looking more than usual like Justice Oliver Wendell Holmes. "I don't hold with these English wigs and heavy robes, but I do think we have to show the public, which is so irreverent and flippant today, all jazz and comic strips, that we represent the sanctity of Justice."

"Dignity, hell!" Judge Flaaten protested. "Every time some Norske or Svenske saw me in a black-silk nightshirt, it would cost me ten votes. Besides, robes are hot."

Judge Timberlane put in, "Not very, Conrad. They can be quite light. Besides, Grand Republic is the coolest city in the state south of Duluth. Besides, do you want to have the boys on the bench in Minneapolis go on laughing at us as a bunch of farmer j.p.'s?"

"I don't care a damn what they laugh at as long as the voting Lut'erans like us," insisted Judge Flaaten. He glared at Judge Blackstaff. "Steve, this is a serious matter. Are we going to yield up the high principles of common democracy to the bawds—uh—the gauds of the outworn Old World?"

"Hurray!" breathed Judge Timberlane.

"Cass, can't you be serious?" worried Judge Blackstaff. "This is a special court of protocol, which may go far to determine the standing of the judiciary in Grand Republic for all time to come. Write your votes on the yellow pads, boys, and fold 'em—and give me back those pencils when you get done with 'em. It's a caution the way my pencils get stolen!"

Silk robes for district judges won by two to one, and when autumn came, none of them more proudly showed his robe to his relatives than Judge Flaaten. Judge Timberlane did not care so much. There was only one person for whom he wanted to wear his robe, and by prodigious chicanery he lured her into the court to see it. But—such is life—she only laughed.

12

THE SELECT golf-and-tennis association of Grand Republic was the Heather Club, three miles from the business center, on a peninsula reaching out from the south shore of Dead Squaw Lake. Surrounding it was the smart new real-estate development called the Country Club District, habitat of such gilded young married couples as the Harley Bozards, the Don Pennlosses, the Beecher Filligans, and the playground of Jay Laverick, the town's principal professional Gay Bachelor, who happened to be a widower. The houses were Spanish, like Hollywood, or French, like Great Neck, and the Heather clubhouse was a memory of Venice, with balconies, iron railings, and a canal thirty-six feet long.

To the Heather Club in late June Cass came for one of the famous Saturday Evening Keno Games. Keno (a sport beloved by the more aged and pious Irishwomen also) consists in placing a bean upon a number called out by some swindler unknown, through an unseen loud-speaker, and after you have breathlessly placed enough beans upon enough numbers, you fail to get the prize. It is not so intellectual as chess or skipping the rope, but it is a favorite among Grand Republic's leading citizens, who gather at the Heather Club on every Saturday evening in summer, to drink cocktails and play keno and then drink a lot more.

With only one cocktail in him, Cass was deaf to the joys of keno this evening, and he wished that he were deaf to the crackling voices about him at the dozen long tables, as he somberly put down his beans. Roy Drover's shouts of "Send us a thirty-two, baby, send us a thirty-two, come on, baby, come on, hand us a thirty-two" merely rivaled Queenie Havock's parrot shrieks and Norton Trock's high giggling, while Eve Champeris had a flushed mild imbecility about her lily face. Delia Lent, a purposeful lady though rich, sat beside Cass, babbling about trout-fishing, but presently he could hear nothing that she said. All the hundred voices were woven into a blanket of sound that covered Cass and choked him.

Abruptly, while Mrs. Lent stared at his lack of manners, Cass bolted from the table, charged toward the bar. He would have to have a quantity of drinks, if he was going to survive these pleasures. He passed an alcove in which two grim women, too purposeful about gambling to waste time on keno, were hour after hour yanking the handles of twenty-five-cent slot machines. He passed a deep chair in which sat two married people—not married to each other. He looked into the card room where Boone Havock, Mayor Stopple, Judge Flaaten, Counselor Oliver Beehouse, and Alfred Umbaugh, the hardware king, were playing tough poker in a refined way.

Jinny's spirit walked with him derisively.

He had almost reached the forgetfulness to be found at

the bar when beyond it, in the Ladies' Lounge, he saw Chris Grau, having a liqueur with Lillian Drover. He stopped, in cold guiltiness, and the imaginary Jinny fled.

He had not seen Chris for ten days, and as she looked at him, all her kindness in her good brown eyes, he shivered. But he obediently chain-ganged into the lounge. Lillian Drover rose, tittering, in washed-out imitation of her husband's humor, "I guess I better leave you two young lovers alone, if I know what's good for me."

Chris's smile indicated that that would be fine.

The Ladies' Lounge, which had been named that by Diantha Marl, after having been christened the Rubens Room by the Milwaukee architect-decorator who had done the club in the finest Moorish style known in his city, was a harem, with grilled windows, a turquoise-blue tiled floor, and a resigned fountain. It was suitable to the harem feeling that Chris should be wearing a loose-throated lilac dress.

Cass sat facing her, with an entirely mechanical "Can I get you another drink?"

"Not for me. There's too much drinking here. I'm glad you're so sober. But then, you always are. It's these younger people that are breaking down the bulwarks of society with their guzzling and shrieking and indecent dancing."

"Now, now, Chris, the drunkest person here tonight is Queenie Havock, and she's well over fifty, and I saw Bernice Claywheel, and she must be over forty, out dancing on the terrace with Jay Laverick as though she expected to eat him."

"Ye-es I know, but——You simply love the sweet young things, don't you, Cassy—Cass."

"M?"

"I'm sure you had a wonderful time with your beautiful unknown at the Unstable, two weeks ago!"

"Why, I——Yes I did!"

"And did you enjoy holding hands in the moonlight?"

He tried to be jaunty. "Enjoyed it very much. Especially as I don't suppose I'll have another chance, alas!"

——Why don't you tell Chris to go to the devil? She's not your guardian.

"So you don't think you'll see her again, eh, Cass darling. Honestly, now—honest*lee*—you know I'm not the nagging sort of girl that would even ask who she was, and certainly I'm not the kind that would go around hinting and whispering that a man who isn't so young any more——"

"What do you——"

"——is making a fool of himself over some young tramp. I was just teasing you about this girl. Of course I *know* you'd never fall for her, whoever she is. So let's not say anything more about it, dear."

"I hadn't said anything at all!"

"That's what I say. Honestly, I was just joking. Now tell me: will you get the Fleeber-Biskness case in the fall, or will they settle it?"

Now the *affaire* Fleeber-Biskness was a fascinating controversy, to Judge Timberlane, but it had not seemed so to the crass public. It was a conversion case, dealing with the possession of a warehouse 28' 7" × 62' 8". Cass was glad once more to see what a sympathetic brain Chris had and, as he looked at them again, what sleek legs. As the palace of pleasure rang with the bacchanalia of keno, he explained to this willing hearer the low tricks Mr. Biskness was accused of having played with a carload of clay. He stumbled as she crossed her legs and he realized that, with innocent spinster boldness, she had come without stockings.

This was in the prim pre-war era of 1941, when it is true that bathing-suits had been reduced to an emphasized nudity, but when perfect ladies still did not display naked legs in public rooms. The Judge was a person of decorum and modesty, but he was interested.

——Chris would give a lover such solid affection—probably much more than a filly like Jinny Marshland.

Not unmindful of the careless lilac-colored skirt but determined to be high-minded, he went on with the case, winding up, "You understand, that's only Fleeber's version, and it's a matter of record. I'm not giving away any secrets."

"Sure. I know you never tell tales out of court," said Chris, fondly.

"If I ever did, you'd be the one person I could rely on. What's say we have a drink?"

"I'd love to," gurgled the strange woman in lilac.

An Assemblage of Husbands and Wives

THE ZEBRA SISTERS

THE QUIMBER GIRLS, better known to the ribald of Grand Republic as the Zebra Sisters, belonged to a real family, lively and devoted, full of anecdotes that began with laughter and, "Oh, do you remember the time when." Their father, Millard Quimber, who was still alive, aged eighty-one, was the city superintendent of schools from 1895 to 1928. He was referred to in the press as "one of our greatest builders," because during his reign there had been erected three red-brick school-buildings which looked like red-brick school-buildings. He was also known as a "profound scholar," because he continually quoted Bobby Burns and Henry Van Dyke and the first two lines of the Iliad, almost in the original Greek.

His three daughters were named Zoe, Zora, and Zeta; they were born between 1890 and 1900; they were fine, big, bouncing hussars of women, hearty at winter sports, discursive about their husbands, all philoprogenitive, all ardent Presbyterians, though with secret desires to be Episcopalians and chic. Their favorite words were *family, chickabiddies, earnest, expensive, womanly, jolly*, and *ice cream.*

Their several husbands were derisively referred to at the Heather Club bar as the Brothers-in-Law, Incorporated.

Zoe, the youngest daughter, was married to Harold W. Whittick, the owner of radio station KICH and of Whittick & Bruntz, a two-room advertising agency which existed chiefly to tell a house-hungry world about Wargate Wood Products. When the chairman of a Rotary Club luncheon at which Harold W. was to speak (about Progress) asked him what to say in introduction, Harold W. wrote a description of himself which may stand as modest and accurate:

"Not only the most streamlined but the most up-to-the-second moderne citizen of Grand Republic."

But Harold W. was, as the chairman laughingly said—you know, kidding him—not himself in Rotary, because he was National Assistant Treasurer of the rival Streamlineup Club, a service organization distinctive in that it had all the speeches *before* lunch, when everybody was "still on his toes, full of ginger and not of hash."

Zora, the middle Zebra, was fondly wed to Duncan Browler, first vice president of the Wargate Corporation, in charge of manufacture. Unlike Harold W. Whittick, he did not make speeches.

The oldest, Zeta, was married to Alfred T. Umbaugh, a gentle and predatory soul who admired his brother-in-law Harold and who, more nearly than the other two husbands, endured the demands of his wife that he be jolly and amorous. He was the chief owner of the Button Bright Chain of Hardware Stores, twenty-seven of them, all shiny and yellow, scattered through Minnesota and the Dakotas, with one far-flung outpost or consulate in Montana. This imperial standing made him, like Browler, eligible to the Federal and Heather Clubs. Naturally, Whittick had also been admitted to those twin heavens, but with a warning from the committee that he would do well not to get oratorical and forward-looking after his fourth highball, and while he was at the table of the blest, he was about ten feet below the salt.

Harold, Duncan and Alfred were unlike in tempo, but they were all true husbands to the Zebra. All three of them were irritated by their wives but never thought of quitting them, all of them had sons and daughters, all were devoted to golf, fishing, musical-comedy movies, motor boats, and Florida, and all of them had new houses, in the Country Club District, of which they were fiercely proud and for which they would have done murder. None of them was eccentric, except that Harold W. Whittick—just for a josh, everybody said; to show off and try to be different—asserted that he had once voted for a Democratic candidate for the presidency, Mr. Franklin Delano Roosevelt. And all of them, though grumblingly, consented to be ruled and extensively discussed by The Family.

They all dined with Grampa Quimber every Sunday noon;

and each Thursday, one of the three sisters was hostess to the others and their broods, with the one great-grandchild in The Family, that of the Umbaughs, asleep upstairs. At these feasts, Harold W. Whittick usually told the story about the Irishman and the cigar-counter girl; and there was a good deal of innocent laughter about the time, in 1936, when Mr. Browler got drunk at an Elks' Convention and bought a small red fire engine.

An unusual feature of the Zebra gatherings was the fifteenth-century frankness with which the sisters reported on the progressive feebleness of their husbands as lovers. They were rugged and healthy girls, and expected a lot, and did not get it. However, they sighed, it was something that neither Harold W. nor Alfred T. nor Duncan "ever so much as looked at any woman outside the home."

That's what they thought.

The Brothers-in-Law, Inc. jointly made business trips to Minneapolis, where they stayed at the magnificent Hotel Swanson-Grand, with three connecting bedrooms and a parlor. Of the uses to which these rooms were put, the Sisters knew nothing. The Brothers-in-Law were stalwarts, pledged and reliable, and so were their Grand Republic friends who managed to be in Minneapolis at the same time.

Half an hour after the Brothers' arrival, the parlor was turned into a complete bar. Within half an hour more, the girls had arrived—not traditional young blondes who glittered, nothing so frigid and boring, but dependable young women of thirty, who worked in offices and banks and stores, who understood hard liquor and liked men.

By two next morning there was a tremendous amount of laughter and communal undressing, to the nervous delight of such Grand Republic visitors as Mayor Stopple, Harley Bozard, Jay Laverick, and Boone Havock.

New York and Chicago and London visitors to Grand Republic, particularly if they were journalists renowned for shrewdness, concluded that Harold W., Alfred T., and Duncan were the most conventional, most standardized, most wife-smothered and children-nagged citizens of our evangelical land, but in truth they belonged among the later Roman Emperors, and he that has never seen Duncan Browler, elder of the Presbyterian Church, standing in his cotton shorts, a lady telephone-supervisor clasped in his right arm, a half-tumbler of straight Dainty Darling Bourbon Whisky waving in his left hand, the while he sings "It's Time to Go Upstairs," has only the shallowest notion of the variety of culture in our Grand Republic, a city which, in different dialects, has also been called Grand Rapids and Bangor and Phoenix and Wichita and Hartford and Baton Rouge and Spokane and Rochester and Trenton and Scranton and San Jose and Rutland and Duluth and Dayton and Pittsfield and Durham and Cedar Rapids and Fort Wayne and Ogden and Madison and Nashville and Utica and South Bend and Peoria and

Canton and Tacoma and Sacramento and Elizabeth and San Antonio and St. Augustine and Lincoln and Springfieldill and Springfieldmass and Springfieldmo and Ultima Thule and the United States of America.

13

JUDGE TIMBERLANE had heard of middle-aged satyrs who worked their will upon frail maidens by promising them riches and magenta-colored cars but never introduced them to the respectable families of their circles. But the Judge himself wanted his entire world to know his fleet Jinny. He stopped in at Miss Hatter's, he discussed with Tracy Oleson the import of wood pulp, then got Jinny aside to whisper, "I'd like to have a buffet supper for you and have you meet my friends—you needn't like 'em if you don't want to. And maybe you'd like to invite Tracy? He's quite a bright fellow."

Perhaps he sounded condescending, without meaning to, for she answered irritably, "I don't want to meet a lot of rich people looking for somebody to snub!"

"But very few of them are rich and none of them are snobbish. I meant people like Abbott Hubbs, managing editor of the *Banner*. I'll bet the owner, Greg Marl, doesn't pay him enough to afford breakfast. And my sister, Rose Pennloss, and my old chum, Bradd Criley—good lawyer and the best dancer in town. People that you'd love, if you knew 'em."

"I don't want to be shown off, Cass. I'm perfectly happy right here where I am, and if I do ever get anywhere else, I want to do it by myself."

It took him five minutes to persuade Cinderella that the glass slipper was pretty and then, just to keep him entirely confused, she said that she would *love* a party, and if she had sounded grudging, it had been only because she was surprised.

The buffet-supper for her was to be at the Heather Club, which was crowded only on Saturday evenings. When he picked her up in his car, she did not expect him to take Tracy Oleson, that muffler, along with them; and she was not prudish when he suggested that, as they were early, they could stop at his house on the way. (It was not on the way.)

At Bergheim she stepped out wonderingly under the wedding-cake carriage-porch and pronounced, "Oh, I love it! Like Walter Scott!"

She was wearing again the little black net dress in which she was so pathetically grown-up, and the one silver rose.

Silent, head turning quickly to one side and the other, she preceded him into the dolorous hall, into the drawing-room, which was too long, too narrow, and too high, and in one corner surprisingly darted off, under a varnished pine grill, into a semicircular alcove which was the lowest story of the tower. It was an ill-lighted room, with wallpaper of Chinese pagodas and bridges, with overcarved and unwieldy furniture upholstered in plum-colored plush and ornamented with a Michigan version of Chinese dragons; a room profuse in

Chinese vases, Aztec pottery, embossed brass coffee tables, Venetian glass lamps, and colored photographs of Lake Louise; a room that was unutterably all wrong, and yet was stately and a home.

Jinny stood in the middle and looked about, neither awed nor ridiculing it, belonging to it as (Cass fondly believed) she would belong to any setting she might encounter.

Then Cleo came bossily into the room on delicately haughty feet, wanting to know who the deuce this was in her house.

Jinny gave a passionate little moan, a sound not so unlike a cat's, soft and imploring, and knelt before Cleo, smoothing the side of her jaw. The kitten recognized her as one of the tribe, and spoke to her in their language. Jinny sat crosslegged then and Cleo perched on her knee like a small brave statue. Acrobatically, not to disturb the kitten, Jinny reached out far for the evening purse that she had dropped, looked up at Cass apologetically, and brought out a tiny crystal model of a cat-goddess of the Nile.

"It's my talisman. Dad gave it to me years ago, as a toy, but I almost let myself believe that it was alive and now—I know it's childish, but I always take it everywhere—you know, so it can see the world and get educated, poor thing."

"What's its name?"

"Different names at different epochs. All of them silly. Just now it hasn't one."

"Why not call it——The kitten is also an Egyptian national,

and named Cleopatra. Why not call your statuette Isis?"

"Isis. 'Slim, undulant deity Isis, mistress of life.' Okay. Let's see if Cleo will have sense enough to recognize a high-class goddess and worship it."

She placed the crystal Isis on a mat made of her handkerchief, on the cabbage-rose carpet, and Cleo before the shrine. They watched gravely, Cass's hand on Jinny's shoulder, while Cleo walked three times around the goddess, sniffing, then, with a careful paw, pushed it over and glanced up at them, much pleased with herself.

"They're friends, anyway," said Jinny.

"Like us."

"Uh-huh."

He kissed her, without prejudice.

He herded her into the kitchen, and announced, "Mrs. Higbee, this is my friend Miss Marshland. The house is hers."

Well, Jinny smiled, Mrs. Higbee smiled, Cleo, sticking around and quietly running everything from behind the scenes as usual, made a sound that corresponded to smiling, and the augury was bright.

Then Cass remembered that Mrs. Higbee liked Chris Grau, also, and that Chris would formidably be at the buffet-supper tonight.

They drove up to the Headier Country Club, which

resembled the Home of a Famous Movie Star, and Jinny was apparently delighted by its yellow tile roof and its grilled windows and blue plaques set in white plaster walls. They crossed the clattering stone-floored lobby to the outdoor terrace on which, this fine June night, the supper was handsomely set out: a baked ham, with cloves stuck all over its sugary bulk, lobster salad and chicken salad and cold salmon, and an exuberant ice-cream mold decked with spun sugar. These treasures were assembled, like a jovial combination of Christmas and Fourth of July, on a long table at one end of the thatch-roofed outdoor bar. At the other end of the bar was the real business: a case of Bourbon, half a case of Scotch, and a cocktail-shaker of the size and menace of a trench-mortar, all guarded by the club bartender, who knew all the amorous and financial secrets of the members. As to wine, most prominent citizens of Grand Republic, including Cass, were unaware of it except as something you nervously ordered on a liner.

There were to be twenty-six at the supper, and six tables, lacy and silver-laid, were on the terrace, with Dead Squaw Lake swaying beyond them, and the pine-darkened hills and the red-roofed yacht club visible on the farther shore.

But none of this luxury did Cass behold. What he saw was Chris Grau, happily arranging the flowers, and her happiness chilled him.

He had not told Chris nor any one else that this supper was to be the introduction of a Miss Virginia Marshland to his friends, and it was assumed that this was another of the duty dinners which unmarried favorites like Cass and Bradd Criley and Jay Laverick give—the technical word is "throw"—now and then when their social obligations have reached the saturation point. Chris had insisted that he let her order the supper, be the hostess.

She was busy now, in her fresh cream-colored linen dress, her gaudiest costume jewelry, arranging the huge bunches of peonies. At Cass's footstep, she looked up with a smile that went cold when she saw him with an unknown wench who was too airy and much too pretty.

The oratorical pride of the Bar Association could do no better than: "Chris—Miss Grau! Miss Marshland—uh—Jinny Marshland."

Both women said "Jdoo" with good healthy feminine hatred, and Cass was rather surprised.

In making up his list of guests, he had not been able to avoid having Roy and Lillian Drover, though he did not expect Jinny to like them. He thought she might like his sister Rose and the Gadds and Greg Marls and the Abbott Hubbses and the Avondene girls and even the giggling Scott Zagos. He was sure that she would like Bradd Criley and once, a few days ago, before he had lost his innocence, he had hoped that Jinny and Chris might "hit it off nicely," having no sounder reason for that hope than that it would be considerably more convenient for him if they did. And Eve Champeris, of Paris, California, and Grand Republic, the most exquisite and linguistic woman in town—he himself had never been comfortable with Eve, and he had invited her entirely to impress Jinny.

He had been more daring than anyone can know who does not live permanently in Grand Republic in leaving out Boone and Queenie Havock—daring and sensible, since at one macaw scream from Queenie, Jinny might very well have started walking home. But the Havock scion, Curtiss, he had invited. Curtiss was a bulky, cheerful, unmarried, somewhat oafish young man who was supposed to work in the Blue Ox National Bank but who was more earnest about fast driving and who was supposed, for reasons incomprehensible to Cass, to be attractive to young women.

Especially for Jinny, he had asked Tracy Oleson, Fred Nimbus, announcer at Station KICH, Lucius and Erica Fliegend, and to keep the Fliegends from feeling chilled at the Heather Club, in which they had not been present five times in ten years, he had invited that intelligent young couple, Richard and Francia Wolke (the Chippewa Avenue jewelers) who had *never* been in the club. Chris had not seen his list and now, as she looked over the party, she tenderly thought that she had never known her Cass to show so superbly the trusting social ineptitude for which she loved him and wanted to mother him. Curtiss Havock would insult the glibly handsome Fred Nimbus who would annoy Eve Champeris who would be insolent to the Wolkes who would bite the Zagos who would nauseate Dr. Drover who would be rude to the Hubbses who hated their bosses, Gregory and Diantha Marl, while Chris herself would have been just as glad if he had not invited Stella Avondene Wrenchard, that impoverished and aristocratic young widow who was so resolutely after Cass for herself that she went around saying, "I adore Chris—poor dear."

And when Chris found that he had added this unknown young fly-by-night called Miss Virginia Mushland or something, then she was almost as irritated as she was tender. So far as Chris could see, he had done everything to insure his social ruin in Grand Republic except to invite the local labor-organizers.

This Mushland doll was evidently too awkward and untutored to be of any use, and Chris went ardently to work at what is called "making the party a success." While Cass filled the unwanted girl's plate at the buffet and sat beside her at table, shamelessly beaming, Chris maneuvered the guests to suitable tables, kept Curtiss Havock from having too many drinks and the Fliegends from having too few, had Jinny switch seats with Stella Avondene, to prevent scandal and to keep Cass's errant fancies on the move, got Fred Nimbus, the radio genius, to sing, got Fred Nimbus to make a comic speech, got Fred Nimbus to start the dancing—with Jinny.

Chris saw to it that Jinny also danced with Bradd Criley, Curtiss Havock, Dick Wolke, Greg Marl, and only twice with

Cass, to the end that Jinny, who had at first been embarrassed by the strangers, had a lively evening and loved Cass for it—Cass, not Chris.

All this good sacrifice Chris made for Cass, and was sorry only that he did not see it.

But Cass did see it, and he knew now how a burglar felt when he was facing Judge Timberlane.

He understood Chris's loyalty and her plump charms. He wondered why the Fates should so arrange it that he could feel only amiable toward Chris, who wanted him, and be wan and adoring with the Jinny who as yet considered him merely another traveling-man.

With a jar he found that Jinny, too, was seeing everything that she couldn't possibly see. When, long after eleven, he had his second dance with her—he had watched the match-unmaking Chris throw her to such dogs as Fred Nimbus—Jinny said with an affection he had never heard from her:

"Dear Cass, I am having such a gay time, thanks to you and to your Miss Grau. That nice woman. She does try so hard to hate me, but she doesn't know how. She tried to snoot me by asking how I liked 'working in a factory,' but before she got through, I had her longing to get off her chaise-longue and be big and brave and punch a time-clock. Cass, you are so good and so bungling. You know I'm just a stray cat, like Cleo. I wouldn't want to—because I am so fond of you—I wouldn't want to make any trouble between you and Chris the girl-friend. Honestly."

He made the suitable arguments.

He knew that, seen as just one of the "country-club bunch," he had lost for her something of his dignity as a Public Figure, but he also knew that she was now responsive to him. He was proud of her debut. She had been so easy with even the most difficult of his guests, with his over-inquisitive sister and with the roaring Roy Drover. Bradd Criley had informed him that Jinny was a "lovely, intelligent girl, and a stepper." That was news!

14

WHEN THE PARTY had meandered to its quiet ending, when the older pleasure-maddened citizens had gone home to bed and the stoutly drinking remnant had moved indoors to escape the chill, Chris gave up her impersonal rule as mistress of the revels and settled down at a table with Cass, Jinny, Tracy Oleson, the inebriated Hubbses and the soused Curtiss Havock, and began to pay loving though discouraged attention to Cass.

He was alarmed. No more than any other man did he want to face the unwed lioness robbed of her wish-dream cubs, the chronic wife who resents the straying of her husband just as much when he is not yet her husband. He had hoped to slip away wjth Jinny, and perhaps be invited in for an incautious moment.

Curtiss belched. Hubbs said, "I agree." "Then I'll take you home," said Mrs. Hubbs. Tracy rose. "Judge, I can save you a trip. I'll drive Jinny back—I have my little bus here."

Treacherous as all sweethearts, Jinny babbled, "Oh, thank you, Tracy. Judge, I did have such a good time. Thank you for inviting me. . . . Good night, Miss—uh—Miss Grau."

Cass was alone with Chris.

"I think they all enjoyed it, don't you, Chris?"

"Yes?"

"Due mostly to you, though. You were the perfect hostess. I was amused the way you kept steering Curtiss away from the bar."

"Yes?"

"And I don't know how you ever managed to coax such a beautiful supper out of the steward, and when you think——"

"Cass!"

"What is it, dear?"

" 'Dear'! Cass, have you fallen for that young female grasshopper, that Marshland girl, at your age?"

"What d' you mean, 'At my age'?"

"I mean at your age!"

"I'm the second youngest district judge in Minnesota!"

"And probably you're *the* youngest octogenarian. I know you can still play baseball and dance the tango, only you don't. You like the fireside and your books and chess."

"So I'm that picturesque figure, the venerable judge. Why don't you put in slippers, along with the fireside and the books—you mean *old* books, that smell of leather!"

"Well, your books mostly do, don't they? I just can't see you with a gilt-and-satin copy of 'Mademoiselle Fifi,' or whatever it is your Virginia reads."

"I'll tell you what she reads! She reads Santayana and Willa Cather and, uh, and Proust! That's what she reads!"

"Does she? I didn't suppose she could read. She certainly doesn't show any stains from it."

"Just because she doesn't go around showing off like a young highbrow——"

"Oh, Cassy—Cass, I mean—I'm sorry, I truly am. The last thing in the world I meant to do was to start scrapping with you." They were on a couch in the club lounge. A bartender and four late bridge-players and the two female slot-machine addicts were still present, and he felt that otherwise Chris would crown her humility by kneeling before him, as she went on:

"It's just that we started twenty years ago, when you were a veteran of twenty and I was a worshiping brat of ten, no, eleven, that could hide her reverence for you only by being saucy, and so I got the miserable habit of jabbing at you and——Cass! Do you take this little Marshland girl seriously? An exquisite little thing she is, too, I must say, and probably fairly intelligent and even virtuous, curse her! I mean, damn her! Do you think you're a little in love with her?"

"I think I'm a good deal in love with her. I agree with you in saying 'damn her'! I didn't want to be in an earthquake. You're dead right, my dear; I do prefer quiet. But I'm simply God-smitten."

She sighed then, sighed and was silent, and at last she talked to herself aloud:

"If I had been more brazen, if I hadn't been so scrupulous,

I could have married you several years ago, my friend. Right after Blanche. I'm the only person you've ever really talked to about Blanche. Isn't that true?"

"I suppose it is."

"And how she made fun of you and hurt you? Maybe you like to get hurt. You're going about getting hurt again in just the right way. Now don't tell me that your Virginia wouldn't want to hurt anybody! I'm sure she wouldn't—intentionally. It's just that all you overimaginative men, who try to combine fancifulness with being clock-watching executives, are fated to be hurt, unless you love some kind-hearted, sloppy, adoring woman like me—the born mistress! Well, as Dad always said, *'Nun, so geht's.'* Good night."

He would not run after her, and before he had stalked out to the automobile entrance, she had driven away, in her fast, canary-colored coupé. He stood frozen, realizing that he was free of his past.

An Assemblage of Husbands and Wives

DROVERS AND HAVOCKS

ROY DROVER was born on a farm just at the edge of Grand Republic, and his father was at once a farmer and a veterinarian.

When Roy was a medical student at the University of Minnesota, a beer-drinker and a roarer by night but by day a promising dissecter, he met the tall and swaying Lillian Smith, daughter of a stationer who was refined, tubercular, and poor. He saw that here was the finest flower he was likely ever to acquire for the decoration of a successful doctor's drawing-room. Also, it tickled his broad fancy to think of seducing (even if he could do it only legally) anything so frail and sweet as Lillian.

She was overwhelmed by him, though she did break off the engagement once when he used a certain four-letter word. He reasonably pointed out, however, that either she did not know what the word meant, in which case she could not be shocked, or else she did know, in which case she must have got over being shocked some time ago. She was conquered, though for years afterward she worried about that logic.

By the time they had been married for five years and Roy had practised for seven, Lillian's father was bankrupt, and Roy had the daily pleasure of telling her that, though her "old man might be so cultured and polite, he was mighty glad to get eighty bucks a month from his roughneck son-in-law." That pleasure continued for years after her father had died. At medical conventions or among strangers in a West Coast Florida hotel, Roy would jovially shout, "My ancestors were Vermont hill-billies, but my ball-and-chain comes from the best stock in Massachusetts—such a good stock that it's got pernicious anemia, and I've always had to give it a few injections of gold."

He continued to feel physical passion for Lillian—as well as for every gum-chewing hoyden that he picked up on his trips to Chicago, and for a number of his chattier women patients. Perhaps his continued zest came from the fact that it amused him to watch his wife shiver and reluctantly be conquered. To her, the whole business of sex had become a horror related to dark bedrooms and loud breathing. Sometimes in the afternoon, when Lillian was giving coffee to quiet women like the Avondene girls or the Methodist minister's wife, Roy would come rampaging in, glare at her possessively, growl "H'are yuh" at the guests in a way which said he wished they would get out of this, and as soon as they had twittered away, he would rip down the zipper of her dress.

She often thought about suicide, but she was too blank of mind. She was always reading the pink-bound books of New Thought leaders, those thick-haired and bass-voiced prophets who produce theatrical church-services in New York theaters, and tell their trembling female parishioners that they can accomplish anything they wish if they Develop the Divine Will Power and Inner Gifts. . . . Sometimes Roy threw these books into the furnace.

Lillian never contradicted him. She was mute even when he teased her about her dislike for having dead mallards or pheasants drip blood on her dress when she went hunting with him.

At the beginning of our history, the Drovers had been married for thirteen years. They had two sons, William Mayo and John Erdmann Drover, aged eleven and nine. Lillian was devoted to them, often looked at them sadly, as though they were doomed. She begged them to listen while she read aloud from Kenneth Grahame and her own girlhood copy of "The Birds' Christmas Carol," but the boys protested, "Aw, can that old-fashioned junk, Mum. Pop says it's panty-waist. Read us the funnies in the paper, Mum."

Like their father, the boys enjoyed killing things—killing snakes, frogs, ducks, rats, sparrows, feeble old neighborhood cats.

When Roy and the boys were away, she stayed alone in a shuttered room, in a house that rustled with hate, in a silence that screamed, alone with a sullen cook and a defiant maid. She did not read much, but she did read that all women are "emancipated" and can readily become "economically independent." She was glad to learn that.

Roy and Lillian were often cited by Diantha Marl as "one of the happiest couples, the most successful marriages, in Grand Republic; just as affectionate as the Zagos, but not so showy about it."

The same authority, Diantha, publicly wondered whether

Boone and Queenie Havock, though by 1941 they had been married for thirty-five years, would not "bust up," as the technical phrase was. When, at their rich parties, Queenie got high and screamed that Boone was a "chippie-chasing, widow-robbing old buzzard," he frequently slapped her. She was almost as large as he and even louder, and she retorted spiritedly by spitting at him, and sometimes when he was entertaining Eastern Financiers or other visiting royalty, she yelled at him, "Oh, shutzen Sie die mouth," which she believed to be German.

But in private, with their great arms about each other, these shaggy gods sat up all night making fun of their neat neighbors, drinking and shouting and cackling like pirates. When Boone was almost indicted for stealing one hundred thousand acres of Eastern Montana prairie, Queenie joyfully announced, "I'll come cook for you in jail, you cutthroat!"

He answered admiringly, "You probably will, too, you catamaran, but if you get any more finger-marks on my César Franck symphony records, I'll bust your ole head open."

Dr. Roy Drover often said, "My experience is that it's all nonsense to say that marriage is difficult just because of complicated modern life on top of the fundamental clashes between the sexes. Yessir! It's all perfectly easy, if the husband just understands women and knows how to be patient with their crazy foibles. You bet!"

15

CASS HAD BECOME embarrassed over calling up her boarding-house and having Tracy or Wilma answer, "Who do you want? Who? Oh. Who wants her? Oh!" followed by a shadow of a giggle, and a half-heard: "It's the Judge again. Can you beat it!" So in early July, to invite her to the Svithiod Summer Festival, at which he would be the guest-speaker and say a lot of enthusiastic things about Swedish-Americans, which might impress a girl with a fancy for high words, he wrote a note to her.

She answered, and for the first time he saw her writing.

Now to an expert, her script may have looked like that of any trained stenographer, correct and round, but to Cass this was a secret message from the captive princess in her tower. On the envelope, he was "The Hon. Cass Timberlane." His name had never looked so stately. Could he really be that monumental object to *her*? Or, sudden jagged thought, did she consider the title pompous?

Her *T* was bold, like a knight riding, and the *o* was precise yet sweet, not too unlike a kiss. (That sentimentality he strongly thrust from him, and shamefacedly took back again.) The square envelope and the letter-sheet were of good linen, with a small square "VM" which, his thumb told him, was printed. (Splendid! Engraving would have been extravagant for her.)

Of the letter itself, of her first letter to him, he still had not read a word. He was shy about it. He might know now whether she loved him or considered him a bumbler. Then, breathing deep, he plunged:

"Dear Cass."

——That's good. Not "Dear Judge." She thinks of me as a friend, anyway. Of course "Darling Cass" would have been better.

"Darn it, I have a date for your evening with the Vikings——"

——Hard luck. Certainly is hard luck. She won't hear me make my speech. I'd hoped she would. Still, her letter is cordial—oh, it's more than cordial, it's really affectionate. And some originality to the writing. Not stilted.

The letter continued:

"So I shall not be able to hear you. But I know you will be wonderful. Call me up soon. Sincerely yours, Jinny."

——She really wants me to go on telephoning her! And she signs it "Jinny," not "Virginia" or "Virginia Marshland." She does like me!

During his first five readings of the masterpiece, he twice decided that she liked him, once that she loved him furiously, once that this was merely a routine answer with all the romantic flavor of payment of a gas-bill, and once that she was bored by him and intended, on his evening of oratory, to go off dancing with some treacherous swine like Eino Roskinen.

He did nothing so puerile as to keep the letter in whatever pocket was nearest to his heart; he merely thought about it. He contented himself with locking it up in the steel box that contained his will, his passport, a picture of his mother, a certificate for a hundred shares of the late Overture Silver Mining Company, and a photograph of his former wife, in a 1929 hat, which he did not remember owning.

——Hm. Funny-looking hat. I wonder if the present-day hats would look just as——Lord, I'd forgotten Blanche was so beautiful. But she looks so calculating and possessive, where Jinny is like a living brook. Poor Blanche. I'll bet her new English in-laws snub her. Huh!

He had many walks with Jinny, on Sunday afternoons, and he discovered that he did not know the city of which he was supposed to be a leader. They found a lath-and-mud slum, with starved widows and children living like war-victims upon property belonging to his friend Henry Grannick, second richest man in town. On Jinny's initiative, he went fot the first time in two years into the museum at the Wargate Memorial, which was three and three-quarters minutes' walking-time from his chambers, and they saw the Indian war-bonnets, the models of fur-trader's canoes, and were swollen and proud with their own history.

They chattered all the while. The buffet-supper had given them more of a common background, and they talked of "Chris" and "Roy" as well as of "Tracy," for they were true Midwesterners in referring to everybody up to the age of ninety-eight by his given name.

They were as garrulous as two old friends at the Poor House, and all through it he was unceasingly on the point of proposing to her, yet never quite daring to. In her bright young ruthlessness, she might dismiss him forever.

He was constantly stirred up by her iconoclastic though slightly second-hand political creeds. As a mild and benevolent Republican, who had to be a politician once every six years, however little he liked cigars and the histories of Coolidge and Harding, he collided with the fact that, early conditioned by her father's sympathy with the Farmer-Labor Party, encouraged later by Eino's internationalism, Jinny was Young Revolution at the inquiring age.

As they explored the city's unrecognized slums, she wondered aloud about the competence of the Prutts and Grannicks to control a city, while she denounced the local "isolationists" and insisted that America must join in the war against Germany, which had just invaded Russia.

She was probably disappointed at the readiness with which Cass agreed with all her challenges; she was probably unable to understand that the Judge Timberlane who seemed to her so conservative was considered by his neighbors, by his colleague

Judge Blackstaff, as a riskily radical young man.

He agreed that America is only at the beginning of democracy; that the super-salesman, with the stigmata of his early toughness or rusticity blandished away by barber and manicure girl, stands with the workman whose face is pitted with soot and grease only at the saloon, the polling-booth, and the grave.

If he was distinctly more leftwing than Jinny thought, he was distinctly less so than he thought. He innocently considered himself, even after election-day, democratically one with the farmer, the section-hand, the pants-presser, yet he had always been so occupied with members of the Federal Club and the dwellers on Ottawa Heights that he was as detached from his constituents as any country squire. A kind man, a just judge, an honest citizen who believed that there must be plenty of public schools and no graft in the water supply, he had not yet gone many years beyond the Good Old Massa dynasty. And golf at the country club is a sweet odor in the nostrils and a dependable anesthetic.

In the fresh air that Jinny always bore about her, he wanted to defy his own ancestral cautions. She did not know, possibly he did not know, how much he enjoyed cutting loose and being more of an outlaw than he was. Later he was to believe that he might really have become the rebel whom in these honied months he enjoyed impersonating, if Jinny had really been the bold economic Amazon she considered herself. It has always been the masculine version: "She did not tempt me enough, so I did not eat."

Meantime, more innocent than ever, he made love not apropos of swords and roses, but of the poll tax, the school system, and German bombers.

In July she went home to Pioneer Falls for her two-weeks' vacation, and he begged for an invitation to come up for three days. Her mother wrote to him, welcomingly.

He had always liked his assignments to hold court at Pioneer Falls, county-seat of Mattson County, because from the windows of the court room he could see the re-echoed heavens of Lake Bruin. Here there were none of the wild river valleys of the Grand Republic country. The falls of the Sorshay River were only three feet high, a sporting ground for minnows. A wedge of the old hardwood country had been thrust northward from the base of the state to Pioneer Falls, and the trees were not pine and poplar but oak and maple and ironwood and basswood. Most of them had been cleared away by the fine, high, destructive industry of the frontiersmen, and the country was now an upland wheat prairie, and Pioneer Falls a characteristic grain-belt village. The streets were flat but sheltered by spacious elms and maples that had been planted by the Yankee and German settlers.

The Marshland house was white and comfortable and simple, except for an upstairs balcony with a triangular window behind it, and Jinny's father, Lester the druggist, was simple and comfortable, and Mrs. Marshland a darling. They wore baggy clothes and loved their friends and they thought that Judge Timberlane was a tremendous man and that their "little daughter" was a "mighty lucky girl to have him take an interest in her and her art career." That he could ever marry her or be her lover seemingly did not occur to them.

He was embarrassed by their friendly desire to have him hold forth like a pedagogue upon her talents—and her unpunctuality, to have him give her measured advice about how to become a real big-city cartoonist or a dress designer. He was even more embarrassed by the fact that Mr. and Mrs. Marshland were only fifty-three or -four, somewhat nearer to his own age than was Jinny. He kept hinting that he belonged to her generation, not theirs, but Jinny bedeviled him by mocking, at family dinner (fried chicken and asparagus and peas from our own garden), "I wish you three would now straighten me out about the Polish question and the use of lipstick."

"Don't play with your food, Jinx," said Mrs. Marshland fondly, at every meal.

Cass and Jinny picnicked on a bluff overlooking Lake Bruin, in an old pasture of short worn grass and scattered oaks. Their table was a slab of rock, splashed orange with lichens; their divan the springy moss. They were idle and relaxed and in love, and they did play with their food, with the hard-boiled eggs, the finger rolls, the lemon-meringue pie eaten with fingers which were vulgarly wiped on the flower-starred moss.

He looked like a woodsman, in laced boots and breeches and mackinaw shirt of black and red and yellow. She wore moccasin shoes, with slacks, but she made up for it by wearing a tight sweater.

Reclining on the moss, replete and exquisitely sleepy, he argued, "Put your head on my shoulder."

She looked mute and sulky; then she rubbed her cheek against his shoulder and lay still. His arm was about her and it may have been by accident that his hand touched the unbelievable smoothness of her naked waist under the sweater. He snatched his hand away, but his finger-tips kept the memory of that living satin, the tender warmth of her soft side. In some panic he knew that he was afraid of her and shocked by himself, but he protested, "Don't be such a prude. Of course you love touching her. That's what it's all about."

But any ideas he might have had about trying to betray her seemed wondrously absurd.

He slipped his hand again about her unbodiced waist, and she let it lie there warmly a moment before she detached it, gentle and unoffended. And that was all that happened of fleshly love-making. Yet now, with her head against his shoulder, they had been converted, united, sanctified.

"Darling!" he said only, and kissed her lightly, and her head settled back in contentment.

It was a poet, not a very skillful one, who began talking:

"Dear Jinny, do you know how lovely you are to me? I love your eyes and your hair—it's very reckless today and it smells so newly washed—and I love your childish fingers—do you suppose that indelible-ink spot will ever come off?—and I love your riotous and pretty undependable humor and your curiosity, like Cleo's, about everything, and your honesty and your disinterest in money-making and your talisman, your crystal Isis—did you bring her back to Pioneer Falls?"

"Certainly. Wrapped in a lovely nightgown. She insisted on coming. She's as fascinated by men and their line as I am."

"You don't think I'm merely following a 'line' in what I say, do you?"

"No! I think you're dear and good, and I think you really like me."

They said nothing about being engaged, but like children they made plans.

"Know what I'd like us to do, soon as the war between Great Britain and Germany is over?" he urged. "Sail for Norway and Sweden, which are the source of so much of the life around here, and then go through Finland and dip down into Central Europe and up to Moscow and then China and especially India. I've always been crazy to see India, since I read Kipling as a boy."

"Wond'ful."

"And then we'll come back here and get settled down. We'll live in Grand Republic in the summer and fall—most beautiful Indian Summers in the world—and have our winters in Beverly Hills and Havana and Rio de Janeiro."

"So we're just going to be hoboes and wasters, are we?"

"Sure—in our dreams. Look here, comrade, have we got to have social significance even in our *dreams?*"

"I think I'll have to get a ruling on that. Meanwhile, what are we doing all this *on?*"

"Can't I just as well dream myself two million dollars and a year's leave from the bench, while I'm about it?"

"You're so heroic—in our dreams."

"Plans okay then?"

"Approved. Cass, maybe we really *could* do some of those things, even without being rich."

"Certainly."

"But why is it that nobody ever does do any of the things that he's free to do?"

In that counsel of doom he was suddenly frightened out of his spurious boyishness, and clutched her hand, as if to protect her.

They silently looked out from the shadowing oaks to the summer-enchanted lake. The farther shore was swampy and in the July light was a gold-streaked utter green, with blackbirds bending down the reeds. There was peace over all the land, and their fear melted, and suddenly she was telling him, as she never had, of her childhood in the white house in the prairie village:

"I was such a serious kid, always so busy. I had to keep track of everything. I had note-books and note-books; I put down the temperature of my dolls, every day, like a hospital chart, and all the bright things they said—I made 'em up, only sometimes I stole 'em from the other kids. And I collected birds' eggs and made the most elaborate notes on just which tree I'd found them in—I drew plans of the trees, with lovely arrows pointing. I was sure that some day those notes would be terribly important to some ornithologist. I suppose I'm still the greatest living authority on snipe around Peterson's Slew.

"And then as fast as I learned a hymn in Sunday School—I was a Congregationalist, like you—I wrote it down on a card, with my notations about what words to come down hard on, like *'Bringing* in the *sheaves'*— only, I thought it was *sheets*.

"I didn't have any brothers or sisters, so they let me have the attic all to myself, and up there I was the busiest man of affairs, rushing from one thing to another: arranging my world-collection of fans, two paper ones and one lace, and my gallery of movie stars, and polishing a brass handle to something—I found it by the road, and to this day I don't know what it was for—and writing down the name of every new language that I heard of. I got up to sixty-seven, and I intended to learn them all, including Swahili and Liukiu.

"And then pets—our old cat, Percival, and a lot of other

cats and dogs and rabbits and a pet squirrel and a very inappreciative garter snake. I used to have an animal drug store and try to cure all their ailments with sugar-water. I don't think I was so successful.

"Maybe a lot of the things that I did were to educate the little blue Bromo Seltzer bottle, the forerunner of my Isis, that I sneaked out and took everywhere so it could see what was going on. Oh, I must have been almost as silly at ten as I am now.

"And I took lessons on the mandolin. I could play 'Down Mobile' and the Russian national anthem on it. I was so busy and so secret. Nobody ever knew; Dad and Mother were swell about not prying. And sometimes I had the most money that ever was—an entire penny. I would go into Dad's store and he would pretend he didn't know me, and he would advise me, very earnestly, and you'd be surprised how many kinds of candy you could get then for a penny: maybe one red and two striped and a licorice lozenge. I'll never have that much money again, never."

"No, there never are any pennies like that after you are ten," said Cass. "And now you're as old as I am. I used to think of you as eons younger, but now I feel as though we were the same age, except that you aren't so cautious."

"And I think of you, Cass, as just my age, except that you have more sense."

With an absorbed I-want-to-think expression, she wandered

off, along the shore, and he watched her sleepily. She looked mature and thoughtful, till, throwing up her arms, she started violently hop-skipping, all by herself, singing what sounded like a jazz version of Celeste Aida, and then she seemed to be all of ten again, and he reached into his pocket for a penny to give her.

16

AFTER THE BUFFET-SUPPER for Jinny, his sister Rose and Gregory Marl said, "What a nice girl that was; like to see her again," but Cass wondered that more people did not comment. He need not have wondered; they did.

Everybody in town—it being understood that everybody-in-town includes some three hundred persons out of the 85,000—discussed Jinny, by telephone, by letter, over the directors' table, or at the Paul Bunyan Bar. But they did not reveal this to Cass, for he was a man not overfond of being tickled in the ribs.

But after he had ventured to Pioneer Falls, before he had yet pressed, in a volume of Supreme Court digests, the buttercup that Jinny had given him, then everybody concluded that they must rush in and rescue him.

He was to play bridge at Boone Havock's, and before the fourth player, Eve Champeris, arrived, Boone and Queenie, with her voice like a flat trolley-wheel, set out to save him with the solicitude of a couple of pigs eating their young. That they had never yet seen Jinny made them no less authoritative.

Boone struck:

"Sit down, Cass, and take a load off your feet. Have a snort? Don't be a fool; of course you will. Now, Cass, I want you to listen to me and don't go interrupting and shooting off your mouth just because you think you're such a high-brow and a judge and all that junk while me, I never got through fifth grade. You haven't any better friends in the world than me and Queenie."

"You're damn tootin'," confirmed Queenie, then remembered that she was being refined and humanitarian this evening, and caroled, "Are we everl Oh boy, I'll say we are! A lot of bums are always yessing you, Cass, because you're in politics, but me and Boone are good-enough friends to tell you the truth. You know. For your own good."

Cass had really come over to play bridge, not to have things done for his good, and he was not a meek man. But he was their neighbor, he was used to them, and in a frontier civilization you are not offended by a neighbor if he does nothing worse than throw tomahawks. He listened to Boone with only a slight biliousness.

"Cass, what's all this we hear about your going nuts over some fifth-rate stenographer?"

"Some low-grade tart on the make," added Queenie, virtuously. After all, Queenie had some background for her opinions on lowness. Her father had kept some of the best saloons in Northern Minnesota.

"I don't know what you two are talking about, unless you mean Miss Marshland, a brilliant young artist in whose career I have become slightly interested."

" 'Slightly' is good!" jeered Queenie.

Boone roared, "I don't suppose you take her out to that gyp' joint, the Unstable, more than three times a week!"

"I do not!"

"I don't suppose her and you were snooping around those tenements on South Greysolon Avenue! You didn't tell each other they were 'a disgrace,' and 'somebody ought to do something about 'em!' Well, I *own* those tenements, and if you want 'em I'll be glad to give 'em to you and see what *you* can do with 'em! Lot of Finns and Communists and Poles and Svenskas in there, never pay their rent and use the banisters for firewood! But let that pass. I'm so used to trying to do something for this community and never get one word of thanks that I don't even pay any attention to a lot of Red bellyaching, and I don't care *what* you said about Havock Haven. But I do care when I see an old friend making a fool of himself over a cute little gold-digger that just hangs around to see what she can get out of him—and then probably goes back to the boy-friend and they laugh their heads off at the old goat!"

Cass broke.

"I wouldn't let you talk like this even if what you said were true, but it isn't. Miss Marshland is decidedly a lady. No, that's a bloodless word—she's an angel."

"Sweet little gold angel with blood in her eye!" screamed Queenie.

"You sleeping with her?" Boone grunted.

"I am not! And even if——"

"Now don't go and get gentlemanly on us, son. We're only trying to help you. You made a portion of a horse of yourself before, marrying that high-hat Minneapolis snob with her phony Boston accent, and we don't want you to do it again."

Cass must have said something confused and not impressive, for Boone was unsquelched.

"There'd be some excuse for this new girl if you were doing a little advanced necking with her, but if you're thinking about marrying her—a cutie half your age——"

"She is not!"

"——that has an idea it would be swell to be Mrs. Judge Timberlane, and expects you to stay up all night and dance with her, or sit around and watch her dance with the younger guys, why, then you're a worse fool than I thought you were, and I've always rated you pretty high in damn foolishness ever since you gave up what might of become a fifty-thousand-dollar law-practice to sit on your dignity on the bench."

Queenie neighed, "Now you listen to me. A woman's heart knows. None of these young girls want to be of any help to their husbands. They just get married for the excitement of it and for what they can get out of it, the little tramps, and so immodest—showing their knees! If you *got* to get married, Cass—and I don't see why; ain't there any lady clerks that know the answers in your court house?—then why don't you pick out some dame of thirty-five that'll stay home and take care of you, like I would?"

He did not, as he longed to then and all through the ordeal of bridge, slap them and walk out. But for a year it broke his habit of the Havocks.

"He's spoiled—touchy as a pregnant woman," said Queenie Havock to Eve Champeris, who said it to Chris who said it to Cass who said it to himself.

He expected Roy Drover to be even more boisterous than the Havocks, but Roy, when he caught Cass in the quiet reading-room of the Federal Club, sounded like a physician, competent and impersonal:

"Son, I hear you've fallen for that pretty little monkey you brought to the Country Club. It's none of my business, but why don't you try some ugly woman with a lot of passion, instead of one of these anemic kids? They haven't any gratitude. I take it for granted you don't intend to marry this chick—her a rank outsider, that none of us know. You're not *that* haywire!"

Cass tried to believe afterward that his retorts to Boone and Roy and two or three other foul impugners and mongers had been in the manner of a stately "Sir!" followed by a challenge. It is doubtful. That would not have gone well with Radisson County duck-hunters, especially when they loved him enough to risk his wrath.

The one gentle effort at his salvation was that of Stella

Avondene Wrenchard.

The Avondenes were a Family, fond and unshakable. They were impoverished aristocracy who were unconcerned about it so long as they could be together in their old whitewashed brick house. The head of the family, Verne Avondene, had been born, in Grand Republic, to a million dollars in timberlands which had been acquired, possibly honestly, by his grandfather, the great Indian agent, who seems in the histories to have had no Christian name other than "Colonel." Verne went to Yale and the English Cambridge and was just looking into diplomatic careers when the family money blew up. He did not complain; the game had been worth any golden candle, and he had a comforting knowledge of Balzac and Monet and Old English balladry, even if he could not earn more than thirty-five dollars a week.

That sum he received in the insurance office of Scott Zago, where he was respectfully entitled "office manager," meaning clerk and assistant bookkeeper.

His wife, still slim and beautiful at sixty-five, said that Verne was the greatest gentleman, the most gallant lover, and the most amusing companion in Grand Republic, and she was a fair judge.

Their two daughters lived with them. Stella had married an engineer, Tom Wrenchard, but had been widowed by an accident within the year, and come home. Her marriage had been so brief that most people forgot it, and she was usually called "Miss Stella Avondene." She taught domestic science in the Alexander Hamilton High School. Her spinster older sister, Pandora, gentle and affectionate and given to flowers and sketching and playing the piano, which under her mild fingers sounded like a spinet, was in charge of the children's department at the public library. Both girls treated their parents as their equals, and the low white brick house was full of fudge, cats, new novels, Delius, water-colors, charades, omelets, and other people's children.

Stella had always thought well of marrying Cass, but had stayed home from hunting in loyalty to Chris Grau. Now, she invented a lovely theory: Chris had, probably for discreditable reasons, jilted Cass, who in wan loneliness had turned to some pretty girl or other who had no virtues. Except in a state of solitary madness, a steady man like Cass could never marry out of Our Class, that ancient aristocracy of Grand Republic, hoary with tradition, which had been going on now for more than seventy-five years.

Stella wanted to save him.

The Avondenes had him in for supper. As they had a maid only when Verne had had a lucky bet on the races—the last time had been in 1939—they did all the housework, and they let Cass help them wash the dishes (which he did unexpectedly well, being a camper) while they all sang "Sweet and Low." Then Stella mended the lining of his coat, poor girl. As his own housekeeper, Mrs. Higbee, was very inspective and efficient about that sort of thing, he suspected that Stella had made the small rip in the lining herself, and he loved her for it.

He might have married Stella then. Perhaps he should have married Stella, and grown peaceful to the point of Double Solitaire, but it happened that either God or Cass Timberlane had made of Jinny Marshland the eternal image of beauty walking with silver feet the waves of dawn. Dear Stella Avondene, teaching in your Sunday-school class at St. Anselm's, and smiling, in the white kid gloves you cleaned at home, singing and a little sad and very kind. You will never walk the waves at dawn. Dear Stella!

He heard something of the town rumors about Jinny. Apparently Mrs. Webb Wargate had said that, though she honored Judge Timberlane and would probably receive any ragtag of a wife that he might drag in, yet she was regretful that such a man should be planning to marry a girl whose real name was Marshandsky, whose father was a drunken teamster on the Range, who had been a waitress in the Pineland Hotel and an itinerant hired girl, and who was in general a threat to the Best People of Grand Republic, so intimately related to the Best People of Albany and Philadelphia and Hartford.

The early Minnesota had its families with the correct and rigid manners, the Emersonian scholarship, of New England, with an annotated Horace and a frivolous fiddle lying upon the pious parlor organ. It had its Romans like General Sibley and, in Grand Republic, the Avondenes and Grannicks. But lesser and brisker tribes like the Wargates had taken their togas.

Cass considered the Wargate peerage.

Old Dexter Wargate had started out in Minnesota in 1881 by conducting a hardware-store and selling nails across the counter to lumberjacks and half-breeds. He had married the daughter of Simon Eisenherz, from Pennsylvania, who had come to Minnesota in 1854, to acquire furs from the Indians in exchange for brass pots and bootleg whisky, with some effect upon the number of murdered white settlers, before he discovered how to steal millions of acres of timberland.

Cass was not pleased when a family founded upon a whisky keg in a log cabin felt superior to a girl crooning over her collection of three fine fans in a village attic, secret and eager and alone—so alone and helpless against the chatter at the cocktail-hour.

He had only one moment of treachery to Jinny: when he wondered whether to others she was as clearly divine as she was to him. He remembered that the Juliet Zago who to him was a wiggling nuisance was a fair young thing to her Scott, and that Boone Havock seemingly felt no distress when his wife yelled like a buzz-saw. Were there barbarians who might think that his Jinny had a touch of the Zago whimsy, with her circulatory Isis? To him, she would forever be a flame, but could his friends see her glory?

He was aware that Jinny had a temper. She was, he thought, unconscious of what the Havocks and Wargates whispered, but if she learned it, he was certain that she would reject him along with all his clansmen forever. He had not planned to venture upon any talk of marriage until they should have had a year of building up a common background. But he felt now that he must not risk her discovery of the gossip till she should be bound to him, protected by him, and on an August evening when he was to take her to the movies, he drove irresolutely toward her boarding-house with the nervous intention of proposing to her.

The living-room at Miss Hatter's was empty. When Jinny appeared, ten minutes late as usual, he sat in the preposterous patent-rocker of 1890, and ventured, "I think we've done all the traditional things that lovers do, even moonlight and picnic by a brook, up to a point."

"But we aren't lovers, Cass."

"We might be."

"M."

"So I want you to come sit on my lap."

"Oh, dear no. That's very outmoded and reactionary, Judge."

"You sit on my lap!"

She did. He felt the pleasure of her body's closeness, but he found that he was remarkably uncomfortable. She was heavier than she looked, and there was extreme danger that the rickety chair would fall over sidewise. He wished that he could think of some polite way of telling her that it would be all right now if she went over and sat on the couch. She sighed blissfully and moved closer and his fingers tightened on her knee, and he was at once in ecstasy and conscious that his right leg was cramped.

In that mingled state he said quietly, "Darling, you know how I want to marry you."

"M."

"We must be married, and soon."

Silent.

"Will you?"

Silent and motionless.

"Jinny! Please!"

She spoke as quietly as he, with no tint of blushing in her voice. "No, Cass, it's impossible."

"Why?"

"We could never make a go of it. I'm terribly fond of you, maybe I'm a little in love with you, but if we were married, it would be too much of a strain."

"Difference in age?"

"Oh, you're not so much older. I've almost fallen in love with men much older than you—one antiquated buzzard of fifty, in Pioneer Falls when I was a kid—an evangelist he was, and was he full of It! No. You're really younger than Tracy or Eino or that Curtiss Havock lug; there's something awfully young and touching about you. But I never could stand your set, not even your sister, though she's nice, or that caramel sundae, Mr. Criley. They're all a bunch of furnace-regulators, and they talk about their Middlewestern Hospitality but none of them invite Mr. Fliegend to their houses. I couldn't do it, I honestly couldn't. But——"

She was actually traditional enough to wind up with, "But let's be the best of friends."

He pushed back her chin with angry fingers and kissed her angrily, and she relaxed to it; a kiss long and confessing. Then, to his shock and to the danger of his flopping over in the patent-rocker, she sprang from his lap and stood smoothing her hair, murmuring. "Somebody——"

There were footsteps. By the time Eino Roskinen came in, Jinny was sedately sitting on the couch and Cass had straightened his summertime blue bow-tie.

Jinny twittered, "Oh, Eino, the Judge wants to hear about the new state dairy regulations. He was just asking me."

Eino was distressingly informed and accurate, and he produced a fireworks-display of figures until Cass, to his annoyance, really became interested. But he felt flat and baffled. How could he persuade Jinny of the joys of a life-time of furnace-regulation? He bravely put her out of his mind forever—forever until they sat at the movie and her hand slipped unasked into his.

So the lover started all over again his daily task of being crushed.

17

HE HAD, for Jinny, dinner at his house, with Rose and Donald Pennloss and Abbott and Hortense Hubbs. Cleo went mad trying to take care of them all.

Rose informed Cass, after dinner, "I do like your Marshland girl. She's the cleverest of all your girls."

"*What* girls?"

"Oh, you know. How would *I* know? And Cass, she's so pretty!" Then Cass loved his sister, whom he had not infrequently considered a nuisance.

He had persuaded Jinny to bring in a portfolio of her Fliegend Toy drawings, that his friends might see that Miss Jinny was not only the most beautiful but the most talented young woman living, and he pressed them on Hubbs.

Abbott Hubbs was the neurotic, young-old newspaperman who hated newspapers, who drank too much and smoked too many cigarettes and was too snappishly cynical, and in the privacy of his meager home, read poetry aloud to his wife, who loved and slapped and, during hangovers, nursed him. He was always shaky, dropping cigarette ashes on everything: a thin, wizened, black-haired, extraordinarily honest and generous man, a victim of the days of war-bulletins and smug syndicated columns and cameras and high finance in newspapers.

Jinny had prepared sketches for a pasteboard political Punch and Judy show. Hubbs looked at her piggish Mussolini, her melancholy Hitler, her bulldog Churchill, her mocking Roosevelt, and he cried, shaking ashes all over the sketches, "These are fine, these are mighty fine. Jinny, could I take some of 'em and show 'em to Greg Marl, at the paper?"

Cass noted, along with his pride in this discovery of Jinny's genius, that this was the first time that any of his friends had addressed her as "Jinny."

Next day, Gregory Marl, large and soft and diplomatic, spoke to him at the Federal Club.

"We think well of Miss Marshland's drawings at the *Banner* office, Cass, and we're losing our cartoonist. He's going to enlist in the Army—thinks America will get into the war, maybe by the middle of 1942."

"*You* don't believe that, do you, Greg?"

"Oh, no, not a chance. We'll go on furnishing supplies to England, but we'll never enter the war."

"Maybe we ought to."

"Maybe—but we won't. But you never can persuade these crazy youngsters like my cartoonist. So I would like to talk to Miss Marshland. Does she understand reproduction processes?"

"Must—working at Fliegend's."

"Confidentially, do you know what they're paying her?"

"Uh—thirty-five a week."

"Uh—I guess the *Banner* could hike that to forty-five."

Cass told himself that he was pleased that she could command all this wealth.

When Jinny went worrying to Lucius Fliegend about the *Banner* offer, Lucius insisted on her taking this nobler job.

On her last afternoon at the factory, in late August, they gave Jinny a riotous party, with speeches by Mr. Fliegend, R. Ogden Hathawick, the shipping clerk, the society reporter of the Grand Republic *Banner*, and District Judge Cass Timberlane.

Her first cartoon for the *Banner* depicted an American eagle meditatively though rather acrobatically scratching its beak with a claw, as it gazed at a two-headed eagle with two crowns. Spirited and original, felt Cass, and he made it the occasion for taking her to dinner at the Unstable.

Where hitherto she had worked on the Southwest Side, now her office was in the center of town, only three and a half blocks from the court house, and as his fall term opened, Cass was demanding that she lunch with him, at Charley's or Oscar's or the Pineland or the Ladies' Annex of the Federal, at least three days a week. But she, who a month ago had been a flying-haired working girl with gingerbread and an apple for lunch in a flowery pasteboard box, was now a gray-suited, demurely coiffed young career-woman, and Cass was heavy with worry and a certain jealousy as he found that she had no longer to depend on him to meet the Important Factors in the Commercial and Professional Life of Our City, but was invited to lunch by Abbott Hubbs, Curtiss Havock, Fred Nimbus, the announcer, and Dick Wolke, the jeweler. When he met her now, it was as likely to be she who had the "inside track on the news"—she called it that—news about Norton Trock's extra-legal speculations or Bernice Claywheel's lovers or the more secret plans of the Turkish Army.

To his tenderness for her Cass added wondering admiration of her knowledge. She knew just how much false hair Madge Dedrick wore, and precisely what plans, in a secluded tent on the African desert, British agents were making. . . . Hubbs had told her, and Cass mustn't let it go any further.

She reported all her professional triumphs, and Cass was proud but worried, as they walked in the chilly September evenings, with the first of the Northern Lights like a gigantic glass chandelier swaying in the ceiling of the heavens.

He was in a trance of absolute love, and such practicalities as marriage seemed trivial. He wanted nothing except what she might want. His responsibility as a judge, his devotion to his friends, his zest in hunting and swimming, his reverence for learning, these must remain in him, for they were indestructible parts of him, but they were minor and obvious facts, not worth noting, compared with his worship for this slight, swift-walking girl.

But he did not think of her only in terms of divinity, of altars and silver wings. He hoarded a bus-transfer ticket that had been crumpled in her hot hand, a pencil sketch of himself which she had made on a paper napkin.

The Quiet Mind that he had always sought he had found now in Jinny's cool presence. She was to him not lovely flesh alone, though wholesomely and urgently she was that as well, but peace and reality. With her, he might never accomplish strange adventures, but with her the commonplace life of a Grand Republic lawyer might become as beautiful as sunrise on a prairie slew.

The rumor that "Judge Timberlane has fallen for some skirt or other and is going to get hitched" had spread from Ottawa Heights to the distant wilderness fully five minutes' drive away, where dwelt nobody at all except the clerks and factory workers and repairmen and women and children who made up nine-tenths of the population of Grand Republic.

Into the mind of everyone who wanted everyone else to do something beneficial for all the rest of the people and do it right away came the same inspiration. If Judge Timberlane was going to be married again, and apparently this time to a tempting little piece who would keep him absorbed, then he would be less affable about giving contributions, making speeches, sitting on committees, signing broadsides, and listening to the local Adam Smiths read aloud, from mimeographed sheets, their plans to bring about international peace by having the Lenin Institute of Moscow, the University of Berlin, and the University of Indiana combine. They must get to him at once, and if George Hame had not been agile at the corridor door of the Judge's chambers, they probably would have done so.

They had to be content with writing to him, though they would have preferred to bolt in and shout, "I know you're a busy man and I just want three minutes of your time," and then stay for three eloquent hours.

Daily Cass had letters from organizations to keep us out of the war, to get us into the war, to support the labor unions, the manufacturers' unions, the farmers' unions, and the Dickens Fellowship, and crusades to glorify the American mother or to persuade her to stop talking.

He felt guilty about all of them but instead of answering them, now, he went out to lunch with Jinny.

He had little of her fantastic imagination, whereby, in her *Banner* cartoons, Rumania became a sinister cat like her own Isis, but he nourished that imagination in her, along with every happiness and tranquility. He looked at her cartoons even before the European war headlines or the court notices, and when she had failed, as unfortunately she frequently did, he winced, and prayed for her success. Oh, yes, he did sometimes pray, to a Liberal Congregational God who was interested in world peace and the welfare of share-croppers.

He walked with Jinny, they played poker at Miss Hatter's—Tracy Oleson had the astuteness about straights to be expected from a Wargate Corporation man—and once, when a carnival came to town, Cass and Jinny attended it and shot rifles at clay ducks and had their weights guessed and their photograph taken, arm in arm.

In the belief that she had enjoyed somewhat rowdy sports like bowling with Eino and Tracy, Cass conceived it to be his duty to show himself boisterous, and he rode the merry-go-round with her, boldly reaching for the brass ring, while the electors of Radisson County stood in a circle yelling, "Ride 'em, Judge" and "Good boy, Judge; you got it." He looked triumphantly at Jinny, on a gold and aquamarine unicorn beside him, but her face was compressed and disapproving.

He got off the merry-go-round as soon as possible. "I thought you'd enjoy roughhousing with me," he puzzled.

"It isn't dignified. Nor for a judge."

"But I thought you didn't like it when I was too dignified."

"I don't, but still——People recognizing you and staring at you cutting up monkeyshines! Your own constituents!"

"Why, Jinny, I gained five votes for my next election every time they saw me go round!"

"Yes—maybe—but still——"

He had thought that in Blanche he had encountered all the feminine unreasonableness there was to know. The student of precedents sighed, "Overruled again."

The first occasion on which they were invited out together was a dinner given by Rose Pennloss, with the playful Zagos, that glittering semi-bachelor Jay Laverick and, to Cass's quaking, Chris Grau.

The Pennloss house was as neat as a shop-window and as comfortable as a hotel and no more affectionate than either. The living-room, scientifically the right size for a family of three, was filled with maple reproductions of Colonial furniture, on a machine-made handmade rug, with a New Art wallpaper depicting, with liberties, the environs of Boston, all highly clean and shining, with one relieving vulgarity in a rubbed red-leather couch on which Don took his naps. The excellent dinner, cooked by the excellent Swedish maid and served on excellent china that, in a fainting gray, showed the major churches of New England, tasted as the fine maple furniture looked.

To Cass, social dinners were likely to be either hellish or dull. This was hellish.

But Chris Grau, now first coming on Jinny and him as a recognized couple, was cordial, was easily generous. She asked Cass about the health of Cleo, and she said to Jinny, "I look at your cartoons every day, Miss Marshland. I think they are extremely clever."

As he heard this, Cass suddenly knew that they were not particularly clever, and he felt bleak.

He kept babbling, and Rose had a sorry tale of how little the Reverend Dr. Gadd appreciated her spiritual yearnings, and the Zagos bounced about and waved the stalks of vegetables in the air, but Jinny was as strong as Chris. She was wordless but merry-eyed, and she listened to everybody exactly as though she were listening.

She even kept on smiling when Juliet Zago yelled, "Oh, oop-sums, we dot Baked Alaska for dessertums!"

Rose had thought not badly of Jinny, and looked at her now with politeness, but she wanted to know quite a few fundamental things about her religious beliefs, her virtue, her opinion of President Franklin D. Roosevelt, and how cheaply she could buy clothes.

What, fretted Cass, could any man do against the secret hates and grudging acceptances of women?

Not cowards in the windy forests of night can find such jumpy fears as any lover. When dinner was over, Rose's daughter, Valerie, fifteen and fresh and excited, came in from a movie which she and the current boy had been professionally viewing and judging. She clamped on Jinny as the only bright thing in this mildewed company. The two girls, twenty-four and fifteen, slipped away and could be heard laughing in the sun-room. When Jinny was dragged back, to make up the second table of bridge, she looked at Cass sulkily, and he felt like a wicked old pasha.

He was unreasonably irritated that they expected him to be

grateful to them for accepting as possibly worthy of them the young Diana clothed in light.

An Assemblage of Husbands and Wives

ROSE AND DON PENNLOSS

CASS TIMBERLANE never at any time expected the marriage of his sister and Don Pennloss to last for three months more. He was sorry; he liked them both, and in their informal and impersonal house he was comfortable. But Rose had ambitions for what she called "a richer life," which meant, to her, music and travel and new clothes and being the hostess to visiting lecturers, like Diantha Marl, or living in a New York duplex, like Astra Wargate, sister-in-law of Webb.

Her husband liked making love to her, liked having her around to play rummy and hear his stories. The trouble, or so Rose thought, was that he was common in taste and dull in talk and a small dreariness to look at. She could not endure the heavy monotone of his voice; he quarreled or made love or said the bacon was good or denounced the unions in exactly the same basso, without inflections.

Don was, at forty, a grain-dealer, president of the Aldpen Elevator System, and he made nine thousand dollars a year and liked carpentry, and when you asked him if he didn't think it was a hot afternoon, he told you. Always, invariably, though Rose threatened to scream, he had a nap on the red leather couch when he came home from the office, and invariably he announced his purpose by saying, "I think I'll take a little nap now." Never a large nap. Never a medium-sized nap. Always a little one. And he snored.

On evenings when they were at home alone, he turned on the radio and let it blast away through music, weather reports, lumber-market reports, addresses about South American tariffs, and humorous sketches in which celebrated radio artists said that their rivals—really lovely friends of theirs— were no good at all. Don rarely heard any of it, as he read his newspaper and *The Grain Gazette*, but if she wanted to turn it off he was angry. He mourned, "Can't a man do what he wants to even in his own house? I don't stay out nights chasing around with a bunch of chippies, and I think I might have some consideration."

Rose frequently told Cass that her liveliest desire was to have Don "stay out nights and chase his head off and let me have one quiet evening to think in."

When Rose had married him sixteen years ago—he was twenty-four and she was only twenty—she had reported to Cass, "Don's really the most appealing boy, under his apparent solidity. I'm the only one who understands him. He tugs at my heartstrings."

She complained about Don now rather too much; usually to Cass but not rarely to an intimate lunch of women at the Heather Club. But she never complained to her daughter, Valerie, for whom she planned vicarious careers as an actress or a newspaperwoman.

She said to Cass, in effect, "I want to live in New York and get to know all the intellectuals. But what is a woman who is still good-looking at thirty-six but not beautiful enough to make a career of it, clever enough to know she wouldn't be clever on any job, aware, through reading, of all the glamor and luxuries of life but with no money for them and no rich relatives to murder, active and yet contemptuous of amateur charities and artistic trifling and exhibitionistic sports, untrained in anything worth fifteen dollars a week on the labor market and not even, after years of marriage, a competent cook or nurse, no longer in love with her husband and bored by everything he does—and he always does it!— and yet unwilling to have the thrill of being vengeful toward him or of hurting him intentionally, liking other men but not lecherous nor fond of taking risks, possessing a successful daughter and too interested in her to desert her—just what is this typical upper-middle-middle-class American Wife to *do?*"

When Cass scolded that she had never yet done anything to prove that she was really superior to her cheerful and industrious husband, and that Don might be bored also,

Rose agreed so angelically that Cass felt helpless. And when he insisted that if she really wanted to break away, she must quit talking, take a plain job, study, thoroughly learn some occupation, she agreed just as amiably, and did nothing.

She had once had something like a lover in St. Paul, a musician, a pretentious fool who finally ran off with a weak-minded grandmother, but Rose was still proud of having been caressed by this cavalier. Once, for two weeks, she had thought that she was in love with the brutal powers of Dr. Roy Drover, but then the doctor had gone trout-fishing.

She believed that she liked to listen to spirited conversations between Men of Talent. She asserted that she was "absolutely in awe of geniuses, like Bernard Shaw and Henry Ford" and that she "got such a profound thrill from hearing original points of view expressed." Actually, they never did get expressed when she was around, because if she asked a deep question, she interrupted the answer to it as soon as she had thought up another question. Even the most intellectual exhibit—say, Norton Trock explaining bank clearances—became only a dark background for Rose's spiritual fireworks.

All of this about Rose Pennloss is true, and none of it is quite true, because along with her restlessness, which arose from her feeling that nothing she was doing was important, she was a kind-hearted and attractive woman and an unjealous mother, who would, with a sturdier man, have become a good farm-wife. And, loving Cass, she was willing to believe as strongly as he that in Jinny Marshland there was a witch-lamp and a knowledge of good and evil.

18

THIS OCTOBER WEEK, Cass had a wriggling heap of
divorces in his court, along with a good clean burglary and
one lively carnal-knowledge case. He worked late in his
chambers or at home, and all week he did not once see Jinny.
Saturday, he went reluctantly off on what was supposed to be
a joyful duck-hunting stag, at Dr. Drover's log hunting lodge
near Lake Vermilion.

"Roy's Retreat" had cost a good many appendectomies for
its varnished logs, its fieldstone fireplace, and many a humble
tonsil had gladly sacrificed itself for the Navajo blankets, the
Mexican pottery, the rack of English shotguns, and the hotel-
size refrigerator.

The six hunters in the party were out on the duck-pass at
four in the morning on the day after their arrival. They set out
the decoys and humped over, shivering, in the rain, watching
the bleary water, the thin tamaracks, as a wet dawn crawled
over the swamp of faded reeds. Dr. Drover had two bottles of
brandy with him, and when they drove back to the lodge for
breakfast, at nine, they had only five mallards, but they had
six beautiful jags. Thereafter, though Roy would occasionally
go out and repel some savage duck that seemed to menace
them, they drank and played poker and talked about women,

and not about women in the kitchen or the polling-booth.

The others were gentler men than Roy; they did not roar and they liked novels and the theater, yet all of them, except Cass and Gerald Lent, who had once lived in Europe and who was now the kept husband and social secretary of Della Wargate Lent, belonged to the Big Boys, the solid and hearty fellows, contemptuous of tenderness toward any women except their mothers and their daughters, and their talk about women, as about taxation, marched with the tread of infantry on parade.

Though the biggest and by far the strongest among them, Cass often had an exasperating feeling of inferioritiy to these virile captains. Like a small boy among scornful elder brothers, he babbled things he did not especially want to say, he interrupted them with uneasy questions that he did not particularly want answered. He told wavering anecdotes about the court room, and even during them he thought, "This is a very dull story!" He chattered about Russia, about Judge Blackstaff, about the way to cook cabbage, about every small subject that was sacred to him just now because he had been discussing it with Jinny.

Roy belched, "Oh, shut up, Cass, you're just gossiping. You get me down. How the hell a pansy like you, that plays the flute and reads poetry and is nuts about every sixteen-year-old gal that hits town and even gets chummy with these Farmer-Labor agitators that want to overthrow the Government—how come you can still be the best shot in town is clean beyond me. By God, *that's* injustice!"

That was Roy's way of showing his affection—and of showing what he really thought.

In their talk of women, Roy and Greg Marl said nothing about their own wives, and Bradd Criley had none, but Harley Bozard jeered that his spouse, Karen, was completely frigid, and Marl let them know how successfully, on a Pullman sleeper, he had seduced the wife of a college president.

Gerald Lent ruefully reported, "If any of you boys think it's a cinch to be idle and live on a rich wife like Della, that expects you to yes her relatives and to get hot at two A.M., I wish you'd try it. I ever tell you about the time I had a row with her before I went off to the Arrowhead? When I came home, she'd put all my pictures and clothes and the chest that I bought in Florence out on the lawn, in the rain. The meanest job I know of is to be the little husband in the home, waiting for the big manly wife to come from work. No ditch-digger earns his keep as hard as I do. I wonder when I'll walk out on dear Della. She'll be so surprised! Hey, don't be so tightwad with that hootch."

Through it all the monkish Cass wanted only to repeat the awfully bright things his Jinny had said.

He dared not even question her employer, Greg Marl, about her progress as a cartoonist, lest the independent young woman hear of it and think that he was interfering.

He was certain that these were his good friends and that he was madly enjoying the drinking and the poker, but when they were all out on the lake, one day earlier than he had intended to go, he left a highly perjured note for them and drove back, on a red-gold Minnesota October afternoon, to Grand Republic—to Jinny.

On the way, from a booth in a country store, he telephoned to her, "Starting home—dine with me tonight?" She was at the *Banner* office, where ordinarily she was forbiddingly businesslike, but now she squealed, "Darling! I didn't expect you till tomorrow. I'm so glad!"

"I had a fine time hunting with the boys."

"The boys! Grrrr!"

"I thought maybe I never would come home."

"So did I. I was scared."

"Would you really care if I didn't come back?"

"I think I'd just die. No, no, I wouldn't! But——"

"Darling, I'm so——We dine, then?"

"Of course. Why not?"

"Well—you know—I was afraid you might have a date with Eino or Tracy or Abbott Hubbs."

"Those brats! And if I did—so what!"

"You'd break it for me?"

By now, the ardor that in her surprise Jinny had betrayed had grown more cautious, but she was still friendly as she answered, "I might think about it, anyway."

"I'll be at Miss Hatter's at seven, then."

"I'll be all ready. Seven sharp."

Which, in Jinny's time-schedule, meant ten minutes past seven, not very sharp.

But for once, when he drove up she was out on a flimsy sort of balcony, apparently ready, and she waved to him with a thrilling "Be right down!"

He then waited, in his car, for seven minutes. Four of them he devoted to regretfully watching his fervor cool off, and three to wondering whether she had, upstairs there, some rat of a suitor whom she did not wish him to see.

As she came out of the covered outside stairway, his rapture sprang up again, but now it was Jinny who was reasonlessly cool. She said "Hello" civilly, and nothing more, and slipped around the car and into it before he could give her his hand.

The fatuous lover fretted, as he drove, "I did miss you so, Jinny. No fun with the ducks. You miss me?"

"I guess I did. Yes, sure. But I've been awful busy."

He had the sense to be still, on their way to the Unstable, or to mutter about ducks, a subject devoid (in their case) of emotional strain, and to tell her that Greg Marl had said, "Good little draftsman, Jinny, and a good sport in the office."

Jinny glowed with "Oh, did he?" Yet she was morose again when they faced the excellent whitefish and fried apples at the Unstable, and our poor friend was no longer wise. He protested, "What's the trouble, lamb?"

"Trouble? I don't know what you mean by 'trouble'!"

"Well, you're so silent——"

"Good heavens, can't I ever be quiet a moment without being accused of being deliberately unpleasant?"

"I didn't say you were unpleasant! I never even thought such a——"

"Well, you certainly looked as if you did."

"Oh, Jinny, dear Jinny, what are you quarreling about?"

"I? Quarreling? Oh, this is too much! I get so irritated when you watch me and spy on me and try to find fault with every little thing that I do or don't do and try and show how superior and——I *do*!"

He could only look at her like a mournful hound surprised by the spitting of his friend the household kitten. Jinny ran down. She laughed, she cried for a second—a tear absurdly dribbled down her immaculate nose—and she whimpered:

"It's my old trick. You'll have to beat me."

"M?"

"When I was a kid, whenever I wanted something terribly and then got it, so I was all excited and grateful—like Christmas or a birthday or finally Mother got a dress for me that I was crazy about—then I was scared to let on how happy I was, or maybe I was afraid it would vanish if I believed in it too hard and showed how much I wanted it. So I'd fly off into a horrible little tantrum, and the gladder I'd been, the worse I'd behave. Believe me, it didn't last long, it never did, and if

Dad and Mother could just get themselves to ignore it, I'd be all right. But it did used to surprise them and hurt them. And now—I'm not so violent, but I'm doing something like that to you, and you're so sweet! I've been vixenish tonight just because I *was* glad you'd come back early! Do you think you can put up with it? I know I'll do it again. Even to you. Can you endure such a horrible, childish frenzy?"

Why, of course he could. Meant nothing at all. Just nerves and tiredness, from all her energy——Get right over it. Certainly. Fact, he'd enjoy her tantrums, if she was always so regretful and generally lovely afterward. And *usually*, with *most* lovers, they didn't just have little misunderstandings like this, but actually *quarreled*, didn't they? *They* were *different!*

19

THE RED MAPLE LEAVES and the golden poplar among the pines, and the innocent blue skies that were the autumnal glory of Grand Republic, were gone. Spring was a season too harsh and swift in Northern Minnesota; it was the carnival of colored leaves and the serenity of the long Indian Summer days that the natives of this land would remember sadly, far off in tired Eastern cities. With November, the first snows had brought shouting cheerfulness to children with sleighs and blasphemy to drivers trying to slide their cars up the slippery roads to Ottawa Heights.

The city hunched its shoulders now to the long winter blast. The trees that had given a village gentleness to the long streets were thin and shivering, and the houses were scattered and low, lonely as the old frontier.

Reviving cocktail parties were gay, at the Wargates', Madge Dedrick's, the Havocks', the Bozards', but Cass was not often present. The first scandal of his interest in a Young Outsider had settled to an accepted routine, but his friends resented more than ever his neglect of them, felt in it a slighting of the social glories of their town, about which they were always very emphatic and very insecure.

When he could not be with Jinny, Cass preferred the

habitualness and the validity of his court room, where now the lights came on early and they were snug and content about their business of sending people to prison and were not disturbed by the invitation of green river valleys and the liquid sound of small lake-waves around a fisherman's scow. Often, after court, he talked for half an hour with George Hame, the court reporter, who apparently knew nothing about Jinny, though he had seen her in these chambers, but who, if he had known, would have assumed that any young thing was lucky to get the Judge.

Cass saw Jinny daily, and he was disconsolate in discovering that the course of true love runs in curlicues. He had assumed that persons so sensible as himself and Jinny would march sweetly and directly onward from meeting to understanding to an altar and a beautiful home and six beautiful children all superb in filial devotion and swimming and arithmetic. With Blanche, die progress had been straight enough. She had found his attentions flattering; she had taught him to wear his clothes and his political opinions well; she had met a richer man; and she had got out. What could be better charted?

But with Jinny, even his jealousies ran jaggedly.

He was dining with Jinny and Eino Roskinen in a booth at Shorty's Fountain Café. The prospect was of a forest of hats and overcoats upon a skeleton tree, a woman in dreadful plaid winter slacks, and a Coca-Cola poster showing a nearly naked bathing girl—the Folk Art of America. They were taking the Blue Plate Dinner: a pork chop with apple sauce and French-fried potatoes and string beans made of wood pulp, though afterward they indulged in "pie á la mode," pie crowned with a hard little knob of ice cream. It was an abominable meal and a criticism on their whole civilization, but Eino the torch-bearer did not, for once, perceive this as well as the cautious judge.

Cass had wanted to treat these boarding-house starvelings to what was here called a T-bone steak, but they had refused his patronage. He was trying so hard to be one with them. Eino now called him "Cass," and the Judge winced every time he heard it, though it was he who had suggested it. To be youthful and chummy, he offered a few remarks on football, which apparently bored them, and on the fallacies of religion, which they dismissed as too elementary for their advanced revolutionary standing.

Well, he had done his social duty, and he fell to musing, thinking of an ethereal and more-than-human girl named Jinny, who was far off somewhere and with whom he longed to be, flinging jests like rainbow-hued balls of glass, reverently kissing her flawless hands. . . . Meanwhile he looked absently at the ink-spot on one thin paw of Miss Marshland of the Grand Republic *Banner*.

He came out of his reverie to find that they were talking about the local Little Theater, the Masquers.

"You ought to *make* time for it, this winter, Jinx," Eino was commanding. "Personally I can't act—I'm too much the intellectual type—but you have an energetic fakery that would make you a swell actress."

Cass fumed that she did not resent this, but let him go on.

"Let me tell you the theater could be the greatest instrument for the implementation of social ideals that the world has ever known. If you'd quit sketching a little and reading a little and really go to work and try for a part in the Masquers, you might accomplish something."

"Eino! Do you honestly think I could act?"

"Well, I'd coach you."

——He would, would he? Aah!

——Is she already going back to that Eino? I suspect she was pretty fond of him when I came along, and then I was a novelty! A respectable lawyer prancing around making a comic spectacle of himself over a girl young enough to be his——Well, she *could* be my daughter, if I'd started begetting at sixteen. Perfectly possible. Curse it!

——Sure. I merely offer her whatever dignities I may have, along with all my adoration, and she flies off with the first tom fool that guffaws at her——

——Now that's unfair. She knew him some time before she ever knew me, and anyway, she's merely a loyal friend of his, and he's a fine, hard-working young——

——Does he have to keep on making that horrible noise,

tapping on the table with that crowbar of a finger?

When the children remembered that their Venerable Friend was still present and tried to cheer up the poor old codger by giving him the news that it had been cold today, he wanted to convince them that he was still alive by croaking that, yes, it had been quite cold—for November, that is—and he had noticed it all by himself.

(It had not, by the way, been particularly cold.)

Having thus done their duty by the nonagenarian and having given a talented new actress to the stage, the happy young couple turned to more personal confidences. They said that Tracy Oleson was getting to be as much of a stuffed shirt as Webb Wargate himself, but they—they would just get off in corners and laugh about it. They illustrated, by laughing.

It was part of their creed and time that every so often Eino and Jinny should say to each other, "What's cooking?" and that they should show reverence for jazz and familiarity with such contemporary maestri as Benny Goodman and Peewee Russell. Cass hoped Eino would never learn that he sometimes, in a melancholy and amateurish way, tried to play Purcell airs on his flute. This practice he had begun in college vacations, and it had been extraordinarily ill received by Roy Drover.

Jinny (or so Judge Timberlane believed) smiled guiltily at Eino while she adjusted the straps of her brassiere—known at this time as a "brazeer," or, coyly, as a "bra." But he insisted that it was not Jinny who was damp and treacherous. She was innocent, but this Roskinen was a wolf.

By God, he would protect this child, toward whom he himself had no intentions save to teach her chess! If Eino thought for one moment that he wasn't suspected——

Eino was on his feet, saying with amiable brevity that he'd enjoyed his dinner—leave you two capitalists to wallow in the movies—g' night. Then Jinny was clawing at Cass like an angry Cleo:

"Cass, my dear young brainless baby, I have never in all my life seen such an exhibition of childish jealousy!"

"Me?"

"You, Honorable Timberlane, you!"

"But I disapprove of—I detest jealousy!"

"Then you detest yourself. The way you kept glaring at Eino, contradicting everything he said, but not decently, with words, but with that horrible sniffy silence! And when I yanked at my shoulder-straps, you put on such a production of goggling at me and then Eino that the poor lamb was thunderstruck. And this after he's given up all claim on me! I'm simply not going to stand for such insane jealousy!"

"Jinny! I didn't know I was. Maybe you're right. I'm profoundly——"

"And all over poor Eino! Now if you'd pick out my editor, Mr. Hubbs, to be jealous over——"

"Hubbs? He, too?"

"Oh, very much too. He's what we call in the office a sweetie pie."

Impishly, she waited for him to vomit over the phrase, but he was being too seriously appalled that he should be another of the jealous lovers who brought so much poison into his court. He muttered, "So I really seemed jealous?"

"And how! And when you consider that I almost never see Eino any more. His mother has moved into town, and they've taken a shack together, and he just drops in at Hatter's to see Tracy and Lyra—not me. The fact is——" She wrinkled with a new worry as she went on. "I don't see enough of him, or the rest of my old bunch, either, not even Lyra. I'm so much at the office, and evenings I'm likely to be out with you. And you actually jealous of those eager kids! I've drifted away from them shamefully. I give you all my time, and then you humiliate me by this jealousy. Oh, Cass, I can't stand it, if you're going on like this!"

"My dear, I'm all humbleness. I hadn't realized it. I have only the old excuse that my jealousy is the measure of my devotion to you—and of my insecurity with you. If we were really engaged, if I could only be sure that I had you to do things for, then maybe I wouldn't be so uncertain and so jealous."

"But I still don't see how you can be so touchy, and 'suspect me of the worst'—whatever that means."

"And I don't see how you can endure driving me plain

mad—and ridiculous—by leaving me so baffled. But no matter; even if you do, I won't be jealous. And. don't tell me again that jealousy is an insult to you. I know it is! So—I'm cured."

"Are you?"

"I think so—maybe."

They could laugh slightly, and everything was settled, and with entirely unconscious jealousy he got her talking about this new menace, this scoundrel, Abbott Hubbs.

She, it appeared, was sorry that Mr. Hubbs drank so much, and she believed that his wife was not gentle enough with him. It also seemed that an Important Person in Washington had asserted that Mr. Hubbs was competent to take charge of any newspaper in Chicago or New York. Most devastating of all, Mr. Hubbs—he had such a sense of humor—cut paper dolls out of the exchanges and presented them to Jinny, who had one of them in her purse this moment, along with Isis.

To Cass, it looked like a very bad paper doll. It looked like a piece of newspaper which had been chewed by a puppy of imperfect intelligence.

He said that Hubbs was a "splendid fellow and veiy brainy" and that the paper doll was of unique charm. Blessedly, then, they quit that quest for perfection in each other which is the maddening glory of all true love, and they did a very fine game with matches—you make six triangles with eight matches, only you never do. He stroked her hand, soft tan against the red-rubber tabletop, and they went arm in arm off to the movies.

That night, gravely rubbing Cleo's spine, he told himself that jealousy was the meanest of sicknesses and most contemptible of prides.

Having delivered before himself an address which would have adorned any Bar Association dinner, Cass became rather sorry for this lonely judge, still young, able to love with angelic selflessness, yet kept waiting like a servant by an opinionated young woman with shameless scarlet finger-nails.

Then—some time in his dizzy changes of opinion he must have pulled Cleo's hair, for she yowled and leaped and fled— he fell upon himself for this desecration. No! Jinny was the true goddess, perfect in every part, under law of the miracle whereby a woman who is completely lovely of face is lovely also in skin and limbs and shoulders and voice and walk. She was the divinity inviolable, to say nothing of being a very exciting young woman who said such clever things, and sometimes was a grieved and frightened little girl who broke his heart by her helplessness against the vicious world.

Then, by a descent into hell too swift to have been marked:

——Of course she's all that. But.

——But does she have to fall for every heel she meets? She specializes in heels. First this philandering Little Theater hound and that statistical Tracy Oleson lout, and now this third-rate dipsomaniac, Hubbs.

——Oh, quit thinking in circles! To say nothing of its being a crime against your love for her, which is the one splendor in your whole mechanical, law-grubbing existence.

——But do Eino and she make fun of me and laugh at me when they're by themselves? Do they consider me a solemn owl trying to be a lark? How they must talk and giggle!

——Dear Jinny, my beloved, forgive me for loving you better than I can!

All the next morning, in court, while he was listening to the horror of a woman who had killed her own baby, he kept fighting off a vicious little plan to drop in at the *Banner* office and see how Jinny and Abbott Hubbs acted when they were together. The testimony of the frightened woman burned away all the cheapness of his plan, and he wondered that his self, which mostly he respected, could be so sneaking. On his way to lunch, he saw Hubbs on the street: tall, anemic, moving jerkily. He thought of him, working hard, drinking hard to keep going, watched always with a friendly distrust by that bland Olympian, Gregory Marl.

Then all the sickness of jealousy was gone from him—for a while.

180

20

WHEN THE NOVEMBER SNOWS had halted automobile wanderings, they began a placid habit of evenings at Bergheim. Sometimes Jinny brought Isis along and set her where she could watch. To Cass, this affection for the tiny glass cat was no sillier than Egyptian rites in which Jinny might have been a little wise priestess, her thin hands elevated in prayer to feline mysteries, in the ancient haze of the Nile.

Mrs. Higbee adopted Jinny, and one evening Cass heard them as they explored the upstairs, conferring on what should be done for Him.

"Do you ever have French toast for His breakfast?" suggested Jinny.

"Oh, yes, He likes any kind of sweets. He isn't a heavy eater, you might say, but the way He can shovel in the griddle cakes!"

"We ought to take more care of His health. He's always carrying on about His hunting and tennis and swimming, but wintertime, He sticks His nose in a book and never gets out."

"Don't I know it, Miss Jinny! . . . You, Cleo, you get out from under my feet. What you want to do? Trip me up? . . . I say to Him at breakfast, I say, 'Judge, aren't you ashamed of yourself, big strong young fellow like you, sitting and reading, read all the time, all those big thick books, and not get out for exercise 'cept summer?' But Lord, I can't do anything with Him. I'll keep Him nice and clean and well fed inside the house, but you got to drag Him out on walks."

"I will, too. Gracious, this bedroom of His is gloomy! I'd like to see it all in maple, with blue curtains."

"Looks like He likes it gloomy. I guess judges don't get fun, like you and me."

"I'll educate Him!"

Downstairs, Cass listened blissfully.

He had at first been fretted by the thought of Jinny's presence raising scandal among all the John William Prutts and peeping telephonic widows, but they were so natural and serene and domestic as they sat reading in the small, pipe-scented library that he forgot such alien dangers. He inquired whether she would not rather go out dancing, drinking, and she had to instruct him:

"I don't want to go racketing around all the time. If I really wanted to go out with these young punks, I'd go. It's just as exciting to find all these books here: *The Golden Bough* and August Derleth. Oh, don't *insist* on my being discontented! I can do that so easy by myself. Sweet blessed angel, will you quit your worrying?"

"Yes—yes—oh—sorry—yes!"

——Trying to make her more contented than contentment

itself! That's all a piece with the jealousies I used to feel. Thank God *that's* cured!

——This profession of being a true lover. Can any one master it? That must be God's most sublime joke on the human race; that the more you want to make a woman happy, the more you blunder and bore her.

——Do you remember that Judge Timberlane being profound about matrimony in his chambers? And spinsters and unwed priests giving advice about it. Marriage and the common cold—the two persistent problems of mankind and the ones that have never been solved.

——Lovely Jinny, sitting there with your tongue in the corner of your mouth, reading *Death Comes for the Archbishop* and looking like such a wise child, and all the while more devastating and terrible than war.

——One thing I do get clear about her. She is one of those extraordinary people who are not willing to settle down and wait for death, willing to play cards and yawn and gossip and actually speak of 'killing time,' when we have so little time. What life she has she will always live.

Unconscious of the lecture about her, the girl softly closed the book, slid to the hearth, and curled beside Cleo while Cass's meditations ticked on:

——You baby! Not so much bigger than Cleo, and yet all the while I see you as the eternal Pilgrim. My beloved, can't there be one husband and wife in history whom Time will spare for a moment and who will defeat the worm? Dear Jinny, I wonder if you hear me?

"Cass! You're smiling so tenderly. Are you thinking of something pleasant?"

"Well, something important, anyway."

"Like candy-bars? Or a high dive?"

"Yes, but with a touch of flaming wings."

"Sounds ingenious. Oh golly, I'm tired. I'm going home to bed, my pet."

"Nice words: home and bed. But rarely any flaming wings to 'em."

"Are we as mysterious as we sound?"

"Jinny, we are the most mysterious and frightening things in the world: a man and a woman of whom at least one is in love. . . . Jin, does it scare you to hear the word death?"

"Never! I can't die—not for sixty years at least."

The little cat meowed pitifully at their feet.

When he had driven her home and returned to his library, he saw that she had forgotten to take Isis with her. On a bookshelf the trinket shone in firelight, now diamond-flashing, now ruby, until as he stood there in his rustic coonskin coat and sealskin hat, he was hypnotized and saw a gigantic crystal cave in whose ice-glaring maw crouched a little figure, half-naked, sobbing, terrified by night and death.

21

BOYISH AND OPEN-FACED, blond and wavy-haired, a controlled drinker, a careful but quick-minded lawyer, Cass's old friend Bradd Criley was a pleasant fellow as well as the most valued dinner-guest and bridge-partner in Grand Republic. He was a bachelor, and he never toyed with any woman over forty nor with any girl under eighteen—unless he was sure he would not be found out. He said to men, "I'm sorry, but I've been so busy" and to women, "You're so beautiful tonight." He said, possibly he believed, that Cass was the soundest judge on the Minnesota bench.

He came snowily in one evening when Cass was giving Jinny a lesson in chess; he insisted on reading till the game was finished; and afterward, as they talked, they three became a firm trio.

With his skillful teasing, he brought out from Jinny her opinions on immortality and Gregory Marl—neither quite favorable—and he made them laugh with his stories of the great, somber, dumb Wargate Family, which his firm, Beehouse, Criley, and Anderson represented. Jinny popped corn for them, pretty and flushed as she knelt by the fireplace, and brought cider from the kitchen, and faintly sang a cradle song. Bradd, when he left them together, shook hands with

Cass and said in his frank, fresh voice, "Your Honor, I submit that you two are the nicest family in Radisson County."

Next day, at the Club, he continued: "Cass, when are you going to marry this girl? Let me tell you: if you don't, I will!"

"I'm crazy to. But she's turned me down flat."

"Nonsense. Keep asking her. I can see she's crazy about you and comfortable with you. Naturally—she's still a kid—she wants to show some independence."

"You don't think she's too young for me?"

"No! Got a wise head on her lovely shoulders. Ask her, boy. You'll get a reversal of the previous verdict. But if you don't get busy—I'll give you three months, and if you haven't got her pledged then, I'm in the ring. I would be now, but I haven't a chance. She thinks you're a solid investment and I'm a flash gold-stock. Wonder how she guessed!"

Bradd's encouragement roused him.

Winter night at Bergheim, a northwest wind driving spears of snow from Dakota and Saskatchewan, and in the library, Cass and Jinny toasting and serene.

He laid down his *Life of Lord Birkenhead* and spoke plain:

"That's the sixth cigarette you've smoked this evening, Jin."

"Oh yas?"

"How many do you smoke a day?"

"I dunno. Twenty, maybe."

"How long have you smoked?"

"Since I was seven."

"M?"

"Cornsilk. In the Marshland barn."

"Well, I'll try not to nag. I'm not much of a reformer. I admire revolutionists more than I do reformers. The greatest reformer living is Mr. Hitler, who is trying to reform all Europe. But still——Jinny, you have such fresh lips."

"That's Higgins's Sans Merci lipstick."

"Nonsense. I've kissed you when your lips were damp and bare after we'd been swimming. Such sensitive lips and such a clear throat and sound lungs—I hate to see 'em messed up, hate to see you spoil 'em just for an unconvincing pose of being worldly."

"Maybe I will cut 'em now—maybe."

"Come sit on my lap."

She did not, as once, roost there awkwardly, but lay gently against him, one hand holding his lapel, while he urged:

"Now this is a trial. You are judge and I'm the defendant *and* his attorney. Now Your Honor, I represent the man Timberlane, a lout and slow-witted, but fervently in love with you."

"With the judge? Why, Cass!"

"Now play fair."

"Okay, Counselor. Is this the accused that I see? Does he have to stand so close? Let me look at him. No. He doesn't look so slow, and I'm not too certain about his fervor. After all my experience on the bench, I'd say he was just in love with the picture of himself as a lover."

"No, the fellow is not a romantic. He really thinks about what his young woman wants."

"His what?"

"All right, all right, monkey! His inamorata. His sweet lamb. His perambulatory dream. His virgin immaculate. His princess of the dark tower, and stormy as sunset were her lips, a stormy sunset on doomed ships, and she gathers all things mortal with pale immortal hands and she does not walk in the fields with gloves. His tragic fate, tortuous as the River Vye. His——Oh, Jinny, I'm afraid I have to be serious. You know that I love you utterly."

Her arms gently circled his neck, but after a selfless quiet she sat up on his knee, a hand on each of his shoulders, mocking and combative again.

"I still say I'm not sure you know what you want, Cass."

"I want to see you at breakfast, fresh in gingham."

"Nobody wears gingham any more, and at breakfast, before coffee, I really *am* a stormy sunset on doomed ships. Ships run for Port Arthur when they see me dooming at breakfast. So that's out. What else?"

"I want to be able to come home from court and tell you how swell I was; how my rulings stood 'em in the aisle."

Children of their earthy land and revolutionary time,

flippant and colloquial and compelled to nervous banter, they were yet in a noble tradition of lovers, and there was more of tragic prince than of smug clown in his airy demand; and it was Ruth amid most alien corn who answered:

"I think you got something there."

Then he was grave. "And I want children." Blanche had been afraid of bearing children and she had always "put it off a while yet—till the right time." Cass demanded, almost mournfully, "Do you want babies, Jin?"

"Yes. I love them."

"I'm glad. And I want to travel with you."

"I see. But not to kiss me."

He answered that.

"Well, I just wanted to make sure," she explained.

"But I haven't asked what the things are you want, and whether I can give any of 'em to you, Jinny."

She was silent, then: "I'm afraid you'll learn I'm one of these changelings that can only give things to herself. I'm fond of you and grateful to you for liking me, but I have to travel by myself, for a while anyway. Maybe some day I can come back to you. . . . The cat that walks by herself, and she does get lonely in the night woods, but she has to see every shadow for herself and not be told by anyone what it's the shadow of—tree or bear or hunter or maybe a ghost—shadow of a ghost. I have to look for myself."

His "Darling!" was a sound of helplessness.

Then, so suddenly that it was almost pain, not joy to him, she said, "But that doesn't mean that I may not marry you, before long, and go away now and then and come back to you when the woods get too scary."

Arm around his neck again, she kissed him voluntarily, and on that there walked into the room Mr. John William Prutt, Mrs. Henrietta (Mrs. J. W.) Prutt, and their sound filial investments Mr. Jack Prutt and Miss Margaret Prutt, with ten thousand ancestral shades of correct and banking Prutts in superb gray Pruttery behind them.

"Oh!" said Mr. Prutt.

"Your maid didn't explain——" said Mrs. Prutt.

Mr. Jack Prutt whistled.

Cass had felt Jinny's body stiffen as she prepared to leap from his lap, but when the Prutts had spoken, she relaxed and stayed where she was, indolent and insolent, throbbing with laughter.

The Prutts bumped rigidly out. Cass put Jinny gendy on her feet—fairly gently—and rushed after them to the hall, coughing, "We're engaged, you know . . . You know . . . Engaged."

Mrs. Prutt said reverently, "But alone? In your house? At night? Unchaperoned? Strange, Judge."

"Very strange, I should think," said Mr. Prutt, and they were gone.

Mrs. Higbee was wailing, "They walked by me like I was

dirt, while I was trying to say, 'The master's in there kissing his girl.' Just walked by me!"

"Nev' mind," hastened Cass, and galloped into the library, where Jinny stood fist-clenched and angry.

"I knew it all the time! I should never have come to your house! I'll never be alone with you again. Oh, I don't blame you, especially, Cass, but I never shall again!"

"But if you're going to marry me——"

"I'll never marry you! Don't ever speak of it again!" She was in a panic, reasonless but overwhelming. Not for the first time had Pruttery been too powerful for a child of light.

"Sit on my lap again for a moment and quiet down and then I'll drive you home."

"No! No! I don't want you to. I'll take a bus."

He had to use all the arts of the legal chambers to quiet her, to say "Now stop it!" as though he knew professional mysteries that she could never understand, before he coaxed her into his car. All the way to Miss Hatter's he was awaiting the verdict of death to love. On the boarding-house step she said, "I guess this is good-bye forever. I don't think I shall see you again."

"Jinny!"

"Really."

"I won't take that. To say good-bye to you is to say good-bye to life."

She was clear and a bit sardonic: "You're the great legal star. You'll get along all right. You always have."

191

"If the legal star has to go on shining by John William Prutt's permission, then I'll chuck starring and everything else except being with you."

"You mean you'd give up being a judge for me, if you ever had to?"

"I certainly do."

"I wouldn't want you to. Good night."

She was gone.

He knew that hers was not merely the perverse rudeness of a lover. He had an excellent chance of losing her. Blanche had been right; he should never have let himself be baked into a pie of Pruttery and Roy Drover's intolerance and the generous avidity of Chris and the Avondenes. The springtime days of companionship with Jinny were past, and he was afraid that she would never again come to bring April light into his dark old house.

An Assemblage of Husbands and Wives

GILLIAN BROWN—VIOLET CRENWAY

GILLIAN BROWN was a business woman, a career woman, but she was human, and she had decided that for such a premature phenomenon as herself, there were but five matrimonial choices: to marry a man who was her superior and who would either cheat her or leave her flat, to marry an inferior whom she would pet and despise, to marry an equal, which would happen only by a miracle comparable to Jonah and his also undependable marine companion, to lie unwed and rigid, or to have company. She had tried all five. The last seemed the most reasonable now, in the 1940's, when she was assistant manager of Harley Bozard's shop for women's clothes, on Chippewa Avenue, Grand Republic.

With her men, some half-dozen of them, she was good-natured, tolerant of drunks up to a point, but scientific about finding out when that point had been reached. She made coffee for them, and she lent them an electric razor of the very best brand.

Gillian Brown, Mrs. St. George Brown, had been christened Mabel Chiddy, in White River Junction, Vermont, in 1898. She was the composite portrait of half the American Career Women. She wore smart suits with lace-trimmed blouses, her hair looked young, and so did her face, as far down as her mouth. She broadcast a weekly fashion report on Station KICH, and her voice was liquid chocolate, lazy and lenient, except when a salesgirl had talked back to her, or after she had had five drinks. Then it was liquid brass.

She was ambitious, and her ambition was to make enough money to buy a horsy country place near Chicago, next-door to a gentleman farmer who would look like an English colonel and would fall in love with her, permanently, not just on option. Then she would become "normal and domestic."

The store was open on Saturdays, except in August, and on Saturday evenings she got drunk, but only introductorily, with The Girls, business women of her own fate. On Saturday mornings she lay and sighed that she would never have her country estate or her Colonel. On Sunday afternoons she got drunk in mixed company, and preferred to sing "Dixie." On Sunday night she brought a male—almost any male, and chosen as often out of pity for his being starved as out of her own simple passions—home to her orderly flat, which was touchingly feminine in its china figurines of cats and lambs and Columbines.

In her bathroom were forty-three kinds of cosmetics. Many of them, she knew from selling them, were useless, but she liked the bottles. But she was always careful to get them wholesale.

She was shrewd, and preferred to be honest, and with equal reverence she read Catholic, Christian Science, and Unitarian magazines, 1890 novels about the indignantly virtuous daughters of widows, and treatises on playing the stock-market.

She admitted to having been married and divorced twice, and boasted of having lived in New York for three years and Paris for three weeks. Actually, she had gone through the valley of matrimonial humiliation three times, but the first had been to and from an aging Vermont farmer, when she was Mabel Chiddy and only seventeen.

Her latest attempt to escape had been St. George Brown, a Brooklyn dress-salesman, whom she was still supporting. She had helped to support all three of her husbands, and though they had varied from small and tidy to lank and furrowed, they belonged to the same pattern: they were all weak and fond of cards and liquor and they all held their heads sidewise.

She despised two things in women: taking alimony, which she regarded as a form of looting the conquered city, and the pretense that you are going to satisfy a man without intending to go through with it.

Therefore, though she associated with them, drank and snickered with them, she detested two women in Grand Republic: Sabine Grossenwahn, divorced niece of Boone Havock, whose Louisiana-plantation-style bungalow was known as "Alimony Hall," and Violet Crenway, Mrs. Thomas Crenway.

Violet was as luscious and perfumed as her name, fetching of eye and uncommonly white of skin. She was renowned for raising funds for noble institutions: St. Anselm's Church, the Red Cross, the Salvation Army, the Republican Women's League. She went into men's private offices, wearing white gloves and a gardenia, looking around intently and panting a little, and the men sent their stenographers away and pushed a chair out for Violet and stood beside it. She came out with the gloves, the gardenia, the funds, and her virtue all intact, leaving the men surprised and blasphemous.

She said that she did adore men, the dear funny things, but wasn't it amazing, their masculine vanity and the way they thought that every Girl who smiled at them expected to be kissed! She boasted that she could come nearer to being kissed without any casualties than any woman since Delilah— though in the comparison she did not mention Delilah but Joan of Arc.

Gillian Brown said that she was interested in being with Violet Crenway because she was the most evil woman in town, and said that among the men whom Violet teased was Mr. Thomas Crenway, and Mr. Crenway did not like it.

Gillian had reason to know how Tom felt about such things.

22

TWO DAYS AFTER the army of the Prutts had landed and devastated the coast, Judge Stephen Douglas Blackstaff came into Cass's chambers after court.

"Cass, I have been listening to that banker fellow, Prutt, expiring of sunburn from his blushes of modesty on the telephone. He's a fool, but he is a symptom. A rustle of scandal is beginning to follow you. Son, you and I are both men of the world—from a strictly Calvinistic point of view, of course—but we are also lawyers, and we both know that there must never be any shadow of scandal over the judicial office. Do you care so much for this girl that I've seen you with? Would you rather resign than lose her?"

"Yes, I would, Steve."

"Nonsense, son. Absolute mongery. Why the devil don't you marry the girl?"

"Why don't I?" Why *don't* I? Because she's refused me. Twice."

"My esteemed Rhoda refused me almost continuously, over a period of two years. She refused me on Rye Beach, she refused me in the Brothers and Linonia Library of Yale College, and refused me once during a communion service—somewhat abruptly, I thought. But still I triumphed—at least, that's the accepted theory. Cass, you're a good young man. Don't risk your honor and the honor of the State for a sentimental fancy! People are sometimes evil, and they are not going to believe that you could not marry this young woman if you desired, and if nothing will make her wed you, there have always been the soundest precedents for consigning her to the devil."

Judge Blackstaff's long and rigid back completed his admonition, and Cass sat wondering whether for Jinny, that lightly dancing figure on a fan, he would really give up his judicial dignities.

Yes, he would, if he must do so to guard one higher dignity—plain humanity. He had no right more imperious than to be with his girl, married or not, and for this he would certainly resign, at need. He had reached this uncomfortable resolution when Jinny herself, not knocking, came flying into his chambers; and before he had planned what to say, he had sprung up, he had kissed her, and she was sobbing:

"Cass! I've lost my job!"

"Oh no!"

"I didn't think I ever could. I was so proud—the girl cartoonist!"

"What——"

"Mr. Marl fired me. For incompetence. I wish it could have been for drunkenness or bigamy. I did so want to be independent, and I thought I was such a whiz—everybody said they liked my cartoons, and I thought they were all looking for them in the paper. I was so busy, and I was enjoying it, like a fool, and Mr. Marl called me in and first he said Mrs. Marl and he wanted me to come to dinner, all by myself—was I ever proud! Then he asked me how come I didn't have a cartoon ready for day-before-yesterday. I hadn't been able to get a good idea, and I'd ruined two drawings. Then he said he'd already hired a new hand from Minneapolis and he was so sorry, so awful sorry, but I was through. So now I'll go back to the factory and eat dirt. I was so proud and silly and now I'm all washed up——"

She was weeping, against his shoulder.

As George Hame entered the chambers, Cass said to her, "Now you're going to marry me."

"Am I? Maybe."

Judge Blackstaff said, yes, it would be a little inconvenient to have Judge Timberlane away from court during mid-term, even for a honeymoon. "But," said the senior judge, "it will be a noble inconvenience." He patted Cass's shoulder. "Son, I am glad that you thought my advice over and decided to take it. I may no longer be the sprightly beau I once was, but you see now that I understand women."

"Oh, thoroughly, Stephen."

"By the way, my boy, take a Bible on your honeymoon. You yourself may not read it extensively, but it may implant some ideas in the pliable mind of your bride. I assure you that it is full of the most admirable advice to females to be thrifty, industrious, chaste, and *silent*. One of the most useful books to husbands. And whenever I travel I find it much safer to take some pulverized coffee."

The Jinny whom Cass had expected to want only an informal wedding, with the mayor officiating and Eino and Tracy racketing around and beer and melody afterward, demanded a formal affair, with all the clergy, trains, white flowers, unreconstructed relatives, and champagne available. Cass was touched by the thought that she did not intend to come into the heraldic haughtiness of Ottawa Heights by the back door. She was so small and alone, and the Prutts so large and firm and multifarious. All right. His fairy princess should come in with as large and brassy a band as he could muster.

But again he felt, "I can't go on carrying everything alone. I must have someone to help me." He turned to his sister Rose and to Mrs. Higbee. He was not worried about the attitude of Cleo; he felt that she would be for anything that brought gaiety and ribbon-trailing and mouse-fetching cake into the somber house.

He sat gravely at the oilcloth-covered kitchen table, with Mrs. Higbee seated across, and urged, "I hope you'll be happy with Miss Jinny here."

"Judge, would you like me to quit, so I won't get in her way?"

"Good Lord, no! She loves you, same as I do. The question

is whether *you'll* be happy."

"Very. A lot of bosses never think of it, but a house is a servant's *home*. I couldn't imagine myself anywheres else, but sometimes it has been lonely. I'll be real pleased to have her here, and that quick way she walks, almost runs, around the place. I hope I ain't intruding if I say it's grieved my heart sometimes to see you poking around so lonely. I prayed about it in church." She laughed. "I hope the Lord consulted you to see if it was all right, before He sent Miss Jinny in answer to my prayer!"

"Yes, He consulted me. Thank you for Miss Jinny."

"Well, she was about the best I noticed around this town— of course it isn't a very big place."

"That's so."

While Jinny was in as much of an orgy of dressmaking as any Wargate, Cass nervously conferred with Rose about "redoing the house."

"Leave it to Jinny," she said.

"And then there's a matter—I don't quite dare to ask her, Rose, about—about rooms——"

Rose answered with the coarseness that only a truly good and wedded woman can achieve. "You mean, do you think she'll want the favors of the same bed with you every night, or to have a room of her own. Of her own, of course; same as any woman born since 1890. If you knew how Don gurgles all night long, and when he turns over, he sits up straight and then moans in terror and shakes himself like a wet dog and then he doesn't just lie down again—he makes a dive at the pillow—a belly-flopper dive. Give her the northeast bedroom, Cassy; the one I had as a girl. It's smaller than that funeral parlor of yours, but it gets the sun."

"It's a go!" said His Honor, the learned judge.

He felt very clever and efficient.

His Honor, the learned judge, who had heard the details of maniac sex-murders and been bland enough in discussing them with psychiatrists, approached Jinny like a freshman:

"You know, just at first, we might—uh—we might not want any children, and I believe there are precautions—uh—is there a woman clerk in your father's drug store that would—uh—I hate to speak of this but——"

"You poor dear lamb! What do you suppose girls talk about nowadays?"

"Do they really? I didn't know."

"There, there, Mother's glad you've kept your innocence."

As a politician, Cass did possess the correct morning clothes, but there was a crisis in the matter of the top hat, that symbol, that grotesque crown made of rabbit's fur, that more than the coat of arms or the broad A or even the dollar sign distinguishes a gent from a fellow. In Grand Republic, they rate with bustles, and while Cass did own a top hat, he had last worn it at a Plattdeutsch funeral, and it had long rested in the attic, a nest for mice.

He begged of Jinny, "You don't want me to wear a stovepipe hat, like Abraham Lincoln?"

"Yes, I do! I've never seen one, except in the movies! Let's be gaudy for once. I don't expect to get married but just this one time in all my life."

"Fine!"

He had the Piccadilly Gents' Ware Shop send for the hat. When he had put on the whole armor of a knight, the high silk helmet, steely white shirt, linen gorget, dark-gray coat shaped like a calla lily, and studied himself in the full-length mirror on the back of his bathroom door, he was delighted.

His best man, Dr. Drover, along with Boone Havock, Bradd Criley, Judge Flaaten, Frank Brightwing, and his other ushers had talked of a bachelor dinner, but he had no mind to endure their heavy jokes. The thought of Jinny was to him as frail and muted as a distant flute in the autumnal dusk.

He spent his last evening before the wedding alone with Cleo in the quarter-lighted library.

Was Jinny in love with him at all? Did she love him enough to endure his longing to give her everything that he was and had? It is more difficult to receive tolerantly than to give gladly. Of Jinny's mother and grandmother the question would never have been asked, but did Jinny, or any girl of her era, really attach herself to her husband and his fortunes, sick or in health, richer or poorer, avid for bright noise or content with the quiet mind?

He was apprehensive.

Cleo, who had been asleep upon his knee beside the dead fire, came suddenly awake, twitching and terrified, and leaped from him. He could hear her protests as she roamed the dark house, up and down, searching for something he did not understand. He sat uneasy, and when the telephone assaulted his ears, he gasped.

It was Jinny. "How are you darling? Are you scared, like me?"

"Bless you for calling. Scared stiff."

"Well, and very right, too, Cass. Both of us ought to be; both of us these disgusting Sensitive Souls, looking for a chance to be hurt and likely to get sore when we *don't* get hurt, because that shows nobody cares enough about us to hurt us. But what are you sitting in the dark for?"

"How did you know I——"

"Because I am, too! Good night. Oh, Cass, we're going to have a lot of fun being married. I'll really learn chess, even. I've ordered a chess costume: plaid, with rabbit-lined boots. Good night, my dear!"

He was convinced that this spirit of fire and mist might some day love him like a breathing woman. But through the house Cleo was still searching, still whimpering reproachfully.

Jinny was not so avid of grandeur as to want the reception that Rose Pennloss longed to give for them. She agreed with Cass that it would be wise to take the train directly after the ceremony. But that ceremony itself was ducal.

Not since the wedding of Della Lent, and her a Wargate, had there been a richer gathering of all that was noble, virtuous, and of five-figure income than at the union of Miss Marshland and Judge Timberlane; and the Rev. Dr. Gadd wore a new Geneva gown and had a Lutheran pastor and an Episcopal priest—pretty young, but of the very highest church—for collaborators in the conjuring whereby the little wild hawk was turned into a Grand Republic matron.

There were even Prutts present. It was more fun to attend and look doubtful than to stay away.

Through the forest of mink and broadtail, Cass saw Jinny coming down the aisle with her father. He noted, as casually as though he were studying a jury, that Mr. Marshland seemed timid and shrunken and shabby, against all the sleek furriness, and that Jinny, in cloudy white, was of the precise loveliness and inviolability of a goddess.

——God keep her shining and confident as she is now.

Then Jinny was his wife, and she was looking at him trustingly, and there was trust and adoration in his first marital whisper to her, "Let's try to sneak out the back door; we got just an hour and a quarter before the train goes" and in her enchanted answer, "Okay, darling—my husband!"

23

THEY MET AGAIN at the station, in rather-too-new traveling costumes. During the maverick reception on the platform, with champagne served in paper cups, it was not Roy, the best man, but Bradd Criley who was the clown. He yelled, he slapped backs, he kissed Jinny, Lyra Coggs, Chris Grau, and Jinny's astonished mother. The train was going then, and Cass was muttering to Jinny, "It's good to get away from our loving friends."

In their Pullman seats, she boldly held his hand, not caring who looked, and said with a strange little fierceness, "We've started, and I'm incredibly excited and cheerful, and Heaven knows where it will end—maybe China and temple bells."

But she had never been farther East or South than Central Wisconsin, and when they had left St. Paul for Chicago, the bold and Chinaward girl became less confident and Cass was promoted from home-town neighbor to expert traveler, who knew all about altitudes and populations and how to treat dining-car waiters, and she looked at him with 1880 bridal reverence, and asked him about the scenery as though he were a geologist.

There was food for awe: The palisades along the Mississippi, dark giant rock and swooping slopes of snow. The ravines of

Wisconsin, leading to wintry valleys. The North Shore suburbs of Chicago, where at stations influenced by the Alhambra the wives of significant insurance-brokers looked haughtily out from station wagons. Lake Michigan, a relentless ocean. The portentous jungle of Chicago factories and warehouses and slums, the smutted steel insanity of the Loop, and the leather and crystal Pump Room, where she listened admiringly while Cass, who knew nothing whatever about the subject, held a symposium on sauternes with the wine-waiter.

The Liveoak Special, leaving for Florida at one A.M., was a supple serpent of a train, all in crimson-barred silver, with no vestibules breaking its smoothness. The fourth-fastest train on the continent, it had a library car, a bar-room car, a car for dancing, four bathrooms, two stenographers, and a Social Hostess who had once been married to a Russian prince who had once been married to a Hollywood female star who had once been married to practically anybody.

Jinny looked at these conveniences as one of her peasant ancestors might have looked at Kenilworth Castle. It was her Cass who had given her this train. There was a husband for you!

She did not know that he was in the agony of accommodations-trouble.

Like many young people of the day, Jinny was familiar with automobiles but less familiar with trains than her own grandmother had been. She had motored with her parents twelve hundred miles out to Yellowstone Park, confidently driving four hundred miles a day, but she had never spent a night on a sleeping-car and she knew no more about the subtle categories of berths, sections, roomettes, bedrooms, compartments, and drawing-rooms than she did about the etiquette of wedding-nights, so delicately connected with them.

In the Florida rush which was now taking the place of trips to war-barred Europe, the Liveoak Special's private rooms had all been engaged a fortnight before Cass applied. He unscrupulously tried to use the influence of the court, the mayor, the local political bosses, and the department-store owner, but the best he had been able to do was two lower berths across from each other.

They rustled through the Pullman, already stuffy with sleep and green curtains, and Jinny had no surprise when he showed her the two separate cloth-smothered caves. She only said, inevitably, "Do I have to sit on my clothes while I'm taking them off? Mercy! Good night, dearest; wonderful day, wonderful journey. I *like* being Mrs. Timberlane!"

And vanished between the curtains.

He sat on his berth, smolderingly took his shoes off, and thoughtfully rubbed his toes. He was in his pajamas (very refined mellilunar ones, a dark-blue silk with a fine silver stripe) and under the close-tucked bedclothes before he decided that he had to do better than this. He would kiss her good night, anyway. They were married, weren't they? He had some rights, didn't he?

The solid Sioux nose of Judge Timberlane jutted cautiously out into the aisle, and turned right and left and hung there, rigid, as the eyes immediately above it perceived that George the Porter was standing inflexibly in the curving niche of Drawing Room A, on watch.

The nose was jerked inside and its proprietor felt guilty, but also credulous that, through the sound of the moving train, he had heard a delicious flutter of disrobing in the berth across the aisle—so near, so perilous.

Three times the nose came solemnly pushing out. Once it shot back at the approach of the conductor, once at the return of the persistent and unromantic George, but the third time it shot across, and Cass was shaking her curtain, moaning, "Unbutton this—open it up—quick!"

He was safe inside then, but flustered.

She was in pajamas, pale-yellow silk, well curving, and she was sitting up, staring at him. He expected a protest at his wild invasion, but what she said was, "Aren't those the nicest little lights! You can lie awake and read by 'em!"

"Jinny! Kiss me—and in the greatest hurry!"

"Why?"

"If the conductor finds me here——He doesn't know we're married. I should hate a public argument! Kiss me!"

She did, leaning forward. She was in his arms, only the

209

two thin layers of silk between them; and shakily, not at all masterfully, he undid the top button of her tunic and softly kissed her breast. Then she drew back, as far as the thick pillows would let her, and whispered, "It frightens me—you dash in here so quickly—I do love you, but now I'm kind of frightened and so alone—this huge train rushing us along in the darkness; you couldn't escape from it, if you wanted to——Be gentle with me, Cass; I'm such a spoiled baby."

"Yes, I'll always be gentle, I hope. I love you very much. And now good night, dear wife. . . . And don't you sit up and read, either!"

He had shot back into his own berth through green denim space, unconscious of transition or of spying conductors, and he lay awake alternately exultant with memory of how satin-like her breast had been and worrying lest she prove too anemic for ardent love. He had heard that these pencil-wise, half-intellectual girls were often so.

His berth-light was on, and in it he gapingly saw a smooth hand slip between the curtains and begin to unbutton them, and then, grotesquely, there was Jinny cheerfully returning his visit. But with a woman's sense and realism and magnificent vulgarity, she was not playing at furtive lover, as he had. She drew wide the curtains and left them open, and in her pajamas, with the vaguest of negligees merely setting them off, she sat cross-legged on his bed. And she was smoking a cigarette.

"Golly!" said the learned Judge.

Her bent knees were extraordinarily round and suave, he noted, and where was that porter, and would he have to have a row?

"It did seem so unfriendly not to return your call," she said, and her expression was like that of Cleo in one of her better moods. "And I wanted to tell you something—I've always wanted to, but I was too embarrassed—but you must have wondered, I don't see how you could have helped it—of course you were too much of a gentleman to ever ask——"

The porter's voice, not so much shocked as official, came from just beyond Jinny's shoulder.

"Sorry, Miss, but we don't allow any smoking in the berths."

Cass could see the edge of Jinny's affable smile as she turned. "Oh, I am sorry. Porter, will you please take this cigarette and finish it up for me? It's an awfully good one—a wedding present—today!"

The dazed Cass saw the dazed porter carry the cigarette away, at arm's length, while Jinny turned back with:

"Of course you would never even hint at it, but I do imagine you'd like to know, so now I can tell you—and I'm darned if I know whether this is a boast or a confession—but if it interests you, I'm still a virgin."

Suddenly he grew up a little, and he was placid in saying, "Yes, it does interest me, and I'm glad, though I don't think I'd 've been ugly if it had been the opposite. And I love you madly and you go back to bed or I'll spank hell out of you."

"Right here in public? In my pajamas? I dare you to!" she said, and kissed him and was gone.

Infinite pity encompassed him that she should have to grow older and more frail, helpless before covetous men and corroding illness, before poverty and storms that would come halfway round the world to threaten her proud head.

In the morning they had left the snow and were running through level farmlands with a sparkle of frost on gray grass and gray snake-fences. He did not know whether they were in Illinois or Indiana or Kentucky, so for her information he picked the last, as most distant from the center of the world— Grand Republic. She stared out and said joyfully, "Look what you've started! This is my first foreign country. How near are we to China now?"

He had explained that, in preference to the gaudiness of Palm Beach and Miami, he had chosen a plain West Coast Florida resort, for privacy, for adventurous fishing, for bathing and shell-hunting on great lonely beaches. He had never seen the place, but Harley Bozard said the food was excellent and the fishing superb. She'd certainly enjoy catching a tarpon.

Oh, yes. She'd always wanted to catch a—a what? Oh, much better than dancing with a lot of handsome tennis players. Yes, she had brought old clothes with her, as he had directed; she'd wear them—when she wore anything at all.

He did not add, not even to himself—not really—that the place would also be much cheaper.

Thus she was not completely disappointed when, on the morning of December fifth, they came to Baggs City, Charlotte County, Florida, and to the trim, clean, white, and completely dolorous Bryn-Thistle-on-the-Bay Inn. The small lobby was full of old ladies who listened and of geraniums which stared, and their bedroom, just large enough for a double bed and a bureau and two chairs, was adorned with a hand-lettered version of the poem about the man who wanted to live by the side of the road, a pink chamber-pot with forget-me-nots, and a three-color job of a cupid piloting a bomber.

"In here, I wouldn't even let you kiss me," protested Jinny.

"Well, there's a lot of outdoors down here."

They walked through the Inn grounds, which were as suburban as Glendale, but it was magical, two days from the wintry street-hurrying of Grand Republic, to stroll in this rich and scented air. Jinny eyed the crepe myrtle, the roses, the obese wonder of a grape fruit growing, and looked at the Cass who had worked this magic for her.

"My Merlin!" she said.

All afternoon, in a slow, good-natured launch, they fished in a deep salt-water inlet bordered by the shade and jungle brightness of a swamp; they stared at the palms, which meant India and the Congo to these inlanders from the wheat prairies and the pine woods; they relaxed and, cheerful as honeymooners rarely are, they came back to the Inn for supper. But the horrible daintiness of the place enfeebled them at once. It was like being choked with pink bedjackets.

All the widows watched them as they ate a meal consisting of fish and finger-bowls; they had too many invitations to play bridge and too little competition when they did play; three several females nickered about "the little bride"; and when they went up to bed, making it as late as was physically possible after an afternoon spent on the water, the air was so thick with lascivious female glances that they could have climbed it instead of the stairs.

They shut the door against a world of intrusive friendliness. They faced each other, and he understood her shyness and tried to speak as he thought her Gang at Miss Hatter's would speak:

"Well, baby, this is it. I guess we're up against it. But let me explain that I'm not just violently in love with you. I'm also extremely fond of you."

She was shivering, but she tried to be merry.

"They all make so much of this accidental virtue of virginity that you get scared about it, and the wedding-night—I suppose this is our real wedding-night—is a combination of getting drunk and winning a million-dollar lottery and waiting to be hanged. Animals are a lot wiser." Then, more sharply, "I hate being an amateur, in *anything!*"

In a practical way, she had begun to undo her belt, and when he had tremblingly drawn off his jacket, she stood, looking admirably casual, in brassiere and absurd small pants. He could not help kissing her shoulder, which tasted faintly of sun and sea. When she had put on a pathetically gay little rose-colored nightgown that must have come from Pioneer Falls and had mutely slid into bed beside him, he held her quietly, hoping that she would feel secure.

He was conscious of the creeping and thunderous silences of the Inn: hesitant slippered footsteps past the door, whispering in the adjoining rooms, a feeling that an inquisitive world was looking at them through the wallboard partitions. He was tense with listening, and Jinny, in his arms, was as impersonal to him as a pillow, and apprehensively he realized that he could no more make ardent love to her now than to that pillow.

Was he going to be a failure as lover with this one girl whom he had loved utterly?

She muttered, with almost prayerful earnestness, "Was the bathroom the third door on the right or the second? I'd hate to go rocketing in on some old maid!"

He laughed then, and lost his apprehensiveness. But as he kissed her it was she who had become fearful and unyielding, and in pity for her his ardor sank to a gentle stroking of her cheek.

When she seemed to have relaxed a little, to be expectant, his intensity had so worn him that he could only hold her softly, while fear crept through him again, and he stammered, "I've heard of such tilings but I never expected—I find I'm so fond of you, and maybe scared of you, that just now I can't even make love to you."

She answered as sweetly and briskly as though they were discussing a picnic-basket.

"Yes, I've heard of it. Temporary—not matter a bit. Oh, you'd be surprised at all the things Lyra and Wilma and I used to talk about. Don't worry. I love just lying with my cheek on your shoulder—now that I've found a comparatively regular valley among the jagged peaks of your shoulder-blades. Dear darling!"

They were almost instantly asleep and Cass came to life at dawn to sit up and see, on her own side of the bed, curled like a cat and rosily sleeping, his adored and inviolate bride.

24

THEY FISHED AGAIN in the salt inlet, next day; they delightedly though erroneously believed that they saw a barracuda, a threatening moccasin; they felt valiant as only tourists can. They hired a Drive-Yourself car, put in bathing-suits and a bottle of cognac for emergencies, and cruised slowly down sandy roads among the yuccas.

In late afternoon they came to an inlet with a great wash of wet sand and a cluster of whitewashed shacks: over-night cabins and a restaurant for impecunious tourists—the eternal gipsy encampment, the wooden-tented caravan.

"Look! We can get away from the painted bridge-pads here! Here's the place for thwarted hoboes!" said Cass. And Jinny noted that on their journey to China, they had come as far as Tahiti.

The restaurant walls were of upright bamboo, with palm thatch; the interior was cool and dim, with cement floor and loose-looking tables and black-and-white reed chairs. The pine bar was for drinking, not for the display of glassware. The bartender was a Minorcan, with a trim thread of mustache, the waitress was Mexican, and in the shadowed background, letting his planless harmonies drip from a guitar, was an old man in overalls, barefoot and masked with whiskers.

The troubadour waved his straw hat and the bartender greeted them, "H' are you, folks." They had two Daiquiris, cool and silken, and dined on fresh red snapper and a Cuban cocoanut ice cream.

Before dinner they had inspected the bare pine cottages, each with only a double bed, a chair, and a water-tap, yet far larger than the Inn cubicles, and voluptuously furnished altogether, for outside each door was the curving sand and the rolling Gulf of Mexico.

"I wish we were staying here, instead of at that knitting-works," sighed Jinny.

The bar-restaurant half filled, after dinner, with Italian fishermen, Mexican truck-farmers, and such tourists as wandered by flivver and trailer, not to improve their minds or tans or social standing, but just to wander. Cass bought drinks for half a dozen new lifelong friends. Everybody beamed at him and Jinny, not titteringly, as at the Inn, but with an earthy love of lovers, and the troubadour played "La Paloma" at them.

"Let's stay here tonight, in one of the cabins," Cass blurted, astonished at himself.

"With no baggage?"

"We have ourselves."

"Okay."

When Cass paid for a cabin in advance, the bartender took it for granted that they were not married, and was delighted by the whole general idea. So were the eloping Cass and Jinny as, with no bags to unpack, they took possession of their first real home together.

There were no occupied shacks near them, no whispering lady guests, but only the sliding sea. They lay with the door half open to the night, and suddenly he was ruthless with love and she as fierce as he, nipping his ear with angry little teeth, and they fell asleep in the surprise of love.

At dawn, Cass woke her and they ran down the beach and bathed, unclad and laughing, and came back to new abandonment.

Jinny marveled, "We both seem to be great successes. It was a terrible shock at first, but now I do cleave to you and we are one flesh."

"Forever?"

"Forever and ever, beloved!"

Sleeping and waking, waking and sleeping, their open door embracing the wash of the fertile tide, amazed by the curiousness of arms and legs and breasts, redeemed from civilization, they lay about the tousled bed till noon, and dressed and ate fried corn-mush for breakfast, to the commendatory smiling of the waitress. They wanted to be dignified, as suited their unique position in the history of lovers, but they also wanted to guffaw when Jinny said, "Think of what the old ladies at the Bryn-Thistle must be saying—the painted old hussies!"

They were one flesh, truly, and ecstatic with life.

" 'Husband,' " she mused. "I used to think that word sounded funny, but now it seems such a sturdy old word. It takes me back, clear through Walter Scott to King Arthur, back to the Anglo-Saxons and the old woods of Wessex, and I feel as if you and I were in a bark hut, worshiping the old gods. My Druid! My husband!"

"My wife! Yes, there are words that even the radio can't spoil."

"Golly! Were the Druids Anglo-Saxon or Celtic or what?"

"I honestly don't know," he said, in a blissfully shared community of ignorance.

There were no other guests at the tourist camp on this shining Sunday, and during the night Cass and Jinny had had no considerable sleep. Happily frowzy in the shade before their frowzy shack, lying on the long beach-grass with the sea-wind sweet about them, they slept through the afternoon.

They might not have gone back to the Bryn-Thistle at all that night—the night of December 7, 1941—but they were not yet so saved from Pruttery that they could stay on without clean clothes.

They would come down here again, in a couple of days. Certainly.

With her arm injudiciously linked in his as he drove, they returned to the Bryn-Thistle at dusk, and from the porch a woman joyful at finding victims who had not heard the news screamed at them, in delighted horror, "Been away? Then you don't know. We're in the war! Japan attacked our ships at Pearl Harbor today!"

They said nothing till they were in their room. Then, staring at him as though she had found him treacherous, Jinny said sharply, "Oh, curse the luck! Why couldn't I have known a few weeks ago? This time, they'll take women in the army. I could have seen Hawaii—France—Russia! And all the boys will be going—Eino and Tracy and Abbott Hubbs and everybody! And I'll be left home with the old women!"

"And with me, my dear."

"Yes," sardonically, "with you!"

Her tantrum—that was what they had come to call any of her not-too-frequent wild moods—was agallop. She moaned, "I hear they'll make women captains and majors and everything now—in uniform and be saluted—and station 'em with the flyers—young and brave and good-looking!"

——I don't blame her for being disappointed—greatest chance for adventure women've ever seen. But——It certainly does hurt to have her talk as though I were senile. Be careful now—be gentle.

"Jinny, I'm sure you can still get into the war, even if you are married."

"Oh, no. You'll complain about being left alone in your gloomy ole Bergheim."

"We can do war-work—maybe together."

221

"Aaaah! Rolling bandages with Mrs. Prutt, and you being obsequious to that old camel!"

"Jinny! Quit it! If you want to go off to war, you shall. But I'm not going to let you forget last night."

She fled to him and kissed him. "Forgive me for carrying on so. I just meant——You *are* a darling, and I do love you so; I even love you passionately, now, as I never could any other man living."

"More than the jittery Mr. Hubbs, even if he's in uniform?"

"Oh, now *you're* being nasty. Much better than Mr. Jitters. Even more than my cute Eino. But you must admit that you're not as awe-inspiring as a whole army marching together."

"I certainly do. Jinny, shall I try to get into the Army, into uniform—maybe the Judge Advocate's department?"

"No, I imagine they'll tell you that you can do more good right where you are. And maybe me too, where I am. Yes—maybe."

——Now shut up, Cass. She'll get over her disappointment if you just keep still.

He did keep still, but he felt useless, he felt that she did not vastly appreciate his labors as a jurist and a defender of Democracy. He felt, in fact, sulky, and doubtless his sulkiness was visible to her. When he said, with what he considered admirable good nature, "How about our going fishing again tomorrow—haven't tackled that tarpon yet," and she echoed,

"Fishing!" he yelped, "All right then, we won't! Of course we do only what *you* want to, my dear Jinny!"

"And just what is there to do, in this dump?"

That was all of their quarrel.

They did go fishing next day, on a placid-colored inlet, and they were so fond of each other that they almost forgot the war, and everybody forgave everybody everything. But it *had* been a quarrel, and if possibly she had started it, he had been the guiltier in carrying it on. They had had differences before, but this had been their first quarrel, their first drink, their first murder, and so, inevitably, it was the beginning of a series of quarrels interspersed with frantic peace-proposals, while the little crystal Isis listened bleakly.

Their second quarrel rose from one of her "tantrums," comprehensible but unexpected. In the midst of a poor little dance that the Bryn-Thistle was trying to give, with aged gentlewomen tottering around the dining-room dancing together, Jinny demanded, "Have we got to go on staying in this hencoop when people are having such a gorgeous time at Palm Beach? Aren't we good enough to go there?"

"My dear child, we'll go over there any time you want to. We'll go tomorrow. We'll hire a car and a driver."

That was all, and after another dance, she apologized: "I'm sorry I flared up so. I'm sure the dear old things here mean well, but they get on my nerves."

"We'll go up and start packing now."

"You're wonderful, and I'm sorry I was noisy and spiteful—and come on, let's get going! Palm Beach, here I come!"

——Do people who love each other always bicker and scratch and hurt? Must they?

They both felt guilty when all the guests at the Bryn-Thistle came out on the porch to cry, "It's been so nice to meet you both. We just loved knowing you, Judge, and your dear little bride."

It was a hundred miles across the Everglades to Palm Beach, and they sang all the way, hand in hand, behind their sedate colored driver. She was radiant then, a joyous peasant with a red kerchief round her dark hair, and when they came into the American Cannes, where all the people are beautiful, the houses all carven of gold, and the ocean water especially imported from the Riviera daily, by airplane, she was impressed to a blissful awe.

The season was early; they were able to get a suite at the Royal Crown: two rooms filled with white-fur rugs and glass tables and chairs so modern that you sat in them as in a bucket; and Jinny squealed continuously in the high religious passion of absolute luxury, and he ordered up a bottle of Johannisberger Cabinet, in the slow drinking of which they enjoyed everything but the taste.

He telephoned to Berthold Eisenherz, now head of the

very richest family in Grand Republic, who came down to his villa at Palm Beach every winter. Eisenherz was cordial, which exiled Grand Republicans are not always to their fellow refugees, and urged them to come over to the villa for dinner and dancing, that evening.

So for five hours the Timberlanes lived in a Hollywood motion picture: a marble terrace on the starry ocean, a Cuban orchestra, champagne from a portable silver-striped bar, roses on a December night, and young Navy officers who danced with Jinny. The war seemed only fictional. She exulted, "Cass, this is the night I've lived for—this and our night at the gipsy camp. I'm intolerably happy! I'm sorry if I was ever cross. Because I love you!"

"More even than that lieutenant s.g.?"

"More even than that lieutenant j.g.!"

"Champagne, madame?" said the footman, who was a deacon in the Swedish Baptist Church, back home in Minneapolis.

Jinny's husband was so relaxed that for the five enchanted hours he actually let her enjoy what he had so anxiously wanted to have her enjoy. And through the net of Jinny's black evening bag Isis peered out with a benignity that knew not good or evil.

The Honorable Mr. Hudbury, United States Senator Hudbury, should have been in Washington, fighting the war, but as he was a very thick, round, stupid man, it may have been as well that he was taking a week off from statesmanship to repose his limbs, which looked like four fingers of an enormous pale-white glove, as they were displayed upon the sands of Palm Beach. As an ex-representative, Cass recognized the Senator even in the improbable disguise of a bloated violet bathing-suit, with a belt patriotically symbolizing the American flag encircling the globe. Mr. Hudbury's belly being the globe.

Now Cass did not care for Mr. Hudbury, not as a pal. Mr. Hudbury started every sentence with "In my opinion," and he spent week-ends with lobbyists. Cass would not have collected Honorable Mr. Hudbury, or any other accidental celebrity, except to give him to Jinny, but since he had not given her any presents now since ten o'clock this morning—the present then had been a coral necklace which looked like the devil on her—he now picked up the Senator's halo and handed it to her.

Fortunately Hudbury remembered him, and fortunately he did not remember that he had hated Congressman Timberlane after a party caucus at which the fellow had suggested that even Republicans ought to know that there was a new invention called labor unions.

They were a musical-comedy group upon these tropic sands: the Senator tubby and half naked, the Judge stalwart and three-quarters naked, and Jinny, like all the other respectable women at that time and place, almost entirely naked, charmingly naked, with white midriff turning coffee-color. With difficulty could you have found three people more nude or more piously against "this crank theory of Nudism."

"Senator, I don't know whether you'll recall me—Cass Timberlane, formerly in Congress from Minnesota."

"Why, yes, yes, my boy, how could I forget a wheelhorse who has rendered such sterling services to the Party! Sure. You had that house on H Street, and the cocktails made with Swedish aquavit. Perfectly."

"This is my wife."

"Oh, yes, and of course I remember you, too, and the name—ah, ah now, wait, don't tell me—*Blanche*!" The Senator looked confused, but he was used to it. For years and years he had been confused over something or other, and he would continue to be confused until someone in his State discovered that he was their Senator, and had him defeated.

Jinny looked irritated, then winked at Cass, yet she viewed Hudbury not without respect. After all, a United States Senator is a United States Senator, even when he is a hoot-owl. (She still held that innocent theory. She had never lived in Washington.)

The Senator went on making sounds like an empty barrel. "How could I forget anything so charming as your lady, Cass? Ravished to see you again, Blanche."

"Oh, don't be ravished, Senator."

"Yes, yes, I will! I can't help it. Now, folks, I'm about to assume the normal habiliments of a gentleman, and what-say you join me for a cocktail on the terrace of the Choiseul in half an hour?"

Cass looked to Jinny for permission, and said, "Fine."

The truth is that over the cocktails, and how many of them there were, Jinny was proud of being intimate with this aged poop, and if he did reveal himself by saying that "American Business stands wholeheartedly back of the war effort, ready to pledge every dollar to encourage Our Boys," yet he also revealed the senatorial magic by having somehow discovered, while he was dressing, that Blanche's name was now Virginia. It is probable that while he was under the shower he had been speaking to the Federal Bureau of Inquiry by vest-pocket radio.

Calling her "Jinny," pouring his black-molasses charm all over her, he first told her that as a boy he had sold newspapers. That was for him an obligatory introduction to anything he had to say, whether in the Senate, a grocery store, or a parlor house. Then he took them right into the heart of world affairs by confiding that on the very day after Pearl Harbor, he had been summoned to the White House for a small conference of the leaders of both parties. (That the President had noticed that Senator Hudbury was there or, if so, that he had said anything to him beyond "Got a cigarette?" Cass and Jinny never could find out.)

After cocktails the Senator took them on to the roulette club where, but under strictly honest, home-made American conditions, none of your foreign shenanigans, Jinny lost forty dollars.

Here, they were in a spotlight of international chic. The Senator's secretary, a pale young man with constant reservations, who was the Senator's eyes and his ideology, had come with them, and he pointed out, at the gaming tables, the third-greatest radio crooner in America, the fourth-greatest New York banker, the fifth-most-beautiful woman from Alabama, a colonel who was going to be a major general, a major general who was going to be a retired major general, and a gentleman, with a beard, who had been a German manufacturer but was now an exiled French patriot.

Through all of this global low-down, Cass was as grateful as little Jinny, and said as they parted—he did not sound like Judge Timberlane of the Twenty-Second Judicial District— "It was extremely kind of you, Senator, to give us such a good time. I appreciate it."

At dinner, the two of them at their hotel, Jinny pounced:

"Have a good time, Cass?"

"Splendid. How did you like the Senator?"

"He's a fool."

"Yes, he does rathdr bear that reputation. But he's always been clever at picking useful brothers-in-law."

"Why were you so excited by having the old pot condescend

to you?"

"M?"

"He doesn't even know anything about politics, only about politicians. He doesn't know half as much as Tracy Oleson or Mr. Hubbs." Then, clearly as an afterthought, "Or as you. Why did you ever drag in the old idiot?"

"Because I thought he would amuse you."

"Dullness doesn't amuse me."

"I picked him out for you the way I did your coral necklace. I wouldn't want to rub my face against the coral, either. Don't be so youthfully censorious. If you don't care to have Hudbury for your collection, if you don't want me to shoot him and stuff him for you, we'll throw him out. . . . Jinny! . . . Sweet!"

"I know, darling! I *am* censorious. *And* young. And I do try to show off my superiority. I'm sorry. Some day, I'll grow up."

And of that quarrel there was nothing more. But Cass was thinking nervously that for years yet she would be impulsive, hasty to judge him, aggressively independent, like the other children of her Positively Final New Modern Revolutionary Age which by 1970 would have come to seem such a naive Old-fashioned Age.

——Like all these girls, she feels—and how can you blame her—that she must have her own life. Besides that, I'm no longer the family priest to her or a guide or a refuge; I'm just A Husband. And I don't even care much, so long as she'll let me go on being *that*!

There was nothing in the Specimen Hudbury that Jinny had not been able to identify from her Pioneer Falls collecting. In fact he looked like the local pre-motor livery-stable keeper who was still sitting in front of his empty barn, still covered with hay-dust, waiting for this automobile craze to pass.

But she was impressed and a little confused when they went to lunch at Berthold Eisenherz's villa, and so was Cass. At the villa dance they had met Berthold only as a sort of private head-waiter. Now, they collided with him as a personality.

The only thing about him to hint that he was not a gentleman was that he too consistently looked too much like a gentleman. He had devoted the voluminous money that his grandfather had made, as a Minnesota pioneer, by skinning beaver and redskins, to Harvard and Heidelberg and the Sorbolnne and a black-eyed, red-tempered Latvian girl who spoke all languages, in and out of bed, and so had qualified himself for the American diplomatic corps, in which, before he got tired, he had risen to first secretary in a minor legation.

He looked like a German who was trying to look like an Englishman. He had been married, now and then, to the daughters of German-American millionaires, who played pianos and barons. At fifty, he was bald and not officially married; he was bald and erect and soft-spoken. In Palm Beach he wore the monocle that even he did not dare to display back home in Grand Republic, where Swedish and Finnish urchins and Roy Drover and Boone Havock would have made exactly the same rather Freudian comments upon it.

He had the Timberlanes for one of his better Grade-B luncheons, with one actress, one lady pianist, one viscountess, a Swiss violinist, and an economist from New Zealand. At the flower-strewn, yellow-damask covered table, on the terrace looking to the Southern sea, the Timberlanes listened while the viscountess tried to talk faster than the pianist.

Berthold himself talked only to Jinny, asking her questions in a manner that made her feel solid and original.

Afterward, Jinny confided to Cass, "That was fun. The vis-vy-whateveritis-countess was silly, but I think your friend Berthold is wonderful. I always heard so much about him in Grand Republic, but I never saw him before. Will we see him when he goes back in the spring?"

"I guess so. If we want to."

"Isn't he hard to know?"

" 'Hard to know'? Why should he be? Just because he's rich? Back home, we're not as naive as Palm Beach. We know where his money came from!"

"No, I don't mean 'because he's rich'! Because he's wise and charming, and he treats a colt like me as though I were a—you know—a countess, too. And the way he can speak French! And knows all about Bessarabia! And kiss the hand! My hand's still tingling from it. Oh, boy!"

"If you're going out for international society, along with Excellency Bertie, you can't mix your dialects, and say 'Oh, boy'!"

"Okay. But don't you like Bertie?"

"Would you be surprised if I said he's even phonier than Senator Hudbury?"

"I certainly would. And I would be fairly sure—fairly sure that you were going jealous on me again."

He gaped. It was true; he was jealous; jealous of Eisenherz, not because he owned a palace but because with it he had been able to impress Jinny; not that he knew the Deauville patter but that he could make Jinny admire it.

He was quick about getting the proper forgiveness, so *that* could not be called a quarrel.

There came a hot and humid evening, and Aucassin and Nicolette acted like Auggie and Nig. For two days they had been idle, soaked in sun, confidently making love, and that sensible uselessness had been too much for two people so perpetually active.

They drove over to West Palm Beach to see a super and maddening movie, and they were unhappy and nervous. He tried to hold her hand, and she drew hers away. She said it was too damp.

He watched her anxiously, and so she watched him protestingly, and when they had worked up a fine, thick, hateful tension, he wanted to cough.

He felt that she was just waiting for him to do something objectionable like that, cough and whoop and spatter in a public place—and so he couldn't do it, and so he wanted all the more to cough, until the entire subsolar world was one horror of suppressed coughing, and he let go in one gargantuan throaty bellow, and, beside him, she gave off electric sparks of rage. Then, in ostentatious indifference, he crossed his legs, and his garter came loose, and he had to make a public presentation of stooping down to fasten it.

He insisted on a sundae after the movie and naturally, being normally a tidy man, he now dropped chocolate sauce on his white shirt.

"Disgusting!" she muttered.

She sadistically scrubbed it into a worse mess with her handkerchief, and they drove back to the hotel in a great hot silence. So when he was brushing his teeth, he dropped a white spot of toothpaste on his slipper, and she saw it, oh, she saw it, and she said:

"Disgusting!"

She thought it over, with all of a good woman's earnestness, and spoke as to a seven-year-old brat whom even his grandmothers had agreed to murder:

"Cass, can't you ever pay the least bit of attention to your personal habits?"

"Whaaaat?"

"I know you've lived alone so much, but still you're supposed to be an intelligent man, and why you don't even notice it when you act like a pig—your sloppy table-manners and yanking your garter around right out in front of people—why do you deliberately go and pick out garters that are guaranteed to come loose? And dribbling spots on your vest and your dressing-gown, and as for your *lapels*——"

"I deny all of that."

"Dribbling. Constantly."

"I do not dribble! You found one spot on my lapel, a month ago . . . before we'd gone and got married. But if it were true, and I slopped around like a half-wit, I'd expect you to shut up about it. I'm neither a New England housewife nor a pansy. I want your love, but not because of my exterior decoration. If you're going to go on watching me, expecting me to act like an ordinary vulgar Middlewestern male—well, that's what I am. I haven't one single extraordinary virtue except my devotion to you. If you want to take advantage of that, I'm helpless. But beloved, my beloved, don't *you* lose something when you make me into a swine?"

She ran to him, and she was crying, lovely in repentance.

"I didn't realize I was picking on you. I was just letting my big mouth run on, as Eino used to say. It didn't really mean anything more than all the silly kidding that Lyra and Tracy and I used to do. I forgot you're so touchy."

"Am I very touchy?"

"Like a racehorse. But that's why I love you. Oh, my dearest, I'll never let you go into politics or be a judge or anything like that. Your hide is about as thick as tissue paper. Kiss me." Her kiss was that of a naughty child distraught to find that she has hurt her friend. "I truly think you're the greatest man living. That's why I was cross with you about Senator Hudbury: that you didn't realize how much bigger you are than him—than he?—whichever it is. You know, I'm not really ungrateful. I know I'm lucky to——"

"Sweet, don't go on. You're making me feel like a lug for even spitting back at you. . . . I do love you so!"

"Identical, pal." But her effort to be funny was pathetic, and she looked so forlorn.

It was after half an hour of tenderness that Cass said, "I'm sure now we'll never have another quarrel."

"Never!"

"And so I'm going to risk my life and criticize you for overdressing."

"M?"

"At lunch at Bertie's, didn't you notice the rigid millionaire simplicity of that blasted countess? But you had on a boutonniere *and* a necklace *and* two bracelets *and* a comic-dog breastpin *and* a rhinestone buckle on your hat. Too much."

"Too Pioneer Falls, eh?"

"Still, why shouldn't you be?"

"Because I am the wife of a judge that ought to be on the

Supreme Court bench right now, and I mean it!"

She must have slipped down to the lobby while he was bathing, while he was feeling proud of himself for having asserted his power and ashamed of himself for having so priggishly bullied so defenseless a little criminal. For there she was, shyly holding out a small Modern Library edition of *South Wind*, and begging, "It's a repentance present."

He almost wept then, while Isis, on the bureau, stretched herself with ancient despair.

There could never be any more quarrels or jealousy. Never.

On the bathing-beach, when numerous men were attentive to the pleasant sight of her straight smooth legs, and got acquainted with her apropos of a dog, a daughter, a cigarette-light, or the quick sketches of the bathers that Jinny sometimes made in charcoal, then Cass was proud that he felt no jealousy.

——Might as well get used to it. When we get back, probably every friend I have—Roy, Bradd, Jay, Harley, Frank, Greg— the whole bunch of 'em will try to make her. Not a chance, gentlemen. There's no malice, no treachery, no intrigue in my Jinny. Going to be none of this "modern, civilized, urbane" sleeping around and getting complicated in *our* house.

Their first Christmas dinner together was at Eisenherz's villa. It was a Grand Republic dinner and full of the double joy of loving the home town and of being able to get away from it in winter. Webb and Louise Wargate were there, just come in, and Madge Dedrick. There was apprehensive talk about the war, and the Wargates expected to rush home early, but there were also hot rum punch and tangoing and holly and kisses as harmless as 1890—though not more so—and Bertie and Madge said that Jinny was going to be their dearest friend for life, starting about March 20th, on their annual bird-flight back to Grand Republic.

But the real Christmas was later that night, when Cass and Jinny stood on the balcony of their suite, looking at the tranquil glow of Lake Worth, and she sighed, "I'll never forget today. Especially, I won't forget our standing here, us two. And I'm glad we're going back home—us two! I don't really fall too much for this Palm Beach glamor. I know it's just gambling with counterfeit money."

"I'm glad. I was afraid maybe I'm too rustic for all the nobility."

"No, you're too independent. Cass, I'm very happy. I'll always be very happy with you."

They came into the station at Grand Republic in a snowstorm.

An Assemblage of Husbands and Wives

GEORGE HAME & FRIENDS

THE RETURN of Judge Timberlane to his court room was marked by an impassive "Glad to see you back, Judge" from Humbert Bellile, the bailiff, a hand-shake from the clerk of court, and "Now we can get going—nice trip, Chief?" from George Hame, the court reporter.

They were quiet and competent men, though bored, and it appeared evident from seeing them run the court machinery that they had nothing so disturbing in their lives as wives to hate or trust, daughters to be worried about, ambitions to be defended; nothing more complex than the conduct of dull agricultural arson cases.

Hame and Bellile went, after court, to the Cockrobin Bar, and had comforting conversation with Ed Oleson, the barber, and Leo Jensing, the electrician.

"See your boss is back from his honeymoon, George," said Oleson.

"Looks fit's a fiddle. Incidentally, the best judge in the State. Born professional."

"What kind of a girl he marry?"

"Cute little trick, bright's a dollar. Hope she appreciates him."

Jensing yawned, "Those rich guys that belong to the Federal Club certainly do marry the swellest dames. Well, they can have 'em. I'll bet they're all a bunch of headaches. My old woman and I—I always tell her she looks like a constipated chicken, and she says I look like a stubble field—she's dumb and she was brought up a Seventh Day Adventist, but we get along like nobody's business. I cuff the kids and send 'em off to bed and then I get a can of beer and we strip down to our undershirts and sit around and tell lies and yap about what rats our neighbors are and generally enjoy life. The Judge can keep his cutie, and that goes for all the fat boys in the Federal Club. Say, ever been in that club, George? What kind of a dump is it?"

Mr. Hame explained, "I often take papers to the Judge there. It's a pretty swell joint, at that! All wood paneling and the bar's like a chapel, stone arches and floor. But you know what you can do with the whole club! Lot of landlords telling each other Roosevelt is a Communist, like it was a piece they learned at school."

Ed Oleson was eager. "You ask *me* about the Federal Club! I go there all the time, to shave the upper-bracket crooks when they got too big a hang-over to walk. Oh, a lot of 'em are okay; Webb Wargate is a real constructive citizen, and Judge Blackstaff—he's just as good a judge as your boss, George, and tips you four bits, like a gentleman. But Prutt, the banker, he never gives you a cent—explains they don't tip, in a club. Hell,

I ain't a club servant; I got my own independent business and I don't have to shave any cactus-faced old gentleman-virgin unless I feel like it.

"But the worst guy there is that Boone Havock. Say, why decent people ever let him in their houses is beyond me. I've been called in to shave that cut-throat when he was so drunk he couldn't go home and had to take a room at the club, and he told and volunteered and told me that he'd spent the night with a tart in a shack down in the South End and then got her cock-eyed and cheated her out of her five bucks, and he boasted about it.

"My son Tracy, that works for Wargate, has got more brains and financial savvy than the whole club put together. By the way, Tracy knows Judge Timberlane's bride; says she's a high-class girl. And talking of wives, I'm like Leo here: my old girl and I have a swell time, especially now the kids are grown up. We go out hunting and canoeing like a couple of Indians. That's the kind of a wife I like."

George Hame rose, jeering, "Glad to hear there's so many square-shooting wives around this burg. I congratulate you boys."

The bailiff, also rising: "Same here. Fellows that're out from behind the matrimonial eight-ball like you two must have money to spare. We'll allow you to pay for the drinks."

Jensing crowed, "Just to prove it, I *will* buy 'em!"

"Any time you're in for rape, Leo, just remind me that I

used to know you, and I'll get the Judge to let you off with life." said Hame. "Good night."

Bailiff Bellile, as he entered his brown Cape Cod cottage, waited for his wife to say, "Have you wiped your feet? I try so hard to keep things nice here, and then you come home drunk and get everything all dirty."

She said it.

She waited for him to say, in echo of his days as a lumber-camp teamster, "I wish to God I *were* drunk, and maybe it wouldn't make me so sick to look at you."

He said it.

Ed Oleson went noisily into his upstairs half of a two-family house, and his aging wife chirped, "It's the old master himself. Have a good time with the boys?"

"I'll say! Wish you'd been along."

"Whyntcha invite me?"

"Juvecome?"

"Try it and see! Bet I would. Smell something nice?"

"And how! What is it?"

"Real Hunky goulash."

"Now you don't tell me." He kissed her.

"Nice time in the shop today?"

"Fellow here from Rochester, New York, he told me all about how we'll lick the Japs with a secret weapon we got. Say, I'll bet Tracy 'll be in the war, and be a major."

"If his lungs are all healed up. Golly, Ed, aren't you proud of that boy!"

"Say, don't you quote me and don't let the newspapers get hold of it, but I'm nuts about him. The damn little hick—think of him—headed for the top of the Wargate Corporation some day!"

"And let me tell you, Mr. Ed Oleson, they'll be lucky to get him!"

"I'll say. How about lassoing that goulash now?"

"I think you got something there, Mister. Let's go!"

There was no ugly noise between George Hame and his wife, Ethel, when he came coldly into their freight-car of a house, but only an uglier silence. That was agreeable to him, because there was for him a poisonous boredom in what he considered her spiritless and hopeless fussing, her whimpering demands for money.

He looked at her over the Dumas he was always reading. She was hemming a pot-holder made of red calico.

"Much too bright for her," he muttered.

"What?"

"Nothing . . . You certainly will drive me nuts."

"What say?"

"Nothing."

Then another baby yelled. They had five of them, and all unwanted. But there was also their fifteen-year-old daughter, Betty, whom he loved.

He said placidly, "All I exist for is to supply you with brats and lactation."

"And whose fault——"

"Yours. If you'd take a little care of yourself——As Montaigne observes, this place is always obscene with new dripping babies, and smells like wet death."

She knew enough then not to speak. When he mentioned Montaigne—pronounced Montaigny—he was likely to hit her with his seal ring.

Betty came in, round and pert as a bouncing tennis ball.

"Hello, Daddy," she said, as she raced for the stairs, and "Hello, sweetheart" he answered, looking up after her new nylon stockings and old shoes.

His wife was afraid not to speak now. "George! I will not have you looking at Betty that way!"

"So you will not have it! So what?"

He returned to Dumas.

Some day, he thought, Betty and he would run off together to France, to the shrine of Dumas. She looked much older than fifteen, didn't she? He dreamed about this always, and always knew that he would never do it. He knew that he would hold to his wife. She irritated him, but he was lonely without her on the evenings when she was visiting her incessantly sick relatives and Betty was out with one of the neighborhood boys whom he hated. He was lonely not because he had no treasures in himself, for he could renew them out of Dumas or Scott or Washington Irving, nor because he could not take comfort in solitude, but because he was afraid that when Betty discovered how he felt toward her and vituperatively left him forever, then no one in the world but Ethel would stay by him, no one else would blame it on Betty.

He guessed that Judge Timberlane would kick him out, if the Judge discovered his thoughts about Betty, and he was sorry, because, though he considered the Judge a little too naive, he also believed him to be the Archangel Michael.

With the firmness of the will to death, he waited for Betty to come down and pass through the room again. The other children panted in and out, but their noise was so blurred that it was to him like an absolute silence.

"Don't you want any supper?" grated his wife.

"What? I suppose so. I never thought about it . . . Oh, Betty, going out? Get home early now, sweetheart. I'll sit up for you."

"Swell, Daddy," she condescended.

Then he felt gay, and he looked amiably at his wife. When he saw her expression, he froze and returned to Dumas.

25

THAT THEY SHOULD return to Grand Republic on an early January day when the sun came out after a snowstorm, that Mrs. Higbee should be at the door to greet the young chatelaine, that flowers should have come from Diantha Marl and Bradd Criley, and a shaker of already-mixed cocktails from Queenie Havock, that Jinny should coo, "Bergheim is an awfully stately old place, isn't it!" was all so exactly the Judge's idea of what was fitting that it bothered him. There was no responsible worrying to be done!

Cleo, now a proud young cat, came galloping hysterically downstairs when she heard their voices. Then she pretended that she didn't even know them, but had just happened to be passing that way. In fact she stayed about for an hour, to make sure that they saw how she ignored them.

They were content, but they found the town in the war.

Even the citizens who six weeks before had said, "We're going to mind our own business and not get into any war" were declaring, "We ought to have gone to Great Britain's aid two years ago, but now we're in, and we won't quit till Hitler and Hirohito are wiped out."

Eino Roskinen, Curtiss Havock, Jack Prutt, and Jamie Wargate, Webb's second-oldest boy, were already in uniform as privates, and Tom Crenway, in escape from his anesthetically amorous Violet, was a major. Violet herself was the rival of Diantha Marl and Della Lent for leadership of women's war activities: Red Cross, Civilian Defense, scrap-collection. Of the Brothers-in-Law, Inc., the spouses of the Zebra Sisters, Alfred Umbaugh was now a colonel in the department of supplies, and his Zeta was adequately managing his Button Bright Stores chain, while Harold W. Whittick, the advertising man, had taken over the patriotism of Grand Republic as once he had taken over its future.

All of these were anxious and faithful, but there was comedy in the case of that absentee warrior, Fred Nimbus of Station KICH.

On December 10, ult., young Mr. Nimbus had begun a biweekly series of radio stories about the adventures of the Marines, in which he was author, director, and star. They were so lively that even a few Marines liked them, and there was a general feeling abroad that Mr. Nimbus, in his studio, was the most daring warrior in the state and that upon hearing his voice, thousands of Japanese dashed up the palm trees.

All of this the Timberlanes learned as they were starting their career as a decorous and settled Young Couple.

Two days after their return, the cold wave struck; the thermometer was at ten, fifteen, twenty-two degrees below zero; all the separate lawns turned into one snowfield, as though the cold prairie had taken over the town; and snow-devils whirled across them. No matter how they wrapped in fur and wool, their foreheads could not be protected from the aching sting of the cold. But before Jinny could moan for the ease and freedom of the Florida warmth, Cass had her out on skis, flying down the Ottawa Hill, and they were triumphant and alive.

He expected Jinny to turn Bergheim into a magazine supplement, and he was financially armed for it. He had been living on his salary as judge and saving the three or four thousand dollars a year that came from the rents which he had inherited from his father.

"Go to it," he said. "Kick out any of the old furniture that gets impertinent to you."

"No. I'm not going to change hardly a thing." She spoke with a new and matronly responsibility. "I'll just refurnish my own room—which I love, by the way; it's so light, with such a view over the valley. But the rest of the house, the old things belong to it."

He admired and wondered.

"And then, too, all your friends will be expecting the child bride to raise Cain with the household gods, and it's our duty to fool 'em."

He wondered and adored.

"And why waste the money now? Some day soon we'll

get a lovely new modern house of our own, with no smell of Eisenherz furs and sauerkraut."

He adored and fretted.

Her notion of a "lovely new house" would cost a great deal of money. But it did not occur to him to refuse.

She was as practical as laundry soap. Her newly decked room did have a flowery dressing-table with twenty-two small and rather redundant bottles and jars of cosmetics, urban and extremely expensive, but the walls betrayed the small-town girl in its sheaf of photographs and souvenirs: Jinny Marshland at six, with kitten; Cousin Joe Marshland, who was now an insurance agent in Gopher Prairie; Douglas Fairbanks as a movie bandit; Eino and Tracy in astounding straw hats; the program of the Pioneer Falls High School Commencement Exercises, May, 1934, silver print on scarlet paper, class motto "Per Aspera ad Astra," salutatorian, Miss Virginia Marshland.

While her own retreat was being redecorated, she was generously invited to lodge with Cass, and when she crept into his room, her bare feet in woolly slippers like white rabbits, and slipped into his monumental bed, they clutched at each other with a stimulating feeling of danger and wickedness.

Lying with one leg impudently cocked in the air, her toes wriggling, she crooned, "I am Judge Timberlane's little mistress."

"Jinny!"

"And the proudest of his Circassian slaves. The concubines

of the seven Kings of Blackstaff envy my breastplate of onyx and my Abyssinian lace slacks."

"Why, Jinny!"

"Does it shock you when I say I'm your mistress?"

"Well, not—uh—not *shock* me——"

"I see, Venerable. You mean it merely *shocks* you!"

"Yes, it does!"

She giggled.

He was sorry when she grandly started to sleep in her own virtuous-looking narrow bed. Somehow he was afraid to go unbidden into her room, as she never was to enter his.

To her maidenly room he added one gift: a white fur rug. She used to sit with her folded bare feet deep in its fleecy warmth, and talk about immortality.

In the rooms other than her own, her practicality was evident. She had more floor-plugs put in, and replaced the old lamps, which resembled moth-eaten velvet mosques erected upon bronze crutches, with lamps of simple shafts and clear parchment shades. She dismissed teak thrones, and ponderous curtains that for generations had been the graveyards of flies and lightning-bugs. The house suddenly had more light and air and gaiety, and at night you did not fall over relics.

And she installed a popcorn shaker, an electric drink-mixer, an electric washing-machine, a set of dominoes. . . .

Her one Bohemian extravagance as an artist was a highly

modernist design which she drew on the inside of the downstairs coat-closet door, in gold radiator-paint and two shades of red nail-polish. It showed two angels, one holding a banner lettered "C" and one with a "J," joyfully flying together. It agitated the more sober citizenry, but to Cass it was a major work.

He had at last the chance to complete her instruction in chess.

It was an edifying and domestic sight: the large man in a doubtful brown-flannel dressing-gown and red slippers; the girl in quilted pink silk, with her small white woolly slippers; the board and the old ivory pieces which Cass's father had bought in San Francisco; all before the fire in the library, where now a clearer light displayed the blue buckram set of "The World's Most Distinguished Legal Orations, with Sketches of Leaders of the Bench and Bar, Profusely Illustrated."

Jinny took to chess with zeal and lawlessness. She began with an eloquent prejudice against the rooks.

She was a true animist; she believed that all inanimate objects—gloves, flatirons, automobiles, stars, lilies, pork chops—had souls and that all animals had human intelligence; and furthermore she almost one-quarter believed in her own belief.

Brooding over the chessmen, she said that the rooks were smug-looking and flat-headed, with stubbly cropped hair, and she scolded them for loafing in the home rank all through the hottest of the game, and then sneaking out to kidnap some bishop who had been working hard and taking risks, and who looked so slim and neat and friendly.

She developed a surrealist criticism of the chess-rules. Why shouldn't a king be able to castle under check?

"Because it's the rule," said Judge Timberlane.

"Why is it the rule?"

"Because it is!"

"Look, silly," she explained. "The king, bless his poor scared heart—the way he has to skip around, with even these G.I. pawns threatening to bump him off all the time—and so when he's in check, when he's in danger and really *needs* to castle, then you won't let him! Why not?"

"Because it's the——"

"Who ever made the rule?"

"Heavens, I don't know. I suppose some old Persian."

"Persians make rugs. They don't make rules."

"Well, this one did."

"How do you know he was a Persian? How do you know he was old?"

"I don't." She was so spirited a debater, so much more belligerent an advocate than any Hervey Plint or Vincent Osprey, that by now he was half-serious.

"You don't know? Then maybe there isn't any such a rule! Maybe you just dreamed it."

"Well, good Lord, all players keep it——"

"How do you know they do? Did you ever see Capablanca or Reuben Fine refuse to castle just because a king was being bullied by some mean bishop? (And I used to *like* the bishops, silly girl that I was, but now I'm onto them.) Did you?"

"Of course I didn't. I've never seen any master play."

"There! Maybe there isn't any such a rule. Maybe they only have it in Minnesota. We're wonderful in Minnesota about wheat and iron and removing gall-stones, but what right have we got to dictate to the rest of the world about castling?"

"Dear idiot child, you'll be asking next how I know you and I are really married, and who made up the marriage code."

"I do ask it! How do you know we aren't living in sin, according to the Mohammedans?"

"I——"

"Maybe I ought to walk right out of here, and go to living with Abby Tubbs or Jay Laverick or Senator Hudbury, or my sweet Bertie. What's to prevent it?"

"Only me and a shotgun."

"You see? You only believe in violence; you don't believe in the rules of marriage—or of my not castling, either!"

"Just the same, you can't castle."

"Bully!"

"Get on with the game, and don't be so reasonable. A girl that would criticize the corpus of chess-laws would criticize chastity."

"I'm not sure that's so hot, either."

"Get on with the game!"

But the real debate—and he was never quite sure that there was not some reality at the core of her pretended rebellions against Authority—came when he first revealed to her, from among the more appalling secret human motives, that by creeping up to the eighth rank, his pawn had suddenly become a queen, and that she was thus about to be checkmated.

"That's the most ridiculous claim I ever heard in my life! Why? Now don't tell me it's the rule. It can't be. I know that pawn. It's got a tiny nick in its head." (This was true, though Cass had never noticed it.) "It's an unusually stupid, uncooperative pawn. It *never* could be a queen. Impossible! I won't recognize the government!"

"Don't you like rules, Jinny?"

"Well, I like you."

"Let me be didactic, Jin."

"Okay."

"Don't say 'Okay'!"

"Why not?"

"It sounds like a gum-chewer."

"But I am a gum-chewer."

"You are not, and you're not going to be. Look. I don't bully you about many things—I'd like to, but I'm too scared of you. But I want each of us to teach the other something of his attitude: me teach you that there's satisfaction in being a sober grind and mastering even a game, like chess; and you teach me that there's nothing legally wrong about letting go and just having a good time. Can't we?"

They gravely shook hands on it, seeing before them the white highway of pious self-instruction whereon every day in every way they would get not only better but more blithe; assured that he would become a first-class grasshopper and she one of the most social-minded ants in the whole three-foot mountain.

She said, with a slight shade of reverence, "When you lecture me, you sound like a real judge on the bench."

"Does it annoy you?"

"I love it. You know, pal, I'm not too sure I'm going to win this battle of marriage. I get around you by being the gay little girl—the blasted little gold-digger!—but you're too accurate and dependable for me."

"And sometimes I'm fun, ain't I?"

"Ye-es, sometimes—oh, quite often."

"But you won't lose the battle, Jin. The worthy blacksmith hasn't much chance against Ariel."

"You're balled up in your mythology, Judge. Ariel was not a girl."

"Which you distinctly are, my dear."

There was something in the smile with which she acknowledged this alluring fact which made him blush. Then, like a cat, her head low and a little sidewise, she cautiously stalked a pawn with her queen's bishop, and pounced.

Cass wondered where he had heard the theory that people, especially women, who are too devoted to animals are more callous toward human beings. Was it a folk tale or reasoned observation or spite, or all three? Remembering it, he was slightly worried, in a husbandly way, that Jinny was so ecstatic over all animals, from the mounted policemen's horses and the elephant in Wargate Park Zoo to the lone goldfish in a bowl which she sheepishly brought home from the Five and Ten.

To Cleo she gave an attention which gratified that bland and conceited cat. She maintained that Cleo had to have thef best liver, the sweetbread meant by Mrs. Higbee for the Master, and a menagerie of catnip mice. For Cleo she busily knitted a set of mittens, red mittens edged with yellow, each the size of a large thimble, for walks in the snow. When they were tried out, Cleo merely kicked off three of them, but the fourth she pounced on with a yell and chewed to pieces, while Jinny looked forlorn.

The gift of a gold string from some ancient Christmas package was Jinny's greatest success. This was Cleo's private string, daily rescued from the wood-box or a pan of batter or a toilet, and coiled beside her pink wicker basket, near the kitchen stove. She leaped into the air to clutch it, and furiously got snarled in it, and in it was suspended from the back of a chair. She spent hours hiding under curtains, wagging herself, trying to catch the string napping.

Jinny also acquired, within three months, a tragic-eyed cocker-spaniel pup named Alfred, who was terrified of Cleo, a canary which every night Cleo tried to eat, a depraved and miserable lizard, and two lambs made of wool and pretty inactive.

Jinny loved them all and tried to get them to love one another, with about the usual success of missionaries ever since Jonah.

Cass wished, sometimes, that in addition to the gay affection which Jinny gave him, he could have the yearning she poured on Cleo and on that faker and love-beggar, the dog Alfred.

Except when they differed over Jinny's purloining the Master's coming dinner for Cleo, Mrs. Higbee was Jinny's ally in spoiling every mangy feline and hound in the neighborhood, and Cass always had a suspicion that somewhere in the laby-rinthian basement of Bergheim the two women were concealing lost and very valuable pigeons, panthers, and hippopotami.

From his bedroom he heard them conspiring again, in Jinny's cave.

"Miss Jinny, now you got that new traveling clock, why don't you let me have this red celluloid one for the kitchen? Kitchen clock don't keep time."

"Oh, I couldn't, Mrs. Higbee, I simply couldn't! I've had

my little red clock for four years. It came from Pioneer Falls with me, and it waked me every single morning when I was on the job at the factory. Its feelings would be dreadfully hurt if I exiled it to the kitchen."

"Maybe something to that. We'll get the Judge to buy us a new one."

He came out of hiding to examine the two witches: "I'll bet both of you believe in palmistry and astrology."

"Doesn't every nice woman?" challenged Jinny.

Mrs. Higbee reflected, "I don't believe in any of those things, but it's awful funny what you find in a person's hand."

The witches, primitive and powerful, looked at each other darkly, with contempt for the shallowness of this childish inquistor with his books and his pride in reasoning.

In early spring, Alfred the dog died suddenly of cat-fur, only a few weeks after his appearance in history. Cass expected hysteria from Jinny, and plans for a torchlight funeral, but she said absently. "He was such a nice pup; sorry he went. But darling, let's not have another dog for a while. I'm not sure—she's too polite to show it—but I think Cleo is annoyed by dogs. They get so noisy when she merely wants to tease them a little."

An Assemblage of Husbands and Wives

SABINE GROSSENWAHN

YEARS AGO, when Boone Havock was not a railroad-builder but a saloon bouncer, a thoroughly worthless brother had followed him to Minnesota and there died in the odor of rye whisky, leaving a luscious-limbed and just slightly nymphomaniac daughter named Sabine in charge of Boone, who was very rigid and moral about women, that is, if they were his daughters or nieces. He sent Sabine to Sunday school, and in 1929, when she was eighteen, he shipped her East, to a fine rustling school in the Hudson Valley.

At a dance she met and in a dance she married one Ferdinand Grossenwahn, a fat, fifty-ridden New York stockbroker who was later known to Sabine's friends as "Pore Ole Ferdy." On the evening of her wedding-day, she slipped away for an hour with a handsome dancing-man whom she had met that afternoon, and when Ferdy found them and was stuffy about it, she slapped him.

As soon as she had succeeded in the new feminine career of lucratively divorcing her husband, she returned to Grand Republic, where her waved hair, delicate as a sea shell, her sables, and her fifteen-hundred-a-month alimony were greater rarities than in Manhattan.

Besides the alimony, Pore Ole Ferdy had given her a fifty-thousand-dollar cash bonus for leaving him in peace and dignity, and she built a house known throughout Minnesota as "Alimony Hall." It was in the shape of a double L, and the leafy courtyard, on the bluff overhanging the Sorshay River valley, was full all summer long of ivy and syringa and rosebushes, of glass-topped tables and plaid table-parasols and wheeled reclining-chairs like portable divans, with an outdoor grill and an outdoor bar; full of laughter and swing music on the phonograph and women who wanted sympathy and men who called it that. It is to be said for Sabine's good nature that, provided they did not attack her own current young man, she was almost as willing to provide secluded rooms for her women friends and their affairs as for her own.

Most frequent of the Alimony Hall Set were Jay Laverick, Harley Bozard, Cousin Curtiss Havock, Bradd Criley, Fred Nimbus, Norton Trock—but he never bothered women—Gillian Brown, who despised Sabine, Cerise, consort of that earnest young legal prig, Vincent Osprey, and, somewhat disapprovingly, Rose Pennloss.

Norton Trock dated himself by quoting Omar Khayyam at their gatherings, but the talk ran oftener to adultery and gin than to wine and roses.

None of them, except Sabine, Harley, and Cousin Curtiss, who had met him briefly in New York, had ever seen Pore Ole Ferdy Grossenwahn, but they all talked as though he were their oppressive and ridiculous uncle. They referred to her alimony as "our income." While Sabine and Gillian giggled, they debated whether Ferdy was worth more to them living or dead, for Sabine had assured them, "I honestly do think that if the old fool doesn't get married again, he will at least have the decency to leave me everything in his will."

They laughed while she told them about Ferdy s fat amorousness, or read them his current letters, which betrayed him by such puerile phrases as, "Though I never could satisfy you & I sure was not worthy of your spiritual gifts and bright way of talking, you must admit that my solicitude for you is unwavering & sure can count on me always, dear babe o' mine, for such financial assistance as able."

During her affair with Fred Nimbus, who was a couple of years younger than herself and a fine athletic radio-announcer, it amused both of them that her stupid ex-husband would not even know that he was supporting her lover. "Mustn't be jealous of Pore Ole Ferdy or talk naughty about him," she whispered to Fred. "You don't think he was romantic, but he certainly is contributing to a high-class romance now. So shut up and kiss me."

Sabine was not so simple in her moods that she always ridiculed Pore Ole Ferdy. Sometimes for a whole week she spoke of him with repentant reverence: "All of you shut your traps about Ferdy. I'm not altogether sold on the idea that he wasn't worthy of me. God knows he was hard to live with, and a cold fish, but he always treated me with the most scrup'lous honor, and in fact he's a perfect gentleman, and I want to tell you that there's no man on the Exchange that has a more prophetic sense about a bear-market than Ferdy."

But sometimes, to show that she was no parasite weakling, she was resentful and firm with Ferdy. He once wrote that he was hard-up and would like to reduce her "income" for a month or two, and she had the courage and sense of responsibility to answer, "All this is a matter of court record, and if you haven't got the dough now, that's just too bad! And you better hustle around and get it, not do the cry-baby act! I don't know what's gotten into you. I think it might help you come to your senses if you took this right into court. You seem to forget you took on an *obligation* in our legal settlement, and I don't intend to let you try and avoid it. I have been faithful to our agreement and I expect you to be the same."

When Norton Trock explained the idea of the matriarchy to her, Sabine said, "Thank God that could never happen in America."

26

THIS HAPPY MAN and woman, this little world, this precious island in a leaden sea, walled from the envy of less happier homes, this blessed trust, this peace, this youthful marriage, this home of such dear souls, this dear dear home.

This valley of refuge, this refuge without flight, this valley shelter from the wars abroad and the hysteric factions of the land, this close and smiling cheer, this dear dear home.

Thus only could Cass read his *Richard the Second*.

If the world of the twentieth century, he vowed, cannot succeed in this one thing, married love, then it has committed suicide, all but the last moan, and whether Germany and France can live as neighbors is insignificant compared with whether Johann and Maria or Jean and Marie can live as lovers. He knew that with each decade such serenity was more difficult, with Careers for Women opening equally on freedom and on a complex weariness. But whether women worked in the kitchen or in the machine-shop, married love must be a shelter, or the world would freeze, out in the bleak free prairies of irresponsible love-making.

With whatever flaws, his dear Jinny and he had created such a shelter. He hastened back to her from his day in court; she hastened to him from her war work in the Office of Civilian Defense, or from a French lesson with Frau Silbersee, or from a movie with Rose and Valerie Pennloss. He met her with a perpetually renewed amazement that this brisk and well-armored girl would soften to his love. She met him with astonishment that so reserved a man should be so without reserve her worshiper.

They walked on winter nights by the dark river flowing under the ice from dark pinelands; they panted home to read in quiet, with one final ferocious game of chess, and she came into his room to say good night and forgot to go.

Poor Cass was so much simpler than most of the criminals who appeared before his wisdom, and any beslobbered pickpocket knew more about the intrigue of love. He suffered from thinking that his was an entirely reasonable, realistic, unsentimental love—in fact, he suffered from thinking, while Nature was busy with much livelier urges.

So great was her kindness toward his stumbling and beautiful faith in her that Jinny was not tempted to tease him by keeping him away, but she was human enough to bully him. It was in timing that she could, with innocent sweetness, most bedevil him.

He was invariably ready to do whatever she wanted to when she wanted; she usually thought that what he wanted to do was a fair notion, but she always showed her independence by delaying the *when*. She was always ten minutes late, always had been and always would be, and he always protested that she was late, and she always explained that her watch was slow, and the ever-refreshing topic was probably a safety-valve and kept them from more perilous matrimonial topics, such as relatives, religion, and the vanity of too-much lipstick.

He had to face the twin questions of whether she could settle down with his staid set, and whether that set would snub her as an outsider and not come calling. But the entire town (again meaning one per cent of it) was frenzied to know what this girl was like who had captured Our Cass. They did come, and Jinny was pleased, even when she was irritated by the manner of the older worthies, which indicated, "We shall make every effort to have you accepted by our senate, now that you are no longer young and wild, but we must be convinced that you appreciate it."

Queenie Havock came in, at the most inconvenient time available, just when Jinny had started to wash her hair, and gave Jinny instructions on how to keep Cass ardent, and charged into the kitchen, said it was too large and too old-fashioned, insulted Mrs. Higbee, and then won her back by screaming, "Here I am shooting off my mouth again, but I know what a crank Cass is about temperance and purity and all that hooey, the old stiff, and you two girls have to live with him, and I just meant any time I can tip you off about men, you let me know, and how would you like a brace of frozen pheasants?"

265

Less endurable was Diantha Marl, Mrs. Gregory Marl, the handsome and fresh-voiced and amiable. Both as the wife of the *Banner* and in her own right as a committeewoman, a madame chairman, an exhaustive and exhausting talker about foreign affairs, the drama, and the illegitimate babies that all the gayer young ladies in town were certainly going to have immediately, Diantha ranked with Mrs. Webb Wargate, Madge Dedrick, and Della Lent as one of the female rulers of the tribe.

She had worked so hard at an English accent that she had acquired a fascinating combination of Oxford and oxcart, and she was so mannered, so pretentious, that when she met you on the street and said "Good morning," it somehow informed you that she was on her way to a conference with the Secretary of State or with Bernard Shaw, who had secretly slipped into town for that purpose.

She remembered that Jinny had once worked for her husband—how she remembered it! how glowingly and inescapably she remembered it!—and, under her system of private imperialism, she assumed the right to inflict on Jinny, as one of her smaller colonies, a rule of gentle questioning, which would provide her with new dinner-party tattle.

Jinny, proud in her power as young hostess, who could give orders to Mrs. Higbee and often have them carried out, offered Diantha tea or cocktails. She took cocktails, and began to whinny.

How cozy here. Did Cass tell Jinny all about his cases in court?

"Oh, yes," lied Jinny.

Did Cass like to play with her, and was he a generous provider?

"Oh, yes," said Jinny, surprised at being able to tell the truth.

What was Cass's worst fault?

"Why, I imagine it's his thinking that his wife is so bright that she's onto it when people who really dislike her pretend to shine up to her."

Not for months did Diantha decide whether Jinny had meant to be insulting. She then, very erroneously, decided *No*.

She ran through a discourse on the post-war education of Germany (which ought to be taken over by liberal-minded women like Diantha Marl), on trout-fishing (she was one of the best fly-casters in Radisson County), and on what a creeping imbecile Perry Claywheel was to believe that his wife was true to him. So Diantha got easily through the period before she could go home and tell a dinner-party that this Jinny Timberlane was illiterate but harmless.

But Mrs. Nestor Purdwin, wife of the dean of the local bar, just brought Jinny a jar of chutney, and that rangy older hawk, Mrs. Judge Blackstaff, came and sat and knitted with jinny, who was glad then to believe that she herself would some day become an authentic Mrs. Judge.

As a planner, a maker of notes and lists, Cass had anxiously thought over all the younger people whom Jinny might like. He was pleased when the Havocks' daughter, Ellen Olliford, came home from Massachusetts. She was just Jinny's age, and everybody said she was "so amusing."

They would be Great Friends, decided Cass.

Ellen Havock had gone to Smith College, then married Mr. Olliford, an engineer resident in Springfield, Massachusetts, now in the service, a captain. Ellen, with her one baby, had come back to stay with her parents.

She loved and despised her parents, she loved and was bored by Grand Republic, and she spread abroad the news that Springfield (Mass.) was a heavenly city compact with music, French cuisine, silver golf-sticks and bridge-cards beaten out of fine gold, till her father said—but still lovingly—"Then why the hell don't you get out of this hick camp and go back to your codfish?"

Jinny was more terrified by Ellen than by Ellen's strident mother. Young Mrs. Olliford was so artificially slim, so icy, so at ease, so inquisitive; and without saying it, she so clearly said to Jinny, "How did a country girl like you ever marry a man who, however far down the rungs, still belongs to our International Ladder Society?"

Half a dozen other young war-widows also came

reluctantly back to the primitiveness of their native Grand Republic, aftei marrying into such exclusive Eastern centers of culture as Peoria, Bridgeport, and Scranton. They knew their horse-shows and their *Vogue* fashions, and Jinny was as uncomfortable with them as any other fox-terrier with a pack of disdainful greyhounds. None of this did Cass realize; he thought that Ellen and her kind were "nice kids, maybe a little too extravagant," who would be grateful to meet anyone so forthright and individual as Jinny. When she said, no, she did not want to give a party for them, he dismissed them with a comfortable "You're probably right. How about some cribbage?"

Not too discontentedly, he thought, Jinny settled down with Lyra Coggs, Francia Wolke, Cerise Osprey, Hortense Hubbs, Rose Pennloss and, perhaps most of all, with Rose's daughter Valerie who, at fifteen, seemed to Jinny to have more eagerness and integrity than anyone she knew except Cass and Eino.

Webb and Louise Wargate, home early from Florida because of the war, gave the Timberlanes a formal party, but of that Jinny could remember nothing except white shirt-fronts, a swirl of tulle, and the magnificent, the absurd, Great Room in the Wargate palace, with its enormous crimson circular seat with an orange tree on the central pedestal, and the marble fountain imported from Italy.

Their real welcome to matrimony was the dinner of twelve persons given by Dr. and Mrs. Drover.

Jinny had, with difficulty, persuaded Cass that it would be fashionable for them to be ten minutes late, so when they came in—two minutes early—the citizens had all arrived, and Cass could hear Roy and Queenie in an antiphon that seemed familiar:

Nobody at all has any servants whatsoever now, and those who do have pay too much, and so all strikes ought to be stopped by law, because all labor leaders and Democrats are crooks. Cass listened while he waited for Jinny to return from the coat-room, and silently exploded.

——Dear Jinny, I've done a dreadful thing, to trick you into becoming my wife and, for your reward, let you for a whole evening listen to Roy Drover belching. I must have hated you, not loved you. I've shut you in a morgue. Well, I'll take you out of it. I'll take us both out! I'd better, little hawk, or you'll fly off without me!

——Now what kind of a way to talk is that? Jinny is a wise-enough kid to know that these people are the salt of the earth, the friendliest and solidest people living. What the devil! They're not *supposed* to talk like a bunch of actors or professors!

He had got so far in his inward scolding when Chris Grau walked in, with scarf, and looked at him straight—not rebukingly, not pathetically, not tenderly, just straight, her manner saying that he had gone rather far, not so long ago, in making love to her, in drinking in her sympathy, and there was nothing that could be done about it, but she did want to have the record clear.

The Judge quit brooding and became practical. Leaving Jinny comparatively safe with Rose Pennloss and a cocktail, he appealed to Lillian Drover, the hostess. She smiled beseechingly at him, as she always did. "Lil! Can you seat Jinny beside Bradd Criley at dinner—he'll entertain her more than anybody, I think—and let me sit by Chris? I've neglected her."

Lillian blushed and nodded.

He bustled to Bradd. Good ole Bradd! Thirty-nine now but hard to believe it, still looks about twenty-nine; wavy-haired, impudently courtly, handsome in a track-athlete way, slim as a tennis-player, master of every trick of the law court and the poker table and the boudoir, a more smiling friend than Roy Drover and a more sensible one than Frank Brightwing—no wonder he held that ducal office of The Most Popular Bachelor in Town!

Cass urged, "Bradd! Pay some attention to Jin tonight. She's shy of these old crabs, and I've got to soothe Chris."

The dimple, the auick smile, the manly voice, as Bradd promised, "Do you think I'll find that hard? Jinny is the one person here, besides you, that I want to see. I'm delighted that you and she are so happy together. And you can hold her.

She'd be onto a flashy guy like me in ten minutes. You watch me squire her."

Good ole Bradd, thought Cass.

Sitting beside Chris at dinner, he probed, "Well, what do we say?"

"About what?"

"About us."

"You mean about letting me think you loved me, and then sneaking off with this girl?"

"Not sneaking."

"Sneaking! . . . Well, I must say, but regretfully, that I think you were right."

"M?"

"Oh, Cass, I know; I had no youthful passion left to give you. It all went to my father, then for years to Mother, and when——I wanted to hate Jinny, but I'm sorry to say that I love her. I don't suppose I'm more than six or seven years older than she is, but I feel as if she were my daughter. She's fundamentally a shy thing, isn't she? Look at her, trying to laugh at Roy's dirty jokes."

"Well, Bradd will carry her through, on her other side. He's——"

"Cass! Are you a competent husband for any girl as fine and winning as Jinny?"

"I don't know. I hope so."

"You've got to be! For my sake, too. Cass, she's my

understudy. No, she's me; she represents, me, she *is* me, in the only love-affair I'll ever have. Are you gentle enough for her and tolerant enough and imaginative enough and flexible enough?"

"What do you think?"

"I'm not sure you are. You're so methodical."

Then Cass was angry. "I'm sick and tired of this contemporary belief that any man who likes to spend as much as one evening a week home is too dull a breadwinner for any up-and-coming young female who's had such a modern education in science and sociology that she can turn on the radio all by herself! But I do love Jinny to a point of desperation, and however much she may like dancing-men and all these other wonder-boys that are too 'flexible' to be 'methodical,' yet in the long run she'll prefer somebody who's solid, like me or Bradd, and I don't intend to apologize even to *her* because I do brush my teeth and pay my bills!"

"Cass, you do love her, don't you! I'm glad. Do love her. If you ever for one minute wanted to love me or anything in me, then love me now in her!"

Her intensity frightened him; in relief he looked along the table at the placidity of Jinny. He was pleased to see how helpful to her Bradd was being. Bradd was talking low and fast, and smiling.

——Thank God, there's one friend I can trust to give her a good time. Bradd is as young as Eino and as mellow as Steve

Blackstaff, and I wouldn't wonder if he understood women better than some married men.

Jinny was so fortunate as to draw Bradd and the Penlosses for bridge, after dinner; she seemed to have a good time, and Cass was puzzled when she was silent to his query "Enjoy yourself?" during the extensive five-block drive back home and when, in the hall, she threw her silver-fox jacket at the indignant Cleo.

"Come sit on my knee," he said. Somehow that always seemed to him a soothing thing to suggest at these times of sulkiness.

She obeyed, but her head against his shoulder was rigid as a plaster model.

"What's trouble, baby?"

"*Nothing's* the trouble! Good *Heavens*, can't I be quiet without your thinking that——"

"No, sweet, you can't. What's the charge?"

"You seemed to be having a gorgeous time with your old girl-friend, that Grau woman."

She loved him enough to be jealous!

"I *was* having a gorgeous time with her. Do you know what we were talking about?"

"Me, I suppose."

"Don't be so egocentric. But matter of fact, we were. She wanted to hate you, but she's succumbed, like me. She loves you. I said you were a hawk, but she says you're a *lark*, among all these crows."

"Well, now, that's what I call something like it!" She kissed his bent forehead; kissed it again with "That second one is for Chris. I always liked larks better than any other bird; the meadow lark that makes you feel so fresh in early morning, and I want to go to England when the war's over, just to hear the skylark. And yet Chris does———"

She was tense again in his arms, and there was nothing funny, nothing of the bad-little-girl in her grave complaint:

"But you and she were so intimate. You've known her so long—you know so many things together that I never even heard of. I felt so shut out. You two have jokes and memories— maybe of all the romantic passes that you've made at her."

"Not so many and not serious. Why, Jin, you aren't jealous?"

"Yes, I am!"

"You, the crusader against jealousy?"

"I'm not a crusader against anything! I'm only jealous when anybody takes *any* of you away from me. Jealous when I realize, and God knows I try and forget it, that you've had so many experiences with women that I don't even know about."

"Haven't you had experiences?"

"Not really. Eino kissed me very nicely one evening, if you want to know. But when I think of Chris, and especially when I think of *Blanche*, that hell-cat, that female heel———"

"No, she wasn't."

"——then I get mad. You and your Blanche! Actually married to her! I can just see it and hear it: dark rooms, and she on your lap, too——"

She tried to bounce away, but not too violently, and he held her.

"——and you two lying and laughing in the darkness and breakfasting together in pajamas—oh, sometimes I get so furious I could kill both of you, and sometimes it just makes me disgusted and feeble. Cass Timberlane, you got to love me terribly, to make me forget all that."

"Do you want me to?"

"Yes, I do!"

"Do you love me, Jin?"

"Yes, I do. Damn it!"

"How much?"

"Very much. Very very much."

She forgot her distress, and not till late, when she had refused to return to her own room, on the ground that it was wolf-haunted, and lay curled serenely in his vast bed, did he recall from his criminal cases into what frightening shapes a resentment long hidden can twist itself.

27

HE HAD HEARD it often enough from his sister Rose, but he had never thoroughly understood that Jinny, with little occupation beyond asking Mrs. Higbee what she wanted her to want, would become idle, empty and bored.

Her chief employment was in war-work. With the others, she did her Red Cross detail and the entertainment of transient soldiers, but it took no initiative, not with such captains of enterprise as Diantha Marl and Zeta Umbaugh directing her how to address envelopes, how to make layettes for soldiers' wives. She worked conscientiously, but the tasks did not take one-tenth of her time, one-hundredth of her energy.

She had been elected to the Junior League, with its dances and mild benevolences, but she did not feel greatly at home in that self-constituted peerage of the Nice Women.

She read enough, but what to the factory draftsman had been stolen joy was merely grim, as an all-day entertainment.

For a month it had been luxury, after having been a working girl goaded by alarm clocks, to sleep till eleven and to breakfast on Mrs. Higbee's gossip and Cleo's antics with the golden string. Yet, before summer, Jinny was bored to the danger-point.

She hoped that when she had children, she would be

fulfilled, but there was no advice of their coming.

Now of all this Cass was more aware than Jinny knew, aware and bothered. He had realized from divorce cases that boredom can be a slimier serpent in Eden than cruelty or drunkenness, and he saw that snake writhing.

What had Blanche done to keep busy? Why hadn't she complained?

Oh, yes. He remembered now. She had.

And at that, Blanche had been nearer in age to Rose and the Bozards and more companionable, and she had enjoyed impressing Grand Republic by wearing backless dresses and being a great hostess. But when she had not been on parade, she too had been bored.

Cass wondered whether Jinny could, as Blanche decidedly could not, be influenced to take an interest in the technicalities of his work.

He gave her popular books about the law. He came home with stories—even he did not think they came out very excitingly—about what an old stickler Oliver Beehouse, chief counsel for the Wargates, was about rules of evidence, what battlers for justice Sweeney Fishberg and Nestor Purdwin were, and how irritated Judge Blackstaff was when Judge Flaaten referred to their new silk robes as their "overalls."

But he got no spark out of her till he told about the young soldier who had been sent up for carnal knowledge, at which she lighted up and warmly defended the young man without having listened to anything but the more esoteric features of the case. Cass discovered that she was as non-conformist in the judicial system as in chess. Her theory of verdicts was humanitarian and brief.

If a criminal was a nice-looking boy, you imposed the minimum sentence and then suspended it and gave him five dollars to go out and get another drink; and in civil litigation, the judge ought to sneak out into the corridor with the foreman of the jury and tell him to give judgment for all tenants, widows, and all persons over seventy, and against all landlords, employers, corporations, and bald-headed men who smoked cigars and called women "Sister."

"I don't think she'll ever be a rival of John Marshall," decided Judge Timberlane.

It was in early March that he came home to find a girl dancing with pride.

"Darling, know what's happened? Guess. You couldn't guess. Greg Marl—what nerve!—he wants me to go back to work for him. I will not! The idea! Maybe I will. Firing me—the best cartoonist *he'll* ever get! Well, I guess I was sort of bad. Maybe I'll be better now. But I was a pretty darn good cartoonist then, too!"

"Whoa! What is all this?"

"Greg called up. Two of his reporters and his new cartoonist have been drafted. He says he could just use a syndicated cartoon, but he'd rather keep the local touch, and he thinks———"

"Do you want to do this?"

"For a while, maybe. Yes, I think I do. Would you mind terribly?"

"We'll talk about it at dinner. Let me think about it first."

While he washed his hands, gargled, inspected the purity of his collar, put on his smoking jacket, peeped at the war news, called up about the coal, looked at the thermometer to see what time it was and looked at his wrist-watch to see how cold, wrote a check for the garbage-collector, glanced at the sports page, looked into his current detective story to find out whether it was due back at the public library, looked at the furnace, put on his slippers and then, with a feeling that this was his evening to be dignified, put on his shoes again, and then put on his slippers—through all his exigent before-dinner duties, the Judge was voraciously thinking about it first.

At dinner, Jinny spoke with more affection than belligerence:

"I'm not so proud and stuffy that I care especially about seeming independent of you, like Diantha Marl, but this is a shaky world now, and any girl of my age may have to earn her living yet, and she ought to be trained, and I've only started my training as a draftsman. I ought to be really good."

"I agree."

"I wish I could be of some help to you in the law, but that would take years, and I have made a start with drawing.

Honestly, it's all—well, anyway, it's partly because I do love
you and want you to respect me and not consider me just a
kept woman. Can't you see? I mean, work till God or whoever
it is that's responsible sends us some children. Couldn't I?"

"Dear child, you don't have to ask my permission!"

"But I wouldn't feel right——"

"I'm not your tyrant. If you want to do this enough, why,
it's decided. I'll admit I had hoped to have you waiting for
me at the end of the day, and all fresh, not a tired working
woman, but I know I have no right to demand that. So. When
do you go to work?"

"Well—yes—I know—but there is one thing. You see, Greg
wants me—and Hubbsy says I'd be fine at it—and Greg will
pay me more, but he wants me to do some reporting, too, and
that means the hours would be from noon till eight o'clock
in the evening—maybe later sometimes, but not very often.
How do you feel? I'm not quite sure."

He was a sunken man then, but he wanted to be polite.

"Look, Jin. If this were some critical war job, or if it were
going to lead to a blazing career for you, I'd be glad. I'd
merely be wondering how I could help. I know that more
and more millions of women will have to earn their livings
now, and I'm all for having every occupation—especially law
and medicine—open to them completely. But is it any part
of this theological doctrine of the economic independence of
women—this rare new doctrine that only goes back to the

Egyptian priestesses—that women *have* to have independent jobs, even if it cracks up the men they love—or at least the men that love them?"

"Don't look so utterly stricken! Of course I won't do it! Foul idea anyway, out in the rain all evening when I've got you and Mrs. H. and Cleo to come home to. Forget it!"

"But I don't want to forget it. You're right about the passing of the fond, foolish Little Woman. But look. You yourself say you need more training in art. You know this old fellow Bezique, that has art classes at the Junior College? I hear he's quite good—he wouldn't be here but for the war. Why don't you work with him?"

"Maybe I will. Now stop looking so woe-begone. Honestly, I don't insist on solving the entire feminist question right away!"

She rushed around the table to kiss his hair, which was gratifying not only to Cass, but to the highly observant Cleo. She was unusually pleased with him and with herself all evening, while he tried to look generous but masterful, and underneath it worried that, three months after their marriage, she could cheerfully have left him for her own world of young workers, and had been kept from it not by adhesion to him, but by the accident that she would have to work after dark.

He realized that from his first sight of her on the witness-stand, his zest in trying to win her had always been underlaid by the fear of losing her. He realized that in the civilization that he represented officially, if nine-tenths of the people suffered from occasional hunger and constant insecurity, the rest of the community, whom the nine-tenths labored to keep in contentment, suffered from boredom and futility. His problem was concerned not with one light-footed girl, but with all women everywhere in an age that puzzled and frightened him.

And Jinny—with enthusiasm she took up sketching and French literature at the Junior College, in Alexander Hamilton High School, and with more enthusiasm she dropped them, when she found that most of the students in the adult classes were youngish housewives who were more willing to fall in love with the teacher than to study.

But this failure did not so much affect Jinny as her discovery that she was a second Eleonora Duse.

An Assemblage of Husbands and Wives

SCOTT & JULIET ZAGO

SCOTT ZAGO, president of the Northern Insurance Brokerage Corporation of Grand Republic, Inc., suffered from nothing in life except his diagnosis of himself as a humorous fellow.

He was a profound yet ingratiating insurance-man, a collector of shotguns, a talented carver of duck-decoys, a powerful dahlia-grower, a pipe-smoker, a dog-lover, and a faithful husband, and he could quote accurately all the limericks about the Bishop of Birmingham, but he would put on an expectant smile and make puns. He telegraphed "Congratulations on the pappy event" to new fathers, provided they were of an insurable social standing, and to lawyers he said, "How's the great trial-liar today?"

He had a comic name for every acquaintance, and used it whenever he saw them. Loudly. "Lydia Pinkham" was his name for Dr. Drover; he shouted "How's Doc Pinkham this obsequious day?" even in the hushed pomposity of the Federal Club; and he introduced him to male strangers with, "Folks, I want you should meet Doc Pinkham. He'll take care of any female complaints you got in stock today."

He found that Abbott Hubbs was born in Oklahoma, and he gurgled invariably, "How's the oil wells today?" As he was never quite sure whether Oklahoma was to be regarded as Western or Southern, he added either, "Brethren, we will now absquatulate together and sing 'Dixie,' " or "Brethren, we will now absquatulate together and sing 'Home on the Range,' " according to his geographic mood.

But Scott Zago was magnificent as a husband.

Juliet and he made love rapturously and unwearyingly;
they giggled at each other's jokes, and whenever they tried
to quarrel, they broke down and laughed. They had two jolly
children. They called their fake half-timber cottage "The Dolls'
House," and it had a pool table and good beds and two-thirds
of a set of *The Harvard Classics*.

Their amorous delight was only increased by the fact that
Scott was fifty now and Juliet only thirty-seven. She had been
married to him when she was twenty, but she was a chronic
child-wife, and would still be at seventy, if God should blessedly
preserve her as a proof of how unnecessary is intelligence to
romance and fine cookery.

She flapped her pretty little fat hands and beamed like a
fat round little baby and did a fantastic little toddling dance
with her little round feet, and simpered, "Honya, I dess tan't
understan' all de biggy, wisey gwowed-up talk that oo big
mans is saying, but 'ittle Juley can shake up a cuddly 'ittle
Clover Club while oo is doing it."

Her favorite endearment was this "Honya," and she ran
to the infantile in clothes; she wore ringlets, with piratical
kerchiefs flaunting over them, large pink hats, and dirndls and
flat strapped baby-shoes and chains hung with jingling silver
charms. And she poked people in the ribs and squealed at
their wincing.

Juliet was not only infantile but cultured. Every month she
took from the library a volume on some branch of science like

astrology, New Thought, gland-therapy, Freud's translations
from the original four-letter words, or the hidden inner
secrets of Tibet, and with the touching zeal of the young
savant, she quoted the first two paragraphs of each book to
all newcomers. Naturally, like Mrs. Higbee across the way,
she believed in numerology and palmistry, but she had one
superstition that Mrs. Higbee did not share: she put perfume
behind her ears. Also, she never listened to information and
let it go at that. She had to make a witty comment, in the
belief that she was easing the social way for large and surly
professors of biophysics or Burmese history.

Most men knew instinctively that the way to shut up
Juliet was to kiss her. For so plump a girl, she did get more
incidental kissing from entirely tangential gentlemen! They
were deceived, however, if they thought they were going
farther.

After parties, she reported to Scott on the assorted kisses
she had received during the evening, and he tried, under her
direction, to imitate the several categories, as: the butterfly
kiss, the solid brother-in-law, the allergic-to-lipstick, the
short interrogative, the long interrogative, and the vampire-
minatory, meant for ravishing. They bounced around in bed
and laughed a good deal during these imitations, and ended
up in an innocent frenzy which would have astonished serious
citizens like Judge Timberlane, who thought the Zagos were
fools, or sentimentalists like Young Mrs. Timberlane, who

thought they were triflers.

The Zagos came near to justifying all such anachronisms as insurance, cocktails, and houses with shingles imitating thatch.

28

FROM A CAMP in South Carolina, Eino Roskinen wrote to Jinny, "I'm a corporal, I shall be a sergeant, I'll never be a comm. officer, I ask too many flip questions. Now you are married and a woman of leisure, why don't you finally go out for the Lit Theater, you have looks and spirit, tho I doubt whether you have enough inner discipline to take direction, why not try? Furioso the Finn."

She read it aloud to Cass, and said with marked doubt, "What do you think?"

"Not bad. I believe you'd be good at dramatics, and you'd have a lot of fun. The Masquers have had a good reputation, more than ten years now. I couldn't ever imagine myself getting up there before a lot of people and pretending I was a king or a butler——"

"You do every day. On the bench."

"Maybe. Anyway, I'd be delighted."

"I wonder when the next try-out is. I wonder what the play will be."

"The play is *Skylark*, by Samson Raphaelson; it's the last play of the season; the reading will be at Della Lent's next Thursday evening, at eight-fifteen."

"How come you always know everything?"

"Why, I read the papers!"

Rice and Patty Helix were small and active and rather untidy. They were the paid semi-professional managers of the Masquers: directors, scene-designers, ticket-peddlers, borrowers of stage furniture. They were devoutly married, and they were either older than they looked, or more wrinkled than their age. They talked, rapidly and enthusiastically, about "Gene" O'Neill, moonlight-blue lights, and tormentors, and they could make a wind-machine out of an old bicycle, a marble Venus out of a Quaker Oats box.

They had acted professionally, but no one seemed to know just when or where; they said that they had given it up because it was so hard to get engagements together; and before they had found a career in the little theaters, they had tried chicken-farming and clairvoyance and being lecture agents in Texas. Late at night, they were seen running hand in hand. The Boone Havocks received them as somewhere between schoolteachers and bartenders.

But at best they were the upper servants of Della Wargate Lent, who supported the Masquers.

The plays were rehearsed at the various houses of the cast and finally presented in the high-school auditorium, but the try-outs were held at Della's abode, which was by no means the largest house in Grand Republic but had the largest drawing-room, all filled with gilt pianos and majolica.

For casting during war-time the Helixes had enough women among whom to choose, but they had to drag in young men from shops and factories and offices. There were present for the reading of *Skylark* only eleven men from whom to pick the six male characters of the play, and one of these was cross-eyed though spirited, but for the four women characters there were twenty-seven candidates, ranging from fourteen and sulky to sixty-three and still artistic.

All twenty-seven wanted to play Mrs. Kenyon, the lead.

Cass told himself that Jinny stood out among the others as the loveliest yet the most efficient. It was not the fantastic or the playful or the flirtatious Jinny who was here tonight, but a business-like young woman in a snuff-colored suit, a crisp scarf, a small brown hat.

They all tried it, but only two were chosen for a second reading of the part of Mrs. Kenyon: Jinny and Letty Vogel, wife of the county agricultural agent. Mrs. Vogel was three or four years older than Jinny, a thin figure in almost-shabby black, a thin, pale, anxious face with eyes too large.

——That poor Vogel girl. Seems to have a fancy for the theater, but not a chance against Jinny—all fire and ivory.

They tried again, and Jinny's reading was like crystal, her voice warm, every syllable clear—and all syllables exactly alike. Letty Vogel seemed tired and her voice was slightly shaky, but as she read she was not Mrs. Vogel at all but the character in the play: wilful, gay, a little cheap and utterly tragic, a wisecracking angel.

——Now, now, now! This is awful! Mrs. Vogel is superb and poor Jinny, she can't act at all! She reads like a schoolgirl.

And so Cass loved her, passionately and protectively, because she could not act.

Della Lent and the Helixes whispered together, and Rice Helix announced:

"Folks, both these final readings were simply swell, and we all know what a fine, hard-working actress Letty has always shown herself to be in a number of plays, but for this particular society part, we feel that Mrs. Timberlane is not only the best, but golly, what a high-class best, and we honest to God believe that with the careful direction we intend to give her, she will put it all over the original performance that Gertrude Lawrence gave on Broadway. Welcome to our midst, Jinny; you sure are a great addition to the local arts. And now, folks, before we bust up, let's put back the chairs in order that Mrs. Lent has been so generous and, to not intentionally make a pun, has lent us for our little try-out, and I sure am real proud of the showing that *all* you folks have made this evening, not a bad egg in the basket, as the fellow says, and don't be discouraged, if at first you don't succeed, try, try again, and don't forget, put back your own chair where it was, we thank you."

The just Judge was staring, wanting to protest, wanting Jinny to protest, and loving her passionately because she did not know how bad an actress she was.

The first rehearsal of *Skylark* was held in the Cyclopean basement of Cass's Bergheim, with cordwood and ash-cans and shotgun-shell boxes for furniture. The first half of it, Cass did not see, and he was regretful, as he had already forgotten that the flowering of Jinny's dramatic genius might not be so showy an exhibit. But he had to go off to address a dinner of the local Junior Chamber of Commerce: "Eat at six, inspiration at seven-fifteen, home at eight-thirty, all come, special treat this time, Hizzoner Cass Timberlane on 'The Cultural and Architectural Future of Our City.'"

As a judge, Cass was expected to know everything, and as a knower of everything, he was expected to hold forth about it publicly, and as a public forth-holder, he was expected to be a medicinal but tasty digestive tablet after the chicken croquettes and brick ice cream. Oratory is the dearest treasure of the American male as alimony is of the American female.

Tonight, Cass was prophetic. He said that some time the City Planning Commission might really have power, and firmly discourage the citizens of Grand Republic in their constant ambition to erect a two-story red-brick bowling-alley, with offices for chiropractors, between a ten-story limestone bank and the City Hall. The Junior Chamber of Commerce, composed of men under thirty-six who expected some day to belong to the Senior C. of C. and have public esteem, were slightly shocked by Judge Timberlane's communism. They whispered together that "He oughtn't to pull such impractical and uncommercial ideas on a forward-looking group that are expected to mold the ideals for the new age of Business and the American Way of Life."

But his adjectives, his grammar, and the authority in Cass's voice made them forgive him, and at the end they did that mystic rite, that flapping together of portions of their anatomies, like locusts scraping their wing-cases, which is known as applause, and six of them invited him out for a drink.

The Judge thought that these young husbands were strangely desirous of staying away from their wives, on their rare evening out, and after listening to a talking-dog story, he got away from them and hastened home for the end of the rehearsal.

——Keen to see her work. Of *course* Jinny is better than Letty Vogel. Mrs. Vogel is too pretentious and arty. I much prefer to have Jinny keep her voice clear and melodious, and not crack it with all sorts of attempts to be emotional. She'll be wonderful.

——Well, anyway, she'll be all right—as good as any of 'em.

——She could be a great actress or a great anything, if she put her mind to it. Her mind is so flexible.

——Love to think of her hair—the way when you see it from behind, it's scarcely hair at all but some finer fabric. It's dark and sleek at the top, but it runs down into waves that you want to follow with your hand.

——So much!

The author of *Skylark*, who presumably thought that he had written high comedy, would have been astonished to learn that, as enacted by Fred Nimbus, it was a Hollywood demonstration of sultry tropic passions.

Cass came down the dark stairs to his basement and stood to watch Fred trying out "business" with Jinny. He thought that this business of manhandling Jinny was altogether too businesslike. He had no initiation into theatricals nor into midnight studio-parties; he resented her being mauled.

Fred was, under the directive eye of Mr. Helix but apparently not needing that expert encouragement, slowly kissing Jinny, her head back, sidewise and helpless; kissing her long and closely, and letting his tight-pressing hand slip from her shoulder to her breast.

Then Cass came into the lighted basement all in one piece, and Cass spoke.

"Nimbus! You may quit that now!"

Nimbus quit.

"Helix, it is not necessary for this fellow to act like a thug in a bawdy-house in order to rehearse a play."

Poor Rice Helix trembled. "Are you trying to bully me?"

"Of course! But I think that's all the outburst I'll need. Go on with the rehearsal now, and you be a good boy, Nimbus.

Good night, everybody. I'm going upstairs and read the Book of Mormon. Isn't it curious now that I've never read the Book of Mormon? Good night."

And he did read it. He was not much afraid of what Jinny would be coming up to say—not more afraid than of the black plague, or indictment for malfeasance.

When she did come, after the rehearsal, and started with the inevitable, "Well, of all the——" he plunged.

"Dry up, Jinny. I know the line. Ridiculously jealous husband—crass outsider interfering with the arts. Will you answer this: Fred had been pawing you pretty extensively before I came, hadn't he? Huh? Hadn't he?"

She half giggled. "He was kind of exploratory."

"And I'm not going to have my wife declared a general area for exploration, with dog-teams and native bearers. If you'd slapped Fred, as you should have, I wouldn't have had to make a spectacle of myself. Remember that, the next time you go and get modern and courageous on me, will you?"

She tried her best, with:

"You must admit you were rather middle-class and reactionary and——Shouting and bullying and carrying on that way, when if you'd been a man of the world, or believed in the ability of the modern woman to take care of herself, you'd just of tapped Fred lightly on the shoulder and said gaily, 'Ease it up, ole boy.' You know. Something like that. Something—uh—suave."

He laughed at her, and she looked unconvinced of her own advice.

"Jinny! I know I was noisy, but both of you were asking for it. You didn't think he was measuring you for a raincoat, did you? Raincoats don't fit that tight. So! Kiss me."

She grumbled only a little, and she kissed him with surprising devotion.

But he knew that it would not last. He had succeeded for a few minutes in being masterful, melodramatic, insulting, and all the other things that a sedentary professional man, married to so attractive and curiosity-ridden a girl as Jinny Marshland, ought to be, but he was not easy in the role.

29

HE WAS NOT unduly intrusive on the other rehearsals, but merely looked on a moment when he called to drive her home. He was pleased to see how patiently Jinny was working; her part letter-perfect after two weeks, taking direction, merely arguing a little with Rice Helix when he insisted that a Perfect Lady expressed her emotions by showing all her teeth and wriggling her fingers as though a bug was crawling over them. He was even more pleased that she was seeing new friends here: Letty Vogel—who, as she could not play the lead, earnestly built the scenery, Bernice Claywheel, wife of the Superintendent of Schools, Dick and Francia Wolke, the young rabbi, Ned Sarouk, and his wife Nelly, and Jay Laverick, the flour-miller, the only member of the Federal Club besides Frank Brightwing who recognized the Masquers.

Cass was puzzled by Fred Nimbus's intentions. Now, whenever it was Fred's appalling duty to embrace Jinny, he did so lightly, with tapping fingers. But a sour thought occurred to Cass: that Fred might be taking advantage of that most sound and ancient technique of the child—knowing that the safest time to steal the jam is when the family is ashamed of itself for having yelled at it for having stolen the jam. It had never quite come to Judge Timberlane that there are men outside jail who make it a careful and well-funded business to seduce all the pretty women in sight, and that against their expert business-methods, an innocent householder is helpless.

"Oh, quit being so ingeniously jealous and let the girl have a good time," the ardent husband rebuked himself.

He noticed then that it was not the pulpy Nimbus but the gallant Mr. Jay Laverick with whom Jinny laughed in corners and, between scenes, danced the rhumba.

Jay Laverick was the town drunk, the town clown, the town tragedy. He was a widower of forty, and he had inherited the Laverick Flour Mills. He was always polite when he was drunk, but unfortunately he was almost always drunk when he was polite. No dance at the Heather Country Club was canonical without the presence of Jay Laverick, emitting the rebel yell and saying to some aged (and delighted) matron, "Madame, does my reason totter on her throne, or are you actually Queen Elizabeth the First?" When people said, as people immensely did say, "Poor Jay is drinking himself to death," it was not irritably but with affection.

In person he was not the round and beloved comic Irishman but the sallow and villainous baronet, with a thin dark face and a long black mustache. It was to be credited to his inherited Irish constitution that, against the normal rule, excess of alcohol had not impaired his powers of love-making.

He was the best flour-salesman north of Minneapolis, and usually sober in the office.

Not till the rehearsals had Jay and Jinny met, except in crowds. She liked his bitter capering, his tragic flourishes, his lightly touching hands, professional touch of the surgeon, the pianist, the healing saint, or the satyr.

Cass was uncomfortable again—and tired of it.

He told himself: here is this poor girl, business-like in sweater and slacks, sexless as a nurse, working hard to produce something beautiful in a blacked-out world. No gauds and gimcracks; just a sweater and gray manly trousers. But——Did Jinny know how fetching, how conspicuously womanly, she was in a tight sweater?

——Of course she knows it! All women know tilings like that. Their capital is modesty, but how they do squander it.

——Of course she never even thinks of such a thing, you Pharisee. You love her, don't you? Well, then! How can you insult her with such suspicions?

——Oh, nuts! Whoever said there wasn't a lot of wanton in every good woman?

——Well, I don't like your using the word "wanton" and thinking evil of——

——Look here! The monarch who sniffed "Honi soit qui mal y pense" was not of a notably moral character. There's nothing shameful about suspecting that a girl is not displeased when she knows that she's stirring up a few normal biological reactions by all her beauties lily-white. You wouldn't want her to be unworldly to a point of imbecility, would you?

——Sure! I wouldn't mind a bit! Friend, my worship of her *is* unworldly, it has a little of the divine; to me, she is all womanhood, out of every time and place.

——Yes, yes. As you say. But I do wish she wouldn't so perpetually get herself ambushed by Nimbus and Jay. Why can't she talk to a really nice fellow, like Frank Brightwing?

Though Cass saw less of Frank Brightwing than of Roy Drover or Bradd Criley, there was no one in Grand Republic whom he more warmly liked. At thirty-eight, Frank was what is known as a successful real-estate man; he dealt not in harp-playing and the design of angels' pinions, as was his nature and as his name quaintly hinted, but in Lot 13, Block 7; in 2-c garg., r.w., h & c; in abutments and amortizations and easements. He had a plush wife and three medium-grade children, but his excitement was in the Masquers, and if a play ran for two weeks, then for twelve nights he went on believing that the hero was as courageous and the heroine as voluptuous and the comic maid as funny as they said they were.

Being the worst of actors, as is likely with such a worshiper of acting, Frank had to be ticket-seller, stage-carpenter, and assistant electrician, and he was content with life when they let him hold the book at rehearsals.

Being, remarkably, also the worst of critics, he believed and he told Cass that they were lucky to have Jinny playing Mrs. Kenyon instead of Letty Vogel.

"But I thought Mrs. Vogel showed a lot of talent."

"Oh. no, Cass. You laymen don't understand these technical problems. Letty is what we in the theatrical world call 'fuzzy,' while Jinny is sure of herself—a real type. Oh, she's out of this world, Cass."

Over morning coffee, Cass said cheerfully, "Well, Jinny, I guess our friend Nimbus has laid off you."

"Oh, absolutely. Sweet Freddy, he's such an obvious lug that he never gets far."

"You kind of liked him."

"Sure I did. I like all rats. They usually know how to kid like nobody's business, and they have a line. It's their job."

In English, she meant, "Certainly. I like all scoundrels. They are full of amiable banter." Her normal use of the swing-age argot had been increased by association with the violently artistic Masquers, but Judge Timberlane understood much of her dialect, and love enlightened where understanding staggered, and increasingly he used the dialect himself.

"Anyway, I wouldn't ever be half so jealous of Nimbus as of Jay Laverick. I imagine you women find him a dashingly tragic figure."

"I'll say! And how! And has he fallen for me!"

"Don't take it too seriously. Jay is a decent fellow with men, but his record of falling for every female from six to ninety-six is rather extensive."

"Now don't go and tell me you're going to be really jealous

even of your old friend Jay!"

"How could I be? Ho, ho!"

"Sweetie pie, that's the falsest-sounding stage-laugh I ever heard. Now quit it!"

——I told you so! What did you ever bring it up for? You knew just how far you'd get, didn't you?

——I couldn't help it.

Rice and Patty Helix knew their strange art of coaxing people to give up being themselves and become someone else, not so pleasant. The play, when it was presented at the high-school auditorium, actually was a play and not an amateur reading. Cass found himself for moments believing that Jinny was this flashing wife of an acrobatic advertising man and not his own simple girl.

At the opening-night party afterward, at Della Lent's, Cass noted the following expert dramatic criticisms:

Bradd Criley, lawyer: "Honest, boy, she was wonderful. Even I didn't know there was so much fire in her."

Frank Brightwing, real estate & loans: "She was ten times better than Gertrude Lawrence in the role. I never saw Miss Lawrence in it, but I know."

Mrs. Gerald Lent, husband-supporter: "She wasn't bad at all, Cass. But was that Nimbus lousy! *And* Jay!"

Mrs. John William Prutt, spiritual, social and domestic adviser in banking: "Mr. Prutt and I thought she was very fine, Judge. I do hope her playacting and the practising don't interfere with her war-work and the home."

Roy Drover, physician & surgeon: "It wasn't a bad show, and I thought Jinny was as good as any of 'em."

Norton Trock, banker: "Why, Cass, she was simply too, too divine. She was all right."

Fred Nimbus, radio artist: "Honestly, Judge, I never could of put it over like I did if it hadn't been for Mrs. Timberlane's loyal support."

Jay Laverick kept sober through the rehearsals, the six performances of the play, and Della's first-night party. He did not break down and become natural man till the party at the end of the run, a gaudy one at Madge Dedrick's. Champagne. Though not imported. But that night he whooped and held Jinny's hands and fulsomely kissed her.

Cass was near enough to hear her say "You quit that!" in a manner so vicious that Jay released her. She walked over to Cass and groaned, "Sweet darling, if you ever catch me seeming to encourage any man again, you beat me."

"I don't think I'll need to."

She was of a forgiving nature, for before the party was over, she was dancing with Jay, and painlessly.

Bradd Criley muttered to Cass, "For a nice fella, Jay can be such a jackass. It takes Jinny to handle him. What a girl!"

When Cass and Jinny came home at three, she kissed him

boldly. He was glad that, no matter how other men might flatter her, it was to him that she turned for true affection.

At dawn, he heard Cleo crying. When he left the sleeping Jinny and went down to the little cat, she shivered and nestled against him and seemed afraid.

The *Banner's* strictly favorable review of *Skylark*, written by Pandora Avondene, admitted that each actor was either Compelling, Professional, Brilliant, or at least Satisfying. A second account in the paper on Sunday reviewed the play as a Social Event and, whether by accident or through the malice of Abbott Hubbs, wound up with a gasping announcement.

It revealed that Mr. Fred Nimbus, who had shown such Sterling Qualities in *Skylark*, and who had been writing and playing in a series of radio stories about the Marines, over Station KICH, which had been so powerful that he was credited with having gained many recruits, now felt that he did not desire to wait and be drafted, and he was going to enlist in the Marines himself.

The town cheered. But Mr. Fred Nimbus did not cheer. This was all news to him.

He called up Cass, along with other local rulers, and cried that he was being railroaded into the service; that Cass must do something about it; that while he was zealous to go as soon as his number came up, he had first to settle his affairs. He did not exactly have a mother to support, but he did have a maiden aunt.

"They say that if I don't go in voluntarily, the Marines will force me to. That's outrageous and undemocratic!" whimpered Fred.

"Nonsense. Who says they will?" growled Cass.

"Oh, everybody does."

In a way, everybody did. There was very little masculine tenderness in town for Mr. Nimbus. But a number of maidens who had thrilled to Fred's manly crooning of his own poetic prose came to serenade him at his boarding-house. There was no balcony for Fred to come out on, like Juliet or a young Mussolini, but he mounted a folding stepladder-chair on the front stoop, and addressed them:

"Dear girls, you move me more than I can attempt to say. It is to defend the virtue and happiness of girls like you that I want to enlist, and I have arranged to do so tomorrow morning, Room 307, the County Court House, and any of you who care to come, be sure and be there before ten. I don't know why you should care for my poor autograph, but if you'll bring your little books, I'll be glad to do what I can. I am so happy that at last I have been able to arrange my affairs, and I can now rush where the fighting is thickest."

Next morning one hundred and sixteen females, mostly under nineteen, filled the corridor and cheered and wept when Fred appeared at the door of Room 307, looking scared, with a marine sergeant, looking derisive.

He later denied the sergeant's canard that he had applied for office work at Marine Headquarters.

Jinny came giggling in to inform Cass that Fred had telephoned wanting to say good-bye to her privately.

"I'm going to stay right with you all the time he's here! I won't have him bothering you!"

"Don't worry, darling. He's not coming. I told him to go jump in the lake," said Jinny, in a refined manner.

An Assemblage of Husbands and Wives

BENJAMIN & PETAL HEARTH

AS A MEMBER of that earnest sect, the Cross and Crown Covenanters, Benjamin Hearth had read numerous tracts about wives with quarter-loaves and half-candles and starving children who waited shivering at home for drunken husbands, usually coachmen; helpful tracts written in England in 1880 and still circulated in forward-looking America in the 1940's. Benjamin loved to read and to distribute such tracts, and it never occurred to him that in these liberal days, the sexes of the drunks could be switched.

He was the junior partner in Hearth & Hearth, the Friendly Morticians, once doing the finest and most sympathetic undertaking-business in Grand Republic but of late eclipsed by that less artistic outfit, the Larson Funeral Home and Byzantine Interdenominational Chapel with the Revolving Cross. He was fat, and fond of beer and sauerkraut, which afterward he repented, in fits of indigestion and remembered piety.

His wife, Petal, was a slight, spectacled, prim-looking woman. She was also a dipsomaniac, a drunk and a dirty drunk, but to the end Benjamin never acknowledged this.

He loved her and she him. Each orgy he accepted as something that had never occurred before and certainly never could occur again, and, after hearing her regrets and wails and audible hair-tearing, he felt himself a sneak to have believed that it had really occurred this time. Probably her stomach. Or her laudable grief over the sickness of the second child of Cousin Mary, who lived in Indiana.

Benjamin was, in a genteel and Covenanter way, convivial; he loved society dinners at six o'clock, with pickled peaches, and grace said, and a game of mah jong afterwards—but never the immoral cards, which lead to atheism and vice. When Petal married him—she had been substitute telephone girl for the legal firm of Beehouse, Criley and Anderson, and later a clerk in the linen department of Tarr's Emporium—she had stepped into a degree of social prestige beyond her experience.

She had always liked hot gin better than Benjamin could have guessed, but economy and the necessity of working all day had prevented her specializing in it. All of Benjamin's snobbish friends—most of them had detached houses, and one was a professional man, Orlo Vay the optician—said that Petal was quite the lady, with an inspiration in trimming hats.

They did not know her peculiar gift and betrayal: when she was drunk, she could still sound sober on the telephone.

Not much was suspected till, a couple of years after her marriage, within one fortnight she had begged off from three different suppers to which Benjamin and she had been invited, and one that they were giving, always on the grounds that "Some close relatives of mine have just arrived unexpectedly from Indiana, this afternoon."

Her circle felt that that was too many Indiana relatives too unexpectedly. George Hame, the court attaché, an enterprising and agnostic fellow, went creeping up to the Hearth nest after one of these disconcerting refusals and, peeping under a curtain, saw Petal not entertaining anybody at all, from Indiana or elsewhere, but flopped on a couch, apparently snoring, while Benjamin sat by in distress, smoothing his chin.

George reported that to him it looked as though she had "passed out cold."

Benjamin knew that she had had a drink, "for a bad cold or maybe it's intestinal flu," but in a blindness of prospering love he had been fooled by the sobriety with which she had told him that she had not felt well enough to go out, and had invented the Indiana kin to save people's feelings.

He was baffled by the famine of social invitations which now set in.

Petal had enough of the sot's admirable caution to arrange her best escapes at times when Benjamin was off on funeral duty. But with the splendid new friends whom she met in barrooms, now that she had the leisure and the funds, she became less cautious and more thirsty. Once, when she had got home safely from a cocktail-joint in time to get Benjamin's supper and found a note saying that he would be on duty out on a farm all evening, she felt unusually free and happy. She laughed and put on a negligee. She took out her private gin bottle, finished the gin, hid the bottle again, felt dizzy, again found the bottle, and was amazed that it was empty.

In fluttering negligee, she ran out of the house, across the street through traffic, past two red lights, and into a liquor store.

On her way home, with bottle, a policeman stopped her. He hinted that he thought she might have escaped from an asylum, and such was the shock to her that she screamed and sat on the curb, weeping. A young man who had been following her came up to say suavely, "It's my sister, Officer. She's had a kind of delirious fever. I'll get her home."

The crowd laughed at the spectacle of the drunken woman being half carried by the young man, while she wept all over him in gratitude. He did get her into her house, into bed. What could she do then in gratitude but throw her arms about him and kiss him?

The patient Benjamin, at his labors in a windy farm-house, knew nothing of this, ever.

His first enlightenment was later, when he came home from what he felt to have been a "real beautiful funeral," and found water soaking through the dining-room ceiling. Above, in the bathtub, naked and entirely drunk, singing "The Red Light Rag," was his Petal.

The severest thing he said to her afterward was "Dearie, promise me you won't let anybody tempt you to take a drink again. You're such an unsuspicious little silly, sweetheart, that you don't realize what this horrid liquor can do. Promise Benny you'll never touch it again, dearie."

"Oh, I promise, I promise—oh, God, my head!" sobbed the damp Petal.

In sobriety, Petal was a woman most ladylike in her syntax, one who knew that you must never call perspiration sweat and that to refer to a pregnancy by any verbal gesture less refined than "the coming happy event" was a coarse and whorish thing, not to be permitted in Evangelical circles. Yet a week after the bathtub, when George Hame had with some curiosity invited them in for chicken à la king, she slipped out to the garage with George, had five amazingly quick drinks, and went back to turn upon Benjamin and pronounce in a cool, amiable, very sober and interested voice, "Jesus, what a fat——you are. The trouble with you is, your mother took in washing, and the way the cop on the beat used to pay her for it was——So don't ever try and pull any of your Sunday-school stuff on me.

Benjamin was very sorry when she spoke thus. He explained to everybody that she didn't mean it at all. She was just nervous.

He knew now. Yet such was his love for this woman, who was so refined and superior, that he would not permit himself to know what he knew.

Once it was clear that he understood, she became more careless, and he tended her like a nurse in a private mad house. He cleaned the vomit from her shoes, he changed the sheets when she had fouled their bed, and when she struck him, though he was a massive man, he wailed, "Oh, don't do that, dearie! I didn't mean to make you cross."

She had developed this new and fascinating trait of hitting people, hitting them quietly and very painfully. She did it once at their pastor's house, and that ended any possible resurrection of the Hearths' social career.

She blamed Benjamin; she said that people could not endure his vulgar belching. On that theme she shouted for an hour. When he tried to stop her, she shut herself in the locked guestroom, where she had stored half a case of gin. Sometimes she screamed at him through the door, sometimes out of the window at awed neighborhood children.

Benjamin took to staying away from the business, to guard her. They became hermits, the lonelier in sitting together spying on each other. He knew that she was thinking how she could kill him.

His older brother, Robert, head of the firm, told him that he would have to have Petal locked up in an institution, or quit the business.

He quit.

He went to work in the Wargate plant, on war materials, satisfied with the job of running a band-saw all day, except when he thought of Petal's misfortunes. People did not understand her.

For two days, at home, she could get no liquor at all, because he had given her no money and the stores did not trust her. Then she found an old bachelor who was amenable.

When she set fire to their house, Benjamin did have to send her to a private sanitarium. He lives now in a hall-room and cooks his own meals on a kerosene stove, because it takes most of what he earns to keep her in the sanitarium. In his room there is but one ornament: the bridal picture of Petal, in white satin, unstained and lovely. Benjamin sits and looks at the picture or at a newspaper all evening.

The landlady lends him the newspaper. He feels that he cannot afford to buy one.

He says that when his dear wife recovers from her mental

shock, which she sustained upon the death of a beloved relative, they are going out into the country to rent a farm and grow flowers. Benjamin particularly loves all flowers that look like white satin, lovely and unstained.

30

THERE WAS AS YET no wartime gasoline rationing in the Middlewest, and they had driven, for the beginning of their summer vacation, north to Ely and the deep woods of the Arrowhead canoe country, up to Grand Portage, which in the 1790's was the castle of the French and British fur traders. You can still see the ghosts of the voyageurs, in capotes and sashes, toting their canoes at twilight.

They drove back along the vast bright palisades of the North Shore of Lake Superior to Grand Marais, and up the Gunflint Trail to a dark lake curtained with pines, where they paddled under a great sunset that made their voices cleave together in fear of loneliness, beneath that threatening majesty.

They sat now in their car on the Skyline Boulevard, looking far down on the city of Duluth and the blue-and-silver vastness of Lake Superior, that blazing shield of inland ocean. Across this narrowed end of the lake, the Wisconsin shore rose into hills, and on the Minnesota side, to the eastward, the cliffs behind the smooth uplands of the Hollister Hills were cut by ravines meant for a western Rip van Winkle. The air was thinner and more resolute than the earthy odor of their own inland cornfields and valley thickets.

Jinny mused, "It's so exciting and lovely, Duluth, between

hills and the sea. I've loved the whole trip—Grand Marais—the Riviera towns must lie against the hills like that. And you've been so much fun, such a whale of a paddler and fly-caster. I'm much obliged to you, sir."

"Best time since our honeymoon, I think. Look at that ship down there, headed east."

An ore boat, huge as a liner, was hull-down on the milk-white eastern horizon; it flickered in straying sun and was presently out of sight, all but its trail of smoke.

Cass mused, "Tomorrow it will be at the Soo. I always think there's a kind of sadness in the passing of ships that we might have taken to ports with domes and towers and bazaars—and Asian birds. But if I were here alone in Duluth, I'd be imagining that the steamer was sailing off with *you*, at sunset, and I not on it."

"Look! Here I am. I'm not on it!"

"I'm glad."

Silver flaws shivered across the lake, and now another great red ore ship, westward-bound, was coming into sight, with its high pilot's deck and its coal-filled belly for the furnaces of Minneapolis and the Dakotas. Their pensiveness was gone in more prosaic cheerfulness.

"What a lot of coal there must be in that hold for somebody to shovel," considered Cass.

"Look, pie. Let's move to Duluth. More fun than Grand Republic."

"Nope. It's too large. Over a hundred thousand people. That's terrible—bad as Chicago or London, almost. Even Grand Republic is too big. I like a place where you can know people."

"And I like a place where there are some people you can know!"

"Now, now, you know plenty in G.R., and you know doggone well you know you know plenty. Now don't you!"

"Oh, yes, some nice ones. Rose and Francia and Lyra and Valerie, my lively niece, and Nelly Sarouk and the Fliegends and Bradd and Frank and Rev Gadd and Tracy and Chris and the Blackstaffs." She meditated, and added musingly, "And Jay Laverick."

"I could do without quite so much of Jay."

"Oh, do be fair to him. Of course he's something of a pest, but he's such a queer, lonely specimen—he needs sympathy— and I'm sure he admires you much more than he does me."

"He must admire me a lot then. Oh, let's forget Jay."

"Let's. . . . Poor Jay."

The ore boat, thrice whistling, demanded that the Aerial Bridge be lifted for its entrance to St. Louis Bay. And that night they heard, from their hotel in Duluth, the fog horn— sounding first like a moaning calf, then like giants moving their giant furniture.

Fog and snorting tug-boats, thought Cass, and great ships upon the waters! Some day Jinny and he would know them in

Sydney Harbor and Portsmouth and Rotterdam.

They took, for the rest of the hot summer, a lakeside cottage on the north shore of Dead Squaw Lake. It was seven hundred and fifty feet from the cottage shared by those professional bachelors, Bradd Criley and Jay Laverick.

This tiny summer colony on Dead Squaw derisively called itself Mushrat City. There were a dozen yellow or white shacks, running mostly to porches, bath-houses, boat-houses, and wooden-floored tents in which Junior and Sister slept.

Only one of them had a bar, and this was the Laverick-Criley establishment. Inside, there were four cots, and a room containing a divan-bed, ornamented with a silken coverlet and not visibly used.

In the colony were the Pennlosses, the Drovers, the Bright-wings, the Beecher Filligans, Vincent Osprey, that forward-looking young lawyer and his backward-looking wife Cerise, and Scott and Juliet Zago, and into it dipped scores of visitors from the nearby Yacht Club.

The true American is active even in his inactivities. The Mushrat City colonists did not lie indolent watching the slow tides of the water rise and merge with slow-revolving sky till heaven and earth were all one sun-hued dream. No, they swam, they dove, they sailed, they fished for bass, they drove into town for the movies, they played bridge, they cooked steak and fish at outdoor grills, they danced to the radio, they drank considerably and made love cautiously.

Grand Republic was not a singularly philanderous community, but at Mushrat City the more earnest strayers had classic surroundings: deep pine woods, skiffs filled with cushions, and long plank piers on which lounged the nymphs and fauns of Thessaly, with a few satyrs. Yet among them all, only Jay Laverick was ever assailed as an amorist, and his friend Bradd Criley defended him by insisting that Jay merely flirted a little to cover up his one passionate ideal, liquor.

At the neighboring Yacht Club, Dr. Roy Drover said to Bradd, fairly publicly, "So Jay isn't a chaser, eh? I don't suppose you are, either!"

"I certainly am not."

"What about Gillian Brown and Sabine the Gold-digger?"

"Well, what about them?"

"Weren't they seen leaving you two fellows shack at dawn on Wednesday?"

"Not by me they weren't. Did you see them?"

"Not personally."

"Then shut up about it, Roy. I can tell you confidentially, it's a lie!"

"Okay by me, Bradd. It's no skin off my neck, anyway."

The Council of Elders, in the club bar, agreed that Dr. Drover had been neatly answered. They went so far as to declare that, whatever Jay did, Bradd was completely chaste: that is, naturally, he had a few lady friends in St. Paul or Chicago, but he was strictly—and in the long run profitably—pure and impersonal with his women clients, his stenographers, and his friends' wives and daughters.

All day Mushrat City brawled with children dashing into the lake. Most of the men were in town, in their offices, except on Saturday and Sunday, and now, in wartime, many of the women joined them. Jinny and Rose Pennloss drove in every Wednesday and Friday, to serve as waitresses in the soldiers canteen or to take coffee and sandwiches to the troop-trains. Cass, with his court closed, went in thrice a week and served on the ration board and in bond drives. All of Mushrat City was busy, and the only menace to its morals was Jay Laverick.

It was unfortunate, thought Cass, that it was Jay whom Jinny found most entertaining.

But so aboveboard was her liking for Jay, for his dancing, his air of sardonic liveliness, and so frankly did she talk about him, that Cass could see it would be very wrong to suspect her. They could scarce avoid meeting, with the swimming, tennis, canoeing. Jinny was a clean diver, and all afternoon at the Yacht Club, her hands flashed like nimble daggers as she dealt at bridge, but in all of these diversions Jay was the champion, when he was partly sober. Cass assured himself that all this was desirable, and good fun for Jinny.

But when Pasadena Filligan, Mrs. Beecher Filligan, who herself liked Jay, gave to his favorite morning drink, gin and bitters, the nickname of Jin and Jay, and it became current, then Cass was vexed.

It was obvious that the one safe path for Jinny between empty boredom and emptier philandering was to have children. "Let's drop all precautions now and start the family," he blurted.

"Yes, let's," she said.

That was all.

They were having a decorous Sabbath-afternoon walk, Cass and Roy Drover ambling on ahead of Jinny and Jay. The Cass who three months ago would have looked back only to gladden his eye with the vision of his sweet fair one could not keep from turning his head for less tender spying.

He saw Jinny and Jay arm in arm. He saw Jay tuck her hand between his arm and his side. He saw Jinny snatch it away, but not too swiftly, after what seemed to be a laughing debate.

So Cass, the Better Sort of American Husband, unhearing Roy's important remarks on wild rice as duck-feed, wanted to go back and beg Jay please not to seduce his wife—please not—it would be so much friendlier all round if Jay didn't—and would Jinny please forgive him for mentioning it?

He realized that Jay saw his spying. Deserting the girl, Jay galloped up and cried unctuously, "Boys, did you ever have a wild cat bawl you out? That's what I've been getting. Jinny has been giving me hell for trying to make Pasadena Filligan. Depict that, will you? And me never so much as wondering

whether Pas would or wouldn't. All I know is, she's a good
tennis partner. I should chase her, or any other woman in
G.R., when I already got a girl in Fergus. You know I have a
branch office there. Oh, damn all women, even your brainy
wife, Cass. Say, uh, Roy, is the health commissioner going to
get after the sewers down by my mill?"

But Jinny was walking airily, heel and toe, with a small
smug smile as the jaunty banner of her thoughts. She looked
so gay! Cass ached with the sense of all the monsters that
might be coiling around her recklessness.

——I'd hate to have her get involved, and go the smeary
way of all loose women. For my own honor, if there is such a
thing, but more for *her* honor and contentment. It would kill
me to see that secure smiling of hers turn diffident and scared
and appealing. Dear Jinny, don't be a fool. And that's the one
thing I can't ask you not to be.

So these provincial and middle-class and uncomplex
Sunday-afternoon strollers, a rural magistrate and his bourgeois
friends and his little country wife, obviously ungifted for the
passions and spiritual tortures of Bohemia or Mayfair or the
boulevards, straggled through the humble, sun-quivering
balsam aisles, and up to the Timberlane summer-cottage on
the weedy lake-shore.

The cottage, of pine clapboards apparently once painted
green, was airy as a birdcage. The roof sloped out over the
screened porch, which made up half the house and served

as lounge, dining-room, observation-post for recording the doings of the Filligans and the Ospreys, on either side, and as Cass's bedroom, with a frame and mattress swinging from four steel chains. Inside the house were only a squat living-room, with a preposterous granite fireplace, Jinny's narrow bedroom, the kitchen, with a kerosene stove, and a toilet with a homemade shower-bath. Mrs. Higbee and Cleo had a one-room tarpaper shack to themselves, behind the main house. Cleo had become a sinister young huntress, a chipmunk-stalker and a dabbler after fish.

The whole establishment was more camp than residence, and it caught the scent of pines, the breezes that were always fleeing in pretended panic from the lively colored, fresh-smelling lake.

Ah let us to the country hie, and seek an humble home, we little care for marble halls and the woes of Tyre and Rome. Here peacefulness and fruitfulness and family concord glow, and hearts of happy harvesters with simple joys o'erflow. Ah, well we wot, we city slaves, we pay a bitter scot for our tempestuous tragedies: thank God, *they* know them not! *Ibid.*

When they came up to the cottage, Cass looked beseechingly at Jay, hoping that he would have the sense to go home. This was no Fred Nimbus whom he could bully. Jay had enough skill in his trade of village gallant to be able to answer, "I don't know what you're talking about. Do I understand you to mean that your wife, whom I had supposed you to respect and honor as I do, is an unchaste woman, or such a fool that any passer-by can mislead her?"

Oh, yes, he could kill Laverick, but he could never shame him, never frighten him.

"How about a little bridge, the four of us?" Jay said sunnily.

"Not for me. I don't feel like it. I just want to sit and chew the rag with Roy," said Cass.

"Fine. Jinny, here's your chance to teach me some chess. You must have learned enough from ole Cass by now to be fairly good. We'll go up on the porch, like little mice, and not disturb the Big Boys."

"Wonderful!" chirruped Jinny.

Cass and Roy sat sourly out under the trees, on a sawbuck and a wheelbarrow.

Roy grumbled, "It's none of my business, but don't you know that Jay isn't the kind of buzzsaw for little ladies to monkey with?"

"Jay has a good line; he amuses her. But he's perfectly harmless."

"Oh, yeah? Better make sure he doesn't amuse her too much. Now don't get sore. I'm not going to butt in any farther. But just ask Pas Filligan—or better yet, ask her husband—just how harmless Jay is. Well, here's where I go over and turn in and get a nap. So long. . . . Bye, Jinny! . . . She never heard me."

Cass sat alone on the sawbuck, a seat too narrow for comfort but surrounded by spruce chips and sawdust with a friendly smell. He wanted some such small homeliness, for he was picturing a menacing procession.

——Tracy Olesen, Eino Roskinen, Abbott Hubbs, Bertie Eisenherz, Fred Nimbus, Jay Laverick. None of them dangerous, but I wish she weren't quite so enthusiastic about the virtues of quite so many nonentities.

When Jay was gone, Cass and Jinny swam out to the farther float. He had a crawl-stroke, steady and uninspired as the pounding of a freight-steamer, untiring and faster than it looked. She flirted with the water like a sail boat. They sat then on the narrow sand-beach, baking. She was tanned a soft brown; he, in his trunks, chest hard and arching, was of a coppery red-Indian hue. Relaxed thus, it was easier for him to blurt it all out:

"Sweet, I'm not jealous of Jay, but he's around here too much. A bold desperado, that fellow. He always keeps it up till somebody slaps him down. Won't you do it for me?"

"Oh, good Heavens, just because I enjoy playing tennis with him, and he talks amusingly——"

"Quit that!"

"*What?*"

"I know all his virtues better than you do. He's been conspicuously displaying them for a long time now. But you know and I know that he's on the make, and what's worse, he knows perfectly well that we know it, and if we allow him around here at all, we practically confirm his ethics. I wish you'd tell him yourself to quit acting the up-creek Casanova."

"Why, dearest, of course I will, if you want me to, though I honestly don't think he has any yen for me whatever. He's far too much interested in Pas Filligan." Her eyes were suddenly fixed and angry. "Blast her!"

"Why, Jinny, you aren't *that* much taken with him? You aren't jealous of Pas?"

"What? How? Of Pas? Heavens, no! I just meant I was irritated by the whole gang of them—the Filligans and Jay and the whole bunch. Aah! They're so sloppy. You're right. You're single-minded and good."

That night he lay relaxed and secure, listening to the wind in the pines, far in the north beside the lonely lake.

She chastened the petitionary Mr. Laverick simply and with dreadful effectiveness. At a Yacht Club dance, the next Saturday, when Jay was being especially attentive, she yelled publicly, "Why, Mr. La-ver-ick, are you trying to flirt with me? Back to your Irish bogs, ye little black divvle."

She knew that the one thing about which Jay was sensitive was the extreme boggishness of his swarthy paternal grandfather, who had been born between nothing and an east wind. When he had migrated to America, he had worked on a railroad section-gang, and had died in a kennel called The

Pipes of Erin, which was a Swedish-owned German saloon and Chinese chopsuey joint on Washington Avenue, in Minneapolis.

Jay left her flat, and went to the bar. The good Judge was surprised to find how pleased he was by her rudeness.

He spoke to Bradd Criley.

"I wish you'd have a talk with your friend Jay. He buzzes around Jinny entirely too much."

"I certainly will. I'm fond of Jay, and he isn't as bad as he acts, but he is a crazy fool. I won't tell him you spoke to me, Cass. I'll just say I admire Jinny, and will he lay off, or else."

"Thank you, Bradd."

"And of course it's true. I've always loved Jinny like an uncle, and I want to protect her almost as much as you do."

"I'm sure of it, and I'm mighty grateful."

So the truce of God was proclaimed, and Cass and Jinny were trusting lovers again, sitting in the northern twilight, with Cleo slipping ghost-like among the trees.

They settled to village peace by the lake, content with humbler establishments than the summer estates of the Wargates or Bertie Eisenherz, who had a small lake of his own. With Bertie, Jinny had learned what trans-Atlantic passengers learn: that you never see vacation-time intimates except on the street.

When she gave up the ways of dalliance, she went out for swimming so powerfully that she became a threat to the lady

Olympic champions—for two weeks.

At all sports she was more deft and quick-learning and natural than Cass. She dived, played tennis and golf, rode, paddled, with joy and style and innate talent, and with innate sloppiness. Cass was awkward at learning, and he gave no signs of particularly enjoying these games, but he mastered them better than Jinny, and he wanted to keep on picking away at them long after she was bored.

But all such competition vanished in the problems of comparative wealth. Cass had become rich—for Cass.

31

HE CAME BACK from town, he yelled "Jin-nee!" in front of their summer cottage, and brought her tumbling down out of an old crabapple tree where she had been curled up asleep, with Cleo asleep in her arms.

"Jinny," he inquired, "would you think one hundred and ten thousand dollars was a lot of money?"

"I would think anything over five dollars was a lot of money. Why?"

"That is the fabulous sum we now possess."

"Money! Dresses! Singhalese scarfs! A red collar for Cleo! A 'Liebestodt' record! Has somebody been bribing you? Oh, goody!"

"Nothing as interesting as that. Mm. How I would hate to have somebody offer me a hundred-thousand-dollar bribe! I'd have to refuse it———"

"Why?"

"Oh, you know."

"No, I don't! Why?"

"I can't explain why, but I would, of course."

"How about *two* hundred thousand?"

"Now don't go on raising. I just refused one hundred thousand, didn't I? Let's say hastily that we've proved the principle, and get on with the experiment."

"But honestly, what would be your limit?"

"Jinny, how much would you want for selling your virtue?"

"To which man?"

"Say just an average man."

"Do you mean indoors or outdoors?"

"Say outdoors."

"Do you mean on a summer night like this, with a full moon, or a night in January——Ah, poor sweet, you don't really think that's funny, *do* you!"

"But listen now. This hundred thousand that we already have——"

"And ten!"

"*And* ten. My father left me enough so I've been able to keep about fifty thousand dollars ahead, put away in good securities. And he also left me that block of stores and flats down in the South End. Here lately, they were almost empty, paying me almost nothing, but with Wargate's and the other factories doubling war production, there's come to be a big shortage in housing in the South End, and today Frank Brightwing told me he can get sixty thousand dollars for the property, spot-cash, and I'd 've said it wasn't worth more than thirty. Oh, Lord!"

"You're not glad. You don't want to do it?"

"I have done it. I have a nice check for sixty thousand

dollars, minus three-thousand commission, in my pocket."

"Oh, lemme see, lemme see, lemme see, good gracious sakes, let me see that lovely thing!"

Together, solemnly, they looked at the meager slip of paper on which was written "Fifty-seven thousand ($57,000 & 00/100)" and which, by the magic of this credulous era, would trustingly be accepted by strangers in return for brick houses and roasts of beef and tickets to *Hamlet* and safety for death-haunted refugees from tyranny.

Jinny said reverently, "Now is that a pretty trick! Hey— wait! Do you mean to tell me Frank Brightwing gets three thousand dollars of our money? Why, I call that scandalous! But a minute ago——Why were you oh-Lording? A thing like that elegant piece of paper, I should think it would be something that all the angels would rejoice over, and even Ma Prutt would look halfway pleased. Why so pale and wan, young capitalist?"

"Oh, I dunno—to get this increased price—it seems like profiteering on the war. Of course I can put most of it into war bonds——"

No criminal lawyer has ever attacked more fierily than did Jinny. Cass was smothered. She tore him down from thirty-five thousand dollars of war bonds to five, and nearly had him down to three, and within half an hour, without knowing better than any layman how the contract had been put over, he had pledged himself to his boss to invest another five thousand in more speculative stocks, put forty-five thousand into a new house and the appertaining furniture, and devote two thousand to their strictly private blowing-in.

He fretted that Jinny was not overly generous in her patriotism, but then he fretted that none of them were. Like almost every other Good Citizen at any time, he did very little except the fretting.

He did not know that he was committed, beyond the power of the court, to buying the new house and deserting the ancient comfort of Bergheim. He believed that he was "still thinking it over," and in the security of that belief he went to sleep, that night, while inside the cottage she sat brooding for hours, her small hands, so apt at pencil, at golf-stick, at the hammer, clutched ardently, like a child's, round her knees. She stared at a candle till the tallow took shapes of towers and spires, of ocean steamers and flaunting bridges, of studios in Paris, of a great stage in New York and a little exciting figure in the center.

He awoke on his porch-swing to peer in at her, and clumped in to kiss her excited cheeks, her clasped hands. She circled his neck with bare arms, muttering, "Never any one but you, my darling. I do want a lot of silly things, and you give them to me, but I want you more. I wish sometimes it could be I who give, and not always you."

The debate about buying a new house started all over again

next morning, as already-thoroughly-settled domestic debates always do.

Cass said profoundly, "Uh—uh——About buying a new house. And of course, with wartime restrictions, it will be impossible to build one. And I don't honestly see any likelihood of our caring for a house that somebody else has arranged to suit themselves. Do you see?"

"Yes, it——I think this grape fruit and orange marmalade knocks the spot off straight orange. You, Cleo, you get off this table, and don't knock over Isis, either."

"I think it's absolutely superstitious of you, if not infantile, to have that crystal image always in sight, honey."

"Isn't it though! See Frazer, *The Golden Bough*. Yes. You know, we'll have trouble making room enough for all your books in the new house, whichever one we get."

"But I don't——That's what I want to talk about."

"I knew it, I knew it, oh, my pet, I absolutely knew it. I said to a robin, when I woke this morning, I said, 'Robin, I'll bet you two worms that Mr. Timberlane will want to talk about the insanity of buying a new house.' "

"Well, I do."

"Do what, Judge?"

"Think so."

"Think what?"

"That we must consider very carefully whether we really want to do this. We have a very fine old house now, and to get a new one would be spending our *capital*."

"But you can sell the old one."

"I don't know whether that would be so easy."

"But if it's such a grand fine old place as you say?"

"Yes, yes, that's—Have to protect our capital. I might very easily be defeated for judge at the next election, and then what would we have to live on?"

"You might practise a little law and make a—what is it? a modicum?—maybe about five times as much as your present salary, and so we'd get along."

"Maybe."

"Darling!" She stopped being flippant; she spoke like the first young cavewoman in the morning of history who resolved that her mate and she must leave their damp cave on the hillside and struggle down into the bright dangerous plains. "Let's be young while we're still young!"

"I know," he said.

"Let's get a house in the Country Club District—if we can find one, I mean, that isn't too expensive—gay and shiny and lots of light—not like our old morgue in town."

"Bergheim isn't a morgue."

"The corpses never know that a morgue is a morgue."

"I didn't know you felt that way about it."

"I didn't, till this minute. And you know, really the chief thing I'm thinking about is how much more convenient a modern kitchen would be for Mrs. Higbee."

"Overruled."

"Well, anyway, I did think some about it, and some about me entertaining in a Spanish drawing-room, looking like the Duchess of Windsor."

"Baby, you're either as childish as Juliet Zago, or——You really want a new house?"

"Yes."

"I'll think about it."

They knew what that meant.

He drove into town and, as though he had not seen it for several years, he stared at Bergheim, his boyhood notion of a castle, his first citadel as a citizen, a counselor, a judge, the lifelong repository of his dreams, filled with contradictory and devastating memories of Blanche and Jinny.

He clumped through the house—noticing how surprisingly much cat-hair Cleo had managed to leave on the chairs—and he was certain that he would miss these solid walls, these un-cramped rooms, the irregular hallways and unexpected closets. In the backyard he admired the carriage-house with its haughty cupola which, as a boy, he had considered the seal of elegance. He mooned over the espaliered pears, the thick and comfortable backyard grass that takes a generation to grow, the view from the bluff across twin valleys. He knew here a little of the tradition that makes a Leicestershire squire, a Silesian Junker, a gentleman of Touraine quiet and enduring and dangerous.

This Country Club District that Jinny coveted—it was a parvenu colony next to the Heather golf course, on a peninsula thrust out from the south shore of Dead Squaw Lake. This "brand-new, up-to-the-second, streamlined home-development for gracious living" had been planned for the sons of Ottawa Heights, the grandsons of the extravagant mansions on Beltrami Avenue South, and newcomers who had wriggled their way into this three-whole-generations aristocracy. The houses there were sleek and well planned; they had steel-and-glass kitchens and tinted toilet-paper; but they were too close together, too small, too much like hotel-suites.

Thus meditating, he returned to Mushrat City, to coax Jinny please not to buy a house but do a lot of striking things with paint at Bergheim.

She met him clamoring, "Beautiful, Pas Filligan says she thinks we'd like the Simmers house—you know, that Spanish-hacienda number just beyond the Heather Club. She says the inside is wonderful and behind it," reverently, "there's a swimming-pool! Lemme in the car, lemme in! Let's go see it right now. There's a key at the club. Let's go!"

Somehow, as they drove round the lake, Cass could not advocate painting the Bergheim kitchen, and putting tin over the major rat-holes, as a substitute for a hacienda-house with a swimming-pool.

And it was quite a house, too.

From the front they saw a roof of alternate red and yellow tiles, a wooden ox-bow with two ship's-lanterns suspended from it, and an outside cement stairway leading down to a honeysuckle bush that was not really remarkable enough to have a special stairway for it.

——Mm. They probably use the stairs for jumping off into snowdrifts in winter.

He was rigidly silent; she was silent like a head-turning little bird, as they went through the place. The rooms were small and, with tiled floors and imitation-antique beams, as oppressive as cells. Above the Mexican fireplace in the living-room a long crack in the wall showed that, after only ten years, the house was sinking. They considered the kitchen, daintily done in pink, green, dark blue, and bronze, and went out to the swimming-pool, which was a nothingness lined with cracked cement.

Then Jinny spoke, tenderly.

"All right, all right, Judge. I always did think it was a mistake for us to invite Cortez over."

But it seemed to be understood between them that, since she had so freely rejected this horror, he could not suggest that they should not buy a new house at all.

They knew the house hunter's shameless joy of intrusion; of looking into closets full of forlorn clothes, medicine cabinets with surprising accessories, sumptuous wine-closets that contained nothing but a bottle and a half of rye and one can of sardines. They studied and extensively talked about terraces, tennis courts, linen closets, automatic-feed furnaces, "breakfast nooks," and basements which, containing pool tables and home-made bars, were appallingly known as "rumpus-rooms."

Frank Brightwing, their real-estate expert, grew irritable, Cass was exhausted, but Jinny strode on, unquenchable. She could examine the eighteenth closet in sequence with undiminished enthusiasm, and three days later could remember the dimensions of each closet and how many hangers there were in it and whether it had a full-length mirror in the door. It did not, however, occur to Frank or to Cass that, with the opportunity, she would have been a better real-estate man than either of them.

They decided quite suddenly on a house, in the Country Club District, which they had twice dismissed as "too plain" and now saw as dignified in its simplicity: a plaster house with a flat roof and drawing-room windows down to the floor; what Brightwing called "a fine restrained example of the French-type house." It could just as well have been called an English-type house, a Lombardy-type house, or a Salzkammergut-type house; it was, in fact, a plaster house. It had almost as many closets as Jinny wanted, almost as much radiator-surface as Cass wanted, a cubbyhole for Cass's desk, and a good view across the lake.

Jinny said that the long windows would be "nice for a lawn-party—people can run in and out." Cass thought it would be abominable to have people running in and out, whether through doors, windows or chimneys, and he considered floor-length windows a wretched idea for Minnesota winters. But if she was happy, then so was he.

The house had been built for Harold W. Whittick, owner of Station KICH, who had moved into a flat in one of the few apartment houses in Grand Republic, to be near his radio station—or, as he put it, "to the transmission of the critical bulletins of this portentous hour of conflict."

Neither Cass nor Harold W. Whittick knew that Groseilliers and Radisson, possibly the first white men in Minnesota, had camped upon this site in 1660. It is a pity that Harold did not know. He might have given those explorers the most gratifying publicity throughout this rich agricultural and dairying section with convenient access to all railroads and wholesale markets.

In treachery to her years at Bergheim, Mrs. Higbee placidly preferred the new house and the new kitchen, and perhaps Isis did also—she did not indicate. But Cleo was melancholy about it.

Jinny insisted on their taking a special journey from Mushrat City to show Cleo her new home, and when Cass objected that the government wanted them to save gasoline, Jinny explained, "Now do you suppose the President is going to say to the Secretary of War, 'Look, Harry, there's that dratted Jinny Marshland wasting gas on a cat?' I bet they won't even notice."

It was not easy to convince Jinny that Cleo might be so occupied in her office of grand inquisitor to the heretic field mice that she could endure waiting another day.

When Cleo did actually see the place, she was difficult about it. They followed her while she examined every room. She repeatedly stopped to ask "Meow?" in a way that said, "Is this all?"

There were—Cleo counted them—not so many rooms as at Bergheim. There were no unlighted closets, no dark attic stairs, no exquisite dark triangles of space under the eaves, no trapdoors, no earth-floored corners in the basement, no place at all where a respectable cat might expect mice or beetles, or could hide from a harsh and mocking world.

"I suppose you sympathize with that animal," sighed Jinny, in a sad little voice.

"No, no," Cass lied. "Maybe we'll miss the old barracks for a while, but I already love this place more, because you're more in it, in every line."

So Cleo went off in a huff and was found in the empty garage, growling.

They would use but little furniture from Bergheim in the new house; they would leave the old castle as it was, and

339

rent it till it should be sold. They had their sprees of buying, in Grand Republic, in St. Paul and Minneapolis, and then, in mid-August, he blurted out the plan that he had been nursing.

Except for the Florida journey, she had still never been east of Chicago.

"We'll have to wait for all the new furnishings to arrive, and meanwhile, what do you say to our taking another honeymoon trip?" he said.

"Do you think we ought to? Spending so much money— we'll have to economize. Oh. I *must* remember to turn off the lights when I leave a room."

"But later we may not get much chance—be less and less travel with the war on and—suppose the trip I was thinking of was to New York?"

"New York!" she said reverently.

An Assemblage of Husbands and Wives

NESTOR & FANNY PURDWIN

NESTOR PURDWIN was born in an October gale in Illinois in 1871. He came to Minnesota in a blizzard in 1890, and married Fanny Clark during an April freshet in 1891, with the roads deplorable but the horizon clear.

He was next-to-the-best criminal lawyer in Grand Republic, and he was honest. He never knowingly declared that a scoundrel or a man of cruelty was harmless, though he might assert that there were excuses for him. He represented many of the labor unions, but he was also summoned by corporations in civil cases, because they often needed an adviser who could say No.

He was a middleroad-to-leftwing Democrat and a convinced Episcopalian. He detested Sweeney Fishberg for being a Jew, an Irishman, a Catholic, a mystic, and a Communist. In the old days, when he had once been associated in a trial with Clarence Darrow, he had detested Darrow for being an agnostic and a socialist-anarchist-syndicalist-populist. Yet in most suits and on most committees he had somehow found himself standing with Fishberg and Darrow, and when the veteran liberal, Salem Volk, from Queen City, came to town, he stayed, often and argumentatively, with the Purdwins.

He was always roaring. He roared equally against high-church rectors named Cecil and Four Square Gospellers named Pete, against tabloid newspapers and glossy magazines and "fool women who are too lazy to read the papers and magazines."

He had never gone to college, but he read Plato, Voltaire, Alexander Pope, Mencken, Bernard Shaw, and Sir Thomas Browne.

Fanny and he had been married for fifty years, and had bickered continuously in a tart, humorous, satisfied way, and she never failed to defend him against everybody else with whom he bickered.

"Yes, I know how cranky he must've been to you. The man is worse than a bear in a beehive. But don't tell *me* about it. I love him."

When Judge Blackstaff was reported as having said that Mr. Purdwin was "not a gentleman," Fanny mused, "Ain't he? That's good. Neither am I."

For fifty years they had slept in an immense, bosomy double-bed. His parting kiss to her each morning was a testy little peck on the lips, but if he forgot it, she was grieved for an hour—but never for more than an hour—and she never reproached him for it.

Exactly once in the fifty years he had tried an extra-matrimonial experiment, with a hotel stenographer. He had neither enjoyed it, repeated it, nor told her about it.

He loved porridge for breakfast, and every morning, three hundred and sixty-five mornings a year, they had porridge. It was after thirty-two years of it that Fanny reported, a bit reluctantly, "I think I'm beginning to like the nasty stuff."

32

THE TIMBERLANES followed the ancient line of provincial tourists going to the capitals: Boeotians to Athens, Tatar caravans to Tibet, Artie and Mrs. Beppin of the Five Towns to London: excited, credulous, terrified of the boorishness and cheating that they expected to encounter.

The question, ancient before the first woman from Petra went up to Jerusalem, of whether Jinny should have new dresses made at home or get them more splendidly in the metropolis, was as usual compromised. She bought a gray suit that Harley Bozard assured her was a "fast little number, just in from New York," and left the rest for Babylon.

Their train from Chicago to New York was an arrow of light. They had a compartment, this time, and none of their honeymoon apprehension. The train was filled with the most beautiful people, lovely girls, saintly old ladies, smooth but stalwart men with clothes and shell-rimmed spectacles and wrist-watches right out of the magazine advertisements.

Cass let himself relax and enjoy it. In his days in Congress he had not gone to New York often enough to be weary of it, and he was all holiday. He spoke not only to the Pullman porter, to whom it was no novelty, but to a clergyman and a traveling-man, and when a man in herring-bone tweed invited him to play bridge, and chuckled, "I warn you, though, the wife and I are professional gamblers," Cass answered, "My wife certainly is. She gambled on marrying me."

The man thought that was a pretty good joke.

The man said to his wife, "Our new friend here has made a pretty good joke."

She said, "Come on now—don't be a tightwad—what's his pretty good joke?"

"He said the little woman took a worse risk in getting hitched to him than she ever did in bridge."

"Yes, and what a gamble *he* took on getting *you* to handle the rights to his pretty good joke. Let's go!"

They played bridge through sixteen counties and forty-two college towns of Ohio, and had four Scotch highballs and shook hands all round. Jinny had won sixty-two cents and a lipstick, and Cass had lost one dollar.

"I'm a little drunk," he said with self-approval, as they wove into their compartment.

"You get younger every day. When I first met you, you were sixty-one. Now you're a bright thirty-four," she approved.

They were up early. People from Grand Republic do get up at the most surprising times and places. Along the Hudson, the river of Presidents, Jinny was thrilled by West Point, the Taj Mahal, and the leaves of Vallombrosa. Suddenly there was an apartment house twenty stories high, and he exulted, "This is it!" She held his hand softly, and whispered, "I love you!"

But the Grand Central Terminal was too much for her: an underground city in which all the inhabitants were going to a fire. She clung to her stalwart Cass, a fellow who could beat off these shoving maniacs, as they doubtfully gave their precious, so-neatly-packed bags over to a redcap, dotted up an incline, crossed through an incredible room a thousand feet tall, and took a taxicab, not in the wholesome fresh air but in a tunnel. In the taxi she still snuggled close to him for protection, and fluttered, "I'm going to have a magnificent time, but let me catch my breath. Does it get any worse?"

As they blessedly came out into the light, she found that part of the taxi roof was of glass, and she gazed up in beatific idiocy.

"Look! Up there! That must be the Empire State Building or the Wrigley Building or something! Oh, jiminy, they are high. You know—high! I never felt so small. Don't you dare leave me one minute all the time we're here!"

She was less exalted when the taxicab stopped meechingly at the Melchester Arms, which Bradd Criley, as an expert on New York, had recommended. "It's smaller and less expensive, but it's one of the smartest hotels in town," he said. "That's where the real New Yorkers go, say while they're opening up their apartments in the fall." (Actually, the only native New Yorkers who frequented the Melchester were clothes-pressers, jobbing barbers, and telegraph messengers.)

It was a smaller hotel and rather plainer than the Pineland, back home, and the lobby was a block of darkness surrounding a large oak table with piles of magazines about travel and the Y.M.C.A. upon it. The clerk was a short, scaly, ill-disposed man with that thin and revelatory hair which is balder than baldness. He looked up at them as though he was getting good and tired of having strangers come in and speak to him without an introduction.

"I, uh—we have a reservation for a two-room suite," said Cass.

"What is the name?"

"Timberlane. Grand Republic. Minnesota."

The clerk, after having looked painstakingly through a file of cards containing names beginning with I and E, sighed, "What was that name again?"

"Timberlane."

"Oh. I see! With a T. Tamburlaine."

"No, no. *Timberlane*. Tamburlaine is from Marlowe."

"Well, we get a lot of people from Marlowe, too. The Melchester is a great favorite with all you folks from the Middlewest."

As he laboriously went at the cards again, Jinny muttered, "Why don't you tell him you're a judge and an ex-congressman, and give him a good time? He needs one."

"Kitten, in this town, everybody's an ex-congressman. We're just a couple of rural nobodies."

"And how! This suit that Harley sold me—I'm beginning to

find potato bugs and alfalfa seeds in it. But Aloysius here is no Vanderbilt. I suppose New York has the biggest everything—even the biggest hicks. Let me slap him, darling, just once."

The clerk turned to them again and said accusingly, "*Timberlane*, that's the name!"

"That's so," admitted Cass.

"Front!" said the clerk, suspiciously.

The elderly bellboy awoke from his dreams of the Civil War, conducted them to their suite, and gloomily accepted fifty cents. He was barely gone when Jinny protested, "Four bits? For that jerk? I'd of brought the bags up for ten cents! There you go, being the typical tourist you read about, overtipping and hurling thousands of dollars around when you have a greedy wife that could use it for luncheon-sets. Okay. Bankrupt the firm and see if I care."

They had recovered the gaiety which had been dimmed in the hotel lobby, and they went down, arm in arm, to ask of the clerk where they could get theater tickets for tonight.

Maybe there was a ticket agency, over on Sixth Avenue and down three blocks? How would he know? He was busy, and really it wasn't his job——

They left him hastily and at the agency inquired benevolently, like people willing to spend their money and confer a favor, whether for tonight they could get superior seats for *Life with Father* or for *Arsenic and Old Lace*.

The agent said genially, "You folks from out of town?"

"How did you guess it?" Jinny said viciously.

He looked at her, unanswering, he winked at her husband, and he offered, "I can get you tickets for either show for about the middle of next November. What you want for tonight is *Slips and Slippers*."

"Do we?" worried Cass.

"Maybe not. I wouldn't know. All I'm telling you is that it's the best musical in New York for ten years, and I happen to have two good seats, but if you don't want 'em——"

The seats cost $6.60 each.

When they were outside, Jinny begged, "Have you any room in your vest-pocket, now you've taken out all that money?"

"Why?"

"That rat made me feel so small when he winked at you that I could fit right in alongside your watch now. Jinny isn't up to this town. They got street-cars and everything. Could we go back to Grand Republic right after the show tonight? *Slips and Slippers*! Six-sixty! Look! He meant sixty-six cents, didn't he?"

Their train had arrived in mid-morning. All day they viewed New York, by bus and elevated and taxicab. There was so fabulously much to master that they felt they would never master any of it. To them it was all a jungle-spawning of people and buildings, fierce and purposeless. The tempo of the city rattled them: the quick turn of everyone's head, the hard glance, the high nasal intensity of the voices.

They came back to their hotel suite—correct enough in its white paneling, but inhuman—and fell desperately asleep and awakened almost too late for their musical show. Jinny insisted that it was Isis, continuing her education by staring out of the window at the Manhattan streets, who had aroused them.

They reasoned that it would be clever to have a sandwich within walking-distance of the theater, and dine sumptuously at some gaudy restaurant afterward. Cass told Jinny that he had been responsibly informed that in Madrid people dined as late as ten-thirty. Probably even eleven. She said brightly, Yes, she had heard so.

It made them feel that they were already in Europe.

They found a Broadway restaurant the size of Grand Republic, with lovely black and red signs announcing that here one might have sandwiches made of smoked turkey, caviar, deviled ham with chives, or sixteen other rich materials. Nothing like this at home! they rejoiced.

The farther hill-country of the interior of the restaurant was filled with daises, mezzanines, balconies, and quarter-decks, while the valley was jammed with circular bars, S-shaped lunch-counters, wall-seats, divans, and booths, and all of these filled, and twenty people herded at the door waiting, apologetic for wanting to eat during wartime, while the restaurant's private supreme court looked at the trespassers punitively. With the other prisoners waited Judge and Mrs. Timberlane. They felt that there was something obscene about wanting to eat at all, in this choking atmosphere of corned beef and cabbage, among this queue of dehumanized serfs who had no longer any power of resentment.

Jinny answered something that Cass hadn't yet even said with, "You're telling *me* you like Grand Republic better!"

When they were finally herded to a table for two, they found that by merely cutting off one arm and one leg each, and balancing the glass of water on the sandwich plate which rested on the unordered and unwanted plate of shredded cabbage under which were tucked the knives and forks and the paper napkins, they could manage very well.

Their sandwiches were called Oaxaca Specials, and among other ores they recognized bacon, peanut butter, currant jelly, chicken feet and iodine. It cost one dollar.

Each of the sandwiches cost one dollar.

Jinny whimpered, "About that Grand Republic now. I shall never leave it again. Oh, that beautiful, beautiful hash we used to have, back in civilization!"

On the street again, she speculated, "Couldn't we give our tickets to one of these pencil-sellers and magic ourselves back to——Let's go over to the Zagos and have some rummy. I never realized what a wide-browed genius Juliet Zago is. Wouldn't I like to see her and Scott right this minute! Pal, could I please kick the next couple that crowd me into the gutter? I guess maybe it would be wonderful to be in New York, if all seven million of 'em didn't want to occupy the same spot we're walking over, all at the same time."

They arrived in the theater as in a calm haven, but that was the last calm they felt till they were back in their hotel, with Jinny trying to explain it all to Isis.

They never did discover what the musical play was about. From having attended the more salacious burlesque shows in Minneapolis, when he was a student, Cass had a few notions, but Jinny was entirely bewildered. There was, in the plot, a young lieutenant who was serving in Tahiti, but as he was simultaneously rowing on the Vassar crew and selling paper drinking-cups to a Turkish harem, it was hard to follow his stream of consciousness. There was also a pair of funny fellows with jokes about the less attractive vices.

Cass and Jinny sat with hand tight in hand, unsmiling, uncomfortable, wondering what the laughter was about. At intermission, Jinny said only "Six-sixty!" but after the show, as they hobbled away through the funereally festive crowd, "I'm old-fashioned and I like it! Honey, if we got a plane, a very fast plane, maybe we could see Cleo before dawn—and find out if that beast of an upholsterer at Tarr's has the curtains up in the new house yet. You know, they always advertise how fast you can fly to New York, but what would inspire deep public confidence would be to tell how fast and far you can get away from New York. Oh, my sweet, you've got poor Jinny caught and happy in a sun-trap at home for the rest of her life!"

They had read, in the syndicated gossip columns devoted to the gracious doings of café society, about the Marmoset Club, that debonair night restaurant, that Bowery saloon in a velvet evening-cloak, where cigarette-bejittered heiresses are photographed with flyers, and cinema press-agents exchange copyrighted wisecracks with abortionists, but after the Broadway sandwich-abbatoir, they were ready to be disappointed. Yet the Marmoset was even more select, smart, exclusive, fashionable, knowing, chic, gracious, elegant, decorative, glamorous, glittering, glistening, shimmering, witty, sophisticated, mundane, gay, international, deft, urbane, and generally expensive than had been proclaimed by the columnists.

The very small lobby was a jewel-box in which stood a young gentleman with the clothes of a whisky advertisement, the eyes of a detective, the gentle effrontery of a diplomat, and the accent of the Bronx.

"Uh——" said Cass, and again, "Uh—can we get a table?"

"Have you a reservation?"

"N-no."

Jinny said in perfectly clear, sweet, womanly tones, "Let's get the hell out of here. I don't like him."

The palace eunuch instantly recognized her then as a

distinguished movie actress, and he said almost humbly, "I'll see what I can do. I'm sure I can find you something, madame."

He did quite well for them, too. He found a table in the Que-Voulez-Vous Room, the largest of the five that made up the Marmoset, despite the fact that it was almost half full.

Well, and it was a beautiful room, and Cass and Jinny had to admit it; better even than the Fiesole Room at the Hotel Pineland, back home. The walls were lined with gray silk, tucked and flaring; under the crimson ceiling were constellations of crystal; and there was a delicate, rustling quiet except at a center table where a male clothes-designer was breaking a rather elderly lady's heart and in a corner where an authoress was breaking her contract.

Word had been carried by the restaurant's efficient O.G.P.U. that the pretty girl with the white mantle was somebody important in Hollywood and the man with her either a doctor or a major in mufti. This was no sensation at the Marmoset. That new Monte Carlo could really have been stirred only by the appearance of the President with Queen Nefertiti. But it did insure a captain of waiters coming to take their order without disciplining them by making them wait.

However, by the ease with which he sold them a bottle of Peruvian champagne and mushrooms *à noisette* under glass, he could see that here was only another dull pair of uncelebrities. He passed the word, and Cass and Jinny went back into the refrigerator. No one even glanced at them, except the male designer, who looked designing.

Cass saw Jinny's spirit paling in her, and he urged abruptly, "Well, you're the prettiest girl here. There isn't one that has your fire or your eyes or a clear skin like yours."

"And you're the only man here that looks as if he could fight a battle or build a town."

More silence, out of which she burst, "If I saw Boone and Queenie Havock over at a table there, I'd go over and I'd kiss both of 'em. Twice. And I would request Boone, but very nicely, to stand up and holler, 'Do you clams know who this is? This is Judge Timberlane and his young wife, d' you hear me?'"

"And Boone would probably do it."

"And Boone would certainly do it. That's why I adore him—now."

That was Monday evening, the end of Jinny's first day among the revelries of New York.

Comfortingly close to each other, they slept in one of the twin beds, for shelter against the bleak wind of urban indifference, while all night the little crystal cat looked out on the prison wall of the New York street. It seemed very small on the broad white sill.

There is a Grand Republic colony in New York, as there is a Smyrna colony, a Benares colony, a Reykjavik colony, and it is the duty of that colony to be gleeful at the arrival of all visitors from the home town, and to take them to that restaurant at which the ordeal of being cordial can be most quickly got over most inexpensively. Equally, it is the duty of the visitors to telephone to all members of the colony upon arrival and to allow themselves to be becordialed. (There are also cases in which the two parties to the social contract really want to see each other.)

With a notion of being thoughtful and not binding them, Cass had not written of his coming to any of the colonists, nor to Dennis Thane, the only one of his classmates in the University of Minnesota law school whom he knew to be in New York. The stuttering task of finding his old acquaintances he took up on Tuesday morning, while Jinny, cocking her bare toes, commented with ribaldry from the rumpled bed.

Mrs. Byron Grannick? She was still at Stockbridge.

Dr. Cope Anderson, the chemist? He was still at his laboratory on Cape Cod.

Mr. and Mrs. Kenny Wargate? They were still at Easthampton.

By now Cass felt empty and unwanted.

He reached only Dennis Thane (of the law-firm of Crossbow, Murphy, and Thane), who invited them for lunch tomorrow, and Bradd Criley's sister, Mrs. William Elderman, Avis Criley Elderman, who forebodingly insisted on coming into town from her suburban home in Darien, Connecticut, and on performing the rite of taking them to dinner on Thursday evening.

"Anyway, we have two friends in the world, Dennis and Avis, except for Avis," sighed the lonely Judge Timberlane.

He had not quite dared telephone to one former Grand Republican, the only person from their section of Minnesota, aside from Salem Volk the veteran liberal politician, who was famous to the whole world: Berg Nord, the actor-director-producer-dramatist, who had been born on a farm in Radisson County. In fact Nord was so distinguished that every citizen back home was under a compulsion to inform strangers, "Oh, we don't take Berg seriously. We still call him 'Ice Berg.' He don't try to pull anything on us, like maybe he does on you folks. We know him too well."

Nord's latest play, *Feast of Reason*, of which he was author and star, had just re-opened for the second year of its run. Back home, Cass had airily thought of telephoning to Nord about tickets—though he would insist on paying for them, of course—but now, with the baby-tiger purr of New York outside his window, he dared not telephone to Nord at all, but after breakfast trotted meekly to the ticket agency, where the learned vendor condescendingly let him have two seats. Cass held them with pride. . . . He had never seen Berg on the stage, but as a child of three, he had ridden pickaback on the shoulders of the twenty-three-year-old Cousin Berg Nord. Now he asked of the omniscience, "Nord is considered a fine actor in New York, isn't he?"

"Oh, merely the best, after Lunt, that's all!"

Cass had lost another inch of stature by the time he had regained the safety of their hotel and Jinny's presence.

33

THEY NEVER COULD recall how they had put in the rest of Tuesday morning, aside from reading the papers down to the auction notices, but they postponed the duty of reveling in the joys of New York till lunchtime. Then they had the great hours of shopping, and admitted that, in this, New York was superior. Jinny dropped the arm of her protector and stepped out and had a few things to say for herself.

She contradicted clerks, high impressive clerks with handkerchiefs like bishops' mitres in their breast-pockets. She yearned over furs and Irish linens and perfume-bottles with gold crowns for stoppers and folding card-tables so sturdy that you could sit on them—the clerk enthusiastically proved it. (He was fired for it, that evening; the table might have collapsed.) But there was a hard shrewdness in her, and she bought only one per cent of the things that she would die if she did not have.

After dozens of tryings-on, while Cass sat on a plush chair in rooms carpeted to suffocation and wondered if he might smoke, and wished that he had a walking stick to rest his chin on, like the other male sitters, she did pick out a silk dress, a blue suit, and a lynx jacket.

Then she dropped again into panic.

"Cass! Let's beat it! So many shops, so many puss-puss grass-widow clerks, trying to stick you with things you don't want—they all get so blurry and alike. There's no fun like there is at Harley's or Tarr's, where you know all the scandals about the clerks. I love you for bringing me to New York, and I wouldn't have missed it for a million dollars, and I wouldn't ever come here again for a billion. Oh, I do want to settle down now. I promise: I will read my chess manual. I will quit getting my queen taken. I promise!"

He kissed her in the elevator of a department store.

They assured themselves that though the Melchester dining-room did look stuffy, "We better have our dinner here, just this once, and not have to hurry to the theater."

The air of the dining-room had been shut in there, among the Brussels sprouts and the damp napkins, ever since the hotel had opened, in 1913, and the stuffed veal tasted like the air, and the waiter, who was a family man and a commuter, had aching feet.

They spent most of their time at dinner in longing for the gaieties of the John William Prutts, and they went to the play as to an operation.

Cass knew Nord only as a bulky, tow-headed Swede in a loose black suit and an irregular bow-tie, lounging around his father's farm. Jinny had never seen great acting, and she supposed that there would be a good deal of yelling and throwing up one's arms and catching them again.

Bewildered, they learned tonight that great theater is more real than reality. Nord was the Little Man, a clerk who discovers that his boss and his wife and his daughters are all liars, who smashes his world and triumphs in defeat.

Jinny commented only, "Gee!"

Cass said, "I think in these theaters you can—'go back,' I think they call it, and see the actors in their dressing-rooms, and of course I've known Berg slightly all my life——I didn't suppose he was like that! He's an archangel. I'm glad I saw this with you. Well, shall we go back?"

"I'm scared to, but if you're sure it's all right——Course I was born only about six miles from his birthplace—and maybe I didn't tell that to everybody in Florida!"

"Come on. Perhaps he'll go out with us for a drink."

"Don't you dare ask him! Prob'ly everybody from Minnesota and points west comes in and bothers him. Come on! I don't think we ought to go see him, but hurry or we might miss him!"

It was all traditional and tight: the secret alley beside the theater, the stooped and hidden stage door, the doorman aged and Irish and misanthropic.

"To, uh, to see Mr. Nord. Mr. and Mrs. Timberlane," Cass submitted.

"*Judge* Timberlane," said Jinny.

But when they were admitted to the star's dressing-room, it was such a littered coop, and the star, wiping off greasepaint, was just Ole Ice Berg Nord. He looked at Cass a little puzzled.

"You're one of the Grand Republic Timberlanes, aren't you?"

"Yes, my mother was Marah Nord. I'm sort of a second cousin of yours. I'm a lawyer."

"Oh, now I have it straight." Nord, a thick, undistinguished figure in a blazing silk dressing-gown, was cordial. "Cass—isn't that the name? Mighty pleased you came back, Cass. Enjoy my show?"

"We thought it was magnificent." Nord was obviously pleased. "Berg, this is my wife. Just married last year."

"Delighted to see you, Mrs. Timberlane. This your first visit to New York?"

"Yes, it's my first."

"You enjoying your visit?"

"Oh, yes, so much. Well. That is. I don't know as I'd want to live here. We're fond of Minnesota."

"So am I, Mrs.—uh—Timberlane."

Jinny must have seen in Cass's pleased and honest face the prohibited come-out-and-have-a-drink look. Firmly taking her husband's arm, she stated, "It's been a great honor to be able to visit with you, and we must go now. Good night."

And went.

They stopped in the street and shone at each other.

Cass said proudly, "Nice fellow, isn't he!"

"Marvelous."

"Course off the stage, he seems like anybody else."

"Oh, no, I don't think so! I can feel the tremendous reserved power in him. Oh, I could go for him in a big way!"

"Ye-es."

"Let's stop and get a drink some place—a quiet place, if there is one in this town—and then go to bed. Oh, Cass, I'm so tired, all that shopping—but is that plum-colored dress a vision! We certainly have one thing to boast of: we didn't try and wheedle poor Berg into going out with us."

"It might have been courteous to have asked him——"

"Oh, no, you can't ask people like that."

Berg Nord was meditating, "I wish I'd asked those people out for a drink—or they'd asked me. They made me quite homesick. I'd like to hear the Grand Republic news. But they're probably busy on their stay here. I wouldn't want to intrude."

In her own twin bed a little later, talkative and not sleepy, Jinny mused aloud, "Think of how brilliantly he must talk when he's with his real friends."

At Sardi's, Berg Nord was saying to his agent, who was one of his three close friends, "I don't want to be a hog about it, but you tell Hollywood I won't even look at less than two hundred thousand. Know what I'm going to do, some day? Move back to Minnesota and stay there. You New Yorkers are a pain in the neck. Always thinking about money. . . . I'll have another Scotch old-fashioned."

Their lunch, on Wednesday, with Dennis Thane started jubilantly with recollections of law school, each of which began, "Say, do you remember the time I . . ."

Thane was effusive to Jinny.

"Is this your first visit to New York, Mrs. Timberlane?"

"Yes, it's the first time."

"Are you enjoying your visit here?"

"Oh, yes, very much, thank you."

But after that the luncheon was less vivacious.

So they did more shopping and went to museums, thousands of museums, and went to a news-reel.

"Let's take a chance and dine at Twenty-One or the Algonquin or one of those famous places, Jin."

"Oh, I don't know. They're fascinating, but they scare me, Cass. Why don't we just have dinner here at the hotel, where they know who we are, and then take in another movie and go to bed? There's a bang-up movie opened on Broadway last night. I know it's good because it was in Grand Republic two weeks ago, and Mrs. Higbee said it was swell. Would that be okay by you?"

"Certainly would. I never care for more than just so much

horsing around. I thought eight days would be too short a
stay here, and New York does wake you up and give you a
lot of ideas, but I'll be kind of glad when we get away next
Tuesday. I've enjoyed every second of it, but I won't be sorry
to be home and shoot some golf with Roy."

"And I'm crazy to see how much the decorators have got
done. Oh, yes, I'm *very* glad we're staying till Tuesday, but that
will be about enough."

A Thursday filled with trying on dresses, trying on museums
and churches, and deciding that their feet were too sore to go
up and look at Grant's tomb and the Rockefeller church, those
appropriate neighbors. The day was magnificently crowned
by having dinner with Avis Elderman, Bradd Criley's emigree
sister.

She remembered Cass perfectly, and forgave him for it.

She had glittering jet on her bosom, and she took them to
the Colony Restaurant.

She said to Jinny, "I don't think I ever met you in Grand
Republic."

"No, I lived in Pioneer Falls as a kid."

"Oh!"

It took Avis a minute to swallow this, but she tried again:
"Is this your first glimpse of New York?"

"Yes, my first."

"I trust that you are enjoying your stay here."

"M."

"Mr. Elderman and I are sorry that you are making such a brief sojourn. We had hoped to entertain you in our home. In Darien. In Connecticut, you know. Though of course we practically live in New York City—my husband's office is here, map-manufacturing, and I come in and join him for an evening at *least* once a fortnight, but still, we always say, even the city hasn't a more exacting and delightful social life than Darien. You would enjoy it so much."

"I'm sure of it," said Jinny.

As Cass and she went to bed, Jinny snarled, "The very next time, I'm going to say, 'No. Is it *your* first visit?' "

And, after more meditation, "I thought Bradd was a lovely man, till I met his sister."

When they awoke to devouring rain on Friday morning, Cass rejoiced, "Would I be a barbarian if I said, 'Thank God, we don't have to go out and look at the glories of New York all day long'?"

"Me too!"

He thought, he telephoned down to the porter's desk, and presently he announced, "I find we can get reservations for the trip back home for Monday instead of Tuesday. What would you——"

"Darling! Swell! Grab 'em! I'm crazy to see the new house, and Cleo and Rose and Valerie and Roy and everybody!"

They went back to sleep, lying close together, comfortably and quietly. They breakfasted luxuriously, for the Melchester did unexpectedly run to English muffins and wild-strawberry jam. They got rid of the breakfast wreckage, and told the chambermaid to stay out till lunch-time. Free from the duties of sightseeing, they laughed as pointlessly as schoolchildren.

——Well, if this trip hasn't accomplished anything else, it's got rid of Jay Laverick, and brought her back to me.

They were normally a somewhat restrained couple, but today they reveled in the cheerful vulgarities of the bathroom. She scrubbed his back, in the tub, and laughed, and kissed the wet smoothness of his shoulder. He reached up his arms to encircle her with a sudden need of her, and her giggling died in a passionate quick breathing.

It was on that day of gaiety and benevolent bad weather that their baby was conceived.

"There couldn't be a more wonderful lover than you," she sighed.

They did admit the chambermaid—who looked at them suspiciously—but they did not dress till five in the afternoon, when the weather had cleared.

They had a small walk up Fifth Avenue. While they were out, Berg Nord tried to telephone them. He had their address from Avis Elderman (whom he hated). Nord had hoped to have them join him after the theater, but he did not leave his name. They never learned that he was a lonely man.

They came back to the dreariness of having to decide which urban delight they would work at that evening.

The telephone. Cass answered. "Yes? Timberlane speaking." Then he shouted.

"Jinny! Do you know who it is? It's Bradd Criley! He's just landed here in New York, and he's right here in the hotel, and he'll be up here in five minutes!"

She sang, "That's the most beautiful thing that ever happened to me in my life!"

As Bradd came in, like a fresh wind from the Sorshay uplands, Cass thought that Berg Nord might be a sturdy trial lawyer, and Bradd, with that wavy hair that provides its own vine leaves, that round pale face and automatic smile, might be a romantic actor. But he got no further with the study, so excited were they all three, two men and a girl, the trinity of friendship—and of danger.

"You're the best sight for sore eyes I've seen since we left home," said Cass.

"You two look pretty good to me. What about you, Jin? Are you as glad to see me as your old man makes out he is?"

"My favorite brother, Bradd!" glowed Jinny, and kissed him.

Bradd summed it up, presently. "You have till Monday then—tonight and all day Saturday and Sunday? Can't we all play around together? I'm here for the Wargates, but I don't have to do a thing till Monday morning, except a few telephone calls."

"Perfect!" said Jinny.

"I really came on a couple of days early, hoping to catch you two."

"Oh, Bradd, you didn't!" whispered Jinny.

"What's your plans for tonight?"

"Not a thing."

"Managed to see *Life with Father* yet?"

"Impossible to get tickets."

Bradd crowed, "Not impossible for *me* to get tickets! It's a cinch, if you know the ropes. And I know every strand of the little ole ropes in this man's town."

"I'll bet you do," worshiped Jinny.

Bradd was already telephoning. "Berbetz? . . . This is Criley, from Grand Republic. . . . Fine. Just got in. Now listen, my young friend. I want three for *Life with Father* for tonight, and I want good ones, get me? . . . Fine. I'll pick 'em up at the box-office. I'll be seeing you."

Jinny was looking at him with admiration.

He ordered briskly, "Now I'll run down and have a quick shower and be ready in half an hour. Let's have an early dinner and have plenty of time to talk. We'll go to the Algonquin or the Plaza, and then after the show, I'll take you to Twenty-One or the Stork Club. Been to any of those places?"

Cass sighed, "We tried the Marmoset, but we felt like a

couple of outsiders."

"You won't with me. They know me! I'll be seeing you."

When he was gone, Jinny triumphed, "Now we'll have a tremendous time. But——I adore Bradd, but he is kind of a faker, isn't he!"

"What?"

"About this hotel being so out of the world. About getting these tickets that you can't get. The way he does it, he just pays some speculator about three times what they're worth. And about being such a sweetheart to all the night-clubs. It's just going there often enough, and tipping more than enough. The wise guy—the great man about town! Why, you're twice as distinguished as he is, and you look it!"

"Oh, now, Jinny, you're dead wrong. He isn't a faker."

"A show-off, then."

"But he isn't! Now, Jinny! I see him in the court room. He likes to make a jury laugh, but there isn't a steadier or better-prepared advocate in the district, and same way with his approach to his friends. He has the heart of a boy, and it pleases him so when he can do things for you that he just bubbles over. You've got to like Bradd!"

"Oh, I do, lots. I just meant——It irritates me if anybody thinks we're hicks just because we don't spend all our time doing New York—on a Wargate expense-account!"

"Don't let his fun and high spirits fool you. You'll come to love him."

"Anything for peace," she said. "All right, I'll love him then."

"Good!" said Cass.

At the Algonquin, Bradd pointed out one timid drama critic, one savage playwright, and two bored actors. Then they settled down to the news from Grand Republic. . . . Harley Bozard had been seen at Austin with a handsome woman from Minneapolis. Major Umbaugh had been promoted to lieutenant-colonel. Jamie Wargate was now a flyer.

Then Bradd spoke seriously.

"New York seems to have brought you two even closer together. Jin, I'm glad you've got the Jay Laverick nonsense out of your system,"

"I never had any in it!"

"Oh, yes, you did! Jay's an attractive heel, and a good friend of mine, but I wouldn't trust him across the street with a deaf virgin aged seventy. He does the sympathy racket. Listen, young lady: Cass never would jump you properly about Jay, because he's a sensitive gent, Cass is, and he's afraid of you. I'm not. So—just how strongly did Mr. Jay express his ambition to make you?"

Cass was surprised that he was not indignant at this intrusion, and Jinny merely sputtered, "He never expressed anything of the kind! I wouldn't let him!"

"You couldn't help letting him. Didn't he ever say anything—

very whimsy and make-believe, the little darling!—about you and him starting an arty tea-room together—he put up the cash and you the good taste?"

"Ye-es, he did make some cracks about my talent for watercress."

"That's his standard line. I know you have too much sense to fall for him really, but still, you did let him stick around, and you better cut him out and cleave only to the dumb breadwinners like the Judge and me. We won't let you down. Now you can tell me how I've been butting in."

"Well, you have! And I won't be bullied!"

"Tut!"

"I'll fall for whom I like. I'm a free woman."

"That's what you think."

"Oh, you make me tired," she said, so feebly that Cass and Bradd smiled at each other, and presently she was smiling with them.

If Cass found it too breathless, Jinny was exhilarated by the different New York that Bradd disclosed to them. He took them to three night-clubs, in which he was cordially greeted by, if not with, fatted calves, and on top of that, he injected them, at one o'clock in the morning, into a pent-house party being given by a man who, Bradd explained, was a very important, high-class man, with a lot of influence in Washington, the representative of a chain of Western banks.

Jinny decided that, after all, she had been born to pent-house life; to the glass bar and the Dali drawings and the couch long enough to seat eight people, to the garden outside and the nervous lights in the skyscrapers that formed its mountainous horizon; born to the attentions of gallantly drunken gentlemen.

Thousands of men were telling Jinny that she was beautiful; thousands and tens of thousands of ageless women were shrieking that she must have another drink immediately, till the coils of people inside the pent-house seemed thicker and darker than the coils of cigarette-smoke. Suddenly even the gregarious Jinny could not endure the blare of voices, and she slipped out on the terrace.

So she beheld a New York new-born and celestial.

She was astonished to come out not to a light-pointed darkness but to the rising sun. Four hours had gone in four minutes.

The pent-house was thirty stories up, on an apartment-house on Central Park West, looking eastward to Fifth Avenue and the park. To the northeast, incomprehensible waterways led through a golden mist to the open sea of Long Island Sound, and over them the bridges arched and vanished in a smudge of factories and airfields. The bulky castles of Fifth Avenue and beyond seemed but a narrow strip of gold-touched black floating upon the waters, and for a moment the ponderous city was as graceful as Venice.

To southward a thousand towers reached toward the sun, while just at her feet, far down, Central Park was still a dawn-dark labyrinth, with the reservoir like one of her own Northern lakes.

At her shoulder, Bradd's voice murmured, "New York can be beautiful, eh? It's London and Paris and San Francisco all in one."

"Yes, I didn't know how beautiful till you showed it to me, Bradd. I was scared of it, but I think I could love it."

He kissed her, and in gratitude she responded recklessly.

Bradd drew back. "We didn't mean that! It was just an accidental salute to the sun. Don't you ever tell that priggish Grand Republic lawyer about it."

"Cass is *not* a prig——"

"I didn't mean him. I meant that——what's his name?——Bradd Criley? The fellow who thinks you're his sister. Are you?"

"Yes!"

Elbows on the parapet, they were talking quietly when Cass came out to find them. He was pleased when he saw their fresh, dawn-cooled faces.

"You two are the only people here that look as if you've ever slept, but as it's tomorrow now, how about thinking of going home?" he chuckled.

"Fine!" said the artless Bradd.

On Saturday and Sunday, Bradd was the most conscientious pleasure-giver since Dennis the hangman. He took them to two theaters, for a drive in a victoria in Central Park. On Sixth Avenue he bought a dozen of the marzipan cakes that Jinny loved even more than candy, and they three walked down the street boldly eating them out of a paper bag. Sunday, they drove to Jones Beach and on to a restaurant with tables on the terrace.

By now, Jinny considered New York just as good as Grand Republic. But not Cass.

Bradd paid his share of all the bills, but he did not show off by trying to pay more. In all their arguments he took Cass's side against Jinny or Jinny's side against Cass, with equal cheerfulness. And he bought for her the first orchid of which she was ever the proprietor.

She confided to Cass, "You were entirely right about Bradd. He wasn't trying to impress us about how well he knows New York. He just has a lot of fun exploring it, and he loves to have his friends share it."

When Bradd had seen them off on the train, on Monday, Cass said to her, "Now you really begin to appreciate Bradd."

"Yes—thanks to you."

They returned to Grand Republic; they moved into the new house; the fall term of court opened; and the first case over which Cass presided was the divorce-suit of Beecher Filligan against his wife Pasadena, with Mr. Jay Laverick warmly referred to in the testimony.

An Assemblage of Husbands and Wives

FILLIGAN VS. LAVERICK

BEECHER FILLIGAN had only a minority share in the ownership of Havock & Filligan, contractors, but he also played at architecture and he had inherited a brickyard and a cement works. In the peerage of Grand Republic he rated as a viscount, with the highest distinction in the playing of backgammon. He was forty, and a friend of Bradd Criley and Jay Laverick.

His wife Pasadena, born in that Oxford of the Pacific Coast, was probably beautiful. She looked like a poor color-reproduction of a Botticelli goddess of rather late spring. She was derivative in everything except her make-up, in which she showed talent, care, and diligence.

Beecher was sick of her, sick of her mildly clattering tongue, her extravagance, and her monotony in bed. He wanted to get rid of her, and since he had no legal reasons, he set about creating them.

He knew that, despite her cow-like amiability when she had everything she wanted, she could be shrill and stubborn if she thought she was being cheated, so the fault had to be seemingly hers, and his the forgiveness or the vengeance.

Jay Laverick took notice of every halfway-pretty woman who seemed obtainable, and Beecher saw to it that Pasadena should appear extremely obtainable.

She was a Talking Woman, and like most Talking Women she was too busy babbling to notice what was happening about her. Her telephone calls, to announce that she would come and play bridge next Thursday, took half an hour. By going out to the kitchen and being orally helpful, she could get any cook to quit during the first fortnight, and Beecher usually went to sleep to her inane discussion of something that would have happened if it had only happened.

Beecher was not utterly to be blamed for his cold plotting against her. His plan had started one evening when, after he had complained absently about her extravagance and her astonishing tendency to get accidentally kissed at country-club dances, she had sneered, "Well, if I'm so lousy, why don't you *do* something, and not just yap about it?"

Not till two years later, when she was already married to the reluctant Jay Laverick, did she realize that Beecher had done something.

Beecher, in the oldest and simplest of tricks, began his work by having Jay at the house for three-handed rummy and being called out to the cement works at ten P.M., then telephoning at eleven that he would not be able to return till two. Venus and Freud did the rest.

Beecher's careful labor was almost ruined by Jay's getting interested in a much prettier and livelier woman, young Jinny Timberlane, so he had Jay for house-guest at his summer camp on Lake Winnemapaug, was called away "for two days," and returned late that same night. He despised Jay for an amateur Don Juan when he found them both in her bed, and asleep.

He said to Jay, "I ought to kill you, and I do happen to have a loaded rifle here, but I think the only decent, civilized way out of this horrible mess that you two have dragged me into is for you to marry her as soon as I divorce her."

Jay said, Why certainly; that's what he had intended to do, all along.

Pasadena, with her rouge smeared, was very distasteful to Jay.

Later, in chambers, Pasadena reported to Judge Timberlane, "Beecher practically cried over all that he had tried to do for me, and I just despised him. After that, I was sure I wanted to many Jay, who is a real man, not a whiner. But I will say for Beecher that he did manage to make me feel like considerable of a heel."

She was distasteful to Judge Timberlane in any state of make-up. He said, "But, Pas, any husband must sense it at once if his wife even begins to stray, and what I don't understand is how either you or your husband could be taken in by such an obvious wolf as Laverick."

"Don't you dare say anything against Jay! He's a gentleman, even when he's drunk, and he's going to marry me."

He was, and he did.

34

THE TIMBERLANES had been married for a year now, and they were fondly accustomed to the new house, to the gray furniture and mulberry carpets and curtains, the yellow leather pouf, the fireplace set flush in mirrors, in the pert living-room, as arranged by Jinny. Isis was presumably happy on a teakwood pedestal on a small glass shelf. The pictures were mostly nameless flower pieces; there were tall portfolios of Impressionist painters; and on a small flat desk were Jinny's precious tooled-leather stamp-box and a useless yellow quill pen. It was all very gay and comfortable and contemporary, even if it was a little like a model room in an expensive furniture store.

Cass thought highly of the oil furnace and the electric washing-machine, though he was not altogether contented in his new study. It was a cigar-box of a room, handsomely paneled, with a small fireplace reluctantly let into the pine walls, but there was room for only a quarter of his books, and the rest were lost in dark hallway-bookcases and the pinched attic.

"Oh, well, most of 'em I only look at once in a while, anyway," he sighed, as he lugged them to the attic. Strange that so few books can require so many staggering struggles up the ill-lighted stairs.

Jinny was joyfully busy. Now that she could organize her own house, and Mrs. Higbee could no longer hide spices and Canadian bacon and corn-flour from her in cavernous unknown cupboards, she was an exemplary housewife, busy with errands to the new Byzantine meat-market and the new Cordovan grocery-store, which made up the business-center of the Country Club District. She went on entertaining soldiers at the canteen, and once she stood on the running-board of a car on Chippewa Avenue and made a speech for the sale of war bonds.

"No," said Cass, afterward, "no, you were a very good speaker. I wish most lawyers would sum up as clearly as you did. Sweetheart, you're beating me at oratory as you do at everything else. Except maybe chess."

She was unquestionably beating him at one thing. She was pregnant.

He was delighted.

It was she who insisted that they must be economical, after the New York journey and buying the new house, now that Owen or Emily was coming.

She had picked out this choice of names for the baby, without discussion. She explained it to Cass:

"I'm glad about the infant. I feel like looking up at you as languishingly as any Dickens heroine. This is real creation.

I guess a baby is about the most modern and revolutionary thing a girl can do. I intend to be a wonderful mother. I know that if it's a boy, he'll be as sturdy and honest as you are, as your father must have been, so I want him to be 'Owen,' after your father. And if it's a girl—I had an Aunt Emily—so gentle, but awful smart.

"I did think, 'way back six months ago, when I was young, that I'd like to have a daughter named 'Lark.' I knew it was kind of a fancy name, but I want her to be what I always wanted to be and never could—swift and clean and belonging to the upper air, not touched with earth. Wait, wait now! Don't tell me a lark has to come down and sleep on the earth after it's got done soloing. I guess an expectant mother has a right to her own metaphor, hasn't she?

"But then I got to thinking about what her classmates would do to the kid, with a name like that, so I said to her, 'All right, you're going to be a sweet, simple Emily, and *like* it!'

"Cass, I am going to adore that baby!"

Cass said to Roy Drover, "She's so sort of serene and adjusted now."

Roy Drover said to Cass, "You mean she's got some of the damn nonsense knocked out of her by morning sickness."

Bradd Criley said to Cass, in Jinny's active presence, "Our girl is more lovely than ever now. How I envy you two!"

Chris Grau said to Jinny, with Cass philanthropically

listening, "How I envy you, dear! Did you ever know that once I thought I was a little in love with your dear husband, myself? Oh, Jinny, you must give him a lovely baby."

Mrs. John William Prutt said to Mr. John William Prutt who, in a gray flannel union-suit, was sitting on the floor, cutting his long pale toenails, "It is perhaps my imagination, but I cannot help feeling that it may have been our influence as their former neighbors that has changed Mrs. Timberlane from a really quite scatterbrained and, I might almost venture to suggest, flirtatious young woman into an apparently responsible young Grand Republic matron."

Boone Havock, the distinguished ex-saloon-bouncer, said to Judge Blackstaff, at the Federal Club, "Cass must of gone plumb crazy. Probably from working too hard at loving that hot little wife of his. Not that it's her fault, poor kid. I thought at fust that she was from the wrong side of the railroad tracks, but she seems to have settled down to being a nice little lady and a good war worker. But Cass—why, I hear where, right in this classy new house of his, he entertained this flannel-mouthed Vogel, the county agricultural agent, that's a Farmer-Laborite and practically an under-cover gumshoer for the co-operatives that want to ruin every decent business that we've given our lives to building up."

"Oh, no, no, Boone," insisted Judge Blackstaff. "I find Judge Timberlane a sound and loyal colleague. I think it's just that his wife—after all, she is young, and she probably enjoys experimentation and wants to meet all these cranks and freaks and reds and fanatics, just to see what they're like. Once she has had her baby, she'll settle down and be just like your wife and mine."

"I certainly hope so," said Boone.

For Eino Roskinen, who was serving somewhere in the Pacific, Cass and Jinny packed a Christmas box: fruit cake, candy, cigarettes, and a thin-paper edition of *Farewell to Arms*.

"We do so little and he does so much. I feel we ought to both be out there with him," fretted Cass. "I'm going to kiss you for *him*." That kiss was strange and disembodied, as though it were indeed the caress of a spirit.

On this, their second Christmas together, everybody decided that the Little Mother—as they all called her, to Jinny's fury—ought to stay home and be visited and relentlessly loved and cherished, and they all did it: the Drovers, Havocks, Blackstaffs, Flaatens, Gadds, and an alternately shrieking and hush-hushing gang of half a dozen more families, while for Christmas dinner, with much holly and silver, there were Bradd, Chris, Cleo, and the three Pennlosses. George Hame diffidently brought in a pair of woolly mittens, embroidered for Jinny by his daughter Betty, and a family whose son they believed Judge Timberlane to have saved from prison sent a goose from Four Mile Pine.

Jinny announced that she was now domesticated and contentedly settled for her whole future life.

Drowsy with Christmas turkey and claret, Cass and Jinny and Bradd, the others gone, hunched down in their deep chairs. Every five minutes one of them said, "We ought to take a good brisk walk." Busy as a squirrel, Jinny ate a chocolate, sipped Benedictine, gulped a glass of water. She complained, "I have the most awful thirst."

"Of course, you baby, eating all that sweet stuff," yawned Bradd.

"Let's see if we can catch die Philharmonic on die radio and then go out and take a good brisk walk," said Cass.

But first on Station KICH came the war-news bulletins, to which they listened with the indifference into which civilians fall. But they sat up as they heard a bulletin:

"I have to announce the sad news that another of our boys has given his life that democracy may live. One of our fine young men, an expert on dairying processes, Eino Roskinen, was killed in an airplane crash somewhere in the Pacific on Christmas Eve."

Bradd said quite cheerfully, "Didn't you know him, Jin?"

She gasped, and they half heard her groan, "I hardly let him kiss me. I wish to God I had!"

Bradd stirred with electrified interest. Cass was filled with pity. He went over to touch her hair, muttering, "A brave boy."

He felt struggling far down in him the rebellious thought, "How do I know I wouldn't have been just as brave, if it had been my job to fight?" But the thought never came to the surface, as she mourned, cheek against his sleeve:

"We never think that death can come near *us*. But I feel as if it were in the room now."

In the silence, they breathed uncomfortably. They could hear the cat as it leaped from a cupboard toward the mantelpiece. It almost missed and, clawing, upset the bracket on which was Isis, who toppled from her little teak standard and fell to the tiled hearth, with a tiny noise of breaking. Jinny hastened across the room and picked up the crystal cat-goddess. One of its miniscule legs was broken clean off, and Jinny held it out for Cass to see, sobbing like a bewildered child.

35

CASS HAD INTENDED to keep their life from falling into a prosperous-middle-class routine which would bore Jinny as it bored his sister Rose, but now, he felt, "just for a while, a Certain Amount of Routine will protect her."

He was correct in calculating that their routine did add up to at least a Certain Amount.

The routine of his court room, workmanlike and busy, and the routine of his return home, the welcoming kiss, the "What you been doing all day?", news on the radio and reading—sometimes aloud—of the *Banner* editorials, the game of chess, the game of dominoes, the game of gin-rummy.

The routine of bedtime and Cass's "Golly, I didn't know it was so late—guess it's about time to turn in," and in the morning, "Almost eight o'clock—time to rise and shine."

The routine of food: steak, chicken, veal chops, corned beef, pork chops, fried pike, steak; and of reports about the weather. The routine discussion of shall we have soup? He was pro-soup, and she was anti.

The routine of dining with the Pennlosses every Sunday noon.

The routine of love-making, which became a routine and not a storm as soon as they wondered how much longer it was safe to continue it.

But he knew that Jinny was no amateur of such regularity, and he pondered upon the production of mild and antiseptic amusements. The best of these seemed to be the encouragement of the Pennlosses and Bradd and Chris to come in whenever they could. Somehow, the busy Bradd was able to "drop in" much oftener than the others.

He was such a safe, comfortable, cheerful friend to have about. He was ready to play cards, to talk, to listen, to pat Cleo, to admire Jinny's knitting and Cass's legal opinions, to tease Jinny when she was petulant and Cass when he was irritable, and to bring ice in for the highballs from the kitchen refrigerator. Bradd was a singularly neat remover of ice-cubes, refiller of ice-trays, and wiper of highball glasses, and he agreed with Jinny on the necessity of using, always, the Chinese brass coasters under the glasses, to protect the tables.

It was Bradd who affably took charge on the evening when Jay Laverick came in to show off his new wife, Pasadena, and was drunk enough to hint that there had been other ladies, quite recently, who had craved his competent affections.

So Bradd became the *tertium quid* in the household: Cass's friend and admirer, Mrs. Higbee's admirer and beau, Cleo's teacher of protocol, and Jinny's brother. He was a combination of grandfather, son, investment-counsel, assistant judge, trained nurse, thoughtful patron, and pet dog.

Cass did not realize—surely Bradd could not have realized—

just how often he was there.

Cass would have said that Chris Grau appeared just as often, because when Chris did come, you noticed it. In forty-five minutes she would change from Cass's thwarted sweetheart to protector of Jinny against Cass's gross passions to sweater-knitting friend.

Bradd also read aloud from a very imaginative little manual of psycho-analysis. He kept begging Jinny not to be shocked by these cases from real life.

She was not shocked. She was interested.

It was a comfort to Cass that on evenings when he had to go out speech-making, to the Masons or the Montenegrins or the Mensheviks, he could count on Bradd to entertain Jinny at home or take her to the movies. Occasionally, when Cass was kept late in his chambers and Bradd felt that poor Jinny might be dull, he drove her down to the Unstable for a drink before dinner.

This, however, seemed to Cass unnecessary.

They had a serene evening, Cass and Jinny alone, discussing the future of Owen-Emily.

"It excites me and it scares me," said Cass. "He—she—will be able to fly from Grand Republic to London in eight hours, and he may see the whole world one state, or see it an anarchy starving in caves."

"Well, before he starts revolutionizing the world," mused

Jinny tenderly, "I'm going to see he's a good swimmer and tennis player, and says 'Thank you, Mother' nicely."

"Reactionary!"

They were cheerful then, but when Cass came home the next evening, he found a Jinny irritable as a cat-haunted robin.

"Why, what's the trouble, dear sweet?" he bumbled.

"Don't be so disgustingly forgiving and paternal!"

"All right, I'll be unforgiving. Go on."

"Oh, it's just——I went out to the Unstable for lunch with Gillian Brown. She had an idea I might do some sketches for their fashion show at the Beaux Arts. And maybe I will, too. And——I hadn't meant to take a drink, but I felt so blue, shut in here all the time——"

"You aren't!"

"Yes I am too! I don't know as it can be helped, but I am. And I had this mean thirst that's been bothering me lately—I suppose that's pregnancy, too—and so I had a highball, and I felt better. And Bradd just happened to drop in, and he came over and joined us, and he felt like taking the afternoon off, and so he and Gillian decided they'd go to Alimony Hall and get drunk, and they asked me would I like to come along, and I said, Yes, I certainly would——"

"You know——"

"Oh, yes, yes, yes, I know *exactly* what you think of Alimony Hall and Sabine Grossenwahn, but there isn't any law in the

Constitution, is there, that I have to accept *all* your opinions? Sabine is amusing, and if she sleeps with everybody in town— except you—I *hope*—that isn't any of our business, is it?"

"I rather think———"

"Oh, don't talk like John William Prutt! Like Mrs. Prutt! Like the whole world of Pruttery! That's how they felt about *us*, one time. Sometimes often you're just as priggish as the Prutts. I much prefer a roughneck realist like Boone Havock. *Or* Sabine! But anyway: I wanted to go, but I knew you and Roy would have a fit, so I said, No, I wouldn't. And so Bradd and Gillian kidded the life out of me for being such a Puritan, and I think they were right, too; I think I'd of felt a lot better if I had gone and lapped up a lot of Sabine's Miracle Mash Bourbon. Roy is crazy. He's just an old woman—like all obstetricians—and he isn't even that—he's a surgeon. By golly, if there were one in town, I'd get me a nice sympathetic young obstetrician that would *prescribe* hell-raising! Now go on. Be horrified. I guess it's very choice and high-class to have a husband that can quote Milton and Veblen, but I get awful tired of living in a diving-bell. So now you can be horrified all you want to!"

"But I'm not, and as soon as Owen comes———"

"Emily!"

"Emily, then. Then I'll go to Sabine's with you."

If indeed he was "horrified," it was only that the trusty Bradd should have been willing to take her to that amateur brothel. Then:

——Oh, sure. I've got it. He didn't want her to go at all, and he just pretended he did to gentle her down. Still, I would like to ask Bradd what he really said.

But, worried over Jinny, worried by the war news, he forgot to ask.

He reached home before Jinny, that evening in early March. He sat in one of the detestably neat gray-leather chairs, bending his newspaper. He heard her at the door. She did not halt to take off her furs; she was in the doorway, her hands flat against either side of the frame, her face wincing, no youthful wife but a frightened woman.

He sprang up.

"Cass! I'm sick, I'm really sick, and it isn't just pregnancy. I may die."

He held her arms, wet with melting snow.

"I've just been to Roy for my examination. Cass, I have diabetes!"

"Oh, no!"

"Yes. And I could die from it."

"It's not serious, Jinny; it couldn't be!"

"Not *too* serious, Roy says. I don't even need insulin, not yet anyway, he says; just proper diet and take care of myself. But could anything be worse than taking care of yourself all the time, like an invalid?"

"I'll do it for you."

"You will, O God, how you'll take care of me! It'll be worse than dying. Wrapped in cotton, all night, all day—and expected to be grateful!"

"Now, now! Let's get your coat off. Here, let me rub your hands. Lord, they're cold! There, there——"

"Now, now, now! There, there, there!" she mocked him. "Sweet, sweet chick! Enjoy your beddie-weddie all day long! You and Roy will have me as sappy as Juliet Zago in a month!"

He had sense enough to ignore her sputtering. A girl had the right to be a little testy at the threat of death! He yelled out to Mrs. Higbee to delay dinner fifteen minutes, and to bring two martinis, quick. He got Jinny settled on the couch, with Cleo soft between them, and demanded, "Now tell me exactly."

"Maybe it isn't too bad. Roy says it's diabetes, all right, but very mild—says if I just have a little common sense—but of course that's like saying, 'If you just have the genius of Beethoven,'—and if I take care of myself, I could live to be ninety and scarcely know I had the thing. . . . And be just as good-looking! I mean—you know—not ugly, I mean . . . But doesn't it sound coarse. Diabetes! Sugar in the urine! Aah! Why can't I die of something romantic, like Camille or Mary, Queen of Scots? Diabetes!"

"Call it 'diabetes mellitus,' then. That sounds fancier."

"So it does. Oh, I do feel better, now I've told you, and I know it will be wonderful, the way you'll take care of me. I'm not really ungrateful. I'm just blaming on you the faulty action of my Islands of Langerhans, blast 'em! I have some nerve back now. I *will* live to be ninety—and you'll be a hundred and four and still trying to get me to eat less candy—and I'll crab all the time, and love you for it!"

But she was frightened. It quavered in all her flippancies, and he concentrated on her fear, not on his own below-zero terror that she might die and all his own life die with her.

As she hastily drank the cocktail he had ordered, he mused, "I suppose Roy has forbidden all alcohol."

"Yes, this drink is my last. Say, how did you ever get as gloomy a friend and physician as Roy? He doesn't even enjoy seeing his patients die when they disobey him. Yeh, no alcohol, no candy, no cake, very little meat. He wants to keep me alive only technically. His theory is that it's better to be alive and miserable than dead and happy. Not even one tender, confiding little cocktail."

"Well, this evening I'll also give you one stiff highball, and starting tomorrow morning, we'll both of us go on the water-wagon, absolutely. Both of us. You realize that?"

"O God, yes, I realize it. When the Judge raises his voice like that, the boys run right out and get the rope."

"Darling, it won't be so bad. We'll have lots of pleasant substitutes for sweets and booze."

393

"As how? *Chess?*"

"No, we'll think of a lot of things."

"Always ending with chess!"

"Now don't be so contrary."

"A girl that's going to die has got a right to be contrary."

"She certainly hasn't any right to say 'has got' for 'has,' and if she claims all her rights and has a husband like me, who's too weakly adoring to spank her and put her to bed, she's in danger of having him become devious and control her by slyness instead of by healthy bullying. You can't win, now that I've started to take care of you, and I want no more pretty nonsense out of you."

"Gee, at that, you may be a better wife-manager than I thought."

"I may. And by the way——You spoke of my court attendants running for a rope. You know, don't you, that actually there is no capital punishment in the State of Minnesota? What are you smiling at, dear? Have I said something naive?"

During dinner, she was cheerful, and in her old voice of affectionate derision she read the regimen that Dr. Drover had given to her.

"Avoid worry. . . . Doesn't say how; just avoid it—*you* know—ole worry come, throw it out of the window. Gee, the wonders of medical science. . . . Warm clothes. . . . Drop in at some lumberjack store tomorrow and buy me a nice red-flannel union suit, will you? That'll keep all the men away, and so I'll also avoid one of the worries, anyway. . . . Warm baths. Mm. Massage. . . . That depends on the masseur. Do you know any handsome young gentlemen masseurs? They *could* be blind. I still think Jay Laverick would make a fine, conscientious masseur, but I never could get a meeting of minds with you on that topic. . . . Diet. . . . Me on a diet! Me that in my prime tossed in banana splits and pickled pig's feet at the same orgy. . . . Saccharine for sugar. . . . Cereals. . . . Leafy vegetables. . . . How I do hate leafy vegetables—the leafier the nastier, I always say. I hate to get my teeth into a mess of leaves. . . . Beans, broccoli, cabbage, cucumbers, endive, okra—okra!—squash, tomatoes, turnip-tops, watercress—I ask you! Could anything sound more loathsome? Just make sure that I stick to that diet for two months, and I'll run away with Boone Havock and go reeling down State Street with the fumes of two steaks and a mutton chop rising to my befuddled brain. . . . Oh, darling, can you stand making me stand it?"

"Sure!"

36

AT THE END of dinner he coaxed, "Now I want you to skip right up and get into bed, and I'll come up and talk to you, and we'll play a good game of—of dominoes."

"Now you look here! I do not intend to start being an invalid, in bed all the time. I'd rather die first! Roy didn't say——"

"No, no, just tonight. You're overwrought. So am I, for that matter. I'll talk to Roy about it, but I presume that ordinarily you'll be able to stay up till ten-thirty or eleven every evening—maybe till midnight, after Baby comes."

"No, tonight especially *not*. If I relaxed, I'd be too scared."

"Tell you what I'll do. I'll get some lively soul to come in and gossip and cheer us both up. I'll get Bradd! He'll have to know, sooner-later, anyway."

"Yes, you phone him, and I'll put on my most languorous nightgown and receive all you boys in bed. Like a queen. . . . Oh, Cass, I was going to be such a good, strong wife, and I'm just a sick, whining child, to bother you."

She sobbed, head against his substantial shoulder, for a long time. When she went up the stairs, still whimpering softly, he looked up after her, and her climbing was that of a naughty child who has been punished.

He did not tell her afterward, but when he telephoned he did not find it easy to capture Bradd. He had to drag him out of a poker game. Bradd sounded not too willing, and Cass insisted that Jinny was ill and really needed the skillful cheering of the man-about-town.

When he went up to sit awkwardly by her bed, in the new gray-and-pink chamber, he reflected that Bradd had never seen her here, and he regretted having invited even his old friend into the sanctuary. She was miraculously feminine tonight; the baby was going to be tiny, and she was scarce swollen; there was no hint of it as she sat up in bed, huddled under the pink silk coverlet. Her throat was fair above sinful laces and ribbons, her hair was softly shaken out, her cheeks were flushed, by nature as well as art.

——Um. That was a mistake. But too late now to stop Bradd. . . . And she really does need some clown like him, tonight. . . . My lovely, warm, terrified girl.

He fumbled, "Before Bradd comes, there's one slightly embarrassing thing—I don't know whether Roy spoke of it or not, but I wonder—and of course we have to think of your health beyond any other consideration——"

"You dear old lady! You wouldn't be chastely referring to sleeping together, would you?"

"Why, Jinny!"

"I could use still more lucid expressions."

"Stop riding me, sweet. I can't help it if I'm shy with

397

you—call it reverent. There are a dozen or so words that Roy and I used to exchange freely, at the age of twelve. I do know them—you'd be surprised! But I honestly don't like to use 'em in your presence."

"Didn't Bradd use 'em, too?"

"Not much. He was a foully clean-minded little beast—then."

"Poor, innocent Bradd!"

"I'd like to get back to our investigation. What did Roy say?"

"He said, situation normal for six weeks or so, and then we'll ha ye to be as chaste as my crystal cat."

They looked at each other so confidingly.

Their old friend Bradd had never been more admirable.

He came in casually; he lightly patted Cass's shoulder; he kissed Jinny's cheek—not overly glancing, Cass noted, at her bosom beneath the foam of nightgown; he sat down and took charge of their muted terror.

"I had a hunch something was wrong, when you called me, Cass, so I phoned Roy, and he says Jin has a very mild case of diabetes, nothing to worry over. Jinny, sweet, our chief job is the agreeable one of keeping you gay as a gopher. Now of course all these docs, even a hardboiled one like Roy, croak about avoiding all alcohol and sweets, and any mental flings more disturbing than buying moth-balls. They exaggerate, because they hope to get *half* of what they order—like a dealer telling you to keep a new car down to thirty. If they tell a patient to cut out alcohol, what they expect is that the dope will cut the intake down to a pint of mule every six hours, with just a dash of canned heat.

"The great thing in curing any of these chronic diseases is mental, so if Cass and you and I have just a couple of drinks and sit around and laugh like fools, that'll be more sensible than acting like a dyspeptic killjoy. How about it?"

"Oh, I'm sure you're right, Bradd," rejoiced Jinny. "I'll be careful, but not get sour and Pruttish."

"Look, you two!" protested Cass.

"Consider it said, sweetie," purred Jinny. "You mean that the orthodox method of not drinking any alcohol whatever is not to drink any alcohol. We young revolutionists don't fall for that any longer. And, Cass, you *said* I could have another drink, after dinner."

"Did I? Well, I think you're getting along fine without it, so let's stick to that."

Bradd and Jinny looked with humorous exasperation at this husbandly spoil-sport, but he was firm.

She refused to have a nurse, but she did, with omissions, "take care of herself." To her the omissions were a joke, a game of thwarting Cass and his co-plotter, Dr. Drover.

To Cass, nothing of all this was a joke. The shock of

comprehending her danger was a delayed contusion, and not till next day did he quite take in the special fact of her illness. Then, all day, on the bench, he was taut and shaky.

He was agonizingly aware that she might die. When he passed a cemetery, cold under March snow, when he heard of the death of another soldier from home, he starkly saw her then, unmoving in a coffin, not to move and speak to him again, ever.

He had never rented Bergheim, and now he refused an offer. He heard himself saying, "If she died, I would take Cleo and Mrs. Higbee and crawl back to the old place."

His most desperate effort was to keep from seeming desperate.

Jinny did not often leave the house, as April came roughly in, promising May. She drove into the country sometimes with Cass or, if he was held in court till evening, with Rose or the Wolkes, but mostly she clung to the house, like the frightened cat with whom Cass was always identifying her now.

Every night she conscientiously tended her feet, stooped over them, bathing and rubbing eveiy tiniest crease or abrasion, while Cass watched her pitifully.

She recited hopefully, "Roy says the great Dr. Joslin says every diabetic ought to have a dog, because a dog never tempts you to break your diet or embarrasses you by being too sorry for you, like your friends. 'Well,' I said to Roy, 'my cat is just as good as a dog that way, isn't she?' and he said, very stiff, 'Joslin doesn't say anything about cats—just dogs.'

"And Roy does lay such stress on the grapefruit. He figures a grapefruit is the diabetic's best friend—next to his dog, of coursel I got to eat grapefruit and like it—that horrible, fat, smug, sickly-yellow lump!

"And Roy says there's no danger Emily will transmit the tendency to diabetes—or Owen either—if there's none of it in *your* family, and he says there isn't any. Poor Emily! To start off with a mother that hasn't got one doggone thing but love for her—no strength and no candy and not much sense. You've got to have sense for both of us, Cass.

"There. If Dr. Joslin himself came right in this room now and looked at those feet, he'd say, 'Jinny, I never saw a slicker job of pedicuring. You're a good girl, Jinny—for a blasted diabetic!' "

"No! A blessed diabetic."

"Oh, yes. And Roy said Joslin said Clemenceau and Edison were both diabetics, and they carried on like sons-of-guns with it."

"So will you."

"But you don't think it will make me reactionary like them, do you?"

"I don't think it will make you anything but Jinny."

"Which is rapidly being accepted by all lexicographers as a symptom for perfection, you mean?"

He wanted to cry.

Sometimes she was little and bewildered and clung to Cass and wanted to be obedient to Dr. Drover's orders. Sometimes she was irritated by the unreasonableness of being ill and turned to Bradd, who chirped, "Cheer up, baby; I'm sure you behave a lot better than His Honor says."

Cass was supposed to be pleased when Bradd could inspire her to a flippant lightness, but he wondered if they did not depend too much on Bradd's friendly presence. Then, in May, the duty of being comic in the sickroom was shared by a discharged Marine—that radio-artistic Fred Nimbus who had once acted himself into the war. Nimbus had an excellent record; he had risen to corporal and been honorably discharged for a mild stomach ulcer. He had gone no nearer to the South Pacific than San Diego, but he came home to his creative labors at Station KICH where, from his experiences as a Marine Corps stenographer, he described to the Far-Flung Radio Audience—flung at least as far as Kanabec County— the fighting on tropical islands, the inside politics of China and India, and the racial mixtures in the Balkans and Peru. He was to be heard at the house of Gregory Marl, explaining everything so vehemently that even Diantha Marl shut up.

There were other returned soldiers in town, but most of them had been wounded and they were strangely unwilling to show off even for such interrogatory civilians as Diantha, and

Mr. Fred Nimbus was their willing Homer.

He remembered that Mrs. Timberlane and he had been chums, and he assumed that in her illness the one thing she longed for was his manly and merry presence. He was often in the house now, forgiving Jinny for having failed him, trying to forgive Cass for having stolen her away, brightening them all up by interpreting the home life of Hirohito.

Round Jinny's chaise-longue gathered, too, the Pennlosses and Wolkes and Tracy Oleson. Cass was disturbed by the very gaiety that kept her cheerful. He wanted, and did not want, to remind her that she was ill, but only when morning sickness overwhelmed her, or dry thirst and a series of itches revealed the lurking diabetes, did she want to be quiet and somewhat less populated. She looked almost too well in frail loveliness, an alabaster lamp.

He hinted, "Why don't you take up your drawing again? That would give you something to do, and not tire you."

"I seem to have lost all ambition. I guess that even up-and-coming young married women do get that way. It's not so much that I'm ill. I'm trapped by happiness. I'm so very proud of Owen."

"Not Emily?"

"No, it's Owen. He stirs quite differently from a girl—more cranky. He'll be one of these men that will take care of their wives even if it kills them!"

Cass was glad of his alliance with Bradd. When the

living-room was full of chatterers, Bradd looked at them malevolently, while Jinny mocked, "Look at those old crape-hangers, Father Cass and Uncle Bradd. You kids better be quiet. I don't dare peep. But I'd like to get up and dance and have a great, big, thick, raw hamburger and four cream-puffs. I am so hungry!"

But if Bradd disapproved of the young people as much as Cass, he could step down into their ribaldry more easily, and Cass admired the ease with which he could say, "We all better get out now and give Jinny a chance to rest."

Cass begged of Jinny, "Do I bore you by asking Bradd to come in so often?" and she consented, "Oh, no, I like him almost as well as you do."

He kept from caressing her, for fear of his own wild possessiveness. He perceived again that none of the spectacles of the world, not the pride of war nor the pomp of religion nor thrones and towers and banners, was so exalted or so tragic as that love between men and women which had been greeted always with trivial welcome or with shameful jesting.

She began to make a business of understanding that she was ill and could not live on pity. He was proudest of her one late afternoon when she reported, "I got out a little today—went over to see Mrs. Purdwin. She's been having terrible arthritis—she's in pain most of the time, awful wrenching pain—it wakes her up. She says it's like a whip-lash; it just takes all the humanity out of her and she becomes an animal.

"So then I quit being so sorry for myself. I'd been feeling as if I were set aside from all normal people; as if I were a condemned man, with no hope. But after I'd talked to Mrs. Purdwin I got to thinking about people that are *really* up against it: men without jobs in cities, farmers with mortgages and the crop has failed again and the kids are hungry and cold; all the awful things that we first-class passengers never know.

"So I decided you're not going to be afflicted any more by having a whiner around. I'm so virtuous now, it hurts!

"But when I do slip and start whining again, you'll put up with it, won't you?"

37

JUDGE TIMBERLANE, a sensible man, explained it lucidly to himself on the train:

——You're only going to be gone five or six days at most, and Roy is right there at hand, and Rose and Bradd will look in, and Mrs. Higbee is better than any nurse. And if anything did go wrong—but nothing could—how could *you* help?

——Just as well not to be around and mooning over her all the time. Be reasonable. And don't keep telephoning her longdistance every minute, either. When you get to your hotel, can't you get settled first, and not phone her before you even take off your hat?

He apparently could not.

Jinny said, No, nothing really critical had happened to her in the three hours since he had left her.

He had been summoned to Duluth to give help with a crowded court-calendar. Now, in April, the trees that embraced the city in summer had not yet blossomed, but Lake Superior was free of ice, with something like terror in its steel beauty. His hotel was just above the lake, and all evening, his business in court finished, idle and lonely and full of the lack of Jinny, he listened to the sounds of the inland seaport.

From his window, across the narrowed end of the lake, he saw the "diamond necklace" of lights on the Allouez ore-docks, and they filled him, the steamers' whistles filled him, with divine restlessness.

Jinny and he must not stay forever in the inland ruts of Grand Republic.

After two evenings of dining with fellow-judges and coming back to the hotel to read briefs and try to think of important reasons for telephoning to Jinny, his bachelor state seemed deplorable. He was pleased when in the hotel coffee-shop he saw that enterprising business woman, Mrs. Gillian Brown of Grand Republic, come to Duluth on propaganda for that fine, clean-smelling, domestic perfume, Mourir pour Amour, of which Harley Bozard was state missionary.

She waved to him invitingly. He liked Gillian, and he moved to her table.

She was in a fine ribald mood, and she also told Cass that he was a graceful swimmer, which no one seemed to have noticed before. They went to a motion picture, and Cass felt that he was expected to slide his hand along Gillian's beautiful arm.

Well, he did and he didn't.

Gillian said cheerfully, "I've got some especially good Bourbon in my suite at the hotel. Come up and have a drink."

In the full elevator, he was pressed against her. As they

entered her suite, she threw her coat at a chair, and looked at him blandly. Her look said that she had always liked him more than he had guessed, and that, poor man, he must be living in the most undesirable chastity. All of her movements were swift and efficient. She mixed two highballs, without spilling a drop, she put them on the low table before the couch, without a bang, she touched his arm and drew him down to a place beside her on the couch. He knew that he was almost inevitably going to kiss her.

But she made one mistake. She said, "Let's have a drink, first," and gulped half her glass. As she set it down, she stared with simple surprise and fury, for Cass had warily popped up from the couch and was, in abject retreat, heading for his hat.

"W——?"

"Gill, you're extremely attractive, and good night!"

All the way to his room he snarled, "All right, I *am* a Puritan! I'm sure Gillian is much more sensible. . . . Jinny!"

During the last month of Jinny's pregnancy, her mother came down now and then from Pioneer Falls, but she was a remarkable mother-in-law; she believed that it was her daughter that Cass had married, not herself. She came in and looked approving and told Cass that he was a fine man, a good husband, and went home.

Except for a tiny lesion on her left foot, over which Dr.

Drover croaked unbecomingly (she said), Jinny got through easily to her time of confinement. She again refused a nurse.

"The woman would just butt in between you and me, and I want us to be so close now, because I am kind of scared. I don't even want Mother or Rose or Bradd around. Don't you dare try to duck out of your responsibility of being my guardian angel!"

"I'll put on special wings."

"You better! And what's this nonsense about your going off to what you call a 'court' every day? Is that kind? Is that necessary? Do you really want to go on with this business of making people unhappy just because they've acted naturally and killed people or raped people or robbed people that were just asking to be killed and raped and robbed? Doesn't your court sound pretty silly, when I put it that way? No, you stay home with me."

He did, as far as he could.

That fair June evening, they sat out on the small screened terrace at one end of the house, Jinny wrapped in a silken coverlet.

"I don't mind much, but it does go *on* so!" was her only complaint.

He coaxed her to sleep early by going off to bed himself. His body ached with hers. Asleep, he dreamed that she was on a steamer pulling out from the pier on which he stood, and he frantically wanted to leap the growing gap. He came sharply awake at a wail from her room. Not quite sure that he was not still dreaming, he was standing beside her bed without seeming to have walked there.

She smiled, but with a twitching tic in it. She wavered, "The pains have started. Would you mind phoning Roy? What time is it?"

"Just a second. . . . Seventeen minutes to three."

"Emily is the most inconsiderate child!"

Nothing was real to him; everything was a fantasy in hard steel colors, in the night chill. He had not believed that he could love Jinny more, but love so filled him that he could in no way express it. He stooped to kiss her fleetingly, and he stated baldly, "Everything is in order. Relax now."

Roy Drover's voice, answering oh the telephone, was watchful.

Cass was dressed and back in her room in six minutes. She was feebly flapping around with a girdle.

"Here, this is plenty wardrobe." He wrapped a quilt about her and carried her downstairs to the car.

"But my clothes, my lovely new clothes that Mr. Timberlane bought for me!" she sighed.

"I'll have Mrs. Higbee pack some and I'll bring 'em later."

She was almost asleep again, exhausted from the pains, as he lifted her into the car, and she nuzzled against him with none of Jinny's pertness.

Grand Republic was proud that its St. Agatha Hospital was as tiled and shiny, as tricky in its surgical technique, as anything in Chicago. But it was also as bureaucratic. The night desk-clerk, a young lady whom the war had unfortunately lured from the farm, had never heard of Mrs. Timberlane, Judge Timberlane, or pre-engaged private rooms, and it is doubtful whether she had ever heard of obstetrics, though she should have. While Jinny sat in the lobby, a small bundle of acute pain hugely covered with comforters, and Cass roared at the clerk, suddenly Dr. Drover made a stage entrance, growled, "I'll take care of her," and lifted her up onto a wheeled stretcher which he seemed to have slipped out of his pocket.

Cass looked at Roy's placid, bulky power with reverence. This was not the old friend; this was their god. That the doctor could ever have done anything so lacking in cold divinity as sleeping and snoring that night seemed impossible. He was the machine that impersonally dealt out birth and death and relief from pain.

In a hygienic, hateful private room, he lifted Jinny to the high bed. Against the meager hospital pillow her hair was stormily black, but her face was thin and small, jerking with agony.

For more than an hour Cass stood clumsily about the room, in a fire of terror. It was at dawn that Roy nodded to the nurse, with "Take her in now." He did not even look at Cass, who was suddenly doing a lockstep up and down the corridor, shut out from her pain. Roy did so far recognize him as a human being as to come out of the delivery-room and nod, but Cass knew that there was danger and difficulty in there, beyond the smug glazed door.

He heard no wail of a new-born infant, no cheerful slapping of its back, none of the traditional joys of childbirth. Roy came rapidly stalking out, authoritative in white gown and mask, followed by an orderly wheeling a stretcher, on which was just seen the tiny unconscious face of Jinny among the covers, and the nurse carrying an anonymous wrapped bundle.

Cass had pictured the baby lying beside the fond mother, and Jinny awakening to love it. But the nurse took the bundle off to a room down the hall.

"Girl," said Roy.

"How is Jinny? How is she? How is she?"

"Oh, she'll be okay. Got more stamina than you'd expect from such a skinny kid. She'll be under anesthetic for a few minutes yet. But the baby——Some trouble there; obstructed gut or something, don't know what yet; not breathing the way I like. May have to operate."

They stood on either side of Jinny's bed, and Cass cloudily tried to associate that diminutive face with his radiant and expansive girl. He felt that they were all in a dream, anxiously doing unseen things in a valley of fog.

Roy was yawning, "I'll go take a look at the baby now. Say, see last night's paper?"

"Yes."

"Those Japs are making us a lot of trouble. You know what I'd do, if I was commanding the Navy? I'd just ignore all these outlying islands and land right on Japan itself. I don't suppose I'm any military and naval expert, but I bet I could do a lot better job than most of these professionals. A surgeon is a fellow that has got to get right down to brass tacks. Of course it's these Roosevelt politics that are hampering———"

From the bed, the tiniest of protesting sounds: "Are you boys going to go on talking all day?"

To Cass's startled, wheeling look, her beady eyes were somewhat malevolent.

She demanded, weakly, "Where's my baby, Roy?"

"You'll see it in just a li'l' while now, honey."

"A girl?"

"You bet!"

"Emily, my darling baby. Now I'll really live!"

The nurse had edged in through the door. Roy clumped over to her, listened to her whispering. He turned, with more tenderness in his beefy face than Cass had seen for thirty years, and said, "Jin, your old man here is about as all in as you are. I'm going to take him down and give him a drink. Come on, boy." In the corridor, hand on Cass's shoulder, he muttered, "Son, you got to have courage. For her. The baby is dead."

For four hours, while she kept falling asleep, they spared Jinny. When she insisted on seeing the baby, Roy told her, with a grave pity, her hand small in his.

She did not make a sound. She lay and stared at them, so defenseless, slowly beginning to cry.

Long after the doctor had left them, she lay with her face deep in the pillow, whimpering like a sick and frightened kitten.

38

THROUGH ALL of the lingering summer, Cass and she were together in a shadowed valley of tenderness.

She would see no one but him; she was uneasy even with Roy and Rose and Bradd. She stayed abed half the day, and followed her diabetic diet with such severity that Roy snorted, "Look here, young lady, don't go getting monkish and neurotic on me. Don't starve yourself. You're having yourself a fine time playacting and being the perfect patient, but I'm not one bit impressed, because I know how easy you can slip and go just the other way."

She was "playacting," Cass knew, but her play was a propitiation of the gods who had so bruised her when she had tried to be grown-up and a normal mother.

Cass and she sat through the summer evenings in a mosquito-proof and canvas-roofed pavilion he had put up under the maples on their lawn. He did not know what she was thinking; she denied that she was thinking anything at all, and he did not press her. The tenderness between them was a language above the clumsiness of words.

She had no wishes of her own. If he wanted to stay home, if he wanted to drive out to the farther lakes, she was willing. He who had feared that ambition and careerishness might steal her from him began now to wish that she had more to do and more longing to do it. It seemed to him dismayingly that she had not grown at all since he had first seen her on the witness-stand.

"Jinny, how about trying an easy part-time job in the fall?"

"I don't think I care to. Why? You're not tired of having me around all the time, are you?"

"I just mean, to keep from brooding."

"I don't brood. I'm perfectly satisfied. I hate these strident, ambitious women who are always clawing at notoriety."

——Did I unconsciously do this to her, to make her dependent on me? A horrible thing to do. I must coax her to see more people. But what if she likes them too much, again, and finally slips away from me? I must take the chance.

She did not like walking with him even so far as to the Country Club, where they would meet people. His sturdy legs needed use, but when he did leave her for a tramp, like a soldier's route-marching, his companion was Cleo.

She was a mature and dignified young cat now, not without affairs of her own, but with Cass she would still condescend to being a kitten and a playmate. She fought beautifully, pretending to chew his finger when he whirled her around on her back. When she walked with him, she was more dog than cat, running through grasses taller than herself, making enormous leaps straight up from the covering jungle, to see where he had got to.

416

When he stopped to rest on a fallen willow by the lake shore, she came trotting up to entertain him, as of old, by chasing her tail. Her vaudeville repertoire was limited, but she always performed it with the most conscientious artistry.

Jinny herself broke her nervous calm. "Darling, I know you're restless, hanging around the house with me all summer."

He did not tell her what picnics he had planned for her and himself and the baby, with enchanting equipments of thermos bottles and rugs.

"I get restless, too, Cass. I go crazy when I listen to that dratted vacuum cleaner, and even your lawn-mower. I know you want me to see more people. I'm trying to get myself to, but they still make me jittery. Let me be a hermit for just a little while yet, won't you. . . . Our baby! I know you wanted her so."

They had driven out to a secret lake, like a highland tarn, hidden among white pines and balsam. It was dark, in late afternoon, and she seemed fragile among the dark pine trunks, beside the opaque waters.

"Chuck the whole bunch of 'em forever, if you want to," he said, and she wriggled to be close to him, and safe.

Suddenly and surprisingly she laughed. "Why don't you teach me golf? If I could be out on the course listening to Boone tell dirty stories, if I could get over being so damned refined and melancholy, maybe I'd be okay."

417

"Fine!" he said, uneasily.

While Cass enjoyed striding the golf course, whooping in the great winds from the cornfields and manfully waving his clubs, she was bored by it and finicky—and showed at once that she could become a much better player. In a year, she would have beaten him, and Roy and Bradd would have made his life hellish. It was not without a guilty relief that he heard her give up golfing.

But at the clubhouse they did meet Jay and the new Pasadena Laverick, and it was the drinking and feverishness of this foolish pair, and their brassy ability to take a snub, that won Jinny and flushed her out of melancholy more than the welcomes of Rose and Bradd and Chris. With Grand Republic devotion to their friends, these more solid neighbors had not wanted to intrude, so long as Jinny desired the privacy of grief. But no such scruples were in Jay and Pas, and they yelled, "Come and have a gin-and-jitters, Jin!"

Cass was prepared to have her snub them, but she said "Swell!"

They shrieked, "Let's all go get drunk with Sabine and the other bums," and Jin answered affectionately, "I think you got something there. I dassn't get drunk—I'm one of these awful creeping invalids—but I would like to hear some swing on the phonograph and see a few human people. Let's go."

Instantly, with no perceptible moment when she passed

from timid refuge to clamorous publicity, apparently without reason or transition, in September, Jinny was wanting a party every evening, whether it was a Pruttish solemnity or a Sabine-and-Gillian debauch, and she was proclaiming again her extreme need of steaks and marzipan, and not all of Cass's coaxing would keep her from having one light highball.

It was not Roy who rescued him, since she felt that it was practically a duty to disobey the doctor, but Bradd, the Husband's Helper.

He barked at her, with Cass blissfully listening, "I'm no Puritan, baby. I can drink six Scotches to your one and not show it. But I know by experience what fools we charming people can make of ourselves, and I think it would be a fine idea for you to stay home and try to be nice to your husband at least one evening a year. Cass is too decent to bully you, but I'm not. If your sense of inferiority to him annoys you, as it often does me, I'll try to lighten things by coming in and playing cards with you two, if you ask me nicely."

"All right, I ask you nicely, you beast!"

She sailed into a haven between brooding and hysteria. There was again a household of three, gossiping, laughing familiarly, and Cass was very happy about it, until he noticed how often in arguments Jinny agreed with Bradd against him, how increasingly she rebuked him for daring to differ with the elegant-minded Bradd.

Then, coming as suddenly as her earlier moods of silent grief and relieving wildness and halcyon serenity, they were caught by an outbreak of quarrels, which are the wars of matrimony, more destructive and senseless than tanks and cannon, wars in which affection is the worst traitor and the most ignoble defeat is victory.

They were going, that October evening, to Madge Dedrick's for dinner at eight, and Mrs. Dedrick was demanding about punctuality. She was not so fanatic as Cass, to whom 8:00 meant 7:58 1/2, but she did annoy society by insisting that 8:00 meant some time before 8:10.

Cass had explained all this to Jinny; oh, he had explained it!

She was well enough to return to Red Cross work. Indeed the only evidence of diabetes was a lightness and breathlessness in her, and a faintly sharpened face which gave her an eager maturity.

She had not yet come home when Cass started to dress. Madge Dedrick was so elevated a personality, so close in station to an archbishop or a woman-author-lecturer, that one dressed For dinner at her house without inquiring. At 7:01 he looked at his watch again, sighed, and took off his coat. At 7:02 he remarked to Cleo, "Now where is your lovely young mistress, cat?" At 7:04 he continued, "Curious that so clear-minded and competent a girl should be late so often," and, after thirty more seconds of removing his vest and contemplatively scratching, "Do you suppose it's just her way of trying to show that she's still an independent human being?"

Cleo said she didn't know.

At 7:07, in one sock and a bathrobe, he tried to telephone to Red Cross headquarters, raging that it was wicked of them to keep his sick wife there so long, but there was no answer.

At 7:26, bathed, shaved for the second time that day, completely dressed and quivering with worry, he heard Jinny bang into the downstairs hall, singing "Roll out the Barrel," and skip joyfully and undiabetically upstairs.

"Oh, *hel*-lo!" she said cheerfully, as he looked into the hall.

He did not say that she was late. Both their glances had already said it adequately. Cleo stalked downstairs as though she would have nothing to do with such a woman.

"Am I in the dog-house!" muttered Jinny, but with no evidence of repentance.

He stayed away from her and from the subject, then, till he had heard her shower-bath and the stillness that indicated she was making up. He ambled nervously into her room and sat down while she, a slightly absurd figure in bare shoulders above a gleamingly hideous satin girdle, was at her dressing-table, penciling entirely needless and imperceptible touches of blue on her eyelids, with as much tranquillity as though she had five hours instead of five minutes.

"Uh——" he said.

"I know I'm late. I'm hustling."

"Not awful fast, dear; do hurry a little. Madge hates to have people late."

"You mean——" In the most leisurely, comfortable way, Jinny inspected her eyebrows and removed one hair with the tweezers, after examining the instrument as though she was interested in the historic evolution of its design and its possible unexplored future uses. "You mean, sweetheart, that she's also a fanatic about punctuality?"

"Well, I don't know as I'd call her a *fanatic*, but she doesn't care much for having the fish-course spoiled."

"You ought to have married her."

"My dear Jinny, considering that she's almost thirty years older than I am——"

"Okay, okay! Then married her daughter. Eve is such a lovely widow, and quite rich, and still punctual. Just the gal for you, my boy."

"See here now! I know I'm probably a crank about punctuality——"

"How did you guess it?"

"But you go too far the other way. Unpunctual people betray the fact that they lack all consideration for other people's rights and feelings."

"Nuts!" She was less merry now. "I'm sick of always being on time myself, and then being kept waiting."

"*When?*"

"When?"

"Yes, when! When did you ever have to wait for other people?"

"Oh, lots of times. I do try to be on the dot, and usually I am, too, but this rigid punctuality—it's like any other bankers-association virtue; it isn't worth making everybody's life miserable for."

"We're going to make Mrs. Dedrick miserable——"

"Not tonight, because prob'ly Bradd will be later than we are."

"Bradd? What's he got to do with it?"

"He'll be there tonight."

"But how do you know he'll be late?"

"Because he just left me."

"Oh."

"And he has to do some phoning, as well as change, before he gets to Madge's."

"You, uh——You saw Bradd this afternoon . . . too?"

"Yes. I just told you. He dropped me here."

"I thought you were at the Red Cross, and that closed two hours——"

"I was, but I got a headache, and I went out with him just to get some fresh air."

"Did you phone him or did he just happen to drop in there?"

"I don't even remember. Good Heavens, why all the fuss?"

"I'm not fussing. I was just wondering. Course I'm glad you

went out and——Where did you go?"

"To the Unstable. Had a drink."

"Or maybe two drinks?"

"Yes, maybe two! And why the cross-examination?"

"Bradd's been an amazingly loyal friend, the way he's backed me up in my effort to get you to take some rest, but somehow it does seem as though it's always he who's keeping you up late, or getting you to take a cocktail—or a walnut-mocha-frozen-cream-puff!"

"Cass! Are you criticizing Bradd Criley? Your closest, most devoted friend, the one man who most admires you as a person and as a lawyer?"

"No, no, good Lord no! I just meant——"

Empires have fallen from wars that began with "I just meant."

She had to hurry now, and they said nothing more, on the way to Mrs. Dedrick's, than that for a warm October evening, it was warm. They arrived fifteen minutes late, to find Mrs. Dedrick malignant—and to find Bradd, placid and smiling, looking as though he had been there for years.

Throughout the evening, Cass was rather dreary, but Jinny was full of lively points. She laughed with Bradd, but no more, Cass noted, than with Harley Bozard or Old Mr. Avondene. He was in a small torment, but not of jealousy; it was a torment of self-castigation at finding himself back in her boarding-house, being schoolboyishly jealous of Eino

Roskinen.

——You took away the poor girl's job and her ambition, maybe took away her health, and now you resent her even having a few gay friends. Bradd and she are so open about liking to play around together that it would be obvious to anybody else that they're entirely innocent in their liking.

——We were on the verge of a quarrel tonight. Be careful. Maybe it's true, as you always claim, that you're never the one that starts a quarrel, but you're certainly the one that never lets it go once you get your teeth into it.

——I trust Bradd. Utterly.

——I just wish I hadn't heard him tell once about his technique with young married women—easing their consciences by praising their husbands.

——He wouldn't do that with me—with Jinny. Anyway, she's too shrewd. Of course he is fond of her. Who wouldn't be? Maybe unconsciously he even likes her *too* much. But never consciously. But maybe it would be a good idea to suggest to him that he ought not to get into a way of thinking he is in love with her.

——Yes? And how would you say a thing like that to as experienced an attorney as Mr. Criley, Judge?

In admission of the fact that Jinny was mildly ill, Cass always took her home at ten—when he could get her away at ten. Tonight, he was amiable and firm about it, and in the car he was unendurably bountiful. It was Jinny, usually an unretaliatory girl though impulsive, who was looking for trouble and ready to start a scene.

She jabbed, "You must have been absorbed in weighty thoughts tonight. You never even listened when Eve was telling us about the Riviera."

"Heard it all before, I guess."

——Careful now! She's resentful over your lecture about punctuality. Be careful.

As they came into the house, he warned himself, "Don't tease her about Bradd's getting there before we did, after all." So he looked affectionately at the heat-regulator, and said aloud, "Well, Bradd got there before we did, after all! We were the last arrivals."

She stopped with her cape in folds about her arms, and launched her burning dart: "Yes, and he'd taken the trouble to put on a clean dinner-jacket, too!"

"Do——"

"Don't you ever look at yourself in a mirror? Don't you ever try to be neat?"

"Me?"

"You've had a spot on your lapel all evening."

He craned at a white speck on the ribbed satin, not one of such dimensions or vile color as to constitute a crime. As he scratched at it with his thumbnail, impenitent, irritated, she laid her cape on a chair and turned on him again:

"Years ago, in Florida, I begged you not to slobber all over yourself. Especially lapels!"

"Yes, we're right back there, Jinny, and you haven't learned a thing."

"What do you mean, I haven't learned a thing? I've learned plenty! I've learned that the more you talk about wanting me to be free and individual, the more you always want me to do only what you want."

"Dearest, I honestly don't know why you started jumping on me."

"You don't? Complaining because I went out for a breath of fresh air with Bradd! Sulking and screaming!"

"My dear girl, you can't sulk and scream at the same time. They're mutually contradictory."

"The judge-language! It's as phony as preacher-language. By the way, poor Eino once asked me whether you would ev6r decide a case against a very rich man, a Wargate, and I said of course you would, but I begin to wonder."

While he gaped at this slander, the astounding irrelevancy of this attack, she marched into the gray-and-mulberry effeminacy of their living-room. He did not want to follow her; he reminded himself again that he did not readily give up a war once it had started.

Then he did want to follow her; he did want to fight the good bad fight.

She was delicately taking a cigarette from a box of glass,

lighting it with relish, staring at the maimed Isis on her pedestal for reassurance, then turning toward him with a cold unspoken query of "Yes, and who may you be?"

She added, aloud, "I'm sure you'd find plenty of excuses for any Wargate."

He was shouting, shouting small but well into the quarrel.

"Yes, if you really want to know, I'm a complete crook on the bench. And have you noticed any other faults?"

She enjoyed it as a good household cat enjoys chewing the tail of a trapped barn-rat. "I don't know why you're bellowing at me merely because I asked a civil question—one that I discussed with Judge Blackstaff."

"And no doubt with Attorney Bradd Criley!"

"Naturally!"

"I suppose I ought to be glad, though, Jinny, that you take even this much interest in my work. You rarely do. You never even ask me, any longer, what cases I've had."

"I know. Poor man. There seem to be two kinds of husbands: those that complain because their wives butt into their business and those that complain because they don't—like you—and your energetic friend Vince Osprey!"

He bit hard on a non-existent gag while Jinny breezed on, "And if you really want to know about your other faults——I don't understand why you were so rude to Old Mr. Avondene this evening——"

"Me?"

"——when he was trying to tell about the early days here, unless it is that you always have to be the center of attention, you always have to be The Judge, and expect obsequiousness from everybody."

That there was five per cent of truth in this did not relieve his injury as she swept on, sweetly, lounging in a couch-corner, her gestures graceful and patronizing:

"You think that everything you say is of so much importance to everybody—not merely to poor untutored me, that you picked up out of the gutter and tried to educate—and you don't even try to make your dictums——"

"Dicta!"

"——clear, and you talk with your mouth full, and then if it ever happens that people get sick of your egotism and turn their heads away from you for even one second, you're furious with them—you're mushy with self-pity because you can't put your importance over!"

He was appalled at her injustice, at her so recent tenderness turning into this poison, yet he did have humor enough to see the comedy of her springing on him when he had been so full of information about *her* faults of unpunctuality and skipping off with every man who asked her. He retreated from his high ground, and said civilly, "I swear, Jinny, I don't know why you started this scene."

"Why?"

"Yes, why?"

"Heaven's sake, don't echo me like a—like a——If you want to know why——I hesitate to tell you, but after the way you rode me tonight——"

"I did not!"

"——and yelled that I simply love to keep people waiting and their damn fish spoiling, I'll tell you. Frankly, my friend, I don't have much fun living with you."

She said it with none of the joyful hysteria of a lovers' quarrel, but so evenly that he believed her. He urged, slowly and miserably, "Jinny, I've given you everything I have, and in return, you are trying to destroy me."

As she casually rose and turned to go upstairs, she answered with one infinitely contemptuous word:

"Piffle!"

That night they slept without having made it up, without having spoken again.

An Assemblage of Husbands and Wives

VIRGA VAY & ALLAN CEDAR

ORLO VAY, the Chippewa Avenue Optician, Smart-Art Harlequin Tinted-Tortus Frames Our Specialty, was a public figure, as public as a cemetery. He was resentful that his profession, like that of an undertaker, a professor of art, or a Mormon missionary, was not appreciated for its patience and technical skill, as are the callings of wholesale grocer or mistress or radio-sports-commentator, and he tried to make up for the professional injustice by developing his personal glamor.

He wanted to Belong. He was a speaker. He was hearty and public about the local baseball and hockey teams, about the Kiwanis Club, about the Mayflower Congregational Church, and about all war drives. At forty-five he was bald, but the nobly glistening egg of his face and forehead, whose arc was broken only by a pair of Vay Li-Hi-Bifocals, was an adornment to all fund-raising rallies.

He urged his wife, Virga, to co-operate in his spiritual efforts, but she was a small, scared, romantic woman, ten years his junior; an admirer of passion in technicolor, a clipper-out of newspaper lyrics about love and autumn smoke upon the hills. He vainly explained to her, "In these modern days, a woman can't fritter away her time daydreaming. She has to push her own weight, and not hide it under a bushel."

Her solace was in her lover, Dr. Allan Cedar, the dentist. Together, Virga and Allan would have been a most gentle pair, small, clinging, and credulous. But they could never be openly together. They were afraid of Mr. Vay and of Allan's fat and vicious wife, Bertha, and they met at soda counters in outlying drug stores and lovingly drank black-and-whites together or Jumbo Malteds and, giggling, ate ferocious banana splits; or, till wartime gasoline-rationing prevented, they sped out in Allan's coupé by twilight, and made shy, eager love in mossy pastures or, by the weak dashlight of the car, read aloud surprisingly good recent poets: Wallace Stevens, Sandburg, Robert Frost, Jeffers, T. S. Eliot, Lindsay.

Allan was one of the best actors in the Masquers, and though Virga could not act, she made costumes and hung about at rehearsals, and thus they were able to meet, and to stir the suspicions of Bertha Cedar.

Mrs. Cedar was a rare type of the vicious woman; she really hated her husband, though she did not so much scold him as mock him for his effeminate love of acting, for his verses, for his cherubic mustache, and even for his skill with golden bridge-work. She jeered, in the soap-reeking presence of her seven sisters and sisters-in-law, all chewing gum and adjusting their plates, that as a lover "Ally" had no staying-powers. That's what *she* thought.

She said to her mother, "Ally is a bum dentist; he hasn't got a single rich patient," and when they were at an evening party, she communicated to the festal guests, "Ally can't even pick out a necktie without asking my help," and on everything her husband said she commented, "Oh, don't be silly!"

She demanded, and received, large sympathy from all the females she knew, and as he was fond of golf and backgammon, she refused to learn either of them.

Whenever she had irritated him into jumpiness, she said judiciously, "You seem to be in a very nervous state." She picked at him about his crossword puzzles, about his stamp-collection, until he screamed, invariably, "Oh, let me *alone!*" and then she was able to say smugly, "I don't know what's the matter with you, so touchy about every little thing. You better go to a mind-doctor and have your head examined."

Then Bertha quite unexpectedly inherited seven thousand dollars and a house in San Jose, California, from a horrible aunt. She did not suggest to her husband but told him that they would move out to that paradise for chilled Minnesotans, and he would practise there.

It occurred to Allan to murder her, but not to refuse to go along. Many American males confuse their wives and the policeman on the beat.

But he knew that it would be death for him to leave Virga Vay, and that afternoon, when Virga slipped into his office at three o'clock in response to his code telephone call of "This is the Superba Market and we're sending you three bunches of asparagus," she begged, "Couldn't we elope some place together? Maybe we could get a little farm."

"She'd find us. She has a cousin who's a private detective in Duluth."

"Yes, I guess she would. Can't we *ever* be together always?"

"There is one way—if you wouldn't be afraid."

He explained the way.

"No, I wouldn't be afraid, if you stayed right with me," she said.

Dr. Allan Cedar was an excellent amateur machinist. On a Sunday afternoon when Bertha was visiting her mother, he cut a hole through the steel bottom of the luggage compartment of his small dark-gray coupé. This compartment opened into the body of the car. That same day he stole the hose of their vacuum-cleaner and concealed it up on the rafters of their galvanized-iron garage.

On Tuesday—this was in February—he bought a blue ready-made suit at Goldenkron Brothers', on Ignatius Street. He was easy to fit, and no alterations were needed. They wanted to deliver the suit that afternoon, but he insisted, "No, hold it here for me and I'll come in and put it on tomorrow morning. I want to surprise somebody."

"Your Missus will love it, Doc," said Monty Goldenkron.

"I hope she will—when she sees it!"

He also bought three white-linen shirts and a red bow-tie, and paid cash for the lot.

"Your credit is good here, Doc—none better," protested Monty.

Allan puzzled him by the triumphant way in which he answered, "I want to keep it good, just now!"

From Goldenkrons' he walked perkily to the Emporium, to the Golden Rule drug store, to the Co-operative Dairy, paying his bills in full at each. On his way he saw a distinguished fellow-townsman, Judge Timberlane, and his pretty wife. Allan had never said ten words to either of them, but he thought affectionately, "There's a couple who are intelligent enough and warm-hearted enough to know what love is worth."

That evening he said blandly to his wife, "Strangest thing happened today. The University school of dentistry telephoned me."

"Long distance?"

"Surely."

"Well!" Her tone was less of disbelief than of disgust.

"They're having a special brush-up session for dentists and they want me to come down to Minneapolis first tiling tomorrow morning to stay for three days and give instruction in bridge-work. And of course you must come along. It's too bad I'll have to work from nine in the morning till midnight— they do rush those special courses so—but you can go to the movies by yourself, or just sit comfortably in the hotel."

"No—thank—*you*!" said Bertha. "I prefer to sit here at home. Why you couldn't have been an M.D. doctor and take out gallbladders and make some real money! And I'll thank you to be home not later than Sunday morning. You know we have Sunday dinner with Mother."

He knew.

"I hope that long before that I'll be home," he said.

He told her that he would be staying at the Flora Hotel, in

Minneapolis. But on Wednesday morning, after putting on the new suit at Goldenkrons', he drove to St. Paul, through light snowflakes which he thought of as fairies. "But I haven't a bit of real poet in me. Just second-rate and banal," he sighed. He tried to make a poem, and got no farther than:

> *It is snowing,*
> *The wind is blowing,*
> *But I am happy to be going.*

In St. Paul he went to the small, clean Hotel Orkness, registered as "Mr. A. M. Romeo & wife," asked for a room with a double bed, and explained to the clerk, "My wife is coming by train. She should be here in about seventeen minutes now, I figure it."

He went unenthusiastically to the palsied elevator, up to their room. It was tidy, and on the wall was an Adolph Dehn lithograph instead of the fake English-hunting-print that he had dreaded. He kneaded the bed with his fist. He was pleased.

Virga Vay arrived nineteen minutes later, with a bellboy carrying her new imitation-leather bag.

"So you're here, husband. Not a bad room," she said indifferently.

The bellboy knew from her indifference and from her calling the man "husband" that she was not married to him, but unstintingly in love. Such paradoxes are so common in his subterranean business that he had forgotten about Virga by the time he reached his bench in the lobby. Six stories above him, Virga and Allan were lost and blind and quivering in their kiss.

Presently she said, "Oh, you have a new suit! Turn around. Why, it fits beautifully! And such a nice red tie. You do look so young and cute in a bow-tie. Did you get it for me?"

"Of course. And then—I kind of hate to speak of it now, but I want us to get so used to the idea that we can just forget it—I don't want us to look frowsy when they find us. As if we hadn't been happy. And we *will* be—we are!"

"Yes."

"You're still game for it?"

"With you? For anything."

He was taking off the new suit; she was tenderly lifting from her bag a nightgown which she had made and embroidered this past week.

They had all their meals in the room; they did not leave it till afternoon of the next day. The air became a little close, thick from perfume and cigarette smoke and the bubble baths they took together.

Late the next afternoon they dressed and packed their bags, completely. He laid on the bureau two ten-dollar bills. They left the luggage at the foot of their bed, which she had made up. She took nothing from the room, and he nothing except a paper bag containing a bottle of Bourbon whisky, with the cork loosened, and a pocket anthology of new poetry. At the door she looked back, and said to him, "I shall remember this dear room as long as we live."

"Yes. . . . As long as we live."

He took his dark-gray coupé out of the hotel garage, tipping an amazed attendant one dollar, and they drove to Indian Mounds Park, overlooking the erratic Mississippi. He stopped in the park, at dusk, and said, "Think of the Indians that came along here, and Pike and Lewis Cass!"

"They were brave," she mused.

"Brave, *too!*" They nervously laughed. Indeed, after a moment of solemnity when they had left the hotel, they had been constantly gay, laughing at everything, even when she sneezed and he piped, "No more worry about catching pneumonia!"

He drove into a small street near by and parked the car, distant from any house. Working in the half-darkness, leaving the engine running, he pushed the vacuum-cleaner hose through the hole in the bottom of the luggage compartment, wired it to the exhaust pipe, and hastily got back into the car. The windows were closed. Already the air in the car was sick-sweet with carbon monoxide.

He slipped the whisky bottle out of the paper bag and tenderly urged, "Take a swig of this. Keep your courage up."

"Dearest, I don't need anything to keep it up."

"I do, by golly. I'm not a big he-man like you, Virg!"

They both laughed, and drank from the bottle, and kissed lingeringly.

"I wonder if I could smoke a cigarette. I don't *think* C_2O_2 is explosive," he speculated.

"Oh, sweet, be careful! It *might* explode!"

"Yes, it——" Then he shouted. "Listen at us! As if we cared if we got blown up now!"

"Oh, I am too brainless, Allan! I don't know if you'll be able to stand me much longer."

"As long as we live, my darling, my very dear, oh, my dear love!"

"As long as we live. Together now. Together."

His head aching, his throat sore, he forgot to light the cigarette He switched on the tiny dashlight, he lifted up the book as though it were a bar of lead, and from Conrad Aiken's "Sea Holly" he began to read to her:

> *It was for this*
> *Barren beauty, barrenness of rock that aches*
> *On the seaward path, seeing the fruitful sea,*
> *Hearing the lark of rock that sings——*

He was too drowsy to read more than just the ending:

> *Stone pain in the stony heart,*
> *The rock loved and labored; and all is lost.*

The book fell to the seat, his head drooped, and his arm

groped drowsily about her. She rested contentedly, in vast dreams, her head secure upon his shoulder.

Harsh screaming snatched them back from paradise. The car windows were smashed, someone was dragging them out . . . and Bertha was slapping Virga's face, while Bertha's cousin, the detective, was beating Allan's shoulders with a blackjack, to bring him to. In doing so, he broke Allan's jaw.

Bertha drove him back to Grand Republic and nursed him while he was in bed, jeering to the harpies whom she had invited in, "Ally tried to—you know—with a woman, but he was no good, and he was so ashamed he tried to kill himself."

He kept muttering, "Please go away and don't torture me."

She laughed.

Later, Bertha was able to intercept every one of the letters that Virga sent to him from Des Moines, where she had gone to work in a five-and-ten-cent store after Orlo had virtuously divorced her.

"Love! Ally is learning what that kind of mush gets you." Bertha explained to her attentive women friends.

39

THEIR AUTUMN SEASON of quarrels was to Cass as
devastating and as senseless as a thunderstorm. Jinny was ill,
and sometimes bored, yet why hadn't she imagination enough
to see that he was often bored and worried as well? Why, when
most of the time she was gay and full of small surprises for
him and seemed tranquilly to love him, did she, under the
horrible black magic of the quarrel, turn in ten seconds into
his enemy, the hearth-fire suddenly burning down the house?

What did Jinny want? Security, scenery, power, the ability
to recognize a quotation from Steinbeck, a ruby-and-diamond
bracelet, a sense of self-discipline, the love of a tangible God,
a red canoe with yellow cushions, an unblemished skin,
venison with sauce Cumberland, many children, a seventy-
five-dollar hat from New York, a request to speak on a nation-
wide hookup, dawn beside Walden Pond, the certainty of her
husband's affection, or an Irish wolfhound? He did not know,
and she was not quite certain. And in which of these virtuous
desires could he most sympathize with her?

It was difficult for each of them to guess the other's
momentary moods. They ought to be labeled, for warning.
He ought to put on the sign, "Stern jurist—be careful" or
"Playboy—willing to dance"; she should bear the direction

"Wistful little girl" or "Termagant—dangerous" or "Sensitive artist who has been drawing in secret but expects her husband to be so discerning as to guess it and congratulate her." Then each of them would know how to start off the evening, and have nothing to quarrel about—except each other's friends, which will be a troublesome topic even among the angels in Heaven, where spirit will say crossly to spirit, "Who was that awful harp-player I saw you flying with last eon?"

There were many springboards for quarrels: he liked the windows open, she shriveled in the cold; he liked pork chops, she liked chow mein; he had been too jocular with Diantha Marl, she too chilly with Judge Flaaten; he wanted to stay home, she wanted to go to the movies—so they went to the movies. And there he dared to consider himself a cinema critic and sniffed at her beloved swing musicians capering as would-be actors. But of them all, there was only one cause: they did not know what they wanted.

There were so many things that could lead to disagreements; there were so many disagreements that could lead to quarrels. As with almost any couple, she would insist on candlelight and he would snort that he liked to be able to see what he was eating. She would devote artistic agonies to curtains, and he would demand why it was that you dug a window through the wall to get air and light, and then covered it over, very expensively, so that you got neither. He would irritably feel that he must have her permission before he invited the

Wolkes in, and discover that she was sulky because she had been thinking that she must have his permission to do the same thing.

Their quarrels always went the same course and always wound up in the same accusations, dreary as slate and vicious as secret poison. They said things they could not possibly have said. He called her a "sponge" and a "torturer"; she shrieked that he was unimaginative, ignorant, and a liar. Usually, somewhere early in the quarrel, was the rueful, "I was just enjoying myself so much, and now you've gone and spoiled it all."

Slights that had been forgotten for months woke up, and they protested, "What did you mean when you said I 'liked to hurt people's feelings' that time—last January, I think it was?" And, "I won't stand any more of this!" with "Is that so!" regarded as a logical answer. The ritual response to "If you're going to be stubborn, I'll just have to show you I can be stubborn, too!" was "You don't have to *show* me!" and to "Now whose fault was *that*, I'd like to know!" the counterblow was "Not *my* fault, certainly!"

And "Of course anything that Bradd or Tracy (or Chris or Stella) does is *perfect*, but if I do anything, it's always wrong." And—once the two of them began saying it at the same time—"The trouble with you is, you're utterly *selfish*." And sometimes, from either of them, the senseless, maniacal "Oh, shut up, shut up, shut up!" or the calmly said, devastating

"I can tell you what *I'm* going to do: I'm going to leave this house right now, and I hope I never see you again. Oh, I mean it—this time. Never!"

None of their slurs meant anything except that each of them was unhappy because the other was unhappy. They were not things said; they were sweeps of their claws, in the jungle; and they were less distressing than the long, thick silences, during the quarrels, when they sat blankly, trying to think what it was that they were trying to think.

When they made up, as they always did, they wailed, "Oh, I couldn't have said that to you. I know I couldn't, because I've never even thought it."

They had said it, though.

"How could we ever have acted like that?" they marveled, and they vowed, "We'll never quarrel again, not over *anything*! Why, darling, you can call me a three-tailed monster, and I'll take it and like it."

She begged, "You take me too seriously, when I fly off the handle. It doesn't mean a thing—it's just one of my tantrums. When I act childish, if you'd just say, 'There, there now, baby,' why, I'd snap right out of it."

She didn't.

He asserted that, if they had to change themselves in order to avoid quarreling, it was she who could change most, because she was less stiffened by the formalism of law and politics. Ah, there, she said enthusiastically, was an idea! For two days she was energetically holy and patient, after which they quarreled because he had not noticed it.

Sometimes in the most heated middle of a dispute, he most loved her, and he was violent and rather unpleasant with her only because he was afraid.

He realized now that it was he who loved the more, but he knew that in love it is truly more blessed to give than to receive, and he was sorry for her that—apparently—she could not know the exaltation of passion for another being.

After every quarrel, when the emotion had burned itself out, he was as confused about what had happened as a man who has been in delirium.

——Just how did I get angry at her, anyway? Just what was it I said, and how did she answer? I seem to have said dreadful things, but I can't remember.

——But it won't happen again. Now that I understand that her moods are never as deep as they seem, I'll be patient. And so will she. She finally *said* she would! The trouble with her is that she's too honest. She has to blurt out whatever she thinks. She couldn't ever conceal anything: a dislike or an unhappiness or a passionate liking. But now that I understand this, we won't have any more disagreements—no more—ever!

40

SHE HAD GONE to bed early, that November evening, purring, "I think I'll get enough rest for once, just to show I can do it."

"Shall I come in and kiss you good night, when I come up?"

"No, I'll probably be asleep. But I'll allow you to kiss me now." Decisively. But quite affectionately. But quite decisively.

That was before ten. He would normally have read—"have caught up on his reading," as he put it—till twelve or one, but he sat brooding about her. He longed to make love to her, he was cold without her warmth, he was lonely without her reaching out for him. All evening he had been lonely for her even while he was in her presence, not ten feet away.

The weather of late autumn was angry, and their cabin of steel and rock-wool and white pine and stucco seemed to be shaking in the gale. He felt snatched back ninety years ago, to the pioneer insecurities of the far-northern winter. He draped the mulberry curtains about him to shut off the light of the room, and looked out, toward a street lamp, through slanting lines of sleet. The blue spruce in the yard was glassy with wet and hateful coldness.

If he could be up there, cozy with her, some miracle might restore the passion she had once felt for him.

He turned back into the room, stared at a gilt clock, stared at the crystal Isis, without seeing them. Cleo came blandly talking around his feet, like a little feline floor-walker in a department store of the affections, but he did not hear her. He was admitting, for the first time unflinchingly, that though they had been married a month less than two years, though his passion was only the stronger, he had become hesitating about revealing it to her, because he was no longer sure how much of it she could return—not sure that she felt any of it at all.

He reflected that she never, of herself, came to his bed now, and that he never went to hers with certainty that her arched and welcoming arms would greet him.

Oh, it would come out all right—there were reasons—she was ill but she would get better—their quarrels had curdled her simple emotions—she was still too interested in other men, Jay and Bradd and Greg Marl and God-knows-who. But in a few years she would grow up and she would be well and then all her ardor would be for him alone.

But he did not want her "in a few years"; he wanted her tonight.

He chased Cleo into the kitchen rather crossly; he put out the downstairs lights, tiptoed up, and guiltily listened outside her door. He heard nothing.

Probably asleep. Well, that was fine, wasn't it? He was glad she was taking care of herself, wasn't he? He'd just undress and read in his dressing-gown. She, uh, she might awaken and want him to read aloud to her. . . . Not that she ever did or ever had. . . . Still, she might. . . . He'd keep the door of his room open, so he could listen.

When he had undressed, he heard from her room the tap of a cosmetic bottle or perhaps a pair of manicure scissors on the glass top of her dressing-table.

She was unable to get to sleep then?

Too bad, but——

He took a long time in going to make a light tattoo on her door. He was restrained by the singularly disconcerting memory of having read somewhere about "The sneaking look that every wife sees on the face of her husband when he ventures into her room."

Damn it, something wrong with both of them, then! So he marched in.

She said "Hello" blithely; she looked up from her dressingtable pleasantly, and most pleasantly she commented, "You going to bed early too?"

That was the trouble; she was so pleasant and safe, and so unmoved by his entrance; she had neither rapture nor wrath nor fear. Well, he didn't expect too much; but she had no *interest*!

"Isn't it kind of late for you to be making up, young lady?

You planning to go to the club?"

"Sure. And dance! . . . Oh, I couldn't drop off to sleep, so I'm trying some experiments with mascara."

He folded his hands round her breasts, kissed the top of her head. Her whole body remained still, unquivering. She patted one of his hands, too amiably, and she turned her head to look into the mirror again, forgetting him.

"Good night," he said sadly, and with the most sweet and devastating carelessness she answered, "Night, dear."

In his great chair, he did not read. He was trying not to think of the name of Bradd Criley.

He had been doubting the entire innocence of Bradd's solicitude for Jinny, and he had been guiltily relieved when the gossiping Madge Dedrick had let him into the secret that Bradd was showing too much interest in Bernice, wife of Perry Clay-wheel, superintendent of schools. Bernice had a pale Swin-burnian beauty; pale beyond porch and portal and movie-theater lobby she stood, hoping that people were thinking how interesting she looked. Even Mrs. Dedrick admitted that she had a "kind of washed-out good looks."

To that information (Cass remembered now) he had objected, "I do hope you're wrong; I hope Bradd hasn't got tangled up with anybody," as sincerely as possible, which was not very sincerely. "Claywheel is anemic, but he's a good scholar and very kind to the kids, and I wouldn't want him to be hurt. I know Bradd is an expert charmer, but I don't think he'd ever be such a poor sportsman, and so treacherous, as to stalk easy game like Bernice."

Madge had jeered, "Your friend Bradd is a busy man, and the only reason he doesn't rope in all the women—including me and my daughter and your wife—is that he can't find time. Don't you think for one moment that Ber-nyce will monopolize him."

So Cass remembered, in his chair.

——I wonder if the explanation of Bradd's recent attentions to Jinny could be that he is pretending to be so taken with her—but in all propriety, of course—in order to mask an intrigue with Bernice?

——Cass, you know you don't believe that!

——I have to. I'll believe anything, except that these two, nearest to me in the world, are beginning to conspire against me.

Bradd did not drop in so often, now that Jinny was not home-bound by illness and pregnancy, but he was even more intimate. He knew where the fuse-box was, and the orange bitters, and the saltines; he knew how to work the electric dish-washer; he knew the fact that Jinny liked a cup of beef tea—that is, she didn't like it, but she was willing to consume it before she went to bed.

On Mrs. Higbee's Thursday-night-out, Jinny had invited

Bradd in for cold supper.

"You sit still and take it easy and Jin and I will bounce out to the kitchen and bring in the chow," said Bradd patronizingly to Old Man Timberlane.

The Old Man was irritated, and at supper not very conversational. His liveliest thoughts were that he hated cold ham and sausage and tongue, and that he considered cold artichoke vinaigrette one of the least excusable substitutes for food.

Bradd rumbled, "Don't disturb the Jedge. He's thinking about *quos Deus vult perdere prius dementat.*"

"Is that legal Latin?" Jinny asked admiringly.

"Well, it could be, in certain cases. And then again, the Jedge might be thinking about the Supreme Court bench."

"Or about his corns!" giggled Jinny.

"Go on, tease me all you want to, children. I'm tired," Cass said good-naturedly. He hoped it sounded good-natured.

"Aw, the old fellow is tired," mocked Jinny.

"Sure. He's all worn out fining lawyers for contempt of court!"

With a nameless melancholy, Cass could not rise to their gaiety. He sat owlishly watching the Bright Young People. He warned himself, "She's having a good time. I mustn't spoil it for her." But he again felt lonely for her even in her presence; he felt left out of it, felt that it was he who was the unnecessary and tolerated third.

They were talking derisively about that earnest young attorney Vincent Osprey and his blundering devotion to his wife Cerise. Cass noted that under Bradd's tutelage, Jinny was increasingly supercilious about people who did not know bridge, *Vogue* magazine, and wine vintages. . . . Not that Bradd or she knew much about any of them, either.

Bradd cackled, "Vince said to me he wished he could get his dear Cerise to come to court and listen to him. He said she admired his tennis, and was all het up about his high diving, and maybe if he could sell her on his oratory, she would quit thinking he was the family cow."

"You don't give Vince credit," Jinny jeered. "He's very important. He's finally proved that virtue is always duller than vice."

Cass burst. "You two superior intellects make me tired! Osprey is no Rufus Choate, but there's nothing funny about the poor devil's adoration of his wife. He'd die for her, and she'd be amused watching him do it."

"Do you think that's very sensible of him?" objected Jinny.

"No, I think it's idiotic, but somehow heroic, in this day of loose affections."

"Tut!" pronounced his wife. "It's idioticer than it is heroic. You know, Cass, sometimes I think Vince Osprey is a burlesque of your own remarkable virtues."

"I find nothing whatever funny about marital fidelity and devotion!"

"Well, I'm sure we're glad to hear that," she said coolly. "I'll get the cake and ice cream."

When she was gone, Bradd seriously admonished him, "You oughtn't to yell at Jinny like that, Cass. I wonder if you realize how sensitive she is, even when she's being funny. You ought not to pick on her so. Well, I better go help her with the dessert."

Cass was exploding with emotions, all colored red. For this outsider to tell *him* that Jinny was sensitive! to tell *him* not to "pick on her"! to pat her pretty back after she had ridiculed every sanctity of love!

He cooled down and thought it all over again. He was angry, and then, as usual, he fretted, "Mustn't spoil her party." But hot or cold, he came always to the same verdict:

"This is just a little bit too much! I don't like guests, no matter who they are, that come in and make over my house!"

He noted that Bradd and Jinny took five minutes to bring in three plates of ice cream and sponge cake. All the rest of the evening he was violently quiet and painfully amiable, and spectacularly did not notice it at all when Bradd kissed Jinny good night on the cheek as though it were anything but her cheek that he was kissing.

When Jinny had gone to bed, Cass thought over the case he had had in court two days before, an accident case, with Vincent Osprey representing the injured workman and Bradd Criley the Wargate Corporation. Bradd had been so suave—too suave. Cass had advised Vince, in chambers, to use witnesses less melodramatic and more factual, but Vince could not get away from the charms of sobbing relatives.

The deft Mr. Criley had won.

After lunch at the Federal Club, Roy Drover commanded Cass, "Come on in the bar. I want to talk to you."

When they were in two red-leather chairs with elephantiasis, Roy grumbled:

"I'm supposed to be a friend of yours as well as your physician, and of Bradd's, too, and I know I'm risking all that by butting in, but I'm not one of these hand-holding bedside docs. I'm too much of a man to sit back and watch you make a fool of yourself."

"What——"

"Fellow, you got to do something about Bradd and your wife. Town's beginning to talk. They're playing a little too much footie-footie."

"Now you look——"

"Hey, hold your horses, Cass. Don't get sore. I want you to look at this in a practical way. Don't get sore at the kid, either; she's fairly young, and a lot less brainy 'n you give her credit for. I just want you to stop all their sweetie stuff before it goes too far. And don't get sore."

"I'm not—really. But it's all nonsense. I know Jinny and Bradd are good friends, but I'm glad of it, and they never even see each other, except at my house in my presence."

"Sure of that?"

"Oh, sometimes they drive down to the Unstable for a drink, but she always tells me about it, and they invite me to come and join them . . . usually."

"What would you say if I told you they were meeting at plenty of other places?"

"I'd say that——"

"Careful, now!"

"I would doubt it. Oh, sometimes by accident, of course—city as small as this—but never deliberately, never, and——Where do they meet?"

"Well, I don't know that they go to Bradd's house, though I've seen her driving that way, all by herself. You're in court all day; you don't get around like I do! And I definitely saw them having lunch together at that God-awful little Italian doggery or fettacheeney or whatever they call it, Lorenzo's, I think they call it, way down on Isanti Avenue, in the South End. I had a patient down there, and I saw 'em through the window in the Italian dump, and I was in the house nearly two hours, and when I came out, the little love-birds were still there, laughing and having themselves a whale of a time. Did she ever tell you about that?"

"No, she——Oh, I don't remember. Anyway, there's nothing to it."

"I know there isn't. There's nothing to having one

pneumococcus in your throat, but when you get a few billion, you're sick. Anyway, they certainly are seeing a lot more of each other than you know or I know."

"Don't be a suspicious old woman, Roy. Get down to fundamentals. Look at their characters."

"I have!"

"Next to you, Bradd is my oldest and closest friend. When the three of us went hunting, as kids——"

"We're not kids any more. At least, I ain't! Sure, Bradd is a good guy—except he thinks he's called to be God's little gift to women. He wouldn't steal your pocketbook—unless it had over a thousand bucks in it—but if he stole your wife, he'd think he was doing her a favor—and maybe you."

"That'd be black treachery, and Bradd couldn't ever be treacherous. I know him in the court room. He enjoys life and enjoys people and he'd do anything for you——"

"Say, for God's sake, is your whole family conducting an advertising campaign for Mr. Criley? Sure, the jolly little playboy, and underneath his whimsy-whamsy, he's the coldest-hearted rich-man's lawyer and the most calculating woman-chaser in the State of Minnesota. You know that. It don't keep him from being a swell pal on the duck-pass, but he's no bishop.

"Now I don't believe they're sleeping together—not yet. But same time, after having her baby and being sick and all the rest, and married to a man who's no infant, she isn't the timid virgin any longer. I don't think she's actually two-timing you, and I guess she'd prefer to run straight, but she'd no longer be as scared of a little romp in the hay as—well, as you'd be. I think you can stop her, and I think you *should*, but first you got to find out what's actually going on.

"Say, I got an idea. Why don't I tell Lillian to snoop around and follow them and find out what they're up to? She's none too smart, but they'd never suspect *her*, and I *will* say you car trust her to keep her trap shut."

Cass was too astonished to be indignant. Of all women living, Roy's shrinking wife was probably the least suited to spying.

"Well, what do you think of the idea?"

"No, I wouldn't want that done for anything!"

"Don't you *want* to know what they're up to?"

"Yes, I suppose I do."

"Don't you think it's important?"

"Roy, it's confusing for a man who's supposed to be reasonably decent to believe that his wife, whom he worships, for whom he'd throw overboard everything and everybody, may be an adulteress."

"There's an old-fashioned word for you!"

"It's an old-fashioned quandary. It goes back to Eve and the serpent. I'm sure the real discussion in Eden wasn't about apples. Hang it, I don't know which is worse: to believe that a woman's adultery is the only form of disloyalty that matters, and she ought to be smashed for it; or to have this new-fangled idea that it doesn't matter at all, that infidelity is all good fun between friends. Both attitudes make me sick. But to have to think of such things about Jinny . . ."

"I always did tell you you had no sense of humor, Cass, and you're a fanatic about your wife. You laymen never understand psychology, like a doc has to. Jinny's all right—I guess—but she ain't the poet's dream you make her out to be, not by a long shot. The sooner you realize it and tell her she can either behave herself or get out, the happier you'll be. Incidentally, she's made you look a lot older."

"That's nonsense."

"It is, eh? That's a guaranteed way of getting old—trying to keep up with a skittish wife. Okay. My only interest in the whole business is that in my own roughneck way—I guess I'm too forthright and scientific for the kind of Eastern, pansy burg that Grand Republic is getting to be—my only concern is, I don't like to see you taken for a ride."

There was more of it, much more, but Cass did not hear him.

He was not sleepy in court that afternoon. He listened with bleak attention to a case involving the theft of a woman's good name and seven pounds of grass seed. He looked grim as a wintertime Sioux warrior as he tacked and skidded his car on the December-bleached roadway.

As he walked into the house, he heard Jinny telephoning:

"I don't know. . . . No, I can't tell. . . . I'll see-ee. . . . Now don't be so naughty, and keep coaxing. . . . Bye, dear."

He did not ask to whom she was telephoning. He knew.

He was attentive through dinner, and then, for the first time, he launched a quarrel intentionally:

"Sit down, Jinny, and be quiet. I want to talk."

"Do——"

"Yes, I intend to start a 'scene'—a bad one. Look. Bradd Criley is around this house too much, and you see too much of him outside. I don't think it's gone too far yet—now listen!—but it certainly will if you don't come to your senses. I grant you all of his charms and virtues, and don't tell me what a good friend of mine he's been—I know it. But he's a thief—a thief of love and a thief of security, a scheming and deliberate thief. He wants what he wants, and he doesn't care much how many lives he may twist in getting it. I don't intend to see him let you down, as he lets down every friend, every woman, when he gets tired of them. That's all I have to say, but I warn you, I mean it."

"Are you quite finished?"

"I hope so. Except that I'm now convinced that it's been Bradd in the background who's been the unseen cause of most of our quarrels. That's all."

"Then let me tell you, just let me tell you——"

"Quit it!"

459

"W-what?"

"Quit being dramatic. Be as nasty as you want to, but don't act Lady Macbeth. Talk sense. Let's not play at murder-trial. I'm in the business."

"Oh, I never hated you before, but when you get so smug, so conceited, so fatuous——'I'm in the business'!"

"Dear love, you know I'm not fatuous—just clumsy. I'm trying to be firm and convince you that I'm not going to tolerate this philandering. Bradd is a closed case."

She was confused and almost meek in her retort of "Oh, you think so, do you!" but she worked herself up into suitable wrath. She punched a pillow and launched out:

"Do you usually try criminals without giving them a chance to defend themselves? If Bradd were here, and you even dared to *hint* at what you call his 'treachery,' he'd knock you down."

"Sorry. He couldn't."

"And when you stood there like a prizefighter, with your manly foot on his chest, you'd expect me to admire you?"

"Sweet, stop it. This has nothing to do with the fact that I will not stand for Bradd."

"Then why tell *me*? Why don't you tell *him*? If you're going to act the noble affronted husband, why don't you *do* it? Make up your mind!"

He remarked, "All right." He crossed casually to the telephone. He got Bradd, at the Avondenes', and said, "I wish you could drive out here. It's quite important. I'll explain when you get here."

During the half-hour while they waited, Cass and Jinny were extremely civil. They said, Have you heard the war news? They said, There's a hole burned in the rug in the sun-room. They said, I don't think the furnace is giving the heat it ought to.

Bradd came in, snowy and smiling. Cass spoke to him with no unusual expression in his voice:

"I wish you'd be careful in answering what I'm going to say, Bradd, and not too touchy, because I don't want to lose your friendship. It's been a valued possession for a great many years."

"You sound serious, Jedge."

"Bradd, you're too attentive to Jinny. People are talking. That's not so important to me as the fact that I'm thinking!"

"You mean to say——"

"Yes. You've gone beyond safe companionship with Jinny, but I believe you can cut it out and we can be friendly again, instead of a pretty silly and nasty triangle."

"What's suddenly started all this?"

"Being forced to admit what I already knew."

"You really believe that I have what the prudes call 'evil intentions' toward Jinny?"

"Yes."

"What?"

461

"I said Yes."

"Really——"

"I don't think she has. But I think you have. Though I also think that you've had so many affairs that you'll never be able to feel very deeply about her or any other woman now."

Bradd rose quietly. "What proof have you of your suspicions?"

"I didn't have any till this second, when you asked that defensive question."

"You call that proof!"

"Bradd, don't be insulted, don't be a comedy villain. There's too little love *or* friendship in life." He astonished Bradd, he overwhelmed Jinny, and he considerably surprised himself by grasping Bradd's arm, and urging, "I love her, and I'm fond of you. I would have gone to you, instead of having the impertinence of asking you to come here just to get bawled out, but I wanted Jinny to know just what I really said. Don't say anything now. You must decide whether you want to hate me or not. But if we three decent people can't get along in honesty, then there's no hope for anybody anywhere."

"Good night," Bradd said flatly, and, as he left them, for the first time in twenty years, he looked confused.

Then Cass turned wearily to Jinny, and prepared to be denounced.

She moved toward him shyly, and muttered, "You're so superior to that fellow! I knew it all along, but I was just being stubborn. I do love you, and he—he's yellow!"

"I don't know that I'd call him yellow. He's really a nice man."

" 'Nice' he ain't! I could tell you a lot of things about him that you don't know. But the point is that you've gone and taken me away from him again, as you do with all my beaux."

"Good!"

"And—uh—Cass, it never did go very far with Bradd and me. Just sort of a careless kiss."

"I'm glad."

"*You're* glad? Gee, maybe I'm not! Sweet dear!"

An Assemblage of Husbands and Wives

PERRY & BERNICE CLAYWHEEL

PERRY CLAYWHEEL, superintendent of schools of Grand Republic and president of its small Junior College, was an enterprising and liberal educator. He fought to have the meager salaries of his teachers increased, and every summer he read several books.

He admired and even liked his lily-pale consort, Bernice, but he was almost impotent to make love to her, and they had no children.

Bernice, that prim wanton, was no nymphomaniac. She said, extraordinarily often, "I think All Those Things are too much discussed." But she did have a normal longing for passion, and she went shyly tripping to Dr. Drover.

"I'm sure you'll believe me, Doctor, when I tell you that I entirely disapprove of immorality, and still more of showing bad taste. But what can I do? My husband leaves me so dissatisfied that sometimes I can't think of anything else, and I'm afraid I'll go crazy. What do you advise?"

"Why don't you try to do your job right and get him interested? You probably scare him off."

"You mean the arts of love?"

"Huh? Yuh, I guess you could call it that."

"To me, Doctor, that would be sordid, and unmodern, like a slave-woman. I must have romance—all the beauty that the movies make an effort to show. I deserve it! And if Perry can't give it to me——It isn't that I want an 'affair,' but if I don't have one, I'm afraid I'll go crazy. I feel so nervous. But if I, uh, go with a man of my own social class, I'm afraid it will get out, and honestly, I wouldn't want to jeopardize my husband's important position. And if I picked up some common person, I'd be terrified of blackmail. Tell me, Doctor—I'm dreadfully ashamed to even ask this, but are there—uh—places where women can go, as there are places where men go?"

"No! Besides, I don't know what you're talking about. That's a problem you'll have to work out by yourself," snapped the virtuous Dr. Drover.

Both Bernice and Dr. Drover regarded themselves as persons who had learned the facts of life.

When she was in this wretched way of feeling, she took some papers for her husband to Bradd Criley. It was late in the afternoon, a rainy October afternoon, and Mr. Criley's stenographer had gone. He remembered, with surprise, that just then he had no affair on whatever, except for an interest in Jinny Timberlane which that fractious girl had never permitted to go beyond flirtation. He looked at Bernice and thought how lovely she was, shining in the putrescent autumn light. He led her to the leather couch and kissed her.

Even with his professional experience, he was surprised by the way in which she instantly went to pieces. She cried "Oh!" and almost smothered him with her reaching arms, and seemed about to eat him up. "Is she hot!" he thought.

They met half a dozen times in a month, and he told himself—indeed, he rather hinted to his friend Dr. Drover—that he was a public benefactor. Bernice asked him whether they were "really doing the right thing," and he assured her—at first—that it was "necessary for her health."

What began to bore him, what made him cut the affair off even more quickly than usual, was the fact that Bernice kept moaning, "Oh, lover, we oughtn't to be doing this to Perry."

"Where do you get that 'we'?" he protested, first to himself but presently to her, and she wept enough, she acted badly enough, so that he was able to break it off with quite a show of indignation.

Now Perry Claywheel had been convincing himself that he was becoming a better lover, recently. There was a teacher, not too young, who thought fairly well of him—not that they did anything really wrong, you understand.

On the night after Bernice's first visit to Bradd, Perry had turned to her, in their golden-oak double bed, with a slight quiver of rapture, but she had said sharply, "Oh, not tonight. Anyway, it's not good for you."

He protested that it *was* good for him, and that he longed for her, and as she continued to refuse him, with more and more resentment, as though he were a preposterous stranger, he could think of nothing but his desire to be with her. He trembled with a conceptive agony that, in his humiliation, was not uncolored with madness.

He did not try to persuade her again. However he might long for her imaginatively, in her presence he became powerless. He had a shameful feeling that he was not quite a man, that his failure was incurable.

He was afraid of her, though he still wanted her to think of him as a possible lover for some time in the future, when she should have got over this curious triumphant mood of hers, which he could not understand. Looking about Grand Republic, he suspected that many husbands were afraid of their wives, quiveringly trying to placate those small tyrants. He wondered if there was any country save America in which a large share of the men were frightened continuously by their own wives.

With all this, he became irritable at school, snapping at the teachers, accusing the pupils, and he no longer enjoyed the intellectual card-cataloging and small prides of his job. He just did not enjoy anything, not even the sight of Bernice and her beauty, for she was suddenly changing, and becoming drab and hesitant, uninteresting even to the young men who delivered groceries and with whom she had once laughed in the kitchen.

When Bernice finally hinted to him that she was willing to return to his embraces, he said bleakly that he had no longer any desire. But he never knew what he owed to Bradd Criley, a man well spoken of for his geniality.

41

MR. BOONE HAVOCK, with Mr. Bradd Criley, his attorney, was attendant in the chambers of Judge Timberlane, in the matter of an injunction against the Sequoia & Hematite R.R.

The Judge and Mr. Criley, though they addressed each other by their first names, were so excessively courteous that Mr. Havock protested, "You boys are awful pplite and helpful to each other today. What's trouble? Been having a row?"

Bradd looked to Cass for a statement which might determine their relationship for many years, and Cass said thoughtfully, "Bradd is my friend, and you can't row with a friend. You might murder him, but you couldn't hurt him. If he did have any faults—no, if a man is your friend, he *has* no faults; he merely has oversights that you know he'll correct when he gets around to it. That's true, don't you think, Bradd?"

"I hope it is—I'm sure it is!"

"God Almighty, you boys getting so noble on me about friendship! You're lucky you ain't in the contracting business! And since you're so het up about friendship, Cass, strikes me you been neglecting your old friends, the Havocks, pretty bad, the past six months. It's that wife of yours—elegant girl but God-awful snooty. Does she let you in under the rope,

Bradd?"

"We're on quite civil terms, I think. She is a very fine woman."

"I guess too fine for us lumberjacks. She's got every right to her opinions, but don't let her take you away from us, Cass. We kind of need you around."

Cass was so inept at the higher lying that he could only get back to the injunction. When they had finished and Boone was gone, Cass dropped his hand on Bradd's shoulder and said, with no particular emphasis, "We want you to come to Christmas dinner. Very much."

"You're sure of it?"

"Yes."

"I'd like to. I'll come and be glad to. And——Look, Cass. I'm never going to say another word about this, but you did exaggerate my feeling toward Jinny. If I was at fault it was just the 'oversight' you were speaking of. I have so much respect for Jinny's integrity and so much appreciation of her humor that I showed it in a way that, I see now, might have been mistaken for a quite improper ardor. But nobody knows better than I do that she *is* your wife. No, no, don't say anything; I just wanted to make myself clear, and I hope that now we three can be friends again. Good night, ole man. Christmas dinner at three?"

Everything was normal and beautiful with this happy young couple, the Timberlanes, now, and there was obviously no reason why their heavenly bliss should not last forever.

Jinny was "taking care of herself"; she got nine hours of sleep, covered as warmly as the doctor advised, she eschewed pastry and looked with sniffs upon more than one cocktail a week. She welcomed Cass to her bed, and wound her arms about his tingling shoulders, and they so rejoiced again in bodily love that they even saw the cosmically bawdy humor in it.

As much as Cass, the reticent Jinny was offended by indecencies, yet she did see that it was demoralizingly funny when the embarrassed young Cass came in expectantly and had to be told that he and his poetic ardor were barred by the lunar rhythm.

She jeered at him then, but tenderly, and revealed the esoteric fact that every woman somehow expects her man to guess that obvious crisis without being told. He lay beside her, his cheek just touching her bare shoulder, and they laughed and were divinely content; the world shut out, the Bradd Crileys shut out, the Boone Havocks shut out, and the dusty court room and the bitter Northern winter and the ghastly speed with which, after you are twenty-five, the whole good day is only one hour long.

They were so commendable. Pricked by Boone's protest, they had the Havocks and the Drovers and the Brightwings and the Reverend Gadds and the Prutts in for dinner. It wasn't really so hard, you know; Jinny's diabetes gave Cass an excuse

470

to invite their guests to go home at ten o'clock.

Their Christmas was as hearty as though no war existed.

They drank lingeringly to all their friends in peril abroad, but then, as every civilian far enough from the battle has done in every war since Troy, they forgot it, and sang carols.

Any strain that might be left over between Bradd and the Timberlanes was wiped out in early January, when Bradd came in to say quietly that he was going to New York to live, permanently.

The Wargate Corporation had bought several plants in New England and New Jersey for its war materials: packing cases, wallboard for barracks, glider bodies, propellers, hulls. They had offices in New York; might even, in some day catastrophic for Grand Republic, move their headquarters there; and in New York they needed Bradd as legal adviser.

He said evenly, "I hate to say good-bye so informally—I think of you two as my dearest friends—but there's a case on, and I have to grab a train tomorrow morning. My stuff will be sent on after me, when I get an apartment in New York. And I have to hustle over to Webb Wargate's now. We have a conference that'll take half the night. So good-bye, and come see me in New York, soon as you can. I'll paint the town for you. And you have a perfectly swell husband, Jinny!"

He shook Cass's hand, he hastily kissed Jinny, and he was gone.

471

42

HE ADMITTED that he had lied to himself in asserting that she had settled down to contentment with housewifery and bridge and dinners and the Red Cross. When they came home from parties they laughed as intimately together and as domestically about their fellow-guests as those guests were then doing about them, and at such a time Grand Republic seemed world enough for her.

Yet she was curiously older. In no feature, not in her throat or her eyes or mouth, could you detect the minute signs of aging, but April was gone. She did not complain. Indeed, when he made the husbandly inquiry, "Are you happy?" she was impatient: "Of course I am. Why shouldn't I be?"

If she was not content, she put up with life, in a static, plodding way. She was only bored when, with that circular conversation of matrimony, the same ideas coming up as bright new ones over and over, he again hinted that she ought to do a little more war work, a little more drawing.

He sighed that he and his cursed domestication had killed so much of that part of her that was peculiarly Jinny Timberlane, and to no end, since he was no more satisfied with three meals in a day colored only by a little passion than she was.

Did all people, everywhere, drift thus into a not-quite-painful dullness? Was it merely the way of the world? Well, if it was, he raged, he would change that world. He would pack up Jinny and Mrs. Higbee and Cleo and Isis and his Nonesuch edition of Dickens and flee.

Where?

That was but one mood. Most of the time, he was at ease as husband and judge. But the twisted mood did come, oftener and oftener.

Jinny had a letter or two from Bradd, in February. She read them aloud to Cass, and apparently she left nothing out.

"Am now one of the dizziest members of café society, and can read menus backwards. Have learned that *Boeuf de Dijon en Casserole* means Irish Stew, and how to answer the waiters, etc., in my best Gr. Rep. French, 'No soap.' "

"He writes clever letters," said Cass.

She sniffed. "Oh, I think they're silly."

He thought so too, and he was much comforted.

"How about a little chess, Jin?"

"I'd just love it."

He was worried. When she just-loved chess, a game which has been truly mastered by no woman since Queen Elizabeth she was hiding things.

His resolve had been subterraneanly forming for two years, but it came to a climax irrelevantly, when he was on the bench during the drawing of a jury.

——My Jinny is going to die, unless I do something to save her. She'll wither and become an old woman early and die. It's more psychic than bodily, her slow fading, no matter what Roy says. I *will* do something.

Only his mechanical judicial mind heard the lawyers. After court, he hastened home in a panic. With his overcoat scarce off, he held her shoulders, looked at her beseechingly, and insisted:

"You aren't getting much out of living the way we do, *are* you? Tell me really. I think it's a perfectly good way, but perhaps it isn't for some people. Don't be heroic or sacrificing. We can do almost anything you want to. Tell me how you feel."

He had spoken without any of the standard domestic questioning, and she answered honestly, "I am getting kind of bored."

"What would you like us to do? I don't care what it is—growing ice-cubes in Greenland."

"Well, sometimes I've wished you were practising law in Minneapolis, or maybe you could be a judge there, still better. Could you?"

"Not for quite a while, anyway. Have to be elected judge, you know. But to go back to practising law——" He sighed. "That would be all right. Might even be exciting. More competition. Minneapolis would be fine. You'd, uh, you'd like it better than Grand Republic?"

"There are too many memories here: Eino and my Emily, and poor Jinny before she got sick—she used to be so excited, such a fool! And there's so little to do here, not even any good restaurants, and in the evening, you can go to a movie—or not go to a movie. But Minneapolis—gracious, a huge city like that—restaurants and the University and all kinds of art galleries and everything! Even a real show right from New York, sometimes. All sorts of wonderful things. You're sure you couldn't get transferred as a judge?"

"No, it's a different judicial district. And the chances are about a hundred to one of my not being elected there, if I even resigned here."

"You asked me to be frank, and I was, and now I want you to be. You do love the dignity of being a judge, *don't* you?"

"Yes, but I love it less than I do you."

"Would it be hard to take up practising again?"

"Well, the commercial end, especially the grabbing off of other people's clients, would be unpleasant. But what would I care about remaining a judge if I lost you?"

"Oh, you'll never lose me! I'll always stick. You haven't a chance. And you would really do this for me, if I wanted to— move to Minneapolis?"

"I certainly would. Only, why Minneapolis? If we *are* going to taclde a more metropolitan place, why not Chicago? Or New York?"

"New York terrified me. I think it did you."

475

"Look, lamb, if Bradd Criley can make a go of it there, I can!"

"Ye-es——"

"I'm at least as good a lawyer as he is—with all apologies to your friend, maybe I'm a little better." He realized that he was betraying a jealousy of Bradd for daring to invade Megalopolis, and he went on more mildly: "I mean, we ought to thank Bradd for showing us the way. We don't have to be Westerners with lariats unless we want to! I don't have to hold court on horseback, and you can come out of the sod hut. We'll pick up New York and shake it."

"Oh, but that headwaiter at the Marmoset Club, with eyes like a wet old dishrag, who looks at you just once and guesses exactly what your income is, and do you know any Astors."

"Maybe we'd get to know a few Class B Astors, if we wanted to, which I doubt."

"I'd love to know *lots* of Astors—big fat juicy ones, and little diamond-studded ones in sables!"

——She hasn't been so gay in weeks. My idea was right.

"Jinny, you shall have all the Astors you want. Have Astors with your corn flakes."

"And cream."

"And extra cream, from the Ritz. God knows even a very rich Astor or Vanderbilt or Morgan, one nine feet tall with a robe made of securities, couldn't be more chilly than our local John William Prutts. Let's look their lodge over. I mean, before we actually decide whether I ever shall resign, I think we ought to go to New York and study it, to see whether, if we had a real home of our own there, we wouldn't enjoy the place."

"And Cleo?"

"Naturally."

Jinny thought it over and said seriously, "And I guess we'd have to take Mrs. Higbee, too, if she'd come. I do get a little tired of her dumplings, but she's the only one we could trust to walk Cleo."

He laughed. "You're already beginning to think of New York as possible."

"Maybe I am. And I imagine that if you did step down from the bench and had to stand looking up at some other old meanie sitting there, you'd rather have it farther away than Minneapolis."

"Possibly."

"You'll get used to being down in the prize-ring again. Beat 'em all up! After all, a referee doesn't have as much fun as the scrappers. . . . Oh, Cass, shall we really try New York?"

"Yes, we'll go see what legal openings there are."

He pondered, not for the first time, that she did not really comprehend what it would mean to him to give up the honor of his judgeship and his belief that in some minute way he was guarding the rights of man, adding to the eternal code of justice. She had not complained about it, but she had never altogether understood why he was willing to take far less in salary than the fees he could make as a practitioner. He remembered that when she had visited his court room, she had been considerably less stirred by the finality of his " 'Jection 'stained" than by Bradd's insinuating address to the jury.

He wondered whether today, as women more and more took on professions of their own, wives in general were less interested in their husbands' work; whether their ears wandered from the men's shop-talk as their eyes wandered from the marriage-bed. Was the sanctity of the profession, to be followed for a lifetime, for many generations, and rarely to be thrown over for a "better-paying job," vanishing from society along with the sanctity of the single family?

It frightened him.

Judges Blackstaff and Flaaten were annoyed when Judge Timberlane wanted to run off to New York for a week during the busy court days of early February. But Roy Drover was annoying.

"Going to see our old friend Bradd there?" he hinted.

"Certainly."

"Your wife going to see him, too?"

"Why not?"

"I wouldn't know. Probably I'm wrong, so please excuse me for living."

43

BRADD CRILEY met their train in New York. He was wearing a black camel's-hair coat and a black Homburg; he who had edified Grand Republic with plaid overcoats and a green hunting-hat with a feather. With Jinny, as with Cass, he merely shook hands.

Naturally, Cass had reserved a suite at that only hotel, the Melchester, but Bradd cried, "Oh, I meant to warn you. I used to think the Melchester was a good joint, but now I realize that nobody but Middlewesterners stay there. I wish I could put you up at my flat, but I have just the one bedroom. Maybe I can get you accommodations at the Gayling. The manager there is a good friend of mine."

"We'll be all right. Only be here six-seven days," said Cass.

If their suite at the Melchester was not the same as the one they had had before, it was even more so, more white-paneled and chaste and monastic. Isis was again set on the windowsill, to see New York. Jinny flushed over worshiping the crystal toy, and turned to Cass with "I *am* silly, I know!"

It was the last time during their stay when he saw her as youthful.

That evening, by the arrangement of Bradd and in Bradd's phrase, they "painted the town red." They went to one restaurant and three night-clubs, and in each place had the same table and the same waiter and the same drinks and the same waiting for their bill and the same excessiveness in the bill when they did get it, and on the whole, if the taxicabs were expensive, still, it did not take them much longer to go three blocks by taxi than to have walked.

In each miniature heaven, Bradd introduced them to the same man, only sometimes this man was fat and had a girl, and sometimes he was thin and had a toupée—and a girl. They all drank, and Cass felt dull. He probably was.

He explained that he was thinking of practising law here. Bradd sounded doubtful:

"Of course you're a swell lawyer, much sounder than I am, but it's hard for me to see you either in a limousine or the subway. You like walking home through the snow too much. Me, I'm a chameleon. I may yet wind up as a tenor. It's only the fact that the Wargates and Boone have always backed me that has kept me from being an ambulance-chaser."

He looked at Jinny, and her eyes said that he was too modest.

"So I can switch from the slow pace of Grand Republic to this hundred-and-four-degree fever tempo of New York and not get nervous. You study a guy for a long time before you accept him as a friend, but I can pick up a hundred new people in a day, and drop 'em just as quickly. God knows it would be wonderful to have you here, but I think you ought to go kind of slow about deciding."

They all became more or less drunk, and Cass could not remember whether, at parting, Bradd kissed Jinny or not.

She slept long after Cass had awakened, next morning, and he was touched by the pleasant sight of her: rosy and half-smiling, with her left index finger clasped in her right hand. Over his solitary coffee, in the parlor of their suite, he saw himself back in a law office, bargaining, arranging, advising, tactfully welcoming new business. . . . There was a long table, and on it the files about a client with a temper and a red-veined nose, and beside it that client himself, and Counselor Timberlane was about to lose his lucrative but distasteful business by advising him that you really can't sue for the possession of property merely because you like the view from it——

A tap, and Bradd came in, in a gray overcoat and a new gray hat and a red chrysanthemum, but closing his eyes in pain.

"Have I got a hang-over!" he moaned. "Were you wise to only drink half as much as I did, last evening! Hope I'm not butting in, but I was too high last evening to make any real plans for us today."

Cass had not known that Bradd *was* to make plans for them.

"The lady awake yet?"

"The lady is awake but I'm not sure she's alive!" floated from the bedroom, and Jinny weaved in, much too pretty in her negligee. She shook hands with Bradd as though they were rival undertakers.

He had coffee with them, and suddenly he was no gilded New Yorker but one of the hometown boys, ready to trade all the shops on Madison Avenue for the lint-smelling aisles of The Tarr Emporium.

"I was kind of pie-eyed and boastful, last evening," Bradd grumbled. "Oh, I *have* met a lot of people here, almost as many as I claimed, but I'm still lonely, and am I glad to see you! I haven't anybody here who's a hundredth as close to me as you two are—nobody whose house I'd drop into uninvited, except my sister's place, way out in Darien. I go out there for week-ends, and Avis is a grand woman, but she is rather sot in her ways. Oh, I'm making a lot of social contacts that will be invaluable later, but I haven't got anybody, male *or* female, that I can knock around with.

"If you're free, I can take the whole day off. Can't you put off seeing prospects for twenty-four hours, Cass? Oh, see if you can't rig it. We'll lunch at the Plaza, and then take a taxi up and look over Grant's Tomb. You always hear about all the visiting firemen going up there, but I never met anybody that has. Maybe Grant's no longer there. He may have left in a huff. We ought to find out, and tell the Associated Press.

"Then we'll have dinner early, at a Hindu place I know of, wonderful curries, and go to a show, *Oklahoma*. Avis will come in town and join us—I've already phoned her—and I have four tickets already. Got 'em by almost you might say a fluke. They're absolutely impossible to get, show is a sell-out, but the agent is a great friend of mine; he said to me, 'Mr. Criley, I wouldn't let anybody else have these tickets, not if it was the President of the United States.'

"So come on, Cass; let's you and I and the girl take the day off and be fancy-free. Time enough to act serious tomorrow. Just say the word and I'll phone my office."

"Bradd, I'm sorry as the dickens, but I have dates with law-firms all day long. Why don't you two skip off together, and I'll meet you and Avis for dinner?"

Bradd seemed entirely cheerful about this desertion. "Just as you say, Boss. I'll squire the lady around and get her back here fairly early and have Avis meet us all here at seven. Be sure and be on time, so we won't miss any of the show, and be dressed——Got your Tux along? Good! I know most of these New Yorkers aren't dressing for the theater, in wartime, but we'll show 'em the kind of speed we're used to in Grand Republic! Be sure and be all ready by seven, so we can have a leisurely dinner. You'll appreciate that cocoanut soup."

"Do I get asked about any of this?" demanded Jinny.

"You do. Do you?" said Bradd.

"I do," said Jinny. They laughed—they two.

Cass croaked, "Well, I got to get started, I'm afraid. Shame I got these engagements."

That was at ten A.M.

At five minutes after ten, Cass went down in the elevator. He had no engagements whatever.

He was ashamed of his suspicions, but he could not help it; he sat in the lobby, in a niche behind a petrified palm, waiting to see when Bradd and Jinny would leave.

Not till this morning had it occurred to the simple husband that, after his warnings about treachery, his wife and Bradd could possibly continue to intrigue against his peace and decency. But he had seen Bradd looking at her in her negligee, he had seen flying between them the glances that do not need words for a body.

He saw them skip through the lobby and out to a taxicab at ten minutes to twelve.

She was in a gray suit with a yellow sweater as lively as a fiesta. She looked, to his sensitized mind, three years younger than when she had left Grand Republic three days ago. She was rosy and excited, and the shadows of her illness and Emily's death and middle-class boredom seemed lifted from her by a new light.

——If that fellow has such a good effect on her, and if I really love her as much as I claim I do, I ought to hand her over to him, even if he doesn't want me to—even if *she* doesn't!

——No! The improvement in her is just travel. She'd go out quite as cheerfully with Greg Marl or Lloyd Gadd.

——But Bradd isn't like them. He can really be evil. There are a few people that actually are evil. He's no good.

——Don't fool yourself, my friend. That's what makes him dangerous. Women love wolves and heels, the way decent men often love insinuating little tarts. And women will sacrifice anything for their compliments—and for their embraces. Real witchcraft. To think that Jinny, who's been clean as a doe in a forest, could stand the bog that Bradd loves to wallow in.

——I won't think that way about either of them!

——I wonder where he stayed in our suite while she was dressing?

——Oh, shame, Cass!

He telephoned and made engagements to see the heads of several law firms. Then he had a horrible afternoon of sitting in Georgian waiting-rooms, dens of knowledge and of contempt, where from the tops of classical bookcases the busts of Cicero and Judas Maccabeus and Roger Taney looked down at him and denied that he could ever have been a congressman or a judge. What had he come in with—samples? Where was the briefcase?

When he finally talked with the Heads, they were less chummy than the plaster busts. They were looking for office boys, not partners.

He lunched by himself at an Automat, remembering how in better days Jinny had loved the magic doors which opened on mince pies. At five he went by himself to a newsreel, and in the war scenes he saw only the faces of Bradd and Jinny and heard only, "Can't you let the poor girl enjoy herself?"

He was back at the hotel at six-fifteen. Jinny had not returned. He was dressed at six-thirty-five, and trying to find the Dick Tracy comic strip in the confusing New York newspapers, which didn't have even the Weather Report in the right place.

Bradd's sister Avis—the refined Mrs. William Elderman of New York and Darien—telephoned up from the lobby at six-fifty-nine, came in, in rich apparel, looked all over the room (fourteen by sixteen) and said accusingly, "Why, Bradd isn't *here!*"

She obliquely let him know that she was not accustomed to being dragged into town like this for every stray tramp from Minnesota. They made talk and looked at each other resentfully, while Cass peeped at his heavy pocket-watch, Avis at her tiny curved wrist-watch. They were increasingly nervous as Time jumped from seven-fifteen to seven-thirty to seven-forty-five to eight——

"But where *are* they?" observed Avis.

At ten minutes after eight, Jinny and Bradd whisked in, very gay. They must have stopped at Bradd's apartment, for he was now in dinner-clothes. Certainly they had had cocktails.

Jinny rejoiced, "My, I'm afraid we're late—most awfully sorry—I'll hustle and change—like a rabbit-hound!" From the bedroom she could be heard as she dressed, in no especial haste.

Bradd said innocently, "Do forgive us, Sister—Cass. I know we're horribly late, but we got to talking and laughing about the Prutts and Queenie Havock, and we didn't realize how late it was getting to be." Then, boyishly and sweetly, "Guess I was sort of homesick for local gossip."

They had a feverishly gulping dinner and missed part of the play, which offended Judge Timberlane's principles of art and of economy equally. And Avis rather spoke about this, later, when they sat at the Marmoset, since she had "gone and taken the trouble to come clear in from Darien, *really!*" In Cass's brain was a pulse beating, "Be careful or you'll lose her—be careful—you'll lose her—be careful."

While Bradd was being sardonic about the audience at the play, who were people very much like Bradd Criley, Cass's head went on beating, "They certainly weren't trying to hide anything, when they came in an hour late! They trust me not to be a jealous maniac. I'll show that I trust *them!*"

He blurted, "I'll have to be seeing law-firms again, all day tomorrow. Suppose you could entertain Jinny, Bradd, or are you busy?"

"I'd feel honored to elope with the lady, but I'll be rushed with work all day," said Bradd; and Jinny, "Matter fact, I'll be rushed myself. Be at the hair-dresser's most of the time."

Cass was so pleased by their casualness that he barely

noticed it when Bradd went on, "But maybe I could snatch just a few minutes, Jin, and grab a quick sandwich with you for lunch," and she, with equal indifference, answered, "We'll see. Call me at the hair-dresser's—Madame Lorraine's."

The thunderstorm was over, the sky cleared, the birds twittering. Even Avis, after two highballs, was sunny, and told them about her first grandchild. She was proud of having one at her age of forty-five, as though it was something special and foxy and quite unsuburban that she had done. At midnight, Bradd put her into a taxicab and returned boisterously.

They moved on to the Jive Hive and there sat or danced till three, and Cass did not suggest their going home, for he was fascinated as Bradd, swiftly drinking, turned into the complete and obvious satyr, and Jinny clearly did not mind. She was excited when by black art, before their eyes, the good housedog, the faithful spaniel, was transformed into an amorous werewolf.

In the 1940's, not even the machines for destroying lives and cities were more ingeniously developed than the novelties in the American vocabulary. The ancient four-letter words pertaining to generation and digestion were brought from the garden fence to the Junior Misses' schoolroom, and in the lower reaches of etymology, there was also a treasury of new labels for the sort of male once described with relish as "an agreeable scoundrel." He could now be referred to not merely as a cad or a bounder, but as a heel, a drip, a punk, a lug, a jerk, a louse, a stinker, a rat, a twirp, a crumb, or a goon. There were exquisite distinctions among the precise meanings of these words, but most of them were allied to "wolf," the contemporary term for a confirmed seducer or amateur pimp, a type well thought of at the time.

Meditatively considering these terms, Cass decided that his old friend Bradd was a heel, a stinker, a rat, and a wolf.

Bradd was, as he became drunk, most whimsical and prankish. He spoke to the waiter in a gibberish which he explained as Modern Persian. He thought it was amusing to steal a silver teaspoon.

He told the Timberlanes just enough of his affair with Bernice Claywheel to give himself a reek of sexual potency. He picked up an anonymous, damply pretty woman at the bar, brought her to their table, told her that he was a renowned Los Angeles psychiatrist, and treated her dipsomania by pouring so many highballs into her that she went off and was sick in the women's toilet.

When Jinny was definitely not amused, Bradd's round face cleared to a look of sober and engaging youthfulness, and he confided, "I ought to apologize to you for kidding that poor sot, but remember I'm a prairie hick, and I can't resist showing up these sophisticated New Yorkers. Cass, doesn't it seem incredible that that slattern and our lovely Jinny belong to the same female sex?"

"Yes—yes—incredible—we'll go home now, Jinny."

In the taxicab, when Cass growled, "Bradd acted like a hobbledehoy," she snapped, "Oh, don't be so picky! He never acts like a judge, if that's what you mean. He loves fun and adventure."

When with long yawns they had reached their bedroom, they undressed in verbal darkness. Cass got what solace he could from the fact that Jinny and he would have dinner by themselves tomorrow evening.

44

MR. CROSSBOW of Crossbow, Murphy and Thane, in which firm Cass's classmate, Dennis Thane, was a partner, was born in Yankton, South Dakota. He thought highly of Middlewestern men and of the Minnesota judiciary; he said Yes, he believed arrangements could be made for Judge Timberlane to join their firm; in fact, they would be honored.

Cass walked a mile up Broadway from Pine Street, out of the district of gold certificates and steamship tickets, dazed that he should have chosen to make his home in this wilderness where grizzlies prowled all night and rattlers lurked all day. He was at once homesick for the stillness of Dead Squaw Lake and proud that he might some day be a millionaire, invited out to Long Island palaces where each guest had three bathrooms.

——Let's see. Jinny wouldn't care for the suburbs. Probably get an apartment on Park Avenue. Maybe on the river. Be interesting to watch the boats—I guess.

He was to meet her at the hotel at six-thirty. They were to dine together, and he rejoicingly had two good seats for Berg Nord's new play.

He pictured himself rushing in to her with the news. That morning he had merely mentioned the voodoo word "diabetes," and she had sworn that she would be back at the hotel by five, and have a nap.

——We won't overdo it tonight. We won't even go backstage and see Berg. I'll send her to bed by half-past-eleven.

She was not in the suite when he arrived. He sat waiting for her till twenty minutes past seven. When she came in, tired and blank, he controlled himself, but the excitement and surprise had gone out of his news and he said methodically, "Well, looks as if we really can stay in New York. I can get a partnership with a good firm. All we have to decide now is when I resign from the bench. Do you want to come here before this summer, or wait till fall, when it'll be——"

"No!" She looked secret and unhappy as she interrupted him. "I don't want you to give up being a judge. I can't do that to you, too."

"How do you mean? *Too?*"

"Oh, just generally disappointing you."

"You haven't. You couldn't!"

"Oh, Cass, don't do it! Take me home—tomorrow, if you can. Please give up this whole idea. I know you couldn't be happy, practising here, and then how could *I* be happy? I was so stupid and didn't realize, but when I see how you writhe— and you should; they're so incredibly packed and vulgar— how you hate these night-clubs, and even the streets, that are so tall and no trees, then I know you mustn't do it. Let's go back *now!* I will try to be satisfied, and I'm sure I can be, now I know how fast and noisy this place is."

"Of course if we lived here quietly, in a nice flat, like most New Yorkers——"

"No, no, no! I want security—and our home—and Cleo. Please!"

"You scarcely have to coax me! Of course that's what I want, too. But tomorrow?"

"Tonight, if we only could!"

That evening he was able to get, for the two of them, one single upper berth on a minor railroad to Chicago, for the next day. He telephoned to his putative new partners, Mr. Crossbow and Mr. Dennis Thane, at their homes, that he would not be able to join their firm. They both said that he had "let them down," but Cass, to whom such an accusation would normally have been occasion for alarm, scarcely heard them.

He was too busy to ask Jinny what she had been doing all day.

"I think we can still make our show, all right," he said happily. (Aspens gentle by the Sorshay River!) "Want us to have some fun, our last evening here. It will be the last for quite a while, I guess."

"Yes—see Cousin Berg——" she said feebly.

But he went on conscientiously, "Or do you think we ought to give up the show and spend the time with Bradd?"

"Oh, I don't think that's necessaiy. We've seen a good deal

of him. Can't we just telephone him?"

He liked that very much. "Sure. I'll try him now."

He did not reach Bradd till after the play, to which he was not veiy attentive, so swelling was he with thought of the coming spring back home, when the top of their blue spruce would be dotted with red buds, like a tiny Christmas tree, the mountain ash starred with white, and the earth-smell sharply clean from Northern rivulets. People here could not understand how proud and separate was his land, nor how completely it drew him back, with no regrets for the heathen wonders of Broadway.

He had Bradd on the telephone at midnight, and said apologetically, "Well, despite all we could do to entertain her, Jinny has decided she wants to go home. Looks as if I wouldn't hook up with any law firm here, for a while at least."

"Won't I see you before you go?" Bradd sounded regretful but not inconsolable.

"Afraid not, till the next visit, but we hope you'll be coming out home soon."

"You bet, Cass; soon as I can."

"Jinny will be wanting to say good-bye now. . . . Here you are, Jin."

She was cordial enough, but so impersonal that Cass was pleased: "Good-bye, Bradd, my dear. It's been fun having you show us around. You're the real rubber-neck-wagon guide! Sorry we won't see you, but I feel a little sick and bothered now—you know—New York is so big—or so I hear! Some day I'll write you, if I don't get too busy with the spring gardening. Good-bye!"

The one flaw was that next morning, when they were packing, they found that the crystal Isis had disappeared. They searched the two rooms, they looked under the twin beds, they summoned the chambermaid, the housekeeper, but they did not find it.

Jinny never saw again the little shining talisman which she had loved so youthfully, so long. She sat crying, her face against her thin arm.

All afternoon and evening, in the club car, he learned the strangest things about Wisconsin cheese and haddock-liver oil and the percentages of grades in the Rocky Mountains, from the indigenous magazines. Jinny was in a mood so sacred that he dared not speak to her. She sat covered with silence as with a veil, hands collapsed but eyes roving sightlessly. It was evident that she was trying to decide something that had to be swallowed with a gulp or spit out angrily.

They had to sleep in the one upper berth; they who had not shared a bed all night for many months. Cass was as embarrassed and guilty and yet excited about it as if they had never yet shared a bed at all. She would undress up there by herself; he would shuck off all that modesty permitted in the smoking compartment, and climb up and finish his undressing after she was tucked in.

The wartime world, accustomed now to every fantasy of travel, saw and was uninterested in the spectacle of the stately Judge Timberlane, in undershirt, trousers, and glove-like Pullman slippers, coming down the aisle carrying coat and shirt and shoes and dangling tie, and climbing to the upper berth, the last public view of him merely a pair of trousered legs waving high in air.

He was not a comic figure to himself, but even the dignity of the reserved unhappiness that had come over him as he had watched her all evening was denied him as he wriggled out of his trousers, into his pajamas, sitting on half the constricted space of the berth, while crowded over on her side under the blanket, her face in the shadow of her pillow, she bleakly observed him. Her right fingers lay touching her cheek; her bare arm was misted with the sleeve of her thin nightgown. She would have been an invitation to passion but that there was neither desire in her look nor any fun of intimacy, but only wariness and a doubt that hinted of fear.

He remembered their honeymoon night, remembered the rowdy adventure of her popping across the aisle and into his berth.

As he crawled under the covers beside her, and hesitatingly, just to say good night, slipped his arm about her scarce-covered shoulders, she flinched away from him. She moved over the inch or two that was her only room for escape. He drew his arm back, muttered "G' night" as indifferently as he could, and pretended to sleep.

Astounding and sudden, he found that there were tears in his eyes, and that he was mourning, "She is drifting away from me. I can't hold her. She and Bradd were loyal to me, but there will be another Bradd, a less scrupulous one, and I cannot hold her. She is drifting away."

The last stage of their journey was on the "Borup," the familiar old club car from St. Paul and Minneapolis to Grand Republic and Duluth. Cass had known it since college days, and for twenty years had known Mac, the old attendant. On it, very welcome, were Diantha Marl and Eve Champeris, brittle and lively and superior in black suits and small pert hats, and Cass was proud of them, citizenesses of no mean city, proofs of home. But Jinny scarcely saw them. There was nothing of her there except her slight body.

But she was still distantly civil as they arrived in Grand Republic toward six, in a dusk that even the friendly sight of the tall Pv elevators could not make anything but cold and dark.

45

FOR CASS and Jinny, when they came in from New York, Mrs. Higbee had ready a supper of hometown superiority: heart-shaped waffles with creamed chicken, potato pancakes, pudding with extra hard sauce.

Jinny looked at it and sniffed, "Tearoom junk."

She had not even asked for Cleo, and it was Cleo whom the fond, habitual husband expected to lure his wayward girl back to contentment. All husbands have such baits, and they are childishly hurt when they do not catch the silver fish of love. Mrs. Higbee "just didn't know where that ole Cleo was at." The animal had taken to wintertime excursions and absences that she never explained. But after supper, while Jinny was looking in a bored way at the *Evening Frontier*, Cass found the little cat in a corner of the garage, half under an old rug, looking up at him questioningly.

"It's all right, Cleo. I'm sure it's going to be all right," Cass insisted.

When Cleo was dropped into her lap, Jinny smiled, and hailed her, "Have you been good, kit? Have you studied your rodentology, and stayed away from the Toms?"

As she said it, Cass realized that it did not mean a thing, and that if she could thus talk to the cat whom she truly loved through a shroud of brooding, then she was distracted indeed. When Cleo leaped from her lap and came resentfully over to him, Jinny did not even notice.

"Tired?" he groped.

"Yes, very."

"Like me to call up Rose or the Wolkes or Jay and Pasadena or somebody?"

"Not tonight."

"Uh—Jinny. I've had a—I think we might drive out and see if Emily's grave is——"

"Please! Don't talk about that, ever. I'll go by myself some time. I don't want to make a parade of it."

"I didn't——"

"Sorry I'm so cranky. I feel all in." Her smile was a wince of pain. "I think I'll go up and get undressed and crawl into bed and read. You can kiss me good night now."

Their kiss was the touch of dry leaves drifting together, and she did not look back as she went out to the hallway.

——She does miss Bradd. It's an awfully good thing I had the sense to get her away from him when I did. Now we can start all over again.

He settled to his accumulated mail, which stirred his usual query whether Democracy could endure the inventions of the typewriter and of advertising. He looked through the unsolicited magazines, the brochure from the Wargate Corporation announcing that right after the war they would be making everything out of plastics—airplanes, egg-beaters, book-bindings, communion cups, the bulletins from the numberless associations for organizing virtue ("please send check or money-order immediately") and all the other mimeographed letters with typed-in addresses which, intimately addressing him as "Mr. J. Cass" or as "Mr. C. T. Judge," announced that they had heard of him as a Leading Citizen, so would he kindly remit.

Lost amid these reminders of an enormous and clashing world which had no interest in the tragi-comedy of married love, Cass looked at his watch and was startled that an hour had sneaked by since Jinny had gone upstairs. He would peep into her room, softly, not to awaken her.

He tiptoed up and to her door. When he eased it open, she was sitting on her bed, crosslegged, adorable in pajamas, her hair reckless. She was so young, so feminine. She tilted her face with a smile, but the smile suddenly closed, as though it were someone else whom she had been expecting.

He stood just inside the door. She said gently, "My dear, it's no go. I love Bradd—I love him! I thought I could run away from him, but I'm going back to him, in New York."

These words took just over nine seconds to say, and they devastated his life and hers completely.

Before he answered he draped a silk comforter about her, so that she was in a little Asian tent. He sat on her pink-lined window seat. The whole room seemed so female and incomprehensible to him. He could no more fight it than he could fight the scent of flowers.

"Going back to him immediately," she said.

"No. You're not. I'm going to hold you." But he was listening to himself critically. "I'm going to fight for you. You're everything that's good."

"Good?"

"Oh, you're not half as bad as you try to be."

"Don't be so smug!"

"I'm not. And I'm not angry, either. Not even at Bradd. He makes me sick, more than angry. But I won't yield. For your sake, too. You're sick; you can't stand this insanity just now. It will kill you."

"It's the only thing that will *save* me. If I can't be with him, I will die. I suppose it does look crazy—kiting right back there, just after our return—but I'll be happy then, and well."

"You'll never be happy with that fellow, not long. You think you're a great adventuress, a great flaunter——"

"I do not!"

"But you're really a pathetic child. I can see you among those big buildings, in the dark streets, trudging along, a little scared figure, so little, with no one to depend on, once Bradd has let you down."

"He'd never let me down."

"You know he will!"

"Well . . ."

"And you always forget you're ill."

"I never forget it. And I want to get well. That's why I must have someone that I love near me."

After this implication, he could say nothing, and she raced on, "It's all arranged. I've just this minute talked to Bradd on the telephone. Oh, should I have done that, from your house? I'll pay you for the call."

"Oh, God!"

She did not heed his cry. "I'm to stay with Avis, out in Darien, and skip into the city once in a while and play around with him—it will be enchanting. Avis knows all about diets, and she'll watch mine, and I'll really look after my health, till you divorce me."

"I'm not going to divorce you."

"I knew it! So old-fashioned! I thought you realized domestic tyrants had gone out. Are you really going to try and handcuff me? Well, let me tell you——"

"Stop it. I won't bind you, except to this extent: I insist on your taking three months to think this over, and to find out what a hard-hearted professional charmer Bradd is, before you file any divorce suit. I'm afraid you'll have to do that back here in Minnesota, unless you want to go to Reno. You won't be a resident of Connecticut, and the only ground in New York State, even if you established residence there, is adultery, and that's a cause which I don't intend to afford you, no matter how obliging I would like to be. If after this three months you still feel you must go ahead, I shan't oppose it—I think. But——"

His law-office carefulness broke down. "My beloved, my dear wife, I never thought I could say this, I thought I had too much pride, I thought I despised acquiescent husbands too much, but I would rather see you go off and be Bradd's mistress for a year and then come back to me than see you divorced and lost to me. Life is worthless without you."

"Life will be worth just as much to you as it was before you ever saw me, and maybe more. I've been bad for you. And I'm sorry, because I have great respect and fondness for you."

" 'Respect and fondness'! God! What d'you think I am?"

"Now don't try to be the hairy-chested brute. It doesn't become you. You *prefer* fondness and respect, and probably what you stand for is much finer than any of the frivolous, dissipated things that Bradd and I like."

" 'Bradd and I'! Please keep that bastard's name out of this."

"But can we?"

"No-o, but still——Look, Jinny. My life *wasn't* worth much, before I saw you. Like most people, most of the time, I was just getting along, satisfied if I wasn't sick or angry or too tired or too lonely, plodding on toward a decent death, with no idea at all what possibilities there were in the human mind *and* body, and——Jinny! I've got to know. I keep skirting around it but——Did you sleep with Bradd?"

Her embarrassment was less than his as she looked down at her hands, slowly rubbed them, and answered "Yes." Then she raised her head. "But never, honestly never, till just the other afternoon in New York, when I went to his apartment. I thought it was just for a drink, and to wait while he dressed for dinner and the show."

It was not at all with a dull ache that he heard the catastrophe, but with a lively sickness and a runaway imagination. He could see what to him was a horror and a blasphemy: Jinny shyly undressing with her sacred body exposed to the gluttonous eyes and cynical fumbling of that libertine, Jinny's breasts against the cold heart of that thief and scoundrel, Jinny glancing up at him as devotedly as she had at her husband.

His black shame for Jinny's nakedness, his black hatred of Bradd, must have shown in his face. She was fluttering, "Now, I guess you *will* divorce me!"

"I would not divorce you even if you became a public harlot. Then least of all. You are my wife—not just a woman who happens to be legally married to me. You can drive me away, but I won't ever turn away, not ever."

A confused "Oh" from her, and a long, blinding silence out of which he struggled:

"I hate your physical contact with another man, and I don't know whether that's out of common jealousy or out of fastidiousness, and I don't even care much—I hate it! Don't make any mistake about that. But I suppose I could make myself forget it. I don't know that your betrayal itself is any worse than the fact that it happened with my oldest friend. And even that is no worse than the discovery that you've lied to me."

"I never lied to you!"

"You certainly did, by implication—you and Bradd playing out that farce of saying good-bye on the telephone, our last night in New York. . . . By the way, I suppose you and he had been together in his apartment *that* afternoon, as well as the one before?"

She did not answer.

——Jinny to wait for Mr. Bradd Criley's condescension in Avis's select suburban residence! What a sordidness of respectable adultery! Civilized divorce. Sophisticated modern sex relations. Exquisite sluttishness. Fashionable bestiality. The intellectual cocktail-hour diversion of smearing three lives with manure.

——Poor, bright, energetic, weak-minded Jinny, with no idea what she'll be up against when she's not so young. I must take care of her, even if I have to lock her in the attic.

Then he was urging, "Jinny! Let's be practical for a moment. You're assuming that after you've stayed for a few months with that delightful hag, Mrs. Elderman, and after I'm used to getting along without you——"

"I hope you will be."

"I hope I never shall! After death, you become used to

505

getting along without a lot of things, but that won't make it interesting. I was saying: What makes you think Bradd will still want to marry you? He's completely unscrupulous in protecting his freedom."

"You don't understand him. You can't. You're too old."

"Oh, come off it. I'm only two years older than he is."

"Not really. As I've told you before, you're fifteen years older. He does things because they're fun."

"Sure. Great charmer!"

"Does charm seem to you such a bad quality for a girl to have in a husband?"

——I'm not coming off so well in the argument. And this is a life-death struggle to hold her, not just a squabble.

"Yes, I think it *is* bad, when it's deliberately turned on and off, as it is with a blackguard like Criley."

"You mean 'heel,' don't you? You know, when you say he's a heel, you're talking like a man, and it doesn't mean a thing to a woman, unless she's half-man herself. Very few women care a hang about the laws or the social rules. What they love in a man is the feeling that he isn't merely *with* them, but that he *is* them, and feels and thinks as they do before they've finished thinking it. What people like you detest about the heels, the outlaws, is that they don't give a hoot for the idiotic rules that you've set up to protect your own awkwardness, which comes from your never really being completely one with a woman, but always remaining a little aside from her, noticing how

good you are or how bad. And expecting her to do what——
Bradd just *laughs* when I'm unpunctual, and maybe *you* can't
trust what he says, but with me he's *always* truthful!"

"Don't you suppose a lot of other women have defended
Criley, too?"

"Oh, don't call him 'Criley'. It sounds like childish spite."

"Sorry. Can't think of him any other way now. How many
women——"

"If Bradd has brought joy to a lot of bored women, is that
against him? Darling, let's not go on bickering. I *know* Bradd!
I didn't want to fall in love with him, and the last thing I
wanted to do was to hurt you. I really tried to run away from
him. I hope you won't remember me as a loose woman. I
couldn't help it. Bradd—he seems to understand everything
that matters to a woman. I do want to be quiet, but I'm afraid
it will have to be with *him*."

It sounded so flat and incontrovertible.

He broke off brusquely. "We could argue all night, but I
guess you'll need some sleep, if you're really taking another
train tomorrow. Good night."

He kissed her blankly and left her.

He sat in his room, rubbing his stocking feet, fertile in
plan, paralyzed in action. He went to bed and, certain that he
could not sleep, he slept. He awoke abruptly, longing for her
and, without meditation about it, padded into her room. It
was dark. He wriggled in beside her, tentatively slid his arm

about her. She whispered, "Oh, my dear, I do love you, too, in another way." She was crying, and. he let her cry on his shoulder.

A current of passion, which seemed to come from far outside them, ran through them both, and her hand which had lain so laxly on his shoulder tightened, and he turned toward her. He knew then that, however demon-ridden she might be, there was something eternal between them.

But when they awakened to early light, she sat up and said with distaste, "You better skip back to your room and let me sleep. I have a long journey ahead of me."

46

"WHAT WE DID last night—that *really* seems to me immoral," she said at breakfast.

"Now look, Jin. Spare me the subtleties. I'm trying to say a tender farewell to an erring daughter—and she *is* erring beyond imagination—and that's all I can manage. This whole business is plain imbecile."

"You've got to admit we've both been honest."

"When a mother loses her temper and beats her child and the child yells, I suppose they're both *honest* enough! . . . Here. I went over to Harley's, before you were up, and raised some cash. Here's three hundred dollars."

"Thank you." Very non-committal.

"I'll send you a check at——Your address will be care of Mrs. William Elderman, Darien? Of all the tragedies played to jazz, that's the worst. Jinny! Won't you wait and think about it?"

"Please, Cass, oh, please! For Heaven's sake! Do we have to go over everything again? I just want to get started."

She remained thus frozen until she had to turn over all her keys to Mrs. Higbee, to whom she hesitated, "You might use the vacuum-cleaner on the curtains in the living-room."

"Yes?" How Mrs. Higbee knew that Jinny was quitting,

they did not understand, but it was evident in her contempt.

"They're very pretty curtains, you know."

No answer.

"I picked them out."

No answer.

Cass was deciding that he would discharge Mrs. Higbee tomorrow, then that he would never discharge her.

Jinny tried again. "And, uh, Mrs. Higbee?"

"Yes?"

"Remember to change the Judge's bathroom mat as often as it needs it."

"I always have, Mrs. Timberlane. Is there anything else?"

"No-o, I don't think so."

Mrs. Higbee clumped out, her back an exclamation-point, and Jinny peered, helpless and frightened, about the room that she had made and that Cass and Cleo and she had come to love.

It was time to go. "I don't think I'll say good-bye to Mrs. Higbee," trembled Jinny. "But to Cleo!"

The little cat had retreated far under the couch, and would not come out to Jinny's pleading. "Kitty, I just want to stroke you once more!" Jinny begged. "Please come out!"

Cass said evenly, "Sorry, Jin, but we'll have to hurry."

In the car, she sighed, "Nobody really cares one bit about me here. All right. The hell with 'em!"

"One person loves you."

"I do love him, too."

On the station platform they kissed and said good-bye, tight-lipped. He recited, "I shall always be waiting for you."

"Don't wait."

"How can I help it? Good-bye, my Jinny."

Then, incredibly, she was in the train, gone from him, just two years and two months, to the hour, after their marriage. He saw her through a car window, so small, so helpless and defenseless, looking around for her seat, and the train had snarled and gone.

"Why did I let her go?" he marveled.

Then, first, he realized that he would have to explain her absence to practically everybody in Radisson County. He heard the whole male world of Grand Republic croaking, "Me, I'd of spanked the little fool and locked her up."

It occurred to him as he stood on the platform, too confused to get into his car, that he could refuse ever to give her a divorce, that she had no grounds whatever.

——But I couldn't do anything of the sort, and I don't know whether I'm a hero or a coward.

——I'll be alone tonight—tomorrow night—every night now, no sight of her reading in her chair, no sound of her voice, no good night to say to her—only loneliness and silence to say good night to.

An Assemblage of Husbands and Wives

HELIXES & SILBERSEES

DR. SEBASTIAN SILBERSEE looked like a tall and wiry Scotch soldier, and his wife Helma like a slender Jewess. Actually, he was Jewish and she born an Austrian baroness of pure Gentile stock, both of which facts she concealed, in Grand Republic, to be the better identified with her husband.

Their closest acquaintances were Rice and Patty Helix, the managers of the Masquers. The doctor believed that they were all drawn together by his 'cello and Rice's ardent but stumble-footed piano-playing, or by their common zeal in pinochle, but, without the men's knowing it, the families stuck together because the two wives were the little mothers of their husbands, and could keep their learned boys happier when they played together.

The four had pick-up suppers, and afterward the doctor and Rice went at their pinochle, feeling superior to the humble wives, who washed the dishes and talked about preserves.

After World War I, the Baron Steinehre, born in a castle, had been as poor and thin as a rabbit. He worked in a Vienna bank and gave elegant little teas with the cakes limited to two per guest. When his daughter Helma, in the clinic in which she was a volunteer nurse, met the ardent but diffident young

Dr. Silbersee, she married him, chiefly because he was so gloomy about the future of the Jews, and of Austria, and of aural surgery.

Leaning on her nervous strength, he was a great researcher; without her, he was a café strategist. They fled from Vienna just ahead of the Nazis, almost starved in London and in New York, and then pushed out to the distant Grand Republic. The doctor gave up notions of aural surgery, and was competent and fairly prosperous as an eye, ear, nose, and throat factotum. If in Vienna he had drunk in the reassurance of Helma as he had his coffee with whipped cream, here on what he considered the frontier (even in the formal gardens of the Webb Wargates, he went on expecting to see grizzly bears), he was kept alive by her and his 'cello and the Helixes.

Helma had to taste everything for him. She rather liked ice-cream soda, comic strips, griddle cakes, baseball, oil-burners, chummy medical salesmen, and the fact that everybody called him either "Sebastian" or "Doc" the second time.

She molded his private life, but publicly, in his office, he was still king, and there Helma revered him as much as the student-baroness had done.

It was the opposite with the Helixes. Publicly, in "show business," he was not very competent, but in private life he was a bit too deft; he cheated at cards, he systematically failed to pay his bills, and he drew and sold astrological charts.

This crookedness his wife accepted, and merely sought to

regulate. She tried to make him see that cheating and voodoo, lovely though they are, and exciting, don't get you any farther on the way to the heavenly reward of a white cottage with green blinds in Wilmette, Illinois.

When they had met, she had been a run-of-the-mill touring-company actress and he the stage-manager, playing small roles and playing them drearily. She had married him because he was the first man who had asked her; he had married her because she had nice ankles and mended his socks, and because he owed her twenty-seven dollars and a half which he could never repay otherwise. It had been a tremendous success; they enjoyed both bed and breakfast together, and the talk about everybody whom they met.

He was not bad as a Little Theater director, because Patty told him whom to cast and, at rehearsals, how to teach the local girls not to walk across the stage as though they were going to the corner-grocer for dried codfish. And she kept their income adequate by doing all the housework, cooking the simpler vegetables so that they seemed edible, and doing odd histrionic jobs on the radio.

With both the Silbersees and the Helixes, husband and wife understood each other and, working hand in hand, they could defy the world. They could exchange opinions about strangers, signals that it was time to go home, or hints that here was a new patient, a new theater contributor, with just a sliding glance of the eye. At any party, Mrs. Silbersee accidentally let the heathen know what a great physician her husband was, and Rice Helix indifferently informed some merchant that if he could get Patty to broadcast on his local program, everybody concerned would immediately make inconceivable quantities of money.

After every party, walking home arm in arm, they would laugh together, little delighted people walking home through the twenty-below-zero Minnesota winter night.

No revolutionary cell, no laboratory team, was ever more secret and loyal and quietly unscrupulous than the Silbersees together or the Helixes together. Yet closer than either pair of lovers were the minds of Helma and Patty when they recognized the golden conspirator in each other, and saw that their two husbands could be coaxed to be allies in the ceaseless warfare between the world and couples who are so presumptuous as to want not wealth and publicity but only love and serenity and a sandwich.

So every night when Rice was not directing a play, the four of them met at the Silbersees' house or the Helixes' two-rooms-over-a-store, and the men made a little music and played a little pinochle, and the two wives gossiped in security.

It probably would not last. The Great World does not permit such unquestioning love and ill-paid truancy.

47

CASS TIMBERLANE was pretending that he was a judge, sitting on the bench in a murder case. What he was really doing was sitting on the bench in a murder case.

The audible case was that of a construction-gang laborer who was alleged to have killed his foreman with a pickaxe, after an argument about Finland and Russia. Sweeney Fishberg, for the defense, showed that there was a question which of the gang had done it, and somehow suggested that it had been a good idea anyway. He had smuggled into the case a confusing dispute as to which of the suspects had worn a mustache at the time of the killing, and for hours there had been the dreary and inexpert testimony of barbers, neighbors, and people who happened to have taken snapshots at that time—at about that time—somewhere near that time—they thought.

Judge Timberlane was attentive enough, but his mind constantly slid off to a second trial that was dearer to him and more agonizing. In this inaudible and imaginary trial, he was the defendant, charged with having killed Bradd Criley.

——Oh, quit your childish day-dreaming! You know that you're too civilized, or too flabby, even to beat him up—as you once boasted to Jinny that you could, you shanty chevalier!

———You don't particularly *want* to kill him. "Vengeance is mine, saith the Lord: I will repay." But you haven't even a good healthy desire for vengeance, the Lord's or anybody else's. You don't see Bradd as an enemy, but as a worm, a crawler into decent men's honest bread.

Suddenly the criminal in the imaginary trial was not himself but Bradd, and he, as judge, was in a splendid, romantic position. Awkward obstacles like codes and juries were cleared away. Bradd trembled (though he had never yet seen Bradd tremble) before the Judge, the very Judge whose lovely young wife he had stolen. He was charged with rape, embezzlement, high treason. The Judge was shining and mighty as an ancient Israelite law-giver upon his throne, and righteousness glowed upon a face dark with honorable wrath.

But his nobility triumphed, and he thundered, "Accused, while I could send you to prison for all your shameful years, I hold the law above my private wrong."

———Rats!

———Of course practically, the way I could get even with Bradd would be to let the Wargates know what sort of a crook their legal representative is. Pull him down, as for years I've helped to raise him up.

———Yes? Now can you imagine what a decent fellow like Webb would say if you came around tattling about one of his staff?

517

——Well, I didn't seriously mean I'd do it.

——You better *not* seriously-mean-it!

Cass would have said that he had small "imagination," but he did have his projections of thought.

What would the ruthless and fickle Bradd do to his girl? Would he live on with her, but so neglect and mock her that she would escape into boozing or scarred cynicism? Would he kick her out, and in that humiliation would she lose every pride and eagerness?

Cass did not at all think that her adultery was a prank to be smiled over. He was raw with the affront. Yet he insisted that there had never been in her any malice, any delight in hurting him. She was fundamentally good, as the pleasant Bradd was fundamentally evil.

Or so he meditated.

The minute Comedy of the Murderer's Mustache, on which hung the life-imprisonment of a human being and the future of his family, plodded on. Vincent Osprey, associated with Fishberg in the defense, was making notes, then plucking at Fishberg's sleeve and whispering into his irritated ear. The master of the court, watching Osprey, reflected:

——I can tell he's been having a row with that grasping wife of his again. He's so nervous and helpful.

Anyway, he would never write to her the long letter which he had instantaneously planned while stooping to drink from the fountain in the court-house corridor that morning: a nasty little piece of literary goods about her new associates in the East being libertines. As he listened to the pounding of the legal machinery, his spite seemed as trivial as it would be useless. This tragedy of his loss was as far beyond his control as this trial was beyond control of the prisoner, and it had less sense and pattern.

Cass's defeat, he believed, came neither from the intentional malice of men nor from the conscious irony of the gods. It merely happened, like a storm, from causes that could be traced clearly enough but still did not make sense. Human beings, who could crush the atom and talk round the world, still could make no more illuminating comment upon the collapse of solid-seeming love than the ancient wailing, "Why—why—why?"

The session closed for the night. In his chambers, Cass wearily took off his silk robe and handed it to George Hame.

"Sweeney doing a fine job," yawned George. "If he had a single bit of evidence on his side, he'd get that Hunky off."

"Believe the fellow's guilty, George?"

"Guilty? Of course he is."

The Judge was thinking of his wife's lover. "What is guilt, George?"

"You want a real definition, Judge—one to go in the textbooks?"

"That would be valuable."

"Guilt is what makes you send for Sweeney Fishberg. Good night."

Cass drove home by streets dreary with the packed and sooted snow of late winter, to finish up the unhappiest labor he had ever known: packing Jinny's clothes and trinkets to send them to her in Connecticut.

It was like preparing a beloved body for burial.

Small white wool socks, "bobby socks" they were called, to be worn with bare legs that were made-up to look tanned. He could see her legs, the gloss of them speckled with tiny dots. He sighed and packed the socks, patting them down in the top tray of her trunk, wondering whether he would ever see them again.

Airy dresses, so flimsy and empty now, yet, as he fitted them on hangers, recalling her swiftness and grace. Blouses and white silk underclothes, which he found decorously folded in her bureau; a boyish scarf, which she had loved for picnicking, and a sweater, straight and prim, the curve of her breast gone from it; scuffed tramping shoes, which recalled to him just when she had got this scratch on one toe as they had bushwhacked through the woods by Dead Squaw Lake. The nightgown which she had worn on her last night at home. Round the shoulders were tiny wrinkles from her sleeping. It seemed to him still warm from her body.

Her sketch-book, with gently spiteful drawings of Boone Havock's bulkiness and Roy Drover's tough jaw . . . and Bradd Criley resting easy and masterful on a golf stick, and Cass himself, put into the costume of a cardinal.

The volume of Yeats that he had given to her and that she had loved: the old edition, the blue cover with the falling leaves, the cross, the mystic rose. He fumbled through it to a poem he had read to her, sitting on windy Ojibway Hill:

> *All the heavy days are over;*
> *Leave the body's colored pride*
> *Underneath the grass and clover,*
> *With the feet laid side by side.*

He saw Jinny lying stilled in the cumbersome earth. As he closed the book, he noticed a comer of paper sticking from it, and pulled out a note:

> How's for a swim this evening? You would comfort the lonely heart of
>
> > Bradd.

Cass grimly replaced the note in the book, packed it, closed the trunk.

But next morning, when the trunk was carried out by the expressmen, it was as though her coffin were being borne out of the house for the last time—the house that would not quicken again to her voice and her light running; carried over the threshold which she had always crossed so gallantly, unaided.

An Assemblage of Husbands and Wives

VINCENT & CERISE OSPREY

PROBABLY NO DULLER nor more careful attorney had ever been graduated from Oberlin College and the Yale Law School than Mr. Vincent Osprey; probably no more devoted or less skillful husband had ever existed; and certainly no more placidly selfish wife has been recorded than Cerise, his consort.

She wanted fine clothes, furs, jewelry, automobiles, perfumes, and English biscuits imported in tins; she wanted power, admiration, and beauty; and neither Vincent's income nor Vincent's influence was large enough to provide them.

Cerise never drank too much, and never fished for anything more than fair words and a handshake from men. She did not expect them to give her the treasures she longed for; she went beyond that, and wanted them of her own right. But she was a collector of celebrities. She simply had to have the great ones of the town—the mayor, the judges, the millionaires such as the Wargates, the Grannicks, and Berthold Eisenherz—at her table, and she expected Vincent to persuade them to leave their nice warm houses to go and eat petrified fowl at the residence of a minor attorney.

Vince did once coax Webb and Louise Wargate to the house for her, but he spent the evening in excitedly overselling Cerise's talents to them, and they did not come again. She very properly punished him, and for a month, whenever he tried to kiss her, his lips reached nothing but her strong white teeth. She said, "Most wives would just let you go on making a fool of yourself, but I happen to be honest."

She went resolutely to his office and examined his books; she knew exactly how much money he had; and yet she charged up bills that he could not meet, and so endangered his small stock of credit and his smaller stock of sanity. He was unavoidably in debt for his insurance, his club memberships, and the installments on the refrigerator, the car, the radio, and even the house, for naturally he was one of those optimistic Americans who acquired these tribal adornments on the installment-plan.

He tried to scold her about it, but she did not spit at him. She had found a retort that was much more dramatic and self-congratulatory: she over-apologized, and admired herself for her humility in doing it. She was sorry; she had been blind, thoughtless, bad; he must think she was a perfect fool; she was sorry, OH she was so sorry!

As she said it, it was evident that she was thinking, "What

a miracle of modesty and good manners I am, to apologize to this little squirt!"

When she had finished, she immediately hastened out to begin running up a new bill or to insult the wife of his best client.

She did not treat only Vince to these improvisations on the theme of humility. She also played her so-sorriness for the neighbors from whom she had borrowed cocktail glasses, table-cloths, and money, which she never returned till the owners demanded them. She was a good actress. She could make her repentances more infuriating than the original injuries.

They had one child, a small son, whom she taught to "forgive his father for his meanness."

Vince was not so sub-human that he did not occasionally threaten a rebellion. Once, when they were driving to Minneapolis and he stopped at a village gasoline-station to fill the tank, she wandered up Main Street and did not come back for half an hour. On her return, he took a strong foreign-office attitude:

"Some day when you do that, I'm going to drive off and leave you."

She looked at him a long time, then: "I hope to God you will. Some of the hicks in this dump look like real men. Maybe I could promote one of them into something better than a title-searcher!"

When the war came, Vince was still of draft age, and he waited to be called. Cerise immediately found an office job in the Wargate plant; learned not only stenography but something about the manufacture of wallboard, and became a real Career Woman, an office politician and an intriguer against the women whose jobs she wanted. Within a year she was receiving seventy-five dollars a week.

Theoretically, she was paying a woman to care for her son, but Vince paid the woman and Cerise blew in on dresses and bracelets all of the seventy-five—and more. She said that they could not afford a maid. She started with the noon shift, and before he left for his office, he laid out breakfast for her. The complaints about her extravagance which he dared not make to her face he hinted about in notes which he left for her in the refrigerator.

She told the women in the office about this cowardly and exasperating trick.

The Wargate staff presently offered her a job in their new Racine plant, at ninety a week, as personnel officer. She went home to tell Vince. She would be going in a week.

"You can't leave me—and the boy!" he wailed.

"Well, I wouldn't mind taking the kid along, if I thought it was good for him, but *you*, my dear Vinsolent, I hope I never hear another of your dear old Yale songs again!"

During the week before she left him, Vince had to talk with someone about the loss of his wife, or go mad, but as he had no other intimates, the only person with whom he could talk was that wife. She was not helpful. He begged her to tell him what to do, and she suggested that he kill himself.

Presumably she did not mean it.

When she was gone, this correct young man, who for years had trained himself to get eight hours' sleep, to do exercises before the window for ten minutes every morning, to swim twice a week in the Y.M.C.A. pool, never to use any word more foul than "Damn," and nightly to kneel by his bed and say "Now I lay me down to sleep" as he had done ever since he was three—this model young lawyer within one week became a haggard hobo, unshaven, staggering, publicly and noisily drunk, slobbering in saloons till he was ordered out.

Judge Cass Timberlane, a man whom Vince revered, though the Judge was only eight or nine years older than himself, came calling on him, where he lay dirty in his dirty bed, and urged him to go away, travel, forget. Vince sobbed that it was too late and he had already "gone to the bad," but the Judge assured him that he, too, had once fallen to pieces, even smaller and worse pieces than Vince's.

He knew that the Judge's own wife was away from him, and gossips were hinting that she had gone for good—and for bad. He cried over the Judge's hand, and promised to be brave. He telegraphed to the man with whom he had roomed in Oberlin, but whom he had not seen for five years, to meet him in Chicago, and they would "have reunion and high old time."

They met, took a room together at a hotel, and had a distressingly dull do-you-remember dinner at the hotel café. After the first spurt, they could think of nothing to say.

Vince excused himself. He was expecting a call from Racine, from his dear wife, Cerise. He would be back in ten minutes. The friend waited half an hour, and went up to their room. The window was open, and twelve stories below, on the roof of an annex, a ragpile of clothing, was Vincent Osprey.

Cerise came to Grand Republic for the funeral, and wept, but she caught a train back to Racine that evening, leaving her son in the care of her sister.

She told this sister that she was a modern woman, and just as clear-minded as any man. And indeed the young man who met her at the station in Racine was nothing like so clear-minded as Cerise, who was paying his room-rent.

48

FOR CASS, the worst, in the late Northern winter, when the malicious cold and the ashen skies had gone on too long, when the white world was speckled with dirt and the snow was spoiled for skiing, was coming home from court to the dusky house that was empty of her welcome. Her absence was not a negative thing, merely a not-being-there; it was a positive and frightening presence, which crept after him and made him turn quickly to see her not-being-there.

He muttered "Jinny?" as he stood in the dark living-room, as though she must hear him and come.

Cleo stoutly accompanied him through the house with her inquiring "Mrawr?" and he talked to her more than to Mrs. Higbee. Once, late at night, when he sat in the living-room alone with Cleo, he heard her reasonlessly begin to purr, and watched her watch an invisible presence in the room. Her eyes clearly followed the unseen figure, to the piano, to the bookshelves, to Jinny's chair, rested there, then, with slowly turning head, she followed the apparition to the door and, half in terror, Cass thought that in the doorway he could see an outline made of air.

——This is bad. Dangerous. I wonder if something could have happened to her? I don't believe in this telepathy stuff, but I've got to telephone to her.

——Don't be a fool!

He felt that he ought to rush out of the house, out of this danger, go to a neighbor's, play bridge, anything. But he could not endure having to explain Jinny's flight. For weeks after she had gone, he was glad when he was invited to dinner, glad to know that he still existed in somebody's affection, yet he always refused. Except for public affairs, where he spoke more impersonally than ever, he dined alone, silent, served by a silent Mrs. Higbee, guarded by an attentive Cleo, whose eyes too often moved from him to follow again the invisible being that slowly entered the room and circled it and vanished.

It had taken him a fortnight to believe that Jinny actually had left him, but as it became contemptuously clear, his state grew worse. All evening, trying to escape into the security of Dickens and Thackeray and Hardy, half-listening to the radio, he kept himself from telephoning to Jinny in Darien.

At every moment through the evening, always calculating the hour's difference in time between Grand Republic and Darien, he was conscious of what she might now be doing. He saw her at bridge with the Eldermans and a neighborhood widower—the widower was imaginary, but Cass pictured him and his sticky little literary goatee, and hated him. Then there were the evenings when the Eldermans were out and Jinny was alone. She was listening to the same network program as himself, and if he disliked it, he still could not turn it off, because she might want to hear it.

He hoped that she was not lonely then, and he wanted to speak to her, cheer her, reassure her. He thought of so many things about which he really *must* telephone her—such as Cleo's casually having kittens—but he dared not try, lest he reach only Avis Elderman or her stupid husband or a Jinny patiently answering his solicitude with "Lonely? Of course I'm not. In fact we're having a wonderful party. . . . *He* is here."

No, no! Surely she would not slap him thus.

But then—she might. He laid down for future generations the discovery: "Love does queer things to people."

His mental dogging of her stopped sharply when his personal Guardian Fiend buzzed in his ear, "And now, my boy, she is having a little love-making with Bradd, your successor and a better man than you."

He was presently able, in a slowly growing self-discipline, to wipe out entirely that picture of them as lovers. He made an injunction against thinking of it at all. He did not, however, persuade himself that Jinny and Bradd were merely playing checkers, or that some day she would raise that lovely face to him and say with tender rebuke, "It was you only that I loved, all along, and Bradd, whom you so unjustly suspected, is my long-lost brother."

His hope was that Bradd was already cooling toward her, and that was at once a vicarious humiliation and a preserving promise. After all, Bradd had never seen in her any peculiar divinity, but only an amusing freshness. Might he not tire of her soon?

He was happiest when the radio played such rustic memories as "My Old Kentucky Home" and "Nelly Was a Lady." He could see himself as a boy of eighteen with a Jinny aged sixteen, on a country hayride in the dusk. They held hands and trusted each other, and suddenly they were both of them eighty, on a country doorstep in the sun, still holding hands, as hue to each other as the coursing rhythms of their blood.

He detested the bland, blond yapping of radio announcers, with their new-world litany of cigarettes and liver pills and bean soup—"yum, *good!*" He resented the fact that he was coming to resemble the college students who cannot study without the narcotic of unceasing radio sound.

But when he turned it off, the house was too solitary in the Northern winter night, too quiet, and he sat listening for Jinny, knowing that she would not come, yet forever listening for her footstep, listening and afraid, not knowing of what he was afraid, not daring to turn his head, afraid and rigid, while Cleo murmured to the invisible passer-by, till he cried aloud and desperately switched on the banal magnificence of a million-dollar band that was right out of the jungle via Tin Pan Alley.

Yet when he remembered that Jinny and he had listened

to the radio with their arms about each other, relaxed and content with love, then the strident gaiety was as intolerable as the menacing silence.

He took to reading detective stories instead of the history which, as the incorrigible Puritan, he felt he *ought* to read. But that was not a soothing dissipation, for after them, in bed, he heard from up in the attic, from down in the basement, from all round the house, Limehouse cut-throats and international agents, and rajahs looking for the idols eye which he had stolen in 1867. He really could hear them, too.

He thought of her loneliness, as well as his. He thought of all the loneliness in the world:

Of widows who for a quarter-century had depended upon husbands and noisy children, but were alone now in cottages where the clock ticked too loudly. Of more prosperous widows surrounded by alien chatter on the porches of gilt summer hotels. Of young men new to a city, too poor for theaters, desperate in furnished rooms. Of other young men, soldiers in strange camps. Of young women with a richness of potential love but with no prettiness about them, alone in the evening, waiting for a telephone call that would never come. Of the lookout on a steamer long in the fog. Of traveling men plodding in shaky cars from country store to store, over the prairie that fled always back from them. Of Pullman porters late at night, the passengers sleeping. Of rich old men, so rich that they were afraid of all their bobbing relatives, invalid and waiting for dawn. Of an old doctor, retired now, sitting in his worn chair, knowing only too well what was wrong with him. Of kings and watchmen and babies left alone to darkness.

If his travels into pity did not make him the less lonely, they did turn his thoughts from himself, and he could endure it again to look about the room that was too quick with suggestions of Jinny's soft being: the lamp whose purchase had been such a triumph; the chessmen that still bore the traces of her fingers. He could endure it then, just endure it, as a patient endures the heart-jab that did not quite kill him—this time—and he could even endure the sound of a distant train whistle, loneliest and loveliest of sounds.

But whenever the radio was not blatting, he was listening for her, hearing her in a sound beyond sound, waiting for her, listening for her, stooped and afraid, listening and afraid, like a man in the condemned cell on the last, slow, irremediable night.

To the public eye—and in Grand Republic that eye can be quite public—he was doing what is known as "bearing up." In court, he had never been so quick and sure; and he had never so often taken briefs home for study. Perhaps, he thought grimly, her absence is very good for my work.

But he knew that if to others his base seemed solid enough, he was out of shape, a figure loose and without pattern.

He carried on an undeclared feud with Mrs. Higbee about eating. He was in a mood to receive sympathy as the lean, suffering, and vitaminless lover, but, with nothing more than a rebuking, "There's some nice lamb chops tonight, Judge, and you didn't eat your lovely chicken last night" as her sole maternal comment, he got no satisfaction.

When she brought him an evening highball, Mrs. Higbee still used the brass coasters upon which Jinny had insisted, to save the mahogany, but when Cass went out to the kitchen, in a dull kitchen-shuffle, to get himself a drink which he did not particularly want, he no longer troubled to bring in a coaster with it, and he rested the glass messily on a magazine, which would have brought retribution from Jinny.

He lost, too, the habit of bringing home flowers, and sometimes, dining alone, he disapprovingly noted his own table-manners, his leaning despondently low over his soup-plate or sitting with his elbows on the table and dipping his toast in the coffee or chasing crumbs about the table.

As intently as a lonely woman fussing over pantry-shelves, he grew absorbed in watching the whirling islands of bubbles on his newly stirred cup of coffee: how handsome some of them were, with one vast bubble-mountain in the center, how the lesser islands were drawn across the current by the mass of the major island, and mystically merged with it. There was the most cosmic of tragedies when the great island crashed and dissolved against the high porcelain bluffs.

"I think possibly you're giving too much attention to the geography of bubbles," he noted.

To the world, he was as proper as ever, yet he saw himself becoming a little queer. He was—for a while—slovenly about "making this shirt do another day—just a little dirt on the collar," and once this fanatical devotee to cleanliness did not shave the duskiness of his jaw a second time before going out to a public dinner, and once he forgot to brush his teeth before going to bed.

His next degeneracy was a look into mystic asceticism. He cut his cigarettes down to fifteen a day and felt that God was counting them and that, as a reward for this abstemiousness, He would give back Jinny's love.

When the ice turned shoddy and went out of Dead Squaw Lake. Cass found that he could be most satisfyingly alone in a canoe on those chilly waters, and one twilight a man walking on the shore incredulously heard the thin complaining of a flute out on the lake, saw a canoe with a figure silhouetted on the leaden ripples.

"That fellow must be a left-over Indian, or else he's crazy," thought the man.

When he was both idle and strained, as he often was now after court hours, Cass was plagued by tunes that chased round and round in his mind, or by "Far on the ringing plains of windy Troy" repeating itself, without his volition. Worst mental parasite of all, ceaselessly whirling like an electric fan at slow speed, was "Silent upon a peak in Darien." That one he had started as a wry pun, but before long it had become a recurrent horror, and it meant for him only Jinny, in Darien, lying in the silence that was death.

When he heard of Vincent Osprey's suicide, he felt that threat menacing himself and, like everybody else now and then, Cass wondered, "Am I losing my mind?" But, like everybody else, he did not believe anything of the sort.

The suicide made him look at his brooding, his own indulgent antics, and abruptly quit all that adult childishness. This sensibleness had its own evils. No longer could the curiously vicious forms of mental solitaire divert his mind from the loss of Jinny. But he had had enough of the exhibitionism of the hair-shirt of morbid love, and when he noticed that he was sloppily leaning over his plate at his dinner, he sighed and straightened himself.

He made himself put away the agonizing memorabilia of Jinny still left in the living-room: the photographs of her, the silver bowl for roses which she had especially loved, the painting of the Sorshay River bluffs—not too good—which she had made on an Indian Summer afternoon. He took to sitting in his tight little paneled study, in which there was room only for himself and Cleo and a portable radio—little room for memories.

But there he could not see her so clearly in his mind, and

this was tragic to him, and he wondered of what future it might be an omen.

Though he was frozen with waiting for her, Cass was also busy with war boards and Republican committees. Sometimes he estimated, "I seem to have come out of my fever of wild-eyed love. But I'm not too proud of that. I'd rather go really crazy than forget her and become free—free for what?"

He was not altogether amused when he discovered that there were times when it was pleasant to go to bed just when he wanted to, as noisily as he wanted to or as quietly; to order only what *he* liked to eat, and to wear the old brown hat.

Early May, this year, was not so much spring as a pallid and invalid winter, and the shutting down of furnaces, the laying away of overcoats, were more conspicuous than any riot of flowers.

Jinny had been gone from him for three months now.

They had written to each other mechanically, once a week. His letters were the most fatiguing documents that he had ever struggled over, and the most exact. He must be neither harsh nor yet a beggar of love; he must leave her free—while trying to trap her with anxious cunning. He wrote fully about Cleo, a little about his court room and the Drovers.

Her small notes were equally competent—and false and lost and pathetic.

She thought that she would establish residence in Vermont

for her divorce, but she did not feel well enough yet for that effort, and Avis was insisting that she remain in Darien till she was quite sure that she wanted to marry Bradd. ("*What?*" exulted Cass.) She wrote "*Dear* Avis," and Cass could hear the fury in it.

As an inveterate between-the-lines reader, he blissfully concluded that she was seeing Bradd only under chaperonage, and he hoped that she was having a dull time, but just when he was sure of it, she wrote about a "gorgeous party that some people that live near here pulled, they are great friends of Berg Nord as well as Bradd: smart women and amusing men and lyric composers and playwrites."

——Darling, you never could spell!

"They were just the kind of exciting people that I *told* you we would meet in and around New York, if we were only patient."

——The hell you did, my dear! You said you hated the place.

"Bradd met all these people through Cousin Berg, whom I introduced to him."

——That is the *worst* impertinence! It's *my* Cousin Berg!

"He is getting to know them so well, they think he is just as witty as they are, and we had a terrific time, charades and cooking at an outdoor grill.

"I'm afraid I did eat too many pastries and drink too much and stay up late, and as a matter of fact, I'm writing this in bed, where I'll have to stay for a day or two, not so well, but still it was worth it."

He was worried to distraction. He wanted to telegraph to her, to telephone, but what could he say? Nothing more than the advice by which conscientious parents drive their infuriated children to lives of vice: "Do take care of yourself." That he must not say.

So he merely wrote to her—air mail: "I assume that after your fine party but a little risky, you will, without being told, see that you must take care of yourself."

Her next note frightened him even more. She wrote, in a script that was not too steady:

Cass dearest:

Cant write much at this time, am still in bed tho getting much better, *honestly*, don't worry my dear am *really* being sensible this time. I have a good doctor here Dr. Liskett, he seems to me much smarter than Roy. He has started me in on injections of insulin which, you know, I never had before.

I hate getting jabbed, like a poor trout with a hook but the Dr says he is sure before long I can leave them off and don't you worry, my dear.

Your bad Jinny

Then he did telephone to Darien.

He was told by a glacial butler that Mrs. Timberlane

539

was now able to leave her bed, that she was taking a short walk, should he give her a message, and what was the nyme, please?

"No message," said Cass.

The word Insulin was a signal of disaster.

49

FROM THE HEARTINESS with which it sought him out and welcomed him back, once she had gone, he ruefully knew how much Jinny had stood between him and his city. He was not at all certain that his hope that she would yet really discover and love his Grand Republic was not as great as his hope that she would again discover and love himself.

His acquaintances did not say much about the highly publicized secret of her absence. He would have liked it if they had said more. They forgot her too easily. He wondered, but dared not ask, whether even the intimates like Rose and Valerie, who had been so easy with her and so chatty, had ever been really fond of her.

Had they considered her too demanding and critical, or had they been afraid of some genuinely superior quality in her, or neither? It seemed to him that it was one of the most marked conditions of her youth that Jinny did not enough prize plain, human, neighborly love and desire to be loved; it seemed to him one of the faults of these same neighbors that they were not patient enough in waiting till Jinny should acquire this humble affection along with her more nimble virtues.

Slowly and shyly the neighbors let him know what they thought.

Judge Blackstaff expressed everything he had to say with a clasp of Cass's hand and a stately, antique, "You look well, son; I'm glad of it"; and Madge Dedrick, Stella Avondene, the Marls and Wargates took imaginary occasion to telephone, "Won't you drop in for a drink this evening?"

They were so kind, he reflected; all his life he wanted to be with them and ever nearer. This Grand Republic, neither too vast nor too rustic, too formal nor too frontierlike, was home.

As was natural for a brooder over betrayed love, at first he combined a resentment that nobody ever telephoned to him at all with resentment when they did telephone, which was continually. When he was invited to dinner, he said nervously, "No, no, I can't—I'm tied up," and the moment he had finished telephoning, he fretted, "Now why didn't I promise to go? I would have enjoyed it."

It was chess which became his surest refuge. The pure abstractness of the game was salvation from his thoughts as it once had been from the worries of his job. But he had few people with whom to play now. He was ashamed to turn again to Lucius Fliegend or the Reverend Dr. Gadd, after neglecting them so long. Every evening he worked out chess problems by himself.

Once, when Mrs. Higbee came in with firewood, he looked at her with an idea.

"How would you like to learn to play chess, Mrs.

Higbee?"

"No, *sir*! Too complicated for me."

She fled. For a while he looked speculatively at Cleo, but shook his head.

Gradually he became easier, and in time he was seen about town as much as that popular young semi-bachelor, Judge Timberlane, had been before he met Jinny Marshland.

Boone and Queenie Havock, out of their fierce partisanship, were the only ones of his hosts who said what they thought. They had him in with Roy and Lillian Drover, and their attack was launched immediately after dinner.

They sat in the magnificent and oppressive Havock library, with its black-and-white marble floor, walls covered with dark-red satin damask, books including the entire library of Sir Ashley Ashelburton (except for such few books as Sir Ashley used to *read*), and the elephantine automatic phonograph, on which a Mozart concerto was faintly purring.

"Judgey," said Queenie, "why don't we get everything out from under our belts? Personally, I think you're lucky. I don't know whether your wife left you cold or you kicked her out—wait, now!—and I don't care, but either way, she's no good. She's pretty, if you like the skinny kind, and she's smart—though not half as smart as Boone's new secretary, that I think he's trying to make, the old false-alarm! But she never appreciated you *or* us. The only kind of guy she ever liked was some mattress-acrobat like Bradd or Jay, or some blues-singer like this awful jerk Nimbus.

"Now you're beginning to get over your love-jag, maybe you can see that Jinny is as stuck-up and bossy and tricky and grabbing as a monkey. We only accepted her because she was your wife. She never had the brains to appreciate your goodness, and she never had the brains to see that a couple of two-fisted high-binders like Boone and me are twice as interesting as some little New York menu-expert. She thinks she knows all the answers because one time she read a book. All right, buddy. Now shoot!"

They looked at him with such affection that he could only say, "Queenie, I suppose you were always the meek little wife that never raised your voice!"

"He's got something there," approved Boone.

Cass said slowly, "All of you have to love her if you love me."

Lillian, the rarely-speaking, exclaimed, "You see, Roy, as I told you, he doesn't just play at loving."

Roy snorted, "Okay, Cass. If she comes back, we'll admit we're wrong. I've done harder things than that for you. I've sat and listened to you trying to tell me that politicians ought to be a bunch of faith-healers."

They all laughed, hastily, trying to sound comfortable.

"And, Cass, don't get us wrong," concluded Roy. "It ain't that any of us think we're superior to the girl. We'll all admit that she plays mighty fast ball, and that she knows a lot—for a girl who doesn't know anything. Say, for God's sake, do we play bridge or don't we play bridge, that's what I want to know, because if things have got so now that when you go out for an evening to play bridge, then you never get around to playing bridge, then I'm going home and catch some sleep."

From that best of mothers-in-law, Mrs. Marshland, Cass received only a letter: "We are hoping with you, dear son, that Jinny will soon realize that candy does not make the best beef steak."

One man Cass rather admired, for his imbecile courage.

John William Prutt, who had never yet informed a widow that he was going to foreclose the mortgage without cordially shaking her hand, spoke to Cass nervously:

"Judge, I trust you will forgive me if I am intrusive and impertinent, but Mrs. Prutt and I have discussed it and we have come to the conclusion that you ought to know that the better element in the community are all in intense sympathy with you."

——I appreciate his good intentions, and Queenie's good intentions, and Jinny's good intentions—I wish there weren't so many good intentions around here. Thank God, Bradd at least has no good intentions.

He was vaguely ashamed, these days, to find out how willingly he, who had always praised Bradd, now listened to the familiar gossip about him as a trifler and a master of pleasing but shifty legal tactics. When Judge Flaaten observed, "I prefer an honest crook like Fishberg to a crooked man of virtue like your friend Criley," Cass said only an impassive "Well——"

He had thought of his niece Valerie as a little girl. He was astonished when the child came calling in the uniform of the Women's Army Corps, a soldier and a woman. (Though she must have lied about her age by a year or two, to get in.) She attacked martially:

"Uncle Judge, I'm off to camp, and I felt I had to come and tell you that you oughtn't to let Aunt Jinny come back here at all."

"M?"

"Now I'm in the Army, I got to thinking, and I thought: People keep saying there's a new world coming, and women's position will change entirely. Well, it's come, and it *has* changed! But there's still ten million dolls like Aunt Jinny, that haven't got guts enough to hold down a job or enough patience to study, and they think that modernity for women is simply being free to skip around with any men they like, and get all the jewelry and embroidered linens.

"I was looking at some photographs of these French guerrilla women. They're so self-reliant; they can sleep in caves and live on beans. Then I got to thinking about Jinny, and honestly, she makes me sick!"

"Private Pennloss! I admire your warrior women—though there's nothing 'modern' about them; the ancient Teuton women were like that, too. But your Aunt Jinny——Do you remember, few years ago, people said our college students were effete—never walk anywhere? Those same boys are now fighting in hell. And if Jinny ever *had* to, she could put on breeches and swing a rifle over her shoulder and march all night as well as any of 'em. Better! She had the courage to know what she wanted to do, and to do it, and to do it openly!"

"Why, Uncle Judge, you do love her, don't you! She's lucky, and she's an idiot. She hasn't heard there's a war on—that for women, there's always a war on."

"Private, I want to see you when you're fifty, and your children are blaming your generation for the next war, as your generation blames mine."

"Darling, you're not that old. You're not a generation, you're a sweetie. Will you marry me if I come home a colonel?"

"Certainly not. You're too efficient."

"You wait and see now. These days, you never can tell."

But with all these accusers of Jinny, there was one accuser of Cass—Christabel Grau.

She came to call on him at home, as informally as Valerie. At thirty-five, Chris looked fresh and kind, bright of eye, tender of mouth.

"Just came to see how you are," she said blankly.

"This is magnificent, Chris! I was thinking about you last evening; what fun we used to have riding our bikes. You used to take me seriously. You'd accept all the fake names I used to give you for the wild flowers. Let's go up and sit in my study. This living-room is too—it's too formal."

As they went up, he was thinking that he had been a fool not to have married Chris, the essential woman, the loving and loyal wife. Jinny and Blanche, who seemed as different as swallow and peacock, were both demanding, both civilly dictatorial, while the rich stream of Chris's generosity wanted only to nourish the land. Could he ever escape his fatal pattern and be courageous enough, original enough, to allow himself to be unharassed?

He sat her in a red-leather chair facing his own, he gave her a cigarette and a drink, and prepared to be cozy. And then Chris attacked like a cobra.

"There's something I have to get off my chest, Cass. I know a lot of people are giving you a hand, sympathizing with you because Jinny had the sense to up and leave you, but I want you to know that I don't!"

"M?"

"When I first saw her, I was jealous. I used to be quite fond of you—in fact, I think I might have fallen in love with you, if you'd ever been able to make up your mind what you wanted."

"M?"

"But then I came to love Jinny. She's only a tiny bit younger than I am."

——Eight years, and you know it!

"But I felt as though she were my baby sister. I was devoted to *both* of you, and I did want you to make a go of this marriage. But, Cass, you were so selfish and inflexible with her."

"M?"

"The way you used to ride her because she was a few minutes late, sometimes. And expecting her to be amused by old stuffs like Roy! Simply intolerable!"

"Chris! I haven't defended myself much, but now I'm going to. I have been selfish to other people—to Blanche, to you—and when I think of how I've imposed on my brother judges to get off on trips with Jinny, I shudder. But Jinny I've loved completely. I've given her everything I had, and I don't see how I could give her anything that I didn't have and couldn't get. And she knew the kind of smug citizen that she was marrying, and she'd met all his smug friends. Nobody fooled her.

"Since you blame me, let me suggest—this doesn't affect my love for her, mind you—that *she* might also have tried to make the marriage succeed. She might have worked a little on her job as a wife. If she was bored by my friends, she might have worked a little harder at finding new ones and bringing them here. I'd 've welcomed them! I married an angel, and I miss her grotesquely, but I did everything to hold her, short of clipping her wings, and you can't do that to an angel!"

Chris had thrown her cigarette at the open fire and was sitting on the arm of his chair, stroking his hair. "I do know how you miss her, Cass. Maybe what I loved in her was *you*!"

He leaned his head against her side, and her stroking hand was still. She would love him so generously, now, without bars——

He stood up abruptly, breaking the petty enchantment, and said, "Let's turn on the radio. Must be time for the Cleveland Orchestra."

He knew what peace and certainty he was gambling away for the fantasy he called love.

That night he thought of Chris too warmly, and he petitioned the spirit of Jinny, "Hurry back to me. I don't want to turn to Chris, but I could."

He remembered that Cleo had made extravagant, rather immodest advances to Chris, though Cleo was no cat-by-night, depending on charm. She was now twice a mother, progressing toward being a grandmother. Her more regular husband was reputed to be the John William Prutts' black and white Tom, a conservative cat if there ever was one, and Cleo had shown a growing conservatism in herself by having her two editions of kittens in the most traditional manner—in a bureau drawer. If Chris had been a cat, *she* would have had her kittens in a bureau drawer, preferably cedar-lined.

Till now, Cleo had obviously preferred the bodiless

apparitions of Jinny to Chris or any other sensible visitor, but she was wavering. She allowed Chris to stroke her.

Did cats forget people? fretted Cass.

An Assemblage of Husbands and Wives

NORTON TROCK

IN SO VAST a city as Grand Republic, with so ancient a history—going clearly back 20,000 years to the first known traces of Indian occupation—there were too many varieties of marriage even to index. Stuart Vogel, the county agricultural agent, and his wife, a skillful high-school teacher, deserve a whole treatise. They met at night, courteous and cheerful, to share in cooking the dinner, in reading plays for the next Masquers production.

They had one sort of "modern marriage," and Norton and Isabel Trock another, also modern.

Before her death, ten years ago, the elder Mrs. Trock often said to the other ladies in hotel lounges with tapestries that she had proved it was all nonsense, this offensive contemporary notion that it was bad for an only son to have a widow mother hovering over him. Look at her boy Norton, that neat and handsome young banker. He had been frail, as a boy, and had shown the sweetest old-fashioned manners, like a little prince, and so neat about hanging up his clothes, yet look at him now: he was a fine swimmer, a splendid boxer, a correct duck-shot—and all the girls were crazy about him.

Then she died.

After her death, it was obvious to her older friends that she had been right. At forty-eight, Norton was president of the Blue Ox National Bank, in which Mr. Boone Havock was chief stockholder. He had two bonny children, and his wife, Isabel, though not too bright and not especially pretty, had the same daintiness as Norton's mother.

He had always, since the age of three, called his mother "Sweetheart," so that it had become her pet name among the choice little set of the more fastidious matrons of Grand Republic, who embroidered altar cloths and explained that they were of pure English descent.

Sweetheart's husband had not been popular with these ladies. He called himself a wholesale chemist, but as a matter of fact he was in the liquor business. He was a coarse, red, bristling man, without taste in altar cloths. Fortunately he died when Norty, as Sweetheart called him, was only five years old, and fortunately he left them almost six thousand dollars a year.

Sweetheart thought of moving to New England or France or Fiesole or the Monterey Peninsula, but she could not sell the house, like a dark stone prison, which her husband had inconsiderately built, and the "wholesale chemist business" needed her shrewd eye.

But Sweetheart and Norty did travel, always the two of them together and always first class. They were not lonely, for they had each other; they could sit talking, lightly laughing, about their fellow-travelers, possibly malicious but always well-bred, from after dinner till after midnight.

She sent Norty to school in Connecticut and to that small but thoroughly sound and Christian college, Toplady. She always rented a cottage for herself near the institution, and Norty lived with her and was spared the coarser associations with the rough male students. But she saw to it that he did not fail to become manly; she had private teachers for him in boxing, riding, swimming, tennis, and bridge; and though vulgar competitors hinted that he won by nasty little tricks, she crowed that he did win. He was also a pianist, and sang French lyrics over which his mother, a broad-minded woman, looked shocked but giggled in an advanced manner.

After his college, they had a leisurely two years abroad, during which they rode on camels and looked up at but did not climb the First Pyramid. For two months they stayed at the loveliest pension in Florence, filled with the most cultured in American and English womanhood. In Lausanne they met an earl. In Canterbury, England, Sweetheart bought a pair of lilac-colored kid slippers, with his help, as usual, and they had to laugh at the strange affection he had for these slippers. "Do put them on, Sweetheart dearest," he begged, almost every evening. He preferred them even to her gold slippers.

He did have the best taste, pointed out Sweetheart.

For three months they had a flat on the Left Bank in Paris and Norty had a friendship with several exiled American poets and novelists that was surprisingly vivid, considering how shaggy their necks were and how many naughty words they used in the books they had published privately.

Sweetheart watched their capital deftly, and when it was diminished to the danger point, Norty and she reluctantly returned to Grand Republic, to the morose stone house, and he started as a clerk in the Blue Ox Bank. He was good. He liked figures. They were impersonal and dependable, they partook of the divine, and yet they could be mastered as the crude, inappreciative people about him could not be.

Naturally, his mother and he lived together, while he looked for a wife, with the assistance of the love, the industry, and the remarkable intuition of Sweetheart. Together they inspected every available girl in Radisson County and in the better (yet not too vulgarly rich) sections of St. Paul, Duluth, Winona, and Minneapolis.

He would go earnestly calling on these buds, he would play the piano and sing the French songs, and stay till ten, at which hour his mother would telephone him, even if it was long-distance, to remind him that he had had a headache that afternoon.

Sweetheart always had the girl candidates at the house, and was kind to them, and asked tactful questions about their stand on homemade puddings, Republicanism, and the reservation of the Host. She had one special test for the chicks. She showed them the bowl of shaving soap which she imported from St. James's Street, London, for Norty, and if the girl laughed or looked puzzled, it was evident that she was a crude provincial.

The young ladies always failed to snare Prince Charming. Without his mother being so intrusive as to point it out, Norty saw for himself that they could never be counted on to warm his pajamas or scrape the mud off his shoes or go out in the kitchen and cook guinea hen or listen to his reading aloud of Ronald Firbank, as Sweetheart could.

Some dozens of girls proved unfit. Norty said, "Sweetheart, I think this whole country has become coarsened and vulgarized. Democracy is all right as an ideal, but why must all the young ladies today be so ribald and impertinent? There aren't any more girls like you, dearest."

"I'm afraid that's true, but let's not give up hope," said Sweetheart.

"Oh, I just don't care one bit about *any* of them!" Norty cried petulantly, and kissed her.

They remained together all evening, every evening. They were invited to dinner together. Norty grew—not older; he could never, in the lulling spell of Sweetheart's tenderness, grow older, but he did grow less young. Sweetheart sometimes said (but laughingly) that he seemed a little bald, and his waistcoat (not his "vest") was more robin-like. He chuckled once, and said that he was catching up to her in age. Some day he would be able to marry her.

Sweetheart thought that was sweet of him, but she worried over it for a couple of days, then hinted, Sorry, but wasn't that remark possibly in bad taste?

He almost cried.

Each year he was neater. He trained Ed Oleson to cut his hair more precisely; his trousers hung even better; there was less danger of anyone finding a cigarette crumb on his sleeve; and to take care of the long-vexing, often-discussed question of how to keep shoelaces and black dress-ties really neat in his top highboy drawer, Sweetheart and he spent two week-ends building an intricate nest of tiny cardboard compartments, which she lined with gold tea-chest paper, kissing each one as she finished it.

"Imagine finding any *young* woman who would give such attention to my needs!" he shrieked.

"Oh, don't say that!" she said, with satisfaction.

She was tireless in trying to coax him out of his moods of violent depression which seemed to increase every year.

She died quickly, of an embolism, in his arms.

It was thought by his friends—who happened, most of them, to be women of his mother's age and understanding—

that Norty would go mad.

Dr. Roy Drover coarsely advised him to "marry the first cutie that makes a grab at you when you tickle 'em." Norty was not offended by Dr. Drover's masculine brutality, as you might have expected. Indeed, he came into the doctor's office frequently and invited him to the house for a drink. The clumsy doctor was embarrassed by these offers of friendship, and growled, "Say, I'm not a nosy psychiatrist that wants to hang around his patients," and the justly offended Norty cut him off. No, sir, Drover might beg all he wanted to, but he was finished with the dull oaf.

After some weeks Norty found an aide and companion: Larry Drome, a large young man who had been a truck-driver, policeman, soldier, sailor. He had once been imprisoned for burglary, but that had been a mistaken-identity case, explained Larry.

He became Norty's chauffeur, valet, and companion at gin-rummy. Together they took motor trips into the Arrowhead forest, and shared a cottage. Someone said that he had seen them together in Los Angeles, and that Norty was introducing his handsome friend as "Major Drome," but that was probably a lie. You know how small-city people talk.

But the talk spread, like honey on your wrist.

The directors of the Blue Ox National, particularly Mr. Havock, thought well of Norton Trock as a banker. He was first vice-president now, in charge of personnel and of loans.

He picked careful assistants, and he could refuse a loan, or call one, with tact. They wanted to make him president, but they were perturbed by rumors, probably spread by his rivals.

Mr. Havock had never heard of Krafft-Ebing or Stekel, but he had run construction-camps filled with hoboes, ex-convicts, and mess boys. While he had never been educated into the history of Greek and Roman culture and morals, also he had never been educated out of a knowledge of hobo culture and morals. He had Norty for dinner, along with Isabel Avondene, cousin of Stella. He had noted that Isabel looked rather like Sweetheart. After dinner, when the two men were alone, with cigars and bootlegged white mule, which Boone preferred to brandy, as being stronger, Boone spoke:

"Nort, we want you to be president of the Blue Ox. But we have to have a man who is a church member and a family-man—you know, beyond criticism. Why don't you marry Izzy Avondene?"

"I don't know that I——"

"You heard me!"

Norty wanted to be a sound husband. He sent his chauffeur, Larry—a rough fellow who might have offended his virginal wife—off to live in a boarding-house. Isabel and he had bedrooms at opposite ends of a rather long corridor, but he did go in to see her, nervously but politely.

They acquired two children in four years, but after that Norty never again entered her bedroom, and he found it was "just too ghastly inconvenient for poor Larry to tramp through all that snow before he drives me to the bank in the morning." He installed Larry again in an attic room of his large house, and again went off canoeing with him.

Isabel consulted Dr. Drover, who was cross.

"Doctor, I loathe talking about such intimate things, but I think I'm going a little crazy. I have such improper thoughts and I don't seem to be able to control them, and I've tried to talk with our rector, but he isn't of much help. My husband never—uh—he never comes near me any more—at night, I mean. He's always so nice and pleasant and he seems quite fond of me, and he's *so* good about playing with the children and entertaining my relatives and so on, but——I do miss something."

"Did you—uh—did you enjoy it when—when he used to come to you?"

"I was beginning to, I'm afraid."

"I'm not a mental doc, Isabel. I much prefer what surgery I can get. But I can tell you this: Don't worry. You women never understand how hard we husbands work, and it's just that Nort gets all tired out, slaving away in that big bank, and so he hasn't—he hasn't much left for you. Uh. He'll be all right again when the pressure lets up. Now skip along, and don't be so impatient with the poor fellow."

When she had gone, Dr. Drover thought, "Poor fellow, rats! Poor *girl*! Nothing I can do. Wonder if these Chicago sex-sharks do really know anything? I must ask some time, when I'm at a medical convention."

Unlike Bernice Claypool, Isabel Trock could not frisk with Bradds and lusty farmhands. After all, she was an Avondene! Whenever she was distressed by lewd thoughts, she prayed. It did not seem to help. So, from having too little of natural human sinfulness, she became as pale and bewildered and hermit-like as the oracular doctor's wife, Lillian, from having too much.

But Norty was blithe and rosy.

50

CASS WAS WORRIED by the pointless possession of two houses. He could not give up the new house—it was hers—but as spring grudgingly came on and he took long walks, he was only too much attracted by Bergheim. He liked to go into that shuttered cavern and sit there, thinking about this whole madhouse of love.

——We're so civilized now that we can kill our horrid enemies—year-old children—two hundred miles away, but nobody except a few rather loveless professors has even begun to understand love. Compared with our schools and churches, which are supposed to instruct our emotions, the shabbiest business, even advertising whisky, has been magnificent in its competence and integrity.

——In the future of married life, will men have to let their wives have as many lovers as they want? The men will hate it; I would hate it, bitterly. Yet all these ages women have hated their men making love to the gigglers. They've had to endure it. Is it our turn now? I don't like it. But what has that to do with it?

——Will the world ever be truly civilized? We always assume so, but will it? Could any caveman be more blundering than this Judge Timberlane, who loses his one love to a fancy-footing shyster named Criley?

——If the world ever learns that it knows nothing yet about what keeps men and women loving each other, then will it have a chance for some brief happiness before die eternal frozen night sets in?

——You cannot heal the problems of any one marriage until you heal the problems of an entire civilization founded upon suspicion and superstition; and you cannot heal the problems of a civilization thus founded until it realizes its own barbaric nature, and realizes that what it thought was brave was only cruel, what it thought was holy was only meanness, and what it thought Success was merely the paper helmet of a clown more nimble than his fellows, scrambling for a peanut in the dust of an ignoble circus.

Thus brooding, remembering Jinny in airy dressing-gown scampering through the gloom of Bergheim, remembering such magnificent trivialities as their supping in the kitchen on scrambled eggs, sadly finding on the back of the coat-closet door the gay angels that Jinny had drawn in gold and scarlet, he was apprehensive under the black spell of the house.

Abruptly, late in May, he committed patricide and sold it.

He sold it to a Scandinavian Lutheran church organization for an "old folks' home." He hoped that the old folks might be quiet there and trustful, and outlive the belief that God was always a man in the dreary black of a Scandinavian preacher.

He went for the last look at Bergheim. Admitting that he

was sentimental about it, he took Cleo along, for her final pilgrimage to that Viking paradise of desperate mice. But Cleo did not like it now. She kept close to Cass, upstairs and down and into the basement, where the Judge, who was a householder as well as a poet, wanted to see again one of the finest oil-furnaces his skilled eye had ever caressed.

They came out on the porch. While he was locking the door, the little cat frisked across the lawn.

Cass heard a barking, and swung round in agitation to see two dogs and some boys chasing Cleo over the grass. Before he could yell, the dogs had trapped Cleo between them. One of them seized her, its long teeth crushing her fragile ribs. It tossed her into the air, and then the other dog pounced.

Running frantically, almost choking the dog who held Cleo, Cass tore the mangled body from him, and held it to his chest.

The little cat half turned her head as if to try to look up at him; then blankness went over her small face, and she was dead. The tall man, like a Sioux chief, plodded to his car holding tight the bleeding body. He was deaf; he could not hear the small boys wailing apologies. As he walked, he was crying.

He drove home—to what had become home now, garish and unloved—with one hand on the wheel and the other holding the light body of the cat, dripping blood on him. Expressionless, he drove the car into the garage, took up a spade, hefted it, and buried the body, so tiny and unrecognizable, under a rosebush. He walked into the house and upstairs. He changed his clothes and brought the stained suit down to Mrs. Higbee.

"Will you have this dry-cleaned, please? It's all over blood. Some dogs killed Cleo. Cleo is dead. Some dogs killed her. I buried her."

"Oh, Judge, it seems like God is taking everything away from us!"

He did not listen. He was trapped in a thought that he knew to be superstitious, but he could not help linking Jinny to the dead Cleo. He could not resist. He tramped to the telephone and dictated a wire for Jinny, in Darien:

Dear Jin, letter from you overdue, am worried, wire if you are all right, love.

He did not expect an answer till the next day, but that evening he dared not stir from the house, and at a little after ten he was called by Western Union.

"This the Judge? Day-letter, signed Jinny, from Darien, Connecticut. Shall I read it to you? All ready? It's fairly long:

Goody this gives me chance annoy my nurse and Avis who might stop me but out of house for dinner. Got sick of having nurse nagging me take my insulin she worse than you ever were darling so laid off injections three days and on bat of candy in New York what a fool I was am back in bed doctor seems worried wish you were here to tuck me in things like this did not happen when with you but honestly would you think four cream puffs equal to one wagonload arsenic love love.

Cass did not smile. He thought for not more than a minute. He called Judge Blackstaff:

"Steve, I'm truly sorry but I must leave for New York tonight, by car. Life and death. Will you phone George Hame for me and take over? Thanks."

He called Alex Snowflower, Sheriff of the county:

"Sheriff? Cass Timberlane. I've got to be in Chicago, to catch a plane East, tomorrow morning. Can you do something illegal and get one of your deputies or somebody with enough gas to get me there?"

"You bet your life I will, Judge. I'll drive you myself. You'll get there."

"Awfully grateful. We want to make sure we won't get stopped, though. I've got to be there!"

"We'll be there. I'd like to see any Wisconsin cop halt Judge Timberlane and the high sheriff of Radisson County! Expect me at eleven."

Cass telephoned to Chicago, to a judge of consequence, who promised that by some means, preferably legal, he would have a seat for him on the morning airplane to New York.

All this time, Cass had been thinking about telephoning to Darien. He could hear himself, only too clearly, bullying the unpleasant butler, then demanding of Avis how Jinny was; hear himself saying with impressive briefness, "I'll be there tomorrow, about noon"; hear Avis floundering, "I don't know that it would be convenient to have you come just now."

No. What he was really afraid of was that Avis would say that Jinny was dead. He did not telephone to Darien.

Mrs. Higbee was lurking in the kitchen. When he plunged in with "I'd like three or four sandwiches in a box, and some very hot coffee in the thermos," she worried, "You look awful fierce and wild, Judge. You going to her?"

"Yes."

She said nothing more.

Sheriff Snowflower came blasting up to the house ten minutes before his promised time. Cass went out to him quietly. They shook hands, saying nothing, and the Sheriff started off through the decorous city streets at fifty miles an hour, which he increased to an unswerving seventy as soon as they had come to the end of Chippewa Avenue—an empty gray shell by night. They crossed the Big Eagle River, soared to the top of the bluffs, and headed southeast, for St. Croix Falls, on the Old North Military Road.

Cass had the familiar illusion that the countryside, unreal with night, was running past them, trees charging at them, a hamlet of ten houses hastily erected while they were coming up and hurled at them, road curves swinging round to avoid them, while they sat secure in this small, dark control-room, motionless, the center of the world.

The more rapidly they drove, the more bulkily quiet was the Sheriff. They were formal with each other at first. Though they were neighbors in the court house, they knew each other only on county business. At the start, it was "I hear Mrs. Timberlane is kind of ill, Judge; we'll get you to her, all right," and "Thank you, Sheriff," but they were both good farmers at heart and good Middlewesterners and first-name-users, and after a hundred and fifty miles it was "I'll tell you, Cass; I know Jinny has got my Mildred skun forty ways for looks and brains, but me I like a plain wife that's a bearcat on kids and dumplings," and "No, I'll argue with you about that, Alex; you've also got to think of what a wife wants for *herself*."

Twice they stopped, and Cass was astonished to see an all-night lunch, materialized out of darkness and actually standing still, not rushing past them, astonished to learn how stiff he was, as he eased himself out of the car. Ten minutes later, the place was gone, lost back in the country that had been annihilated behind them, and he could not remember what he had eaten.

Always he strained his eyes ahead, imagining, even a hundred miles from Chicago, that he saw the city's glow. Yet when rows of green-roofed suburban bungalows began to flow past, then factories and wooden tenements and street cars, he felt that he had been lifted up and instantly put down here.

He caught his plane, he slept all the way to New York, his taxicab hurried into the Grand Central Terminal, and just before one o'clock he was ringing the bell at Avis Elderman's large yellow house in Darien.

The butler, small but swelling with superciliousness, opened the door and said "Yes?"

It occurred to Cass that the man did not recognize him, perhaps did not know that he existed; that he looked dusty and disarrayed; that no one in the house knew that he was coming. But it also occurred to him that a few feet away was his Jinny.

He said impatiently, "I'm Mr. Timberlane."

"Yes?"

"Damn it, Judge Timberlane!"

Everyone on that floor must have heard. Avis popped into sight, down the hall, and the expression on her face indicated only that it was *very* inconvenient to have strangers coming in just before lunchtime.

He did not so much push the butler aside as blow him away with the explosiveness of his "Avis! Jinny?"

"Oh, yes, Cass. Well—no—she isn't very well."

"But what——"

"She is in a coma."

"Does that mean——?"

"Not always, our doctor says. Not with insulin. But it's

serious. He brought her out of one coma, but—well, she's more in kind of a daze now than a real coma. She keeps coming to, and complaining—oh, not exactly complaining, perhaps, but——It's very hard on the household, 1 *must* say, after all we've done!"

"I'm going up to her."

"I don't know that that would be——"

"You heard me! Where is she?"

51

THE UPPEB HALLWAY was heavy with oak and dark-brown velvet window-curtains. It was as ostentatiously modest as a funeral parlor.

When Cass opened her door, there loomed up, to bar him, Dr. Liskett, a plump, disapproving man with eyeglasses, grunting, "What is it?"

"I'm Jinny's husband."

"Whose husband? Look. If you'll just wait downstairs——"

"Get out of the way!" said Cass.

The doctor simply disintegrated, in the too-mahoganized room, and Cass was facing the too-ponderous bed in which he incredulously saw his Jinny, her face seeming as tiny as Cleo's, among the great pillows. As he went nearer, she was slowly opening her eyes, and she feebly held up her arms to him, with a weak but exultant, "Oh, Cass, my darling!"

Her eyes filmed over again. Her arms, too thin and anemic, dropped, and she seemed to have gone.

"Doctor!" Cass muttered.

The man was there, more attentive.

"She'll come out of it again. She's in kind of an intermittent mild delirium, with moments of entire lucidity. Sometimes her mind wanders—you know, wool-gathering—but sometimes she knows me perfectly, and I'm sorry to say that then she isn't entirely polite. You must excuse me for not welcoming you. I didn't realize who you were, when you first——"

"Has she a chance?"

"I think so. I brought her out of coma with insulin, and I believe I have the sugar controlled. She might live five months or five years or fifty, depending entirely on how well she obeys my injunctions."

"From now on, she's going to obey entirely!" Cass said grimly.

"And depending on whether she really wants to live."

"I'll see that she wants to live, now."

"Well, I'll just leave you two together, and be back in a couple of hours. Her nurse is downstairs having her lunch. She'll be right back. She knows all about the insulin and everything—you can trust her—in fact, she's my sister-in-law. I hope you'll be satisfied. See you soon, see you soon!" The sunbeam into which the suspicious physician had now turned withdrew its light from the room.

When the nurse came in, Cass did not even see her. He was sitting rigid, watching Jinny's restless drowsing. He was angrily fretting, "If she only had a real doctor, like Roy. That chintz-covered fellow here just got interested in me when he realized I'll be paying his bill. For *Jinny* to have a medical rabbit like that!"

The nurse looked once at Cass and sat down in appreciative silence.

Jinny moved, then lifted again out of her muted delirium. She smiled at him, and he sat awkwardly on the bed, pillowing her head on the crook of his arm. She spoke clearly, at first:

"Dearest, take me out of here. I want to see our house. I want to see Cleo and Isis. And Rose and Valerie and Roy. And Chris. I don't like these people here. Not any of them. No. I kept wondering when you would come and take me back home."

She slipped into a half-delirium. She thought that they were in Pioneer Falls, on a picnic, and there was no color but rose, no time save youth, in the misty fourth dimension in which she was wandering.

"I love cocoanut layer cake; it is very superior, don't you think? Do they have any in Paris?

"Maybe I can go there—to Paris—with Cass. He is very bright. He knows everything and he isn't afraid of anything. We would go there and sit at a café and talk all day, and if I were scared of all those French people——Do the kittens and dogs in Paris understand French?

"This path leads to a shady place under the birch trees, and I sat there beside him on the moss, and there was a patch of clover out in the bright sun, and we could see a meadow mouse, the tiniest thing but so wise and spry, and I wouldn't like to die, I can't die and go off into darkness before I sit there with Cass again and look at a field mouse, so small and wise——

"Bradd doesn't like sick people. Once I didn't either, they bored me and they smelled funny, I just liked them lively and doing things and that's how Bradd is, but Cass would keep the bats' wings away, he's so serious with his damn books but he would protect me, and how could I die now, when I'm just learning how to live?"

A mumbling, and then she was conscious, asking weakly, "Am I talking nonsense? I sort of hear myself. Am I silly, and disappointing you, after so long away? You know, it's hard to die with much dignity."

"Don't!"

"No, I won't die. I think maybe I would have, if you hadn't come. I *have* been a fool! I was young—but not that young! I do know a little better now. Quicksilver people like Bradd slide away from you so. Take me away from here, Cass, please do!"

"I will!"

"As soon as you can. And then we'll be happy—pretty happy. If you can just manage to hold onto me for one more year, only one year, Cass, I'll learn. Hold me close. They come in here and stare at me and wonder if I'm dead, or if they will have to go on having me here. Hold me!"

Her head was pressed against his arm as she again vanished into danger. She was so still that he thought that had been her

573

last beseeching cry.

The nurse came from nowhere, felt Jinny's pulse, nodded with "She's all right, sir."

Then Bradd Criley was in the room.

He came in with the hasty air of having just arrived from the city and, immediately afterward, the highly uncomfortable air of not having been told that Cass was here.

Cass stood up. He passionately wanted to do three things: to be an honorable judge, to have Jinny love him, and to kill Bradd Criley. He rapidly compromised. He decided merely to hit him. He could feel himself slapping Bradd, like a righteous schoolmaster; he could feel his fingers smack against that suave and treacherous cheek. His arm flew up, but he heard the voice of his law-school dean: "The essence of the law is that the sweets of private vengeance shall be denied."

He said to Bradd, "Oh, get out."

Bradd got.

Cass's fury was ruined then by a cheerful thought, the first one he had had in many days: the thought of how impertinent he had been in kicking Bradd out of this room in his sister's house. He turned to the bed, hoping for appreciation of the ribaldry of the thing—and he got it!

Jinny was smiling, trying to speak. Bending over, he heard her whisper, "I'm sorry you didn't sock him! That's the only thing I dislike about you: you're so blasted patient. He needs hitting, he does. Why, Cass, he's a heel!" She had a pale, self-congratulatory smirk at this huge discovery, but it softened to tenderness. "So irritatingly noble. But, darling, I would have died, if you hadn't come. I really am yours now, Cass."

Then, after minutes of drowsy rest, "Do you think less of me because Bradd has turned me down—him *and* his sweet sister? He's been trying to sneak out of love gracefully, and that's so hard to do. Can you still like me, now that you know I'm just a poor thing, that couldn't hold even a Bradd? I do love you now. Am I too late? I have learned—but why did I have to pick such an expensive teacher—and take all the extras? Dear single-minded Cass!"

It had taken her two dragging minutes to get through this voluminous speech, while Cass stroked her hand and sometimes hesitatingly kissed it, and the nurse knitted in a corner and clucked with approval.

Jinny relaxed then in her first natural sleep.

Yes, said Dr. Liskett, what his patient most needed was rest and quiet, and he seemed to feel some strain here in this house. (The doctor got around a lot, and saw things.) Yes, it might be better for Mrs. Timberlane to be transferred, by ambulance and only seven miles away, to that charming Pleasant Air Inn on the Sound, so comfortable and the prices so reasonable. She need not be dressed, and the nurse and doctor would go right with her. Oh, gladly.

Unscrupulously, Cass wrapped her in the indignant

Elderman blankets and quilt. But he did not, as he wanted to, leave for Avis a note: "Kindly send bill for wife's board & room to C. Timberlane."

Neither he nor Jinny saw any kind of Elderman or Criley as they left.

In the month during which they stayed at the Inn and Jinny became well enough to walk for ten minutes at a time, Cass telephoned long-distance to Judge Blackstaff, offering to resign his deserted post, and was answered, "Don't be silly, son. Come back to us, come back home, when you can. We miss you and—uh—we miss your wife. Good luck!"

His chessmen had been sent on from Grand Republic, along with his clothes, and for chess partners he found a clergyman, a Polish shoemaker, a schoolboy—and Jinny.

"You know," said Jinny, half-puzzled, half-merry, "I think Avis was even more bothered by having to fuss over a diabetic diet for me, and maybe the cook would quit, than over my relationship to Bradd. But I'm sure she kept worrying, 'Why does my brother want to marry a semi-invalid—a diabetic?' "

It was revealed to Cass, shockingly, that Bradd had never wanted to marry her; that he had been as resentful as his sister at being trapped into anything so permanent; and that, just now, he was probably relieved at being rid of her.

In a fortnight, Jinny was strong enough for the inevitable

peace treaty.

She worried, "You honestly do love me, after Bradd?"

"What has that to do with my loving you? I hated it, I loathed it, but that didn't change the shape of my nose or my heart."

"I'm not really the little thrush you thought I was. I'm a good deal of a vixen, don't you think?"

"Yes."

"Oh! . . . Oh, do you?"

"Yes."

"But then——"

"I told you: what has that to do with my loving you?"

"Oh."

"What we have to discuss is: Naturally, I want you to come home to Grand Republic with me."

"And I want to."

"But you'll have to reconcile people; not just Roy and Boone, but even Rose and Valerie. And Mrs. Higbee. Don't be superior—like Bradd. She gave you as much of her life as you would take, and you took quite a bit. Do you think you can stand working at winning back these people, of whom you didn't think too highly in the first place?"

"I guess that after being lost in these Eastern crowds, so indifferent, I want to go some place where they love you enough to hate you if you don't love *them*. I'll try. I will. Oh, Cass, I can't say I'm sorry for everything I did. I couldn't help it. But it *is* all over now. Can you stand it even if I can't make myself all dramatic and repentant?"

"I can."

Jinny had no chance against the ancient wisdom of Mrs. Higbee. When they arrived at the house, that clairvoyant was as cheerful and casual as if they had merely gone to Pioneer Falls for the day. Rose Pennloss and Frank Brightwing and Judge Flaaten met them at the train, and in the house were flowers from the Havocks, the Drovers, the Blackstaffs, and Sheriff Alex Snowflower.

To its fugitive children, Grand Republic will forgive almost anything if they will but come back home.

When she had suddenly kissed Mrs. Higbee, when she had exclaimed over the flowers, Jinny said gleefully, "Now Cleo. Where is that darn animal, bless her?"

Cass went cold. At the Pleasant Air Inn, he had lied about Cleo, but he reluctantly told her now.

Jinny broke, "It was me that killed her, by deserting her."

He sent her off to bed with what empty comforts there are for grief.

Next morning, there were eleven invitations for Judge and Mrs. Timberlane—to come to amner, cocktails, trout-fishing, sailing on Dead Squaw Lake. To his tactful telephonic refusals, eleven hosts or hostesses answered, "Still sick? Oh, the poor girl! Give her my love, Cass."

52

THAT WAS A particularly hot summer in the Sorshay Valley, and Cass and Jinny, keeping close, built up such a community of unimportant interests that he sometimes forgot that she had been away. And, save that she had the annoyance of diet and insulin injections, and had to be in bed by ten, they often forgot that she was ill. They were bound together by the discussion of Mayor Stopple's political ideals, of why the chickens from the Superba market were so tough, and all the other epic insignificances of a pleasant life.

The long, serene Indian Summer was carnival. The hills were extravagant as with Chippewa head-dresses and the far smoke from Chippewa fires. The sky had the curious and innocent blue of the North Middlewest, and the air such cheerfulness that Jinny was filled with renewed joy and submitted to Cass an idea about one—just *one*—party with dancing till midnight.

"No cocktails, no midnight sun," he said, "and don't coax. You're to be in bed by ten even if I have to carry you."

She was only mildly sad about it, just enough to assert her non-existent independence, and he discovered that he had made a psychological advance. He did not worry about that sadness. Once, when she had complained that she "didn't have much fun," he had felt guilty, but now he reassured himself that most sick girls and most judges over forty do get along without much riotous fun.

Possibly both of them would yet grow up.

They walked beside the lake, with an autumnal sunset like a burning forest over the crinkled and lapping water, on which the rowboats stirred and whispered.

When they came home, Jinny was summoned to the telephone, and she returned from the call half-exasperated and half-amused, to hurl at Cass, "The persistence of the amorous male!"

"M?"

"That was Fred Nimbus, our radio friend. Jolly old Fred! Hears I'm much better—ready to be put into circulation, and would I like to have him call around some afternoon?"

They were side by side on the glazed chintz of the glider, on the screened porch. She reached for his hand, and she sounded frightened:

"When I think what his call probably means, I'm scared. Have I a reputation here for being a fast woman, merely because I——Well, I can see how I might. Have I?"

He lied as well as he could.

She had always been reticent about her feelings, but now she brought them out anxiously:

"I do want to try and tell you how——You've been waiting

to have me say that I'm sorry for going off with Bradd. Haven't you?"

"Well, if you want to."

"And I am sorry, terribly sorry, for having hurt you. But I can't honestly say I'm sorry I knew Bradd. He gave me the education—such a bitter education it was, but so thorough—that you'd had before I ever saw you."

"I don't understand."

"I told you once long ago—but you didn't listen—that I've always been jealous of your experiences with Blanche and Chris."

"Oh, not Chris!"

"Sure. She's a woman of character. She may get you yet, and maybe that would be a very good thing for you. *Just let her try it*! . . . But it was your life with Blanche that maddened me. She shared your first love, your first wandering, your first house. You gave her your first eagerness. Even if you did come to hate her, you learned what it was all about with *her*. But I'd never had anybody but you. How could I size up life, size up even you? I thought maybe with Bradd, it would be a new world. Well, it was. A horrible one, but thrilling. And then being with Bradd made me appreciate *you*.

"He's so grasping—in his lively way. He takes so much that finally I saw that I'd always been taking from *you*, and not trying to give much. I will now. I will try. I'm poor in spirit now, but I will give what I have. But if I've learned that, how

581

can I be sorry for anything that happened?"

"You're not poor in spirit. You're so rich——"

"And that's the other thing—your worst fault. You praise me too much. You inform the world *and* me that I'm the greatest beauty, the smartest draftsman, the slickest tennis-player since Leonardo da Vinci, and will I please show my paces. I can't live up to it. When you advertise me so much, it makes me perverse; it makes me want to be vicious.

"But——All these words! I have no skill in them. I just wanted to say that I did have to learn about myself, and I know it almost killed me, as it hurt you, but you brought me back to life, you keep me living, you *are* my life."

She cried a little, and in their kiss her love seemed to be utterly restored.

They had been living like brother and sister. He had not even hinted of love-making. He did not know whether he was fatuous or noble in not demanding his "rights." With Jinny, he felt as much as ever that he had no rights, only privileges.

That night, with his breath in a harsh rhythm not so unlike sobbing, he went into her room, and in the bedside light she stretched out her arms with a passionate "Dear, dear love!"

He still did not quite believe it, but when he lay beside her, she murmured, "We've found each other again, sweet! I don't know how I ever strayed. How could I? Now, I *am* sorry, I am repentant, I do love you!"

Every bond of caution was broken. It was very sweet.

It was sweet until he realized that she had been cheating for generosity's sake, that she could not really respond to him. She was trying to and failing. He was humiliated a moment. Then he was grateful. He said tenderly, "You've been brave and wonderfully kind. But you're still shut off from me, aren't you? You still haven't got Bradd quite out of your system. Don't be afraid to tell me. He still holds you?"

"I'm afraid so. Though I detest him. He's so ruthless. But maybe that made him a good teacher. Wouldn't it be strange if he taught me to give, by his never giving anything! Then this miserable business—I know it was that now—it won't all have been a waste. Can that be?"

"I think so. Jinny! If you're ever moved by your own self, by your own desire, to come to me, I'll be waiting. Will you, when you feel like it? Will you remember?"

"I shall remember."

"And I won't overpraise you any more."

"Now look! You needn't be a fanatic about it!"

They were cheerful at dinner, the next evening. Jinny voluntarily announced that there were times when she did not mind these messes of green vegetables.

"Not more than having your teeth pulled?"

"Not *much* more," she asserted.

After dessert—a bread-pudding in which Cass said there was merit, and Jinny said Yes, but not much else—Mrs. Higbee placed on the table a teapot-cover: no cups, just the pink quilted tent. They gaped at her, and she stood expressionless. They looked at the cover, and it was moving, by itself.

Jinny snatched it up, and beneath it was a little black kitten, all black, midnight black, cocky and independent and purring and kneading with its paws.

"It is—it *is* Cleo!" cried Jinny. She put out her hand and the kitten rubbed against it, and glanced over at Cass for applause, in Cleo's old familiar way.

Mrs. Higbee said indulgently, "It's Cleo's own granddaughter. I got her off the Prutts' cook. Only, I feel like it's Cleo herself. You can't kill people like her, not for keeps."

Jinny smoothed the kitten, while Cass wondered, "Is this an omen that even our Emily may return and we'll have made the greatest human journey—in a circle back to the innocence with which we began?"

When Jinny set the kitten down, it stepped out gallantly across the cloth.

"You get right off that table, Cleo!" said Mrs. Higbee.

On that January evening, Roy Drover telephoned:

"Bradd Criley is going to be in town tomorrow, just for the one day, to see the Wargates. He'll have an hour free, and he's coming to my place for cocktails. I want you and Jinny to show up. Now don't be a mule. Let bygones be bygones. Live and let live——"

Cass interrupted with a sharp, "I'll do whatever Jinny says."

It was at the peaceful time of the evening. Jinny was reading a new book filled with significant social trends and portents: *Dealings with the Firm of Dombey and Son, Wholesale, Retail, and for Exportation.* She was stroking the younger Cleo and, though she had become an absolute Trappist as regards candy, she gave the feeling that she was now and then confidently reaching for a bon-bon.

Cass studied her contentment, and he spoke reluctantly: "Jin, Bradd will be in town for a few hours tomorrow, and Roy wants us to come for cocktails with him."

She stared. "I don't want to see him!" Her violence betrayed that she was afraid to see him, that she longed to see him, that she had to see him.

"I guess he's one fact we'd better face," said Cass patiently.

In Dr. Drover's sun-room, with its pea-green wicker chairs, there were eight people, all friends of Bradd, who with magnificent tact played his role of Home Boy Who Went to the City and Made Good but Will Never, Never Forget His Old Friends.

He kissed Queenie, Lillian, and Diantha on the cheek, and Rose on the mouth, but with Jinny Timberlane he shook hands cordially, exactly as he did with Jinny's reticent husband.

It seemed to Cass impossible that he could either have

loved or hated this fellow. He was too brisk, too obvious, too unfamiliar. This was another Bradd. Success and the great city had claimed him.

He was full of quips and of names which he considered famous. He let them know how chummy he had become with a stock-broker, an aviation magnate, a female columnist formerly a professional lady, but he was not blown with all this social grandeur. He kept yelling, "You don't see any Park Avenue dames as handsome as Queenie," and "Let me know when you hit town, Rose, and I'll get ringside seats for the opera."

After half an hour, Jinny said, "I'm afraid we'll have to go home now."

They shook hands with Bradd and with everybody else available. In the street, Cass said, "Well?"

"I know. Oh, darling, the man is a monkey, a monkey on a stick! I'm so glad I saw him, though. I never really saw him before. That charm-peddler! And I never really saw you before. Cass, I——Don't you see what I'm trying to tell you?"

"Yes."

She was so serious that it was not till dinner that she said, "And that was the *worst* tie he had on. Like these colored pictures of vegetable soup. And I'll bet he spent nine dollars for it. You'll never wear a tie like that!"

Late at night he awoke to find her standing in his doorway, a moth against the light from the hall.

"I thought maybe you would come in and see me. I was very cold," she said plaintively. "Couldn't I crawl in your bed and get warm?"

Then, for her and his love for her, he gave up his vested right to be tragic, gave up pride and triumph and all the luxury of submerged resentment, and smiled at her with the simplicity of a baby.

"Dear Jinny!" he said, and she confided, "I'm going to get new storm-windows on my room, even if I have to put them up myself. I could, too! I'm the best storm-window fixer in this town. You'll see!"

CPSIA information can be obtained
at www.ICGtesting.com
Printed in the USA
LVOW12s1825010616
490796LV00004B/355/P